BENEDICT ARNOLD
in the Company of Heroes

If there is any period one would desire to be born in, is it not the age of Revolution; when the old and the new stand side by side and admit of being compared; when the energies of all men are searched by fear and by hope; when the historic glories of the old can be compensated by the rich possibilities of the new era? This time, like all times, is a very good one, if we but know what to do with it.

— Ralph Waldo Emerson, *The American Scholar* (1837)

Benedict Arnold
in the Company of Heroes

The Lives of the Extraordinary Patriots Who Followed Arnold
to Canada at the Start of the American Revolution

Arthur S. Lefkowitz

SB
Savas Beatie
California

Library of Congress Cataloging-in-Publication Data

Lefkowitz, Arthur S.

Benedict Arnold in the company of heroes: the lives of the extraordinary patriots who followed Arnold to Canada at the start of the American Revolution / Arthur S. Lefkowitz. – 1st ed. p. cm.

Includes bibliographical references and index.

ISBN 978-1-61121-111-5

1. Canadian Invasion, 1775-1776. 2. Arnold, Benedict, 1741-1801. 3. United States—History—Revolution, 1775-1783—Campaigns. 4. United States—History—Revolution, 1775-1783—Biography. 5. United States. Continental Army—Officers—Biography. 6. Soldiers—United States—Biography. I. Title.

E231.L438 2012

973.3'820922--dc23

2012032377

First edition, first printing

SB

Published by
Savas Beatie LLC
989 Governor Drive, Suite 102
El Dorado Hills, California 95762

Mailing Address:

Savas Beatie LLC
P.O. Box 4527
El Dorado Hills, CA 95762

www.savasbeatie.com (web)
sales@savasbeatie.com (email)

Savas Beatie titles are available at special discounts for bulk purchases in the United States by corporations, institutions, and other organizations. For more details, please contact Special Sales, P.O. Box 4527, El Dorado Hills, CA 95762, or you may e-mail us at sales@ savasbeatie.com, or visit our website at www.savasbeatie.com for additional information.

Printed in the United States of America.

This book is dedicated
to my grandson Jonah Goth Lawrence

With the hope that he will help to keep the Spirit of '76 alive

The Arnold Expedition was launched during the first year of the Revolution when the rebel army had few uniforms or standard weapons. American soldiers wore their civilian clothing and brought their personal firearms and accouterments from home. Despite their appearance, these men were tough fighters. Similarly equipped patriot troops inflicted a crippling blow to the British army at Bunker Hill just two months prior to the organization of the Arnold Expedition. *George C. Woodbridge, Author's Collection*

Contents

Contents (continued)

Illustrations and maps have been placed throughout the text
for the convenience of the reader.

Preface

The audacious Arnold Expedition of 1775 has always appealed to me as one of the most amazing stories in American military history. However, I was warned not to write a book on the subject since the campaign ultimately ended in failure and its commander, Benedict Arnold, is the most famous traitor in American history. However, I decided I could give the story of the Arnold Expedition a positive ending by concentrating on the military careers of the men who served under Arnold and survived the grueling campaign. The only Arnold Expedition veterans I knew about when I started my book were Daniel Morgan, Aaron Burr, and Henry Dearborn, but I felt certain that there must have been others who returned from captivity in Quebec and rejoined the fight for the patriot cause.

As I began researching the military records of Arnold's Kennebec Corps, I was amazed at how many Arnold Expedition veterans eagerly returned to the Continental Army, and at their impressive combat records. But as I began to craft my Arnold Expedition book, I realized that its logical and dramatic conclusion had to be their attack on Quebec on New Year's Eve, 1775. The result was *Benedict Arnold's Army*, which told the story of the Arnold Expedition and early American efforts to seize Canada during the Revolutionary War. However, I remained fascinated by the later military exploits of the men of Arnold's Kennebec Corps, and I continued to learn about them.

I also wanted to expand my study of the character of Arnold, who was a great motivator of men and a fearless combat officer. It took a dynamic leader to get a band of starving men to follow him through the Maine wilderness to Quebec in 1775, and to stand and fight against overwhelming odds at Valcour Bay in 1776.

Arnold is also a complicated historical figure, and I followed his career as a British general after he switched sides to provide clues to his character. This book is the result of my interest in the veterans of the Arnold Expedition and its ill-fated commander.

Benedict Arnold in the Company of Heroes also includes a summary account of the Arnold Expedition. I included this information because it is important to identify the names of the campaign's officers and some of the enlisted men in order to appreciate their subsequent contributions to the American war effort. My book *Benedict Arnold's Army* gives a more detailed account of the Arnold Expedition.

Benedict Arnold in the Company of Heroes continues the story of the Arnold Expedition by describing the imprisonment of Arnold's men at Quebec, their efforts to escape, their parole and exchange, and their ultimate return to active military service. It is an incredible story of determined men who remained faithful to the cause of liberty. For many of them, the Arnold Expedition was their first experience of war, and they had the great opportunity to learn from Benedict Arnold, a courageous and charismatic officer who led by example. I believe that they took much of what they learned and observed from their experience under Arnold and applied it to the benefit of the fledgling Continental Army. The men who survived the Arnold Expedition went on to become some of the best officers in the patriot army. This is their story—which constitutes the positive ending to the tale of the ill-fated Arnold Expedition and the future traitor who led it.

Acknowledgments

Writing a history book on a challenging subject is an excellent way to learn and *Benedict Arnold in the Company of Heroes* was no exception. Part of my education consisted of discussing my manuscript with eminent historians and serious Revolutionary War enthusiasts who critiqued my work and recommended sources for additional information. This is my opportunity to thank these people for sharing their expertise and ideas with me.

I have arranged my acknowledgments starting with historians. My definition of a historian comes from my friend the late George C. Woodbridge, who said that a historian is anyone who earns his or her living from history. Applying this formula, I came up with several names including John Ferling. Professor Ferling is the author of a number of important and engaging books about the American Revolution. Among his works is the recently published *Almost a Miracle*, which I believe is the best military history of the American Revolution. Professor Ferling's in-depth knowledge of other periods of American history became apparent to me when he was editing a page from my manuscript that mentioned the town of Steubenville, Ohio. Professor Ferling wrote a *bon mot* on the margin of the page that singer Dean Martin was born in Steubenville, which I discovered to be correct.

The award-winning historian Thomas Fleming was also generous in sharing his impressive knowledge of the American Revolution with me. Mr. Fleming has written numerous outstanding books on the subject. For me, his latest work, *The Intimate Lives of the Founding Fathers*, is among his very best.

I am also grateful to Philander D. Chase, the Editor Emeritus of *The Papers of George Washington.* Professor Chase has encouraged and assisted me over the years, and my new book benefited from his perceptive knowledge of George Washington and his association with Benedict Arnold.

I am also pleased to acknowledge Eric Schnitzer, the acting historian at Saratoga National Battlefield Park. The 1777 Saratoga campaign brought together a number of Arnold Expedition veterans including Benedict Arnold, Daniel Morgan and Henry Dearborn. Eric is an authority on the complicated movements of the opposing armies and I was happy to benefit from his encyclopedic knowledge of the event. I also take this opportunity to apologize to the staff of Saratoga Visitors Center who listened attentively to my question: Why were so many Revolutionary War battles fought in parks?

One of the delights in researching a new book is the opportunity to make new contacts and friends. This project yielded the jackpot, for I befriended Nicholas Westbrook, the Director Emeritus of Fort Ticonderoga. Nick is one of the most knowledgeable and affable Revolutionary War historians I have had the pleasure of knowing. I initially contacted him to discuss the events leading up to the capture of Fort Ticonderoga by Ethan Allen and Benedict Arnold. They argued over who was in command of the attack, which resulted in conflicting eyewitness versions of the event by them and their supporters. A lively exchange of e-mails with Mr. Westbrook ensued, during which he mentioned that his ancestor was Fenner Foote, a Revolutionary War soldier and veteran of the 1775 Arnold Expedition. The date of Private Foote's death caught my immediate attention. It was April 27th, 1847, thus bestowing upon Foote the distinction of being the longest-living member of the Arnold Expedition. Mr. Westbrook shared his extensive research regarding his ancestor as well as valuable information about Capt. William Goodrich, Foote's company commander. Although a minor figure in the Arnold Expedition, Goodrich was of interest to me as I wanted to know if he returned to active duty following the Arnold Expedition and his imprisonment in Quebec. Nick Westbrook also had valuable source material documenting the wartime exploits of Capt. Oliver Hanchet, another officer of the Arnold Expedition about whom little is known.

Touring the historic sites that I write about in my books is productive and always a fun step of the research process. The highlight of my field trips for this book was Nick Westbrook's guided tour of the route followed by Allen and Arnold in their surprise attack on Fort Ticonderoga. We also explored the interior of the fortress including the restored magazine building. It is an imposing three story structure situated on the east side of the fort's historic parade ground. Nick explained that the original powder magazine was blown up when the French abandoned the fort during the French & Indian War. The building was restored under Nick's passionate direction, using remaining pieces of its cellar and outside walls and years of meticulous research. The restored Magazine was opened in 2008 with new exhibit areas and a year-round conference center. The reconstructed Magazine adds to the experience of visiting Fort Ticonderoga and helps to secure its standing as one of the most important historical sites in America.

I next turn to my fellow extreme Revolutionary War enthusiasts, who earn their living from something other than history. These independent researchers are a unique group who continue to publish important books out of a love for the subject. They usually embark upon their research with no publisher, university backing, book agent or publicist to promote and encourage their work. It's a tough business that leaves a lot of half-written books filed away in desk drawers. Among these stalwart independent researchers and writers is David Wilson, who published an excellent book titled *The Southern Strategy*. David earns his living writing advertising copy for credit card companies who solicit your business via direct mail. The next time you receive one of these so-called pieces of junk mail, please be kind as the copy may have been written by a Revolutionary War scholar.

My friend Thomas McGuire is a Philadelphia high school teacher and prolific researcher and writer. He recently published a scholarly two volume history of the 1777 Philadelphia campaign. My book benefited from Tom's critiques and suggestions.

My thanks are also extended to General Dave Palmer, a retired commandant of West Point. General Palmer is the author of *The Way of the Fox*, which is one of my favorite books about the American Revolution. He has published an excellent book about Benedict Arnold titled *George Washington and Benedict Arnold: A Tale of Two Patriots*. My book benefited from the general's in-depth knowledge of Arnold.

I am also grateful to Tim J. Todish, a retired police officer and a noted authority on rangers in the French & Indian War. He is the author of several books on the subject, including *The Illustrated Journals of Major Robert Rogers*. Arnold Expedition veteran Simeon Thayer served in the rangers when he was teenager. Mr. Todish helped me piece together Thayer's probable French & Indian War service record. I also learned from working with Tim that there were numerous other Provincial ranger units in the war besides the famous Rogers Rangers.

Raymond Andrews is another fellow Revolutionary War enthusiast who shared his extensive knowledge of the period with me. Ray is an architect and an avid American Revolution independent researcher and lecturer. I am also grateful to Ed Wimble,another Rev War devotee, who critiqued my manuscript and offered valuable and constructive advice.

My longtime advisor, Dr. Richard Prouty, once again came to my aid with his knowledge of the history of military medicine. Dr. Prouty also laboriously spent hours with me comparing a list of Arnold Expedition veterans held prisoner in Quebec against the pension applications at the David Library of the American Revolution. Names like John Brown were a problem because there were scores of men with that name who saw service in the American Revolution. We did much better looking up possible Arnold Expedition pension applicants with names like Valentine Willey and Theophilus Hide.

David Dougherty from Evening Shade, Arkansas, is a residential land developer and genealogist with much to research. His family tree includes his ancestor James Dougherty who reached Philadelphia from Ireland in early 1775. James quickly embraced the patriot cause and was a rifleman on the Arnold Expedition. Dave generously shared his information about his impressive great-great-great-grandfather. Dave explained that the small number of generations between Revolutionary War veteran James Dougherty and himself is due to the longevity that runs in the Dougherty family.

This is the first book for which I required the help of a computer consultant to resolve the problems created when I constantly revised and moved text and corresponding end notes. My patient and tireless computer hero was Tom Bodall. I also relied on Michael Spingeld for technical support. Mike is an expert in Photoshop software, which was used to convert my digital color photographs into high-definition black and white images.

An important thank you also goes to my publisher Savas Beatie. Everyone there has been very supportive of my work. Managing Director Theodore P. Savas is an outstanding author and authority on the American Revolution in his own right. His firm specializes in books about American military history, and he provides authors like me an important outlet for their work. Publishing has become a profit-oriented business based on quick, high-volume sales of books. As a result, specialized reference authors find it difficult to get their manuscripts published. Savas Beatie is important because it focuses on books that add to our knowledge of history, as opposed to subjects that simply result in quick sales. Savas Beatie's recently published Revolutionary War titles include valuable histories of the Saratoga and Yorktown campaigns, as well as my narrative *Benedict Arnold's Army*. Please review their books online (www.savasbeatie.com) and support their important work.

Much of the research for this book was done at The New York Public Library, which is one of the world's greatest depositories of information. A unique aspect of this world-class institution is that it is a privately run library whose collections are open to the public at no charge. This extensive rare book and manuscript collection is open to researchers who lack academic credentials. I also worked in other institutions, which were eager to help me. These include the Widener Library at Harvard University, the Connecticut Historical Society, The Library Company of Philadelphia, The Historical Society of Pennsylvania, and the David Library of the American Revolution.

And finally, I am grateful to my wife Susan for her encouragement, editing suggestions, and patient endurance of another of my book projects.

Arthur S. Lefkowitz
Piscataway, New Jersey

A Note on the Cover Illustration

The cover art for this book is an original oil painting by artist-historian Dahl Taylor. The front of Mr. Taylor's wraparound cover art shows Maj. Gen. Benedict Arnold conferring with Col. Daniel Morgan on Bemis Heights during the 1777 Saratoga campaign. This was the strong American defensive position that successfully blocked Gen. John Burgoyne's Southern offensive from Canada.

Both Arnold and Morgan were veterans of the 1775 Arnold Expedition. Morgan is shown wearing the same clothing depicted in John Trumbull's painting titled "The Surrender of General Burgoyne at Saratoga." Trumbull served as an officer during the Revolutionary War and accurately depicted uniforms and weapons in his historical paintings. The helmet worn by the mounted dragoon behind Arnold also comes from Trumbull's painting of Burgoyne's surrender. The building in the background is a fortified Dutch-style barn discovered by archaeological excavations to have been on Bemis Heights at that time.

The soldier behind Morgan is a rifleman. He is carrying a folding pike, a weapon proposed by Commissary Gen. Benjamin Flower in July 1777 for use by riflemen whose guns could not mount a bayonet. It is possible that some of Morgan's riflemen were armed with this pike at Saratoga. The illustration on the following page shows the design of Gen. Flower's pike.

The musket horse (gun rack) in the painting is based on a background detail in the 1781 portrait of Col. Walter Stewart by Charles Willson Peale in 1781. The guns on the rack are French Charleville muskets. They were among the shipments of weapons that arrived from France in time to supply Gates' army at

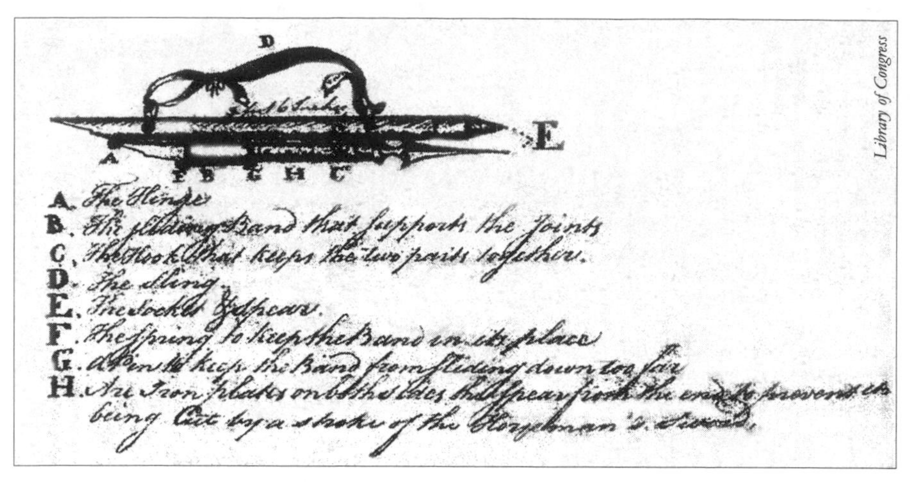

Library of Congress

Diagram of a Rifleman's Pike

Saratoga. The bayonets are fixed to the muskets, which was a logical practice at the time since each musket was handmade and its bayonet custom-fitted.

The two officers behind Morgan are Maj. Henry Brockholst Livingston and his 19-year-old cousin Matthew Clarkson. These men were Arnold's aides-de-camps at the time and their function (aide) is identified by the green ribband-of-office that they wear across their chests. Note that one of the aides carries a dispatch case.

The soldiers standing behind Arnold's aides are members of the First New York regiment. The Saratoga campaign culminated in October and Dahl Taylor takes note of the autumn colors in his painting.

The two dogs in the painting are the author's terriers: Jackson, standing next to Arnold, and Schuyler, who is near Arnold's aides. Jackson gets around. He was last depicted sitting in a bateau on the Kennebec River on the cover of the author's book *Benedict Arnold's Army: The 1775 American Invasion of Canada During the Revolutionary War* (Savas Beatie, 2008).

Chapter One

The Patriotism of Benedict Arnold

"We . . . do Associate under all the ties of religion, honour, and love to our Country, to adopt and endeavor to carry into execution whatever measures may be recommended by the Continental Congress . . . for the purpose of preserving our Constitution [English law] and opposing the execution of the several arbitrary and oppressive acts of the British Parliament."

— *From Benedict Arnold's Declaration of Principles dated "Crown Point, 15th June, 1775"*[1]

The American Revolution lasted for eight years (1775-1783) and, for the first five years of the war, Benedict Arnold was seemingly a staunch patriot and probably the best combat officer in the Continental Army. In 1780, Arnold defected to the British, and his change from patriot to traitor is one of the most compelling narratives in American history. Various explanations have been offered to account for Arnold's transformation, which include his need for money, the influence of his wife, his disillusionment with the patriot cause, and the entry of France into the war on behalf of the Americans. Arnold called the French "the enemy of the Protestant faith" and maintained that, while the

1 Benedict Arnold's *Declaration of Principles.* This 236-word document was written by Arnold on June 15, 1775, to rally the few hundred troops under his command at Fort Ticonderoga and Crown Point. The document was signed by 32 influential men, including the captains of Arnold's New York militia companies and an Albany member of the Committee of Safety. Arnold was the first person to sign the document. Manuscript in the Fort Ticonderoga collections and published in the *Bulletin of the Fort Ticonderoga Museum*, volume II, number 3 (January 1931), 99-100.

Court of Versailles advocated "an affection for the liberties of mankind, she holds her native sons in vassalage [i.e., serfdom] and chains."[2]

Some of these factors may have influenced him, but I believe that Benedict Arnold turned to treason as revenge against his fellow countrymen who had been working to humiliate him since the start of the war. While it is true that Arnold had numerous powerful enemies within the patriot movement, the cause of their hostility was often his own belligerent behavior. In fact, Arnold had been heedlessly destroying his military career ever since the start of the war, due to his lack of diplomacy, neglect in cultivating influential friends in government, and belief that he was smarter than most of the people around him.

As the Revolutionary War progressed, Arnold's arrogance caused his list of enemies to grow. By the fifth year of the war (1780), he was an angry and vindictive man, and, with the encouragement of his 19-year-old wife, resorted to treason to get even. His plan was spectacular in its potential to damage the patriot cause. Arnold used his goodwill with George Washington to obtain command of the strategic American fortress of West Point, with the intent to deliver the stronghold to the enemy in exchange for money and a commission as a British general. When Arnold's treachery was accidentally discovered on September 25, 1780, he managed to reach safety just ahead of the American troops who had been sent to arrest him for treason. He escaped by boarding the ironically named Royal Navy ship *Vulture* that was anchored in the Hudson River.

There is a trend today to treat Arnold sympathetically. His supporters point out that his exploits as an American officer, prior to his treason, were significant. Also, despite his victories on the battlefield and being twice wounded in combat, Arnold was ignored or passed over for promotion by

2 Isaac N. Arnold, *The Life of Benedict Arnold: His Patriotism and His Treason* (Chicago: Jansen, McClurg & Company, 1880), 331. Isaac N. Arnold (1815-1884) was a distant relative to Benedict Arnold. Isaac was born in upstate New York, where he studied law and was admitted to the bar in 1835 at the age of 20. He moved to the boomtown of Chicago the following year to practice law and befriended there fellow Illinois lawyer Abraham Lincoln. Arnold became active in the new Republican Party and won election to the U.S. House of Representatives in 1860, where he was a strong Lincoln supporter. Isaac returned to his Chicago law practice at the end of the Civil War and published a biography (1867) of his friend Lincoln entitled *The History of Abraham Lincoln and the Overthrow of Slavery*. Arnold was criticized for his lack of research in writing his book. He responded to his critics by publishing (1880) his meticulously researched biography of Benedict Arnold. Isaac Arnold died in 1884.

Congress. The alliance between France and the United States had not altered the course of the war, which was dragging on as the British made inroads in the Southern colonies. With the possibility of a negotiated peace to end the war, Arnold may have believed that he had a more promising future in the British rather than the Continental Army.

However, while Arnold's anger may have been partially justified, his treason was reprehensible. It came at a time when American morale was probably at its lowest point in the eight-year conflict. Devastating events just prior to Arnold's intrigue included the surrender of Charleston in May 1780 to General Sir Henry Clinton, with the loss of over 3,000 patriot troops; the defeat of General Horatio Gates by Lord Cornwallis in August of that same year at the Battle of Camden, which gave the British control of South Carolina and threatened North Carolina; the failure of the French to commit their army to the war; growing pessimism; and runaway inflation, exhausted credit, and an American economy teetering on the verge of collapse. Had Arnold's sinister plot succeeded, it might have been the crippling blow that would have ended the war with a negotiated settlement unfavorable to the Americans.

The origin of Arnold's belligerent behavior can be traced all the way back to his formative years. It may have started when his father's humiliating bankruptcy and drinking forced young Benedict to leave school at the age of fourteen to become an apprentice in his uncle's apothecary and general merchandise business. It was under these circumstances that he apparently acquired some of those qualities (industry, sharp wits, belligerence, and an authoritarian attitude) that allowed him to rise rapidly from a lowly apprentice to a wealthy and socially prominent merchant and shipowner in New Haven, Connecticut. Sometimes he took personal command of one of his merchant ships, sailing it to the West Indies or Quebec, where he sold horses. As a business owner and ship's captain, Arnold became accustomed to making decisions, giving orders, and expecting to be obeyed without question.[3]

3 There is a gossipy narrative of Arnold's years in New Haven that describes how he operated his business. It explains that Arnold was apprenticed to Doctor Daniel Lathrop of Norwich, Connecticut, where Arnold was born and raised. After serving his apprenticeship, Arnold established his own business in New Haven. The text then reads, "He then first got with child, and afterwards married the daughter of Mr. Mansfield, High Sheriff of New Haven, much against the will of the latter; who at length became reconciled to him and employed him as a supercargo [an officer on a ship who has charge of the cargo and its purchase and sale] to the West Indies, where he usually went in the spring, and returned in the autumn with molasses, rum and sugar. In winter he went among the Dutch towards the head of Hudson's River, and

With the newly acquired wealth from his business and borrowing on credit, Arnold built a mansion overlooking New Haven's harbor.[4] It was one of the largest and most beautiful houses in the town. He also indulged in wearing bespoke (custom-made) clothing and expensive shoes to gratify his enormous ego and flaunt his success.[5] Business was complicated in colonial America, and it took a smart, quick-witted person to be successful. Arnold's rise to wealth is particularly impressive considering that he began his career as a destitute apprentice.

Although Arnold was a man of vast ambition, he apparently never sought public office or made an effort to cultivate the friendship of influential politicians. In fact, other than his fellow Connecticut merchant Silas Deane, who was a delegate to the Second Continental Congress, Arnold had no powerful friends in public office to speak out on his behalf. Even Deane's support was short-lived as a result of his failure to be re-elected to Congress at the end of 1775. Deane was next sent on a secret mission to France, leaving Arnold vulnerable to wild accusations about his character and military record.

---

into Canada, with various sorts of woolen goods, such as stocking, caps, mittens, etc. etc. and also cheese, which sold to great profit in Canada. These articles he either exchanged for horses, or purchased them with the money arising from his sales. With these horses, which generally made a part of a Connecticut cargo, together with poultry, corn and fish he went to the islands, whilst his father-in-law was selling the rum, molasses and sugars of the last voyages and collecting woolens for Arnold's next winter trip to Canada. It was in these voyages that Arnold became an expert seaman." Marquis De Chastellux, *Travels in North-America*, 2 vols. (London: G. G. J. and J. Robinson, 1787), I:361-362.

4 Following Arnold's treason, the state of Connecticut confiscated Arnold's home and property in New Haven, which were sold at auction. Noah Webster purchased the house in 1812 while he was working on his dictionary, but quickly sold it and moved inland out of a fear that the British might launch an attack against the city during the war. The house, located at 155 Water Street, was later torn down to make room for a lumber company. Emily Ellsworth Fowler Ford, *Notes on the Life of Noah Webster*, 2 vols. (New York: Privately Printed, 1912), I: 450-453, See also "Some of New Haven's Colonial Homes," *The Connecticut Quarterly*, Vol. II, (1896), 93-94.

5 The term "bespoke" dates from the 17th century, when tailors held the full lengths of cloth on their premises. When a customer chose a length of material, it was said to have been spoken for. While all 18th-century purchased clothing was hand-sewn by a seamstress or tailor, bespoke garments used the finest fabrics expertly fitted and sewn to your personal requirements. There is presently a Savile Row Bespoke Association in London. They are a group of tailors whose standards include making a paper pattern for each garment they produce. In modern usage, the word is an adjective meaning custom-made. It has found its way into the high-tech computer industry where custom-made software is also called bespoke software. Anne J. Kershen, *Uniting the Tailors: Trade Unionism Among the Tailoring Workers of London* (Portland, Oregon: Frank Cass, 1995), 4-6.

Besides Deane, Arnold enjoyed the wartime friendship of Maj. Gen. Philip Schuyler, the commander of the patriots' Northern Army during the opening years of the war. Schuyler was a man of great wealth, enviable family background, education, and military experience. He was one of the few men whom Arnold recognized as his superior and, with their common interests in business and military affairs, the two men got along famously. However, Schuyler's army career was sabotaged by the hostility of the New England troops and government functionaries who despised his wealth and aloof character. Arnold's alliance with Schuyler eventually became a liability.

Arnold was also admired for his courage and aggressiveness by George Washington, the most powerful and savvy political player of the era. However, Washington was too experienced a politician to risk his own reputation by getting involved in his hot-headed subordinate's altercations. Where Arnold was headstrong and confrontational, Washington was impassionate and respectful. He methodically built and maintained a cadre of influential friends in Congress and state governments to defend him against his critics. Washington also refused to take the handsome salary that was offered to him as commander-in-chief of the Continental Army. His famous statement that "no pecuniary [financial] consideration could have tempted me to have accepted this Arduous emploiment [sic] . . ." was viewed as a genuine act of patriotism, and protected him from any criticism of trying to profit from the war.[6] While many other American officers insisted on being paid their salary, allowances, and immediate reimbursement of expenses, Arnold in particular gained a reputation as a money hungry crook. With few friends in government to dispute the outrageous stories spread by his enemies, Arnold was viewed as "introducing a series of extravagant charges in his own favor and robbing that very public, which, under the guise of a hypocritical patriotism, he pretended to serve from disinterested motives, and at a great sacrifice."[7]

The concept of honor, or what we would today call reputation, is another important factor in understanding Arnold's personality. His full name was Benedict Arnold V, and his namesakes had been among the wealthiest and most

6 W.W. Abbot, et. al., eds., *The Papers of George Washington, Revolutionary War Series*, 18 vols. to date (Charlottesville, Virginia: University Press of Virginia, 1985- present), I: 1.

7 Jared Sparks, *The Life and Treason of Benedict Arnold* (Boston: 1835), 96-97.

respected men in New England.[8] While every officer and gentleman was concerned with protecting his honor, Arnold seemed obsessed with restoring his family's good name and reputation, and the slightest affront to his character elicited a hot-tempered response.

At the start of the American Revolution in 1775, Benedict Arnold was 34 years old and married (1767) to the former Margaret Mansfield. They had three children, all boys, named Benedict VI (born 1768), Richard (1769), and Henry (1772). Arnold was of medium height, with a muscular, robust body. Dr. Benjamin Rush described him as "low [short] but well made," with a handsome face.[9] He had dark hair and a swarthy complexion, but his most-mentioned physical features were his hawk-like nose and black, penetrating eyes.

Arnold's business connections in the West Indies served him well as the American colonists prepared to defend themselves from what they saw as a "regular, systematic plan of oppression" by the British government to "fix the shackles of slavery" upon them.[10] The Dutch island of St. Eustatius, for example, was a major source for the European-made weapons, tents, blankets, gunpowder, etc., which were offered for sale to Americans by shrewd importers. Arnold's skill at negotiating the purchase of weapons in the islands and his high standing back home got him elected (March 15, 1775) as the captain and senior officer in the 2nd Connecticut Foot Guards, a New Haven militia company.[11] Arnold was typical of the 65 men who joined the unit: young, affluent, and passionate in their belief that England, like Rome in its decline,

8 Independent historian Nicholas Westbrook commented that Benedict Arnold V is merely a convenience of modern historians and genealogists who struggle to keep track of a family which perpetuated the name Benedict Arnold for at least six generations. Mr. Westbrook said that he has never seen any 18th-century documents which refer to a Benedict Arnold V.

9 George W. Corner, ed., *The Autobiography of Benjamin Rush* (Princeton, New Jersey: Princeton University Press, 1948), 158.

10 Bernard Bailyn, *The Ideological Origins of the American Revolution* (Cambridge, Massachusetts: The Belknap Press of Harvard University Press, 1967), 120.

11 The 1st Company Governor's Foot Guard was established in Hartford (the capital of Connecticut) in 1771 for the purpose of providing an escort for Connecticut's governor and assembly. The company was known as the Governor's Guard until 1775 when the second company was chartered in New Haven. This resulted in the Hartford unit being renamed the 1st Company Governor's Foot Guard, while the New Haven detachment became the 2nd Company Governor's Foot Guard. Both the Hartford and New Haven companies exist today as honorary military organizations. Dave Richard Palmer, *George Washington and Benedict Arnold: A Tale of Two Patriots* (Washington, D.C.: Regnery Publishing, Inc., 2006), 72.

had fallen "from being the nursery of heroes, to become the residence of musicians, pimps, panderers and catamites."[12]

Captain Arnold's militia company had the money to hire a British Army deserter named Edward Burke to teach its members how to maneuver as a detachment and load and fire their weapons in formation. Like other militia companies throughout New England, the 2nd Connecticut Foot Guards were preparing to fight to preserve their hard-won liberties should the British troops stationed in nearby Boston attempt any hostile acts. The militia system dated from the time of the establishment of the colonies. With few British troops to defend them against the French, Spanish, and Indians, the colonists had revived the medieval system of armed citizens who could be called out in a military emergency. It is ironic that the system of colonial self-defense, which had been encouraged by the British government, was turned against it, especially during the opening months of the American Revolution.

British troops had occupied Boston since mid-1774 following the so-called Boston Tea Party (December 16, 1773) and the closing of the port of Boston in retribution. Massachusetts was also placed under martial law, with British Army units periodically marching into the countryside to flex their authority. However, the British regiments in Boston were not facing a London mob brandishing clubs and pitchforks, but armed and well-organized militia companies led by officers with combat experience from the French & Indian War.

Massachusetts was a powder keg of pent-up anger, which exploded into armed rebellion on April 19, 1775, when a column of British troops under the command of Lt. Col. William Smith marched 16 miles from Boston out into the countryside to the village of Concord to destroy military equipment being gathered there by the Massachusetts militia. In one of history's most pivotal events, the local militia turned out in force to repel the Redcoats' incursion. The first shots were exchanged in the village of Lexington, and the fighting intensified throughout the day as scores of additional militia companies arrived on the scene. By late afternoon the colonial militia was engaged in a running

12 Bailyn, *Ideological Origins*, 136. Professor Bailyn states that the source of the quote is a letter from William Hooper (a North Carolina delegate to the First Continental Congress) to James Iredell dated April 26, 1774. Iredell was a strong supporter of the patriot cause in North Carolina. In 1790, President Washington nominated him to be an Associate Justice of the U.S. Supreme Court. Iredell's nomination was confirmed by the Senate, and at age 38 he was the youngest of the original Supreme Court justices. A catamite is a boy kept for anal sex.

battle with Smith's column along the road back to Boston. The British had to rush reinforcements and artillery to the scene to prevent a massacre. The day-long event, which became known as the Lexington Alarm, ended with the Redcoats staggering back into Boston, feeling lucky to be alive.

A courier arrived in New Haven on the afternoon of April 21 shouting, "To arms, to arms, the war has begun!" and carrying a hastily written account of the Lexington Alarm.[13] The Foot Guards eagerly gathered on New Haven's village green the following day, determined to march to Boston "for the relief of our brethren and defense of their as well as our just rights and privileges."[14] Passions ran high as some students from Yale College joined their ranks and, with Captain Arnold in the lead, seized additional weapons and gunpowder from the town's magazine.[15] After listening to some fiery speeches and

13 The post rider (courier on horseback) who carried the news of the Lexington Alarm was Israel Bissell. He left Watertown, Massachusetts, on the morning of April 19 and rode for four days and six hours as far as Philadelphia. Bissell stopped briefly at every town along his route, as ordered, to find the local Committee of Correspondence or other town officials, who copied the hastily written message he carried from General Joseph Palmer, a member of the Massachusetts Committee of Safety. Palmer's message is fascinating because it was written just after the British column had fired on the Lexington militia en route to Concord. Palmer's electrifying note reads in part, "Wednesday morning near 10 of the clock—Watertown. To all the friends of American liberty be it known that this morning before break of day, a brigade, consisting of about 1,000 or 1,200 men landed at Phip's [Phipps] Farm at Cambridge and marched to Lexington, where they found a company of our colony militia in arms, upon whom they fired without any provocation and killed six men and wounded four others. The Bearer, Israel Bissell, is charged to alarm the country. . . ." Israel Bissell's ride rivals that of Paul Revere. Bissell's feat is overlooked in history, perhaps, according to one wit, because "Paul Revere" rhymes with a lot more than "Israel Bissell." Adding to Bissell's obscurity is that he is sometimes mentioned as "Trail Bissell." This error in his name derives from the fact that he stopped numerous times along his route to allow local officials to copy Palmer's message. In their haste to copy the note, "Israel Bissell" was sometimes mis-written as "Trail Bissell."

14 Peter Force, ed., *American Archives: A Documentary History of the Origin and Progress of the North American Colonies*, 9 vols. (Washington: Published by M. St. Clair Clarke and Peter Force, 1837-1853), Fourth Series, II: 383.

15 A supply of gunpowder was under the control of New Haven's governing officials (called selectmen) and stored in a public building known as the Powder House. On April 22, 1775, the 2nd Connecticut Foot Guards, under Arnold's command, demanded that the selectmen give them the keys to the Powder House. Arnold's company wanted additional gunpowder and other military stores to take with them to Boston. When the officials on hand refused, Arnold is reported to have said, "You may tell the Selectmen that if the keys are not coming within five minutes, my men will break into the supply house and help themselves. None but the Almighty God shall prevent me from marching." The keys were reluctantly handed over and Arnold and his men took what they needed from the Powder House. This dramatic event is recreated each year in New Haven on a Saturday in April. Celebrated as Powder House Day, the members of

sermons, the Foot Guards' field musicians (on fifes and drums) struck up a lively tune as they set out for Boston, to the hallooing (shouting) and cheering of the local patriots. En route, each man signed articles of agreement drafted by Silas Deane asserting that they "were not mercenaries . . . wading through the blood of their countrymen; but men acquainted with, and feeling the most generous fondness for the liberties and unalienable rights of mankind."[16]

The organizational structure of the rebels following the Lexington Alarm was confusing. Boston was held by the British Army under the command of Gen. Thomas Gage. The rest of Massachusetts was controlled by the insurgents, whose extralegal governing body was called the Massachusetts Provincial Congress. This assembly delegated the Massachusetts Committee of Safety to administer the day-to-day operations of the Provincial Army of Observation, the name given to the militia force from the various New England colonies that gathered outside Boston following the Lexington Alarm. Cooperation between the colonies during these opening weeks of the war was enthusiastic but voluntary. Each colony had its own civilian government, militia organization, and committees involved in the insurrection. Adding to the excitement of the time was a so-called *rage militaire* that was sweeping the colonies: the romantic idea of soldiering for a noble cause. Many young men marched to Boston with their militia companies eager for a chance to fight in an uprising that was expected to last only a few months. Besides defending their liberties, status-conscious Americans such as Benedict Arnold viewed service as an officer in the insurrection as a means of gaining upward mobility and prestige in their communities.

The Provincial Army of Observation, headquartered in the town of Cambridge near Boston, was being supplied by the fervent efforts of

---

the honorary 2nd Connecticut Foot Guard re-enact the event, with one of them portraying Arnold.

16 Force, ed., *American Archives*, Fourth Series, II: 384. The Foot Guard Articles of Agreement are dated "24th of April, 1775," which has led some historians to conclude that the 24th was the earliest date that Arnold's militia company could have left New Haven for Cambridge. But Arnold biographer Clare Brandt concluded that the Foot Guards departed New Haven on April 22 and signed the Articles en route. Clare Brandt, *The Man in the Mirror: A Life of Benedict Arnold* (New York: Random House, 1994), 20. I believe Ms. Brandt is correct. In addition, we know that Arnold arrived in Cambridge on April 29 and that the approximate distance between New Haven and Cambridge is 120 miles. A reasonable daily average march for Arnold's company over the existing roads was 15 miles per day, or a total of eight days for the trek. This information points to the Foot Guards leaving New Haven on April 22 in order to reach Cambridge on the 29th.

Massachusetts and her neighboring colonies. Delegates from all the colonies had gathered the previous year (1774) in Philadelphia in the First Continental Congress to discuss the political situation in America, and had sent petitions to the King and his government summarizing their grievances. A Second Continental Congress was planned for Philadelphia. However, it too was voluntary, a gathering of the colonies with no authority to raise or direct an army. The outbreak of fighting in Massachusetts on April 19, 1775, occurred prior to the opening of the Second Continental Congress, which was scheduled to convene in mid-May. With a New England militia presence building outside Boston, many influential colonists advocated for assertive military action, while others counseled calm and respectful negotiations with the King and his government.

Captain Arnold and his Connecticut militia company marched into this imbroglio on April 29, 1775. The American Revolution was ten days old when Arnold and his Foot Guards joined other New England militia companies under the loose coordination of the Provincial Army of Observation. Despite the army's impressive name, the rebels were a ragged lot, with few uniforms, little discipline, and a hodgepodge of weapons. The Foot Guards were an exception: they were well-armed and disciplined, with new uniforms consisting of red regimental coats with buff facings (lapels, collars, and cuffs) and white waistcoats (vests) and breeches.[17] There were some other similarly equipped and trained insurgent units in the rebel camp at the time, but Arnold's company was one of the most impressive.

After arriving at Cambridge, Arnold devoted his time to finding comfortable quarters for his men. He found billets for them in the abandoned mansion of a Loyalist (as colonists who sided with Britain were called, also known as Tories). Arnold's concern for the welfare of his troops was typical of his command style throughout the war.

After attending to the needs of his men, Arnold turned his attention to the fact that the patriot army needed more and heavier artillery if it was going to force the British out of Boston. He had been told by his pre-war business

17 The uniform of the 2nd Connecticut Foot Guard was adopted on February 2, 1775, as "A scarlet coat of common length, the lapels, cuffs and collars of buff and trimmed with plain silver wash buttons, white linen vest, breeches and stockings, black half leggings and small, fashionable and narrow ruffled shirt." On March 16, cartridge boxes (a box, usually made of leather, that held fixed ammunition), hats and cockades were adopted. The unit's records also state that the soldier's hair was to be clubbed behind and the side locks braided and powdered.

friends in Quebec that there was a stockpile of ordnance and other valuable military equipment at Fort Ticonderoga, the fortress guarding the strategic passage between Lake George and Lake Champlain in upper New York. Arnold had no combat experience or fluency in logistics (the planning and carrying out of the movement and maintenance of forces) and he probably had never seen Fort Ticonderoga, but that did not prevent him from proposing that he lead a detachment to surprise the fort's rumored small, superannuated (i.e., ineffective because of advanced age) garrison and seize its valuable artillery. Quick action was critical because the fortress was expected to be reinforced by British troops from Canada following the news of the Lexington Alarm.

Some additional information about Fort Ticonderoga and upper New York is appropriate here, since the region was the scene of some of the major events in this narrative. Fort Ticonderoga was originally built in the 1750s by the French (they called it Fort Carillon) to protect Canada from a British invasion moving north from Albany across Lake George and Lake Champlain and aimed at the cities of Montreal and Quebec. The British countered by building Fort William Henry on the southern end of Lake George to defend New York and New England from a French incursion; it was subsequently destroyed by the French during the French & Indian War. The situation changed when the British annexed Canada under the treaty ending the French & Indian War. The Lake George and Lake Champlain forts had virtually no military value following the French surrender. Thus, Fort Ticonderoga and the other old forts in the region had fallen into ruin by the time of the American Revolution. Sieges, gunpowder explosions, and fires over the years had accelerated their decay. By 1775, Fort Ticonderoga was a lightly garrisoned depot for artillery and other equipment left over from the French & Indian War.

In Cambridge, Benedict Arnold approached Dr. Joseph Warren and other members of the Massachusetts Committee of Safety with the idea of leading a fast-moving expedition to capture derelict Fort Ticonderoga. They must have been impressed with Arnold's acumen and spirit, for they gave him a commission, dated May 3, 1775, appointing him a colonel in the service of Massachusetts, with orders to raise up to 400 men to capture the post, secure it with a garrison, and "bring back with you such of the cannon, mortars, stores &c. as you shall judge may be serviceable to the Army here."[18] The speed with

18 Force, ed., *American Archives*, Fourth Series, II: 485. Arnold had submitted a report to the Massachusetts Committee of Safety on April 30, 1775, prior to his appointment to command

which Arnold moved on his idea is demonstrative of his alert mind and aggressive behavior. He arrived in Cambridge on April 29—and he had written orders to seize Fort Ticonderoga four days later. Arnold appointed Eleazer Oswald and Jonathan Brown as his junior officers, ranked as captains, with orders to recruit men in western Massachusetts for his new regiment.[19]

Oswald was well-known to Arnold as a fellow New Haven businessman and member of the Foot Guards. Oswald's later adventures would include campaigning with Arnold and serving as an artillery officer in the French Revolution. As one of Arnold's most devoted partisans, Oswald was a key person in the story that follows. In modern parlance, Oswald was Arnold's "sidekick."

Brown's appointment as one of Arnold's officers represented a very different situation. He was a 51-year-old resident of Watertown, Massachusetts, with combat experience as a Provincial captain in the French & Indian War. Brown was also active in pre-war Massachusetts politics, and his military background was put to good use by the colony's Committee of Safety, which sought his advice on a variety of military subjects. Brown was probably

an expedition to seize Fort Ticonderoga. Although Arnold had never seen the fortress, his account was surprisingly accurate. His information was probably supplied to him by his pro-American business friends in Montreal and Quebec City. Arnold's report read in part, "You desire me to state the number of cannon, &c., at Ticonderoga. I have certain information that there are at Ticonderoga eighty pieces of heavy cannon, twenty brass guns, from four to eighteen pounders [the weight of the ball fired by the various weapons] and ten to twelve large mortars.. . . The Fort is in a ruinous condition, and has not more than fifty men at the most. There are large numbers of small arms, and considerable stores, and a sloop of seventy or eighty tons on the lake [Champlain]. The place could not hold out an hour against a vigorous onset." *Ibid.*, 450. Additional details about Arnold's assignment appear in the minutes of the Massachusetts Committee of Safety for May 1, 1775, which read in part, "Voted, That Colonel Arnold, appointed to a secret service, be desired to appoint two Field-Officers, Captains &c., to be allowed the same pay during their continuance in service as is established for officers and privates of the same rank, who are ordered by the Congress of Massachusetts-Bay to be raised for the defense of the rights and liberties of America; the officers and privates to be dismissed by Colonel Arnold, or the Committee of Safety, whenever they shall think proper." *Ibid.*, 750.

19 Arnold's orders were explicit that he was to recruit "in the western parts of this and the neighbouring [sic] Colonies." The reasoning of the members of the Massachusetts Committee of Safety was that they did not want to pay travel expenses for the long march across Massachusetts. Jonathan Brown is identified as one of Arnold's captains in a letter Arnold wrote to the Massachusetts Committee of Safety, dated "Crown Point, 19th May 1775." The pertinent text reads, "I must refer you for Particulars [the raid on St. Johns] to the Bearer, Capt Jonathan Brown, who has been very active & serviceable, & is a prudent & good Officer.. . . " William Bell Clark, ed., *Naval Documents of The American Revolution*, 10 vols. to date (Washington, D.C.: U.S. Government Printing Office, 1964-present), I: 365.

appointed as one of Arnold's officers at the insistence of the Committee of Safety. Apparently, while they were impressed with Arnold, Warren and his fellow committeemen wanted their own trusted representative on the mission to keep an eye on Arnold, as well as to provide him with a mature person with military experience.[20]

Arnold's orders specified that he was to recruit men for his expedition in western Massachusetts and the "neighbouring Colonies."[21] He probably left Cambridge and rode toward the western part of the colony accompanied by Brown and Oswald. At some point they split up, with Arnold riding ahead to gather intelligence on the situation at Fort Ticonderoga while his officers fanned out to recruit men. What happened next turned out to be Arnold's first military campaign. The story is worth describing in detail, as it illustrates Arnold's aggressive personality and how he managed to alienate people in record time. Just as compelling is the observation that Arnold apparently lacked the introspection to learn from the incident and see how his confrontational and abusive manner undermined his military career. Here is the story of Arnold's first military campaign, the capture of Fort Ticonderoga.

Unknown to Colonel Arnold as he rode west from Cambridge, the Connecticut Committee of Safety, acting without authorization from the colony's conservative legislature, had organized its own expedition to capture

20 Jonathan Brown (1724-1797) is an obscure figure from the American Revolution of whom little is known beyond his long list of civilian and military positions. Brown's role in facilitating the ease with which the inexperienced Arnold got his commission to capture Ticonderoga has been overlooked even by Arnold's best biographers. For example, Brown is not mentioned by either Isaac Arnold in his *The Life of Benedict Arnold* or James Kirby Martin in his authoritative *Benedict Arnold, Revolutionary Hero*. The impression we have is that the Massachusetts Committee of Safety was smitten with Arnold. Typical of this theme is Isaac Arnold, who wrote on page 38 of his biography, "Arnold presented the project [the capture of Fort Ticonderoga] so clearly, and such was the impression made upon the committee by his intelligence, energy and enthusiasm, that they immediately and eagerly commissioned him as colonel, and authorized him to raise four hundred troops for the service." The action of the Committee of Safety becomes less emotional when Brown's watchdog and advisory role are included in the story. Besides Brown's numerous civilian posts, he served throughout the Revolutionary War as a militia officer, achieving the rank of colonel in the 7th Middlesex County (Massachusetts) militia. Information about Brown can be found in Henry Bond, *Family Memorials: Genealogies of the Families and Descendants of Early Settlers of Watertown, Mass.* (Boston: Little, Brown, 1855), II: 728-730 and 1064; *Journals of Each Provincial Congress of Massachusetts in 1774 and 1775*, 1838; Secretary of State, *Massachusetts Soldiers and Sailors of the American Revolution* (Boston: Wright & Potter State Printers, 1896), II: 653-654; *Watertown's Military History* (Boston: David Clap & Son, 1907), 18-19, 105-108.

21 Force, ed., *American Archives*, Fourth Series, II: 485.

Fort Ticonderoga. The fact that both Massachusetts and Connecticut had launched uncoordinated campaigns to seize the fort is typical of the disorganization of the patriot movement's disorganization during the opening months of the war. Additionally, Fort Ticonderoga was located in New York, and that colony naturally had an interest in its fate. In fact, at least six political bodies could claim jurisdiction over the fortress: the Massachusetts Committee of Safety, the Massachusetts Provincial Congress, the Connecticut General Assembly, the Connecticut Committee of Correspondence, the Albany Committee of Correspondence, and the New York Committee of Safety.[22]

Realizing that speed was essential to capture Fort Ticonderoga, the Connecticut firebrands drew money from their colony's treasury to finance their expedition and appointed a local militia captain, Edward Mott, to command it. Mott, in turn, recruited John Brown as one of his officers. At the time of his appointment, Brown was a 31-year-old lawyer practicing in Pittsfield, Massachusetts. He was educated, politically connected, and a leader in the insurgent movement in western Massachusetts. Following his graduation from Yale in 1771, Brown became a lawyer and a junior officer in the Pittsfield militia. He was appointed as a member of the pre-war Massachusetts Committee of Correspondence with Canada, on whose behalf he successfully carried out an arduous fact-finding journey to Montreal in February and March 1775 to determine the sentiments of the Canadians. He was recommended for the mission by his friend John Adams. Brown had also made inquiries about the situation at Fort Ticonderoga during his Canadian trip, learning that the place was undermanned. Recognizing the strategic importance of the fortress, Brown wrote in his report that "[t]he Fort at Ticonderoga must be seized as soon as possible, should hostilities be committed by the King's Troops."[23] Mott also enlisted Brown's friend Colonel James Easton, a Pittsfield tavern owner and commander of the local militia, to help him recruit men for the attack.

Despite their enlistment efforts, Mott, Brown, and Easton knew that they would need more troops quickly if they hoped to take Ticonderoga before it was put on full alert and reinforced with additional troops from Canada. The fastest way to recruit men was to approach a frontier brawler and land speculator named Ethan Allen, who at the time was in command of a nearby

22 Brandt, *The Man in the Mirror*, 30.

23 Force, ed., *American Archives*, Fourth Series, II: 243-244.

quasi-military force known sympathetically as the Green Mountain Boys.[24] Allen and his followers had settled in a region called the Hampshire Grants (modern Vermont) which lay between New York and New Hampshire. New York claimed the territory, calling Allen and his renegade army the Bennington Mob or the Bennington Rioters (after the unofficial capital of the Hampshire Grants) and claiming that they terrorized anyone who dared to dispute their land claims.[25]

Through advance emissaries, Allen and his rowdy cohorts agreed to join Mott's expedition. However, upon Mott's arrival at Bennington, and after counting heads, Allen realized that he was supplying the largest number of men to the mission, and demanded to be put in charge. In the spirit of cooperation and realizing that time was of the essence, Mott accepted Allen's arrangement. Besides, it was the long-established custom that the man who commanded the largest number of men was made the leader. Thus the Connecticut-based expedition's plan went forward with Allen as commander-in-chief and Mott, Brown, and Easton designated as his committee-at-war. Mott was officially the

24 Historian Washington Irving called Ethan Allen "a kind of Robin Hood among the mountains." Irving included a vivid description of Allen in his biography of George Washington: "He was well fitted for the enterprise in question, by his experience as a frontier champion, his robustness of mind and body, and his fearless spirit. He had a kind of rough eloquence, also, that was very effective with his followers. 'His style,' says one, who knew him personally, 'was a singular compound of local barbarisms, scriptural phrases, and oriental wildness; and though unclassic [sic], and sometimes ungrammatical, was highly animated and forcible.'" Washington, in one of his letters, said there was "an original something in him which commanded admiration." Washington Irving, *Life of George Washington*, 4 vols. (New York: G.P. Putnam & Co., 1856-1859), I: 442-443. Irving was a great writer and historian, and his multi-volume biography of Washington is accurate and beautifully written. It proved to be his final writing effort; he died shortly after the publication of the final volume. Irving decided to write a Washington biography at a time of growing sectionalism in the United States (culminating in the Civil War) to remind all Americans of their common struggle for independence.

25 The governors of both New York and New Hampshire gave grants to the same land, modern Vermont, because the King had been imprecise in laying out the boundaries of the two colonies. That had not mattered much when settlement was sparse. But by the 1770s New York and New Hampshire were encroaching on each other, and The Grants, as the territory was called at the time, became a no-man's-land. Land speculator Ethan Allen and the Green Mountain Boys defended what they believed were properly their land grants, which clashed with the claims of the authorities in New York. Ethan Allen's family came from Salisbury in northwestern Connecticut, as did many of his neighbors and members of the Green Mountain Boys. Indeed, The Grants were briefly called the Republic of New Connecticut in 1777 when independent statehood seemed a possibility. Nicholas Westbrook, correspondence with the author.

head of the committee, but Allen held the power. Despite their pretentious organization and military ranks, the Connecticut-organized expedition had no legitimacy. Not only were its members lacking written orders from any colonial authority, they were also undertaking an offensive operation into a sister colony (New York) which had not sanctioned their action.

One of the first things that Allen did was to set up patrols on the roads in the region to prevent anyone from trying to warn Fort Ticonderoga's garrison of an imminent attack. Another of Allen's measures was to send thirty of his Green Mountain Boys, under the command of Capt. Samuel Herrick, to Skenesboro to "take into custody Major Skene and his party, and take possession of all the boats that they should find there and in the night proceed up the Lake to Shoreham."[26] Skenesboro was a large estate owned by Philip Skene, a former British Army officer and ardent Loyalist who was in England at the time. There were boats at Skenesboro that Allen needed to transport his men across Lake Champlain. Skene also owned a small schooner (a two-masted sailing vessel) named the *Katherine*.[27]

26 Edward Mott to the Massachusetts Provincial Congress, dated "Shoreham, May 11, 1775" in Clark, ed., *Naval Documents of the American Revolution*, I: 315. Regarding the identity of the officer sent to seize Skenesboro, in his report Edward Mott stated "[t]hat a party of thirty men, under the command of Captain Herrick, should, on the next day, in the afternoon, proceed to Skenesboro, and take into custody Major Skene and his party, and take possession of all the boats that they should find there.. . . " Captain Herrick is identified as Samuel Herrick in Francis Heitman, *Historical Register of Officers of the Continental Army* (Washington, D.C.: The Rare Book Shop Publishing Company, Inc., 1914), 287. His full name also appears in Arnold's expense account in Force, ed., *American Archives*, Fourth Series, III: 344. The Major Skene captured at Skenesboro was Andrew Philip Skene, the son of Phillip Skene, who owned the Skenesboro estate.

27 Captain Phillip Skene fought in upstate New York during the French and Indian War, where he became familiar with the Lake Champlain region. He was promoted to major on July 31, 1759. Skene pensioned out of the army on half pay when the war was over, but even before then he began securing land grants for the territory on Lake Champlain on which he had served. By 1764, he had amassed some 45,000 acres which he called Skenesborough. In early 1776, Skene was in England trying to secure an appointment as Lieutenant Governor of Crown Point and Ticonderoga. He was successful, but was captured on his return to America in June 1775. He was eventually exchanged for James Lovell. Skene is often referred to as Colonel Skene. It was probably a brevet appointment made by Gen. John Burgoyne during the 1777 campaign. Author's exchange of e-mails and correspondence with Nicholas Westbrook. While the Green Mountain Boys were searching Skene's house, they found the dead body of a woman in the cellar, where it had apparently been lying for years. It was the body of the former Mrs. Katherine Skene, the Colonel's deceased wife. He had never buried her because she was the beneficiary of an annuity which she received "while she remained above ground." James

Allen mustered 230 of his followers at Bennington and made a forced march to Lake Champlain, arriving in the town of Shoreham on the east side of the lake across from Fort Ticonderoga. They arrived at Shoreham on the night of May 9, 1775. Allen had excellent, up-to-date intelligence about the situation inside the fort from Noah Phelps, one of Mott's men, who had posed as a farmer and managed to talk his way into the fortress. Phelps returned with an encouraging report that the garrison had no knowledge that fighting had taken place near Boston. Although the isolated fort had been ordered to increase its security months previously, little had been done to defend the place, which lay quiet and peaceful.

However, there was intense military activity across Lake Champlain on the night of May 9 as Allen prepared to attack the fort with hundreds of armed men. The rebels were only waiting for nightfall and the arrival of Herrick's additional boats from Skenesboro to add to the two scows (barges) they had anchored at Hand's Cove, near Shoreham. Allen had a total force of 286 troops poised for the attack, consisting of 230 Green Mountain Boys, 16 volunteers from Connecticut commanded by Edward Mott, and 40 men recruited in the Pittsfield area by James Easton and John Brown.

Arnold was at Nehemiah Smedley's tavern in Williamstown, Massachusetts, on the night of May 8 when he learned that Mott and his men had passed through the village a few days before en route to join Ethan Allen and his Green Mountain Boys in Vermont.[28] Arnold realized that their objective had to be Fort Ticonderoga, so he arose early the following morning and rode north into Vermont to find them. He caught up with Mott, Brown, Easton, and some of their men that evening (May 9) in a tavern in Castleton, Vermont, preparing to join Allen, who was a short distance away in Shoreham with the main column. Everything was set for the entire force to cross the lake later that night, to be followed by a pre-dawn surprise attack on Fort Ticonderoga.

A prudent man probably would have understood the situation and offered to help, in a spirit of cooperation. Instead Arnold raced to Shoreham, where he burst into Allen's makeshift headquarters waving his Massachusetts commission and insisting that he was in command. He based his demand upon

---

Phinney Baxter, *The British Invasion From the North with the Journal of Lieut. William Digby* (Albany, NY: Joel Munsell's Sons, 1887), 217.

28 Brandt, *The Man in the Mirror*, 24.

his commission from the Massachusetts Committee of Safety as a colonel and his written orders to "subdue and take possession of the Fort of Ticonderoga."[29]

Allen recognized the legitimacy of Arnold's commission and orders, but Arnold was accompanied only by a manservant, while Allen had almost 300 armed men ready to attack the fort. The situation required diplomacy and tact—qualities which neither man possessed. After some wrangling, the matter was resolved by Brown, Easton, and the other officers present by recognizing Allen and Arnold as co-commanders. The Green Mountain Boys were unhappy with the arrangement, insisting that they would take orders only from Allen. A mutiny was averted by explaining to them that Arnold's participation gave their mission legal status; but the raucous Green Mountain Boys remained sullen and cynical—an attitude which was aggravated by Arnold's haughty manner.

Meanwhile, the night wore on and the additional boats failed to appear. With just a few hours of darkness left to conceal their movements, Allen and Arnold decided that they would cross the mile-wide lake using their two scows to ferry their troops across the lake in stages. But by 4 a.m. only 80 men were on the New York side. They were hiding on a sandy beach below the fort accompanied by their officers. With daylight fast approaching, the commanders determined that the attack could wait no longer, and they decided to launch their assault with the men they had available. It was at this moment that Arnold decided that he was entitled to have the honor of leading the troops into the fort. Standing on the beach below the fort, he argued the point with Allen, while precious minutes slipped by.

William Gordon, a gossipy raconteur and early chronicler of the war, described the event: "[A] dispute took place between the colonels, Arnold became assuming and swore he would go in first, Allen swore he should not. The gentlemen [officers] present interposed, and the matter was accommodated upon the footing that they should go in together."[30]

Thus the two antagonists advanced side by side at sunrise, with their men following. They reached the main gate of the fort, shoulder to shoulder—only to find it shut. However, the wicket (a small door in the gate of a fortified place, through which men could enter in single file) was open. Apparently Allen went

29 Force, ed., *American Archives*, Fourth Series, II: 485.

30 William Gordon, *The History of the Rise, Progress and Establishment, of the Independence of the United States of America*, 4 vols. (London: 1788), II: 13.

through the door first, because there was a sentry on the other side who fired his musket at him, but the gun failed to go off. Allen said he chased the sentry, who ran deeper into the fort and "gave a halloo."[31] But the rebels swarmed into the fort through the wicket while also scaling the undefended wall on both sides of the gate. There were a few other sentries on duty who, according to Allen, "were so surprised, that contrary to expectation they did not fire on us, but fled with precipitancy."[32] The interior of the fort consisted of a parade (open area) surrounded by barracks on three sides. The Americans rushed into the buildings and captured the British soldiers they found sleeping there. The entire operation took ten minutes and was a complete success.[33] The fort's garrison was soon revealed to be 42 privates, 24 women and children, and three officers.[34]

ne of the captives was Lt. Jocelyn Feltham, who later described the attack: "I was awakened by a number of shrieks and the words 'No quarter, no quarter ' [no surrender] from a number of armed rabble." He said that the rebel assault was a complete surprise: "I never saw a [British] soldier, tho' I heard a great noise in their rooms and . . . that they must have been seized in their beds. . . . When I did see our men they were drawn up [standing in formation] without weapons."

31 Ethan Allen, *A Narrative of Colonel Ethan Allen's Captivity Containing His Voyages and Travels* (New York: The Georgian Press, 1930), 7.

32 Force, ed., *American Archives*, Fourth Series, II: 606.

33 Frank Moore, *Diary of the American Revolution from Newspapers and Original Documents*, 2 vols. (New York: Privately Printed, 1865), I: 78.

34 The classic summary of the garrison's size is in Ethan Allen's letter to Governor Trumbull dated May 12, 1775. The original is in the Fort Ticonderoga collection. The letter reads in part, "I make you a present of a Major [Andrew Skene, Jr., captured at Skenesborough], a Captain [Delaplace], and two lieutenants [Feltham and Wadman] in the regular Establishment of George the Third." In his 1779 *Narrative of Col. Ethan Allen's Captivity*, Allen tells us that he and his men captured "the commander [Delaplace], a Lieut. Feltham, a conductor of artillery [Lt. Wadman], a gunner, two sergeants, and forty-four rank-and-file." There is also a list of the number of officers and men captured at Fort Ticonderoga and Crown Point prepared by Lt. Feltham which states that one captain, one lieutenant, and one conductor were taken at Fort Ticonderoga. Allen French, *The Taking of Ticonderoga in 1775: the British Story* (Cambridge: Harvard University Press, 1928), 53-55. *An Universal Military Dictionary* defines conductors as "assistants to the commissary of stores, to conduct depots, or magazines, from one place to another: they have also the care of the ammunition wagons in the field: they report to the commissary, and are under his command." Captain George Smith, *An Universal Military Dictionary* (London: Printed for J. Millan, 1779), 66.

Lieutenant Feltham also commented on the reckless nature of Allen's Green Mountain Boys. Calling them "rioters," he said they were constantly landing men from across the lake "who . . . came now to join in the plunder which was most rigidly performed as to liquors, provisions, etc., whether belonging to His Majesty or private property."[35]

On the following day (May 11), the Green Mountain Boys captured Crown Point (called Fort St. Frédéric by the French) located ten miles north of Fort Ticonderoga on Lake Champlain. The rebels easily overwhelmed the dilapidated fort's meager garrison, consisting of one sergeant and 11 common soldiers.

The American Revolution was three weeks old when the patriots captured Fort Ticonderoga and Crown Point. Their attack took place just in time, because Guy Carleton, the royal governor of Canada, had been alerted by General Thomas Gage in Boston to rush reinforcements to Forts Ticonderoga and Crown Point from Quebec.[36] Troops from the 7th Regiment were about to depart from Montreal when the Governor learned that the King's Lake Champlain forts had been captured by the rebels. Writing to Gage on May 20, 1775, Carleton said that it was impossible to carry out his orders, since one "Dominick Arnold and certain Banditti [the Green Mountain Boys] settled on the Borders of the Lakes had seized the fort."[37]

Carleton's report was among the few accounts which gave Arnold any credit for the capture of Fort Ticonderoga. Arnold's mean-spirited behavior during the brief campaign had alienated him from Allen and his committee of war. Their opportunity for retribution came in their after-action reports and letters, which either failed to mention Arnold's participation in the attack or denounced him as a demagogue. For example, in his report to the Massachusetts authorities announcing his victory, Ethan Allen praised his officers, including James Easton, "who behaved with great zeal," and John

35 Henry Steele Commager and Richard B. Morris, eds., *The Spirit of 'Seventy-Six*, 2 vols. (Indianapolis and New York: The Bobbs-Merrill Company, Inc., 1958), I: 101-102.

36 James Kirby Martin, *Benedict Arnold, Revolutionary Hero* (New York: New York University Press, 1997), 66.

37 Allen French, *The First Year of the American Revolution* (Boston and New York: Houghton, Mifflin Company, 1934), 147-148.

Brown, who was "personally in the attack," but he did not even mention Arnold's name.[38]

Allen's committee-at-war was even more hostile to Arnold. Its members wrote a scathing letter to the Massachusetts Provincial Congress (Arnold's civilian bosses) requesting his recall. "This is to certify," their letter read, that "said Arnold refuses to give up his command, which causes much difficulty and . . . we think that said Arnold's further procedure in this matter highly inexpedient."[39] In a separate report, Edward Mott added to the condemnation of Arnold: "Colonel Arnold strenuously contended and insisted that he had a right to command them [the troops] and all their officers, which bred such a mutiny among the soldiers which had nearly frustrated our whole design."[40]

John Brown probably inflicted the most damage upon Arnold's fledgling military reputation. Brown was what we would call today a "team player," and apparently was appalled by Arnold's arrogance and lack of cooperation during the Ticonderoga campaign. Serious trouble started for Arnold when Brown was selected by Allen and his cohorts to carry the news of their victory to the Second Continental Congress, which convened in Philadelphia on May 10, 1775, to "determine upon such measures, as shall be judged most effectual for the preservation and re-establishment of American rights and privileges, and for the restoration of harmony between Great Britain and the Colonies."[41] Brown arrived on the night of May 17 in Philadelphia, where he was enthusiastically welcomed. He gave his report to a hushed session of Congress the following day. While there is no known text of Brown's report, accounts of his story appeared in the New York and Philadelphia newspapers—and none of them mentioned Arnold's participation in the successful attack. Historian Justin Smith said that "Brown wielded a special influence against Arnold everywhere."[42] As we will see, Brown's attitude toward Arnold would become ever more hostile as the war progressed.

38 Force, ed., *American Archives*, Fourth Series, II: 556.

39 *Ibid.*

40 Force, ed., *American Archives*, Fourth Series, II: 558.

41 Worthington Chauncey Ford, ed., *Journals of the Continental Congress 1774-1789*, 34 vols. (Washington, D.C.: Government Printing Office, 1904-1937), II: 15. The text is a portion of the credentials given to the New York delegates attending Congress.

42 Justin Smith, *Our Struggle For the Fourteenth Colony: Canada and the American Revolution*, 2 vols. (New York: G.P. Putnam's Sons, 1907), I: 185.

James Easton was given the honor of carrying the news of the capture of Fort Ticonderoga to the Massachusetts Provincial Congress. In his account, Easton lauded Ethan Allen and John Brown, who "behaved with the utmost intrepidity and good conduct," but never even mentioned that Arnold had participated in the assault.[43]

Arnold quickly fired off his own version of the events to his civilian bosses. His report included the following description of the situation in the fort following its capture:

> Ticonderoga, May 11, 1775
>
> There is here at present near one hundred men, who are in the greatest confusion and anarchy, destroying and plundering private property, committing every enormity, and paying no attention to publick service. . . . Colonel Allen is a proper man to head his own wild people, but entirely unacquainted with military service; and as I the only person who has been legally authorized to take possession of this place, I am determined to insist on my right, and I think it my duty to remain here against all opposition, until I have further orders.[44]

Arnold's comment about Allen being "unacquainted with military service" is a bit of bravado, since the sum of Arnold's own military experience at the time was a brief, pre-war stint as a militia captain.

The reality of the caliber of the men who followed Ethan Allen across Lake Champlain became evident soon after the capture of Fort Ticonderoga. They were a rough, impoverished lot who could afford to leave their farms for only a short time. Some of them quickly returned across the lake to their Vermont homesteads—laden with good purchase (plunder) from the fort—while others chose to remain with Allen in anticipation of further easy conquests and booty. Those who stayed with Allen promptly went on a three-day drunken spree from the Fort's rum supply. Despite the departure of some of the Green Mountain Boys and the condition of many others too inebriated to fight, Allen retained the upper hand since Arnold still had no troops under his command.

The situation took a dramatic turn in Arnold's favor on May 14, when Capt. Oswald sailed into view at Fort Ticonderoga at the helm of the *Katherine* with 50

43 Force, ed., *American Archives*, Fourth Series, II: 624-625.

44 *Ibid.*, 557.

men aboard. His fortuitous arrival was a combination of good luck and training from his youth. Oswald's good fortune occurred during his overland march to join Arnold with 50 men that he had "enlisted on the Road."[45] He marched into Skenesboro with his recruits on May 11 to find the place occupied by a detachment of Green Mountain Boys commanded by Capt. Samuel Herrick. Major Skene's valuable trading schooner lay deserted offshore because none of Allen's landlubbers knew how to sail her. But Oswald had learned seamanship from his father, a ship's captain who sailed out of the English coastal town of Falmouth. Oswald was 15 years old when his father was lost at sea. With no particular prospects in mind, he had immigrated to America in 1770, where he became an apprentice to the New York City printer John Holt. He endeared himself to the Holt family, married their daughter Elizabeth in 1774, and moved to New Haven, where he opened his own printing shop. However, Oswald never lost his knowledge of sailing, and he must have eyed the *Katherine* bobbing in Lake Champlain as a golden opportunity.

Captain Herrick was aware that his fellow Green Mountain Boys had already captured Fort Ticonderoga, and in a generous mood he let Oswald have the *Katherine*. Oswald put his men on board, maneuvered her out onto Lake Champlain, and sailed north toward Fort Ticonderoga. He found Arnold upon his arrival at the fort on May 14, four days after it was captured by the rebels.

The appearance of the *Katherine* with her complement of troops gave Arnold the first opportunity of his military career to show his talent for inventiveness, fast thinking, inspired leadership, unwavering determination, personal courage, and bold action. Historian Raymond Andrews eloquently summarized Arnold's innate martial skills as "his ability to understand the moment, terrain and position."[46]

Arnold's ability to grasp a situation and exploit it—understanding the moment—quickly became apparent. He armed the *Katherine* and set sail in search of the king's armed sloop *Betsey*, the largest ship on Lake Champlain.[47]

45 Benedict Arnold to The Massachusetts Committee of Safety, dated "Crown Point, 19th May 1775" in Clark, ed. *Naval Documents of the American Revolution*, I: 364.

46 Comment by Mr. Raymond Andrews in a telephone interview with the author. Mr. Andrews is a member of the New York State Historical Preservation Commission; his special interest is the American Revolution.

47 The term "king's armed sloop" (or ship) suggests that the *Betsey* was under the control of the British army and manned by British soldiers. It would have been referred to as *H.M.S. Betsey* if it was a Royal Navy vessel. The name of the ship is confirmed in a Return by Capt. William De la

He knew—understanding the terrain—that since the Lake Champlain region was heavily forested, with virtually no roads, any large-scale British offensive aimed at recapturing Ticonderoga and Crown Point would have to utilize Lake Champlain to transport troops and artillery. Arnold realized—understanding the position—that achieving naval supremacy on Lake Champlain was the key to defending the forts and preventing the British from launching an invasion against New York and New England from Canada. There were only two ships on the lake at the time, the *Katherine* and the *Betsey*. Arnold had the *Katherine*, and he went after the *Betsey*.

Arnold hastily converted the *Katherine* into a warship while she was berthed at Fort Ticonderoga by piercing her sides to accommodate the carriages for four guns (cannon) and eight swivels (small-caliber cannon) selected from the stockpile of weapons captured at the fort.[48] After renaming Major Skene's schooner the *Liberty*, Arnold, Oswald, and their 50 men set sail for the British-held Fort St. Johns, where he anticipated finding the *Betsey* anchored. Not knowing what to expect, the *Liberty* was also towing two boats armed with swivel guns.

Place, who was in command of Fort Ticonderoga and Crown Point in late 1774. His Return, dated September 1, 1774, includes the following: "I likewise enclose a Muster Roll of the Sloop Betsey." *Military Papers of Thomas Gage* in the William L. Clements Library. The name of this ship has been referred to incorrectly as the *George*, the *George III* and *the King George III*. See, for example, Richard L. Blanco, ed., *The American Revolution 1775-1873*, 2 vols. (New York: Garland Publishing, 1993), II: 1684; Mark M. Boatner III, *Encyclopedia of the American Revolution* (New York: David McKay Company, 1974), 958.

48 "Benedict Arnold's Regimental Memorandum Book, written while at Ticonderoga and Crown Point in 1775" in *The Bulletin of the Fort Ticonderoga Museum*, vol. XIV, number two (Winter 1982), 71. This publication of Arnold's Memorandum Book is from the original document in the collection of the Fort Ticonderoga Museum. *The Pennsylvania Magazine of History and Biography*, Vol. VIII, has a transcription of this document but with numerous errors. Arnold's account reads, "Sunday 14th [May 14th, 1775] The Schooner Liberty [the renamed *Katherine*] arrived at Ticonderoga from Skensbo with Captain Brown [and Captain] Oswald and about 50 men enlisted on the road. We immediately fixed her with four carriage, and six swivel guns, and proceeded to Crown Point with 50 men in the Schooner and one Battoe [bateau: a flat-bottomed, double-pointed boat of simple construction common on the inland waters of colonial America; the plural is bateaux] with two Swivels where we arrived on the 15th." Arnold specifically mentioned that the *Katherine* arrived at Fort Ticonderoga on the afternoon of May 14 in a letter he wrote to the Massachusetts Committee of Safety dated "Crown Point, May 19th, 1775" which included the following: "My last was of the 14th instant. . . . The afternoon of the same day being joined by Captains Brown and Oswald, with fifty men, enlisted on the road, they having taken possession of a small schooner at Skenesborough." Based on his arrival at Crown Point on May 15, Arnold transformed the schooner into a warship in less than 24 hours. Force, ed., *American Archives*, Fourth Series, II: 645.

The enemy fort was a British Army outpost near the northern end of Lake Champlain. Understanding where it was situated is important to following events as they unfolded: Fort St. Johns (today the town of St. Jean) was 25 miles inside Canada on the Richelieu River (also called the Sorel River), which flowed 110 miles north from Lake Champlain into the St. Lawrence River. Fort St. Johns defended the southern end of a portage around a series of rapids on the Richelieu River. The northern end of the portage was protected by Fort Chambly. Montreal was 18 miles overland from Fort Chambly.

As Arnold neared the northern end of the lake, contrary winds prevented the *Liberty* from proceeding further. Anxious to carry out his mission, Arnold loaded Oswald and 35 of their men into the two boats and entered the Richelieu River, proceeding at night with muffled oars (i.e., the portion of each oar that rested in the oarlock was wrapped, usually with fabric, to enable the men to row quietly). Oswald's journal describes how they came ashore within half a mile of the enemy fort at sunrise and hid along the banks of a small creek "infested with numberless swarms of gnats and muskitoes [sic]."

From their concealed position, Arnold sent a man forward to reconnoiter the Fort. The scout returned to report that the fort consisted of some old wooden fortifications that had gone to ruin. The place seemed to be weakly defended, with the *Betsey* berthed in the nearby river. She was a valuable prize, described as "a handy vessel of about seventy tons, carrying two fine 6 pounders of brass [small cannon with brass barrels firing a six-pound ball]."[49] Arnold ordered everyone back into their boats. They quietly maneuvered alongside the enemy sloop and boarded her. With muskets and swords at the ready, Arnold's men easily overpowered the *Betsey's* crew of seven, all of whom were asleep when the rebels boarded her.

After securing the ship, the rebels rushed the old fort, which, like Ticonderoga and Crown Point, was a rotting, neglected relic from the French & Indian War. Its garrison consisted of a sergeant and 12 soldiers who, according to Oswald, "had their arms [were armed and ready to resist] . . . but upon our briskly marching up in their faces, they retired within the barracks," dropping their weapons as they ran. The *Liberty* arrived soon after and was loaded up with everything of value from the fort. The rebels moved quickly because their prisoners told them that their commanding officer had gone to Montreal for

49 Smith, *Our Struggle For the Fourteenth Colony*, I: 157.

reinforcements and was expected to return at any moment. When they had finished looting the place, Arnold ordered everyone to clear out.

The raid was a huge success. Besides their prisoners, Oswald tallied the results of their foray: "the King's sloop [*Betsy*], two fine brass field pieces, and four boats. We destroyed five boats, more lest they should be made use of against us [and] . . . directly hoisted sail and returned in triumph."[50]

After arriving back at Fort Ticonderoga, Arnold put the next step of his plan into action. He armed the *Betsey* with additional cannon and twelve swivel guns and rechristened her the *Enterprise*.[51] Arnold could now use his flotilla to buy time until reinforcements arrived. Oswald made Arnold's intentions clear when he wrote in his diary after the raid on St. Johns: "May 23, 1775. It is Col. Arnold's present design, that the sloop *Enterprise* and the schooner *Liberty* shall cruise on the lake, and defend our frontiers, 'till men, provisions and ammunition are furnished to carry on the war.'"[52]

Arnold had envisioned and executed a brilliant plan that gave him the only naval squadron on the lake. The British would have to build their own flotilla and defeat Arnold's warships before they could launch an offensive from Canada.

Although Arnold was now in firm control of the two Champlain forts (Ticonderoga and Crown Point), Ethan Allen and James Easton remained in the area with some of their followers. The pair arrived at Crown Point on June 10, where they found Arnold using the old British fort as his own headquarters. Easton carried with him an outdated order giving him command of Crown Point, and the situation soon grew into a heated argument with Arnold over who was rightfully entitled to claim command. This time, however, Arnold had the troops to support his authority, and in a vindictive rage he refused to allow Allen and Easton to leave Crown Point without a proper pass—which only he could issue. The savage quarrel resumed the next day when Easton confronted Arnold over the issue. Stories exist claiming that Easton was a coward, and that Arnold tested his courage by challenging him to a duel. According to Arnold, although Easton was armed with a hanger (a type of sword) and a pair of loaded

50 "Journal Kept by Eleazer Oswald on Lake Champlain," entry for May 18, 1775, in Clark, ed., *Naval Documents of The American Revolution*, I: 358.

51 Force, ed., *American Archives*, Fourth Series, II: 714.

52 "Journal Kept by Eleazer Oswald on Lake Champlain", entry for May 23, 1775, in Clark, ed., *Naval Documents of the American Revolution*, I: 513.

pistols at the time, Easton refused "to Draw Like a Gentleman." Arnold, so the story goes, then "kicked him very heartily & Ordered him from the [Crown] Point."[53]

Arnold worked conscientiously at his task of preparing to defend New York's northern frontier, but that meant he remained in a remote fort while his critics in the political and military centers of the rebel movement were spreading ugly stories about him. Adding to Arnold's condemnation was the opinion of some colonial leaders that he had gone too far when he raided St. Johns. They believed that they should be fighting a defensive war to protect their liberties, but Arnold had dispelled that idea when he crossed the Canadian border and attacked St. Johns. Questions were also being raised about why Arnold, who was a Connecticut militia officer, had been given command of a regiment funded by Massachusetts. A glimpse into the criticism of Arnold was a comment by Barnabas Deane, one of Arnold's pre-war business associates, who said that "Colonel Arnold has been greatly abused and misrepresented by designing persons."[54]

Unknown to Arnold at the time, fast-moving events in Philadelphia would further adversely affect his fledgling military career. Alarmed by the high cost of maintaining Arnold's regiment in the Lake Champlain region, which was not even within the borders of their colony, the members of the Massachusetts Provincial Congress wanted the defense of the area to be made at least a shared operation. In late May 1775, the Massachusetts authorities appealed to the recently convened Second Continental Congress for relief. The delegates

53 Force, ed., *American Archives*, Fourth Series, II: 1087; "Benedict Arnold's Regimental Memorandum Book" in *The Bulletin of the Fort Ticonderoga Museum*, vol. XIV, number two (Winter 1982), 77. Writing under the thin disguise of "Veritas," Arnold made his assertion that Easton was a coward based on stories that he was not seen during the attack on Fort Ticonderoga and "not till the soldiers and their arms were secured, he having concealed himself in an old barrack near the redoubt, under the pretence of wiping and drying his gun, which he said had got wet in crossing the lake." Easton later claimed that he was active in the attack on Fort Ticonderoga and had personally accepted the surrender of Captain William Delaplace, the commander of the post. Easton's assertion was published in a newspaper which Delaplace read. After seeing the story, Delaplace apparently wrote to the newspaper: "I cannot, in justice to myself do less than contradict the many particulars therein contained, knowing them to be totally void of truth. Indeed, I am quite at a loss to conjecture what could incline this same Colonel Easton to publish a conversation said to be had with me, except he, knowing that I was a prisoner, and restricted from giving any account at all of this affair, took the advantage of my situation, in order to answer his own purposes.. . . For I solemnly declare I never saw Colonel Easton at the time the fort was surprised." Force, ed., *American Archives*, Fourth Series, II: 1087.

54 Smith, *Our Struggle For the Fourteenth Colony*, I:185.

responded with their first act of wartime coordination by asking Connecticut to aid her sister colony. Congress voted on May 31, 1775, that "the Governor of Connecticut [Jonathan Trumbull] be requested immediately to send a strong reinforcement to the garrisons of Crown Point and Ticonderogo" and that Governor Trumbull should "appoint a person, in whom he can confide, to command the forces" defending the two forts.[55]

Trumbull was an ardent patriot, and he responded enthusiastically to Congress' plea by raising 1,000 Connecticut troops to reinforce the Champlain forts. Col. Arnold seemed a logical choice for Trumbull to name to command this force, since he was already on the scene, familiar with the military situation in the Champlain region, and a resident of Connecticut. But apparently Arnold was never seriously considered for the post. The Governor got his information about Arnold from Ethan Allen and his cronies, and there was no one to dispute their allegations or endorse Arnold for the command. Arnold lost the opportunity to advance his military career when Trumbull selected Col. Benjamin Hinman, a mediocre but politically connected Connecticut militia officer, for the position. Hinman arrived at Crown Point on June 17, 1775, as the new officer in charge. Hinman was a quiet, reserved person—no match for the volatile Arnold, who refused to relinquish command of the forts and his naval squadron. He told the feckless Hinman "that he would not be second to any man."[56]

The response to Arnold's abusive behavior toward Hinman was swift and severe. The members of the Massachusetts Provincial Congress fumed when they learned about Arnold's hostility toward the Connecticut troops. They were eager to reduce or eliminate their spending on the defense of the Champlain Valley, and promptly dispatched three of their prominent members, headed by Walter Spooner, to travel to the region to resolve the command issue and make a decision concerning Arnold's further service as a Massachusetts officer. The so-called Spooner Committee was authorized to dismiss Arnold if he failed to cooperate with the Connecticut authorities.

55 Ford, ed., *Journals of Congress*, II: 74. Congress was already on a wartime footing, having resolved a few days earlier (May 26) "that for the purpose of securing and defending these colonies, and preserving them in safety against all attempts to carry the said acts [unconstitutional and oppressive acts of the British Parliament for laying taxes in America] into execution by force of arms, these colonies be immediately put into a state of defense." *Ibid.*, 65.

56 Force, ed., *American Archives*, Fourth Series, II: 1540.

The Spooner Committee arrived at Fort Ticonderoga on June 22, 1775, where its members learned first-hand from the reticent Col. Hinman about Arnold's belligerent behavior. Arnold was at Crown Point at the time, and the commissioners were in a nasty mood when they arrived there to confront him. Spooner told Arnold that Col. Hinman was in command of the Champlain forts, and that Arnold could retain his command so long as he acted as Hinman's subordinate. Arnold snapped back that, in accordance with military custom, he was the senior officer in the region, since the date of his commission as a colonel preceded Hinman's. Arnold refused to listen to reason, and in a rage he submitted his resignation on June 24. He recorded the event in his memorandum book: "I have resigned my commission, not being able to hold it with honor.[57]

But that did not mean Arnold had given up. He retired to his cabin aboard the *Enterprise*, at anchor on Lake Champlain, where he told various loyal members of his regiment about his altercation with the members of the Spooner Committee. They were fearful that Spooner would disband Arnold's regiment without the back pay that was due to them. Arnold did nothing to dispel their fears, and his men sent a delegation after the Committee, which was back at Fort Ticonderoga conferring with Col. Hinman. Arnold's efforts to create trouble backfired when Walter Spooner calmed down Arnold's men by appointing a new commander for their regiment who would cooperate with Hinman. In a twist of fate, the Spooner Committee named James Easton to command Arnold's Massachusetts Regiment, with John Brown as his second-in-command.

Connecticut militia officer Edward Mott had a field day with the story of Arnold's insubordination toward the Spooner Committee. He expertly twisted it into a horrendous tale for Governor Trumbull, one that added to Arnold's growing reputation as an egomaniac. Mott told Trumbull that Spooner and his fellow committee members "were treated very ill and threatened" and that "they were fired upon with swivel-guns and small-arms by Arnold's people."[58]

Soon after Arnold's resignation, a supposedly unsolicited testimonial from the local residents appeared in the newspapers. The memorial was dated "Lake Champlain, July 3rd, 1775" and included the following comment about him:

57 *Benedict Arnold's Regimental Memorandum Book* in *The Pennsylvania Magazine of History and Biography*, Vol. VIII, 375.

58 Force, ed., *American Archives,* Fourth Series, II: 1592.

"By your vigilance and good conduct, we have been . . . preserved from the incursions and ravages of an enraged enemy, to whose declared vengeance we lay entirely exposed; and therefore we cannot help expressing our sorrow at the approaching period of your removal from us."[59] The testimonial was sent with a thinly disguised letter signed A. B. (Arnold Benedict?), which read in part: "It appears that envy or self-interested views has created Colonel Arnold some enemies, who have, in his absence, artfully endeavoured [sic] to misrepresent his conduct, and give a blamable aspect to actions, which, when fairly examined, will be found to merit the highest approbation of his constituents and the publick. . . . "

Arnold replied to the flattering testimonial with a letter of appreciation on the following day (July 4, 1775). He thanked the writers for their support, then in a self-serving comment added, ". . . and cannot help regretting the necessity I am under to leaving you so soon."[60]

The American Revolution was only ten weeks old when Arnold resigned his commission and prepared to return home a bitter and disillusioned civilian. He departed the Champlain region on July 4, 1775, and rode south toward Albany and home. As he travelled through New York, Arnold heard stories about a great battle that had taken place at Boston (the Battle of Bunker Hill, fought on June 17). He also passed small detachments of troops marching north toward Fort Ticonderoga. They told Arnold that Congress was now in charge of the war and was organizing a national army.

Their information was indeed correct. The Continental Congress rapidly assumed control of the rebellion and raised a Continental Army consisting of men from every colony. While Arnold was soldiering on the frontier, Congress had voted to appoint their fellow delegate from Virginia, George Washington, "to take command of the forces raised and to be raised, in defense of American Liberty. . . ."[61] Congress had also commissioned a number of senior officers for their new Continental Army, including four major generals (one rank below Washington) and eight brigadier generals, as well as filling a number of desirable administrative positions including adjutant general (chief administrative officer) and commissary of the musters (inspector). Although Arnold was known to the

59 *Ibid.*, II: 1,087-1,088.

60 *Ibid.*, II: 1,088.

61 Ford, ed., *Journals of Congress*, II: 92.

members of Congress through his succinct reports to them from the Champlain region, he was never considered for any of the new positions. Any possible consideration of Arnold for a post in the new army was offset by the scandalous stories about him and a lack of supporters in Congress.

Philip Schuyler, the wealthy New York landowner and member of Congress, was appointed a major general and given command of northern New York, including the Lake Champlain region. Congress voted that the Connecticut and Massachusetts troops garrisoned at the Champlain forts were to be absorbed into the Continental Army and put under Schuyler's control. His command was originally called the New York Department, but the name was soon changed to the Northern Department or Northern Army, while the troops under Washington's immediate control were referred to as the Main Army.[62]

The establishment of the Continental Army was followed on June 27, 1775, by a dramatic resolution from Congress ordering Gen. Schuyler to invade Canada.[63] The delegates voted for the measure despite the fact that just weeks earlier they had declared that theirs was a defensive war and that "no expedition or incursion ought to be undertaken . . . against or into Canada."[64] But now, to the armchair generals in Philadelphia, Canada appeared to be an easy conquest. They believed that the colony was lightly defended, that its population was sympathetic to the patriot cause, and that its occupation would be an excellent bargaining chip for negotiating a quick and satisfying end to the rebellion. Also,

62 For use of the term "New York Department" to identify Schuyler's command, see *ibid*, II: 104. The term "Main Army" was used during the American Revolution to identify all the troops under Washington's immediate command. Such troops included Continental regiments, state troops, and militia.

63 *Ibid.*, 109-110. The decision by Congress on June 27, 1775, to invade Canada was based partially on reports that it had received from Arnold about British military activity aimed at recapturing Forts Ticonderoga and Crown Point. The Congressional resolution read in part, "Resolved, That as Governor Carleton is making preparations to invade these colonies and is instigating the Indian Nations to take up the Hatchet against them, Major Gen Schuyler do exert his utmost power to destroy or take all vessels, boats or floating batteries, preparing by said Governor or by his order, on or near the waters of the lakes [a reference to Lake Champlain and Lake George]. . . " On the same day, another motion was adopted: "Resolved, That if General Schuyler finds it practicable, and that it will not be disagreeable to the Canadians, he do immediately take possession of St. Johns, Montreal and any other parts of the country, and pursue any other measures in Canada which may have a tendency to promote the peace and security of these Colonies."

64 Ford, ed., *Journals of Congress*, I: 75.

officers on the scene, especially Arnold, warned them that Governor Carleton was organizing a counterattack against the rebel forces in upstate New York.

A big problem with Congress' decision was that America's resources, especially its supplies of weapons and gunpowder, were already stretched thin trying to maintain Washington's army; there was not enough equipment to support a second front. In addition, the Canadian campaign required a long supply line to transport provisions and equipment to the American base at Fort Ticonderoga. The line stretched from the seaport of New York City up the Hudson River, overland to Lake George, then across Lake George to the portage that led to Lake Champlain. Large numbers of boats, wagons, and horses were needed to move everything to the front, and the Americans had virtually no equipment or men experienced in supplying an army on the frontier.

Faced with organizing an invasion of Canada, Schuyler needed competent officers to help him tackle the enormous logistical problems involved in the campaign, as well as good combat officers to defeat the British troops in the field. Arnold's replacement at the Champlain forts, Col. Hinman, was so inactive that he was given the nickname "King Log." One American officer said that he could have captured Fort Ticonderoga at the time with a pen knife by cutting the throats of the two sleeping sentries he found there, then setting the fort's powder magazine on fire.[65]

As a member of Congress, Schuyler was aware of the informative reports that Arnold sent to Philadelphia. Typical was a missive from Arnold dated "Crown Point, 23 May, 1775" that was read aloud in Congress on May 31. In his report, Arnold stated that "he had certain intelligence that . . . there were 400 regulars at St. Johns making all possible preparations to cross the lake, and expected to be joined by a number of Indians with a design of retaking Crown-point and Ticonderoga."[66] Arnold's good work in the Champlain Valley was more important to Schuyler than the stories about his contentious behavior, and Schuyler probably met with Arnold in Albany on July 11.[67] Schuyler was impressed with the former Massachusetts colonel and wanted him to be his adjutant general. Such an appointment needed Congressional

65 Smith, *Our Struggle for the Fourteenth Colony*, I: 190-191.

66 Ford, ed., *Journals of Congress*, II: 73-74.

67 Willard M. Wallace, *Traitorous Hero: The Life Fortunes of Benedict Arnold* (New York: Harper & Brothers Publishers, 1954), 53.

approval, and Schuyler asked Silas Deane, Arnold's only ally in Congress, to lobby for the post on his friend's behalf.

However, when the influential New York Judge William Duer heard about the pending appointment, he wrote Schuyler a letter dated July 19 critical of Arnold. Duer said that he was "engaged in his [Arnold's] controversy with the Boston [Spooner] Committee" and that "his late conduct at Ticonderoga must have been grossly misrepresented to you; for I am very sensible you would not think of showing any mark of favor to any one whose unaccountable pride should lead him to sacrifice the true interests of the country."[68]

Arnold lingered in Albany, hopeful of getting a post in Schuyler's Northern Army. However, his stay was cut short by a letter he received from New Haven. It was from his sister Hannah, giving him the tragic news that his 29-year-old wife Margaret had died after a brief illness. Arnold left Albany and hurried home to care for his three young sons and to rescue his business.

Following Arnold's hasty departure, Schuyler received a letter from Silas Deane on behalf of his pre-war business friend. An excerpt: "Colonel Arnold has been hardly [badly] treated, in my opinion, by this colony [Massachusetts], through some mistake or other. . . . I wish you to remember him as I think he has deserved much and received little, or less than nothing."[69]

Arnold had proved to be courageous, intelligent, and a natural leader of men; but after just two months of soldiering, his military career appeared to be over. However, he remained at home just long enough to regain his health before leaving his New Haven household under the care of his competent unmarried sister Hannah and heading for Watertown, near Cambridge, on August 1 to settle his accounts with the Massachusetts Provincial Congress.

The settlement of Arnold's account with the Massachusetts Provincial Congress is an ugly story. The congress had advanced him £100 (Massachusetts currency) when he received his commission and instructed him to "procure suitable provisions and stores for the Army, and draw upon the Committee of Safety for the same, and to act in every exigency according to your best skill and discretion for the public interest."[70] Arnold, with his usual concern for expediency and the welfare of his men, claimed that he had "spent an additional

68 Benson J. Lossing, *The Life and Times of Philip Schuyler* (New York: Mason Brothers, 1860), 384.

69 *Ibid.*, 385.

70 Force, ed., *American Archives*, Fourth Series, II: 485.

one hundred Pounds, lawful money [another reference to Massachusetts currency], out of my private purse."[71] He now faced the problem of presenting his accounts and being reimbursed by unsympathetic Massachusetts bureaucrats. As usual, Arnold was aggressive; in this instance he insisted upon being promptly and fully compensated, which launched his reputation as a cheating, money-grasping person aiming to enrich himself through the war.

While the Massachusetts authorities were auditing his accounts, Arnold rode over to nearby Cambridge in hopes of getting an interview with General Washington. Much to his surprise, Arnold was welcomed by the commander-in-chief, who was interested in talking to Arnold about the military situation in northern New York, a subject of which Arnold had excellent, first-hand knowledge. Their meeting probably took place on August 10, 1775.[72] As a member of Congress prior to his military appointment, Washington probably had become familiar with Arnold's well-organized, clear, and concise reports from the Lake Champlain region. Because Washington's administrative style included explicit correspondence, he may have been impressed with Arnold's writing skills. The General undoubtedly liked Arnold for his aggressive and tenacious qualities, attributes that the commander desired in all of his officers.

Arnold's timing certainly was fortuitous, as Washington was considering sending a detachment from his army on a secret mission through the rugged backcountry of the Maine district of Massachusetts (the modern state of Maine) to capture the walled city of Quebec, or the capital of Canada. Washington believed that he could spare the men for what he called "a sudden incursion" into Canada that would either help his friend Schuyler by forcing Carleton to divert some of his troops from the Lake Champlain region to defend Quebec or "suffer that important Place [Quebec] to fall into our Hands."[73]

Washington's mission was not a raid or a reconnaissance mission, but what in modern terminology is known as a "deep attack"—the expedition had to capture Quebec and hold it until Schuyler's army arrived with reinforcements from upper New York and Montreal. Such a bold surprise attack on Quebec

71 *Ibid.*, 1,599.

72 Arthur Lefkowitz, *Benedict Arnold's Army* (New York: Savas Beatie, 2008), 29.

73 Washington to Schuyler, dated "Camp at Cambridge August 20 1775," in W. W. Abbot, et al, eds., *The Papers of George Washington, Revolutionary War Series*, I: 332.

required an officer with exceptional leadership, quick thinking, and good judgment.

Washington picked the controversial Arnold for the coveted independent command and appointed him a colonel in the Continental Army on September 1, 1775.[74] The secret mission which he was soon to command became known as the Arnold Expedition. Thus, Arnold was back in the war—and about to lead one of the most daring campaigns in American military history.

74 Heitman, *Historical Register of Officers of the Continental Army*, 75.

Chapter Two

The Nursery of Heroes[1]

"I have been much deceived in every Account of our Route, which is longer, and has been attended with a Thousand Difficulties I never apprehended."

—Benedict Arnold to George Washington, October 27, 1775

Plans were already afoot to capture Quebec when George Washington arrived in Cambridge on July 2, 1775, to take command of the Continental Army. The mission had been proposed by a group of New England officers who wanted to surprise the walled city by approaching it from the isolated Maine District of Massachusetts. It was agreed that there was a trail through the region, but no white man except a British officer named John Montresor was known to have actually travelled it. Ironically, Montresor was nearby at the time, in Boston—with the besieged British garrison. He had traversed the route with a small party of Indians in 1761 to verify that it was possible to travel between the coast of Maine and Quebec City by following a chain of rivers and lakes.

Montresor's surveying party followed the route in Indian canoes and killed game for food. The rebels had a copy of Montresor's journal (a journal indicates an official record, as opposed to a diary, which is a personal record) of the trip,

1 The phrase appeared in a Philadelphia newspaper description of the American attack on Quebec. Force, ed., *American Archives*, Fourth Series, IV: 706.

which they had stolen from a closet in Gen. Gage's Boston headquarters.[2] But their pilfered copy was missing some key information, such as landmarks and compass directions. This vital information had been purposely omitted from copies of the journal to preserve the secrecy of the strategic route. The original and complete journal was safely housed in London.

Besides missing pieces of the journal, the rebels were unaware that Montresor had written privately that near-starvation and the severity of the trip had nearly killed him. He was famished, he continued, because his party took along only a small supply of food so they could travel light and fast; however, there were fewer opportunities to shoot game than they had hoped. There was more to the story that even Montresor was ignorant of: his Indian guides had purposely taken him over an important section of the route at night so he would not be able to see that they were travelling through a maze of streams that meandered in different directions. Anyone passing through this area, even with Montresor's journal and map, would get lost in the region's tangle of dead-end waterways and swamps. Thus, the Indians safeguarded what they considered to be exclusive knowledge of their ancestral trail.

Washington was briefed by his New England officers on the idea of capturing Quebec by approaching it through Maine. The plan appealed to his aggressive nature, and the timing was right to attempt the enterprise. Auspiciously, Congress had also recently ordered Gen. Philip Schuyler to invade Canada via the Lake Champlain route aimed at Montreal. A second, secret invasion of Canada through Maine targeting Quebec would help take the pressure off Schuyler as well as being a huge victory, if successful, for the rebels. Washington believed that he could spare some of his restless troops for the campaign since Gage's army was barricaded inside Boston and showing no signs of trying to break out. In Cambridge, Washington lacked the artillery to force the beleaguered British to fight or leave.

By mid-August 1775, Washington decided to go ahead with a surprise attack against Quebec through the Maine wilderness. The campaign was planned not as a partisan operation (called guerrilla warfare today), but as what

2 G. D. Scull, ed., *The Montresor Journals, Collection of the New York Historical Society for the Year 1881*, 2 vols. (New York: Printed for the Society, 1881), I: 135. Montresor wrote, "Should the American Colonies be lost to Great Britain, it may be attributed to a variety of unfortunate circumstances and Blunders, &c, viz. General Gage having all his Cabinet papers, Ministers' Letter, &c, and his Correspondence all stole out of a large Closet, or Wardrobe, up one pair of Stairs on the Landing at the Government House at Boston."

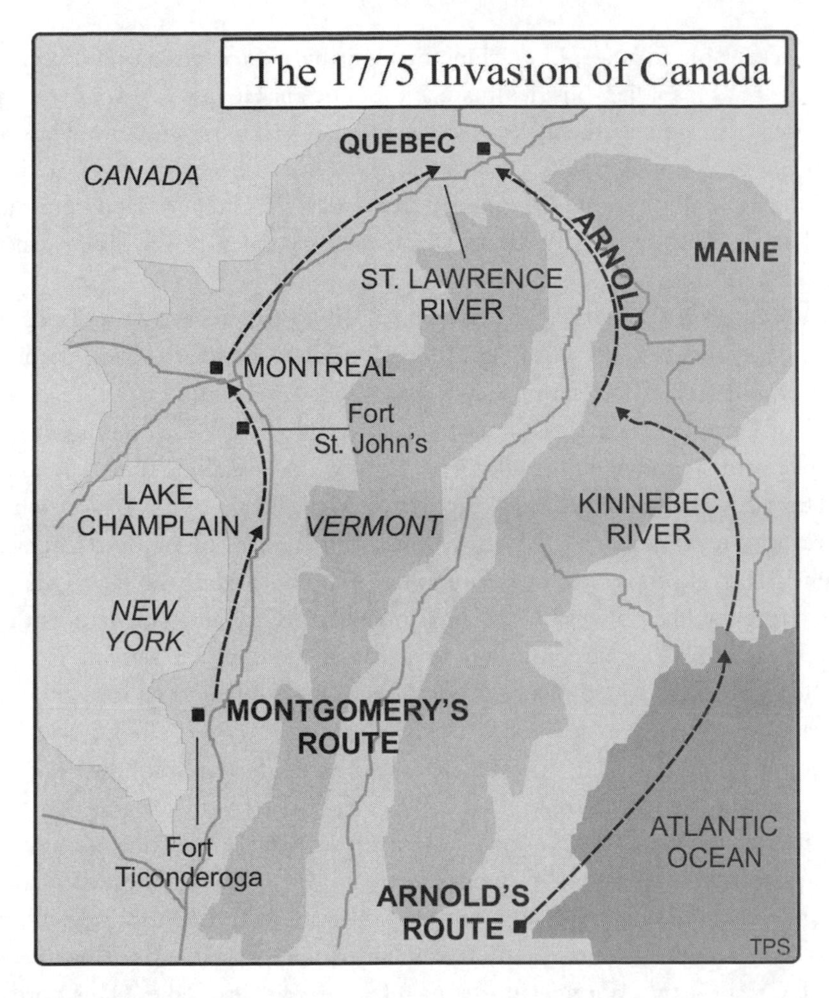

modern military parlance calls a "deep attack" (as noted in Chapter One). A deep attack is an assault against a specific objective behind enemy lines with the intention of holding it until reinforcements arrive. (A modern example of a deep attack is the Allies' seizure of the bridge at Arnhem on the Rhine River in WWII.) Once the detachment captured Quebec, it would have to defend the city against a possible enemy counterattack until Schuyler arrived with his army from Montreal.

Such a campaign (or expedition, as it was called), would require an intrepid commander who could operate independently and improvise as necessary. It was a coveted assignment, and a number of qualified officers were available in the impatient patriot army surrounding Boston. However, the commander-in-chief picked the controversial and relatively inexperienced

Benedict Arnold for the job. Washington made his choice based on his years of experience as a soldier, businessman, and politician. He liked Arnold and was confident that he was the right man for the dangerous assignment. Thus, by mid-August 1775, Arnold's greatest hopes were realized. He was back in uniform as a colonel in the Continental Army and in command of an important combat mission, which Washington began to refer to as the Arnold Expedition.[3]

Washington decided that the Arnold Expedition would leave Cambridge in small detachments and travel over different roads to avoid attracting attention to their movement. The various units would rendezvous at the rebel-held port town of Newburyport, Massachusetts, where ships would be waiting to take them aboard. The expedition's flotilla of ships would sail along the Maine coast and up the Kennebec River as far as possible, to the height of navigation, where there was an old fort called Fort Western (on the site of modern Augusta, Maine). This outpost would be the jumping-off point for the assault on Quebec. The effort would employ a fleet of small boats called bateaux (singular: bateau). A contract for 200 was awarded to a Maine boatbuilder named Reuben Colburn, whose boatyard was near Fort Western. The plan called for Colburn's bateaux to carry the expedition's provisions, ammunition (ball and powder), tents, and other heavy cargo, while the bulk of the men would follow the boats by trekking along the riverbanks.

Relying on their stolen copy of Montresor's journal and map, along with some information from Colburn and others in Maine who had travelled some distance up the Kennebec, Washington and Arnold traced the expedition's intended route. Starting at Fort Western, they would proceed up the Kennebec to the Great Carry, a portage whose main feature was three lakes. This portage led to a tributary of the Kennebec called the Dead River. The expedition would follow this river north to its source, a series of lakes called the Chain of Ponds. This extraordinary waterway formed a pass through the Appalachian Mountains that Montresor described as "beautiful country . . . a chain of lakes to conduct us the great part of the way." Montresor's journal described a stream that flowed into one of the lakes. It was the key to locating a trail over the Height of Land (the last range of mountains) which separated New England from Canada.

3 Washington to Schuyler, "Octr 4th, 1775" in W.W. Abbot, et. al., eds., *The Papers of George Washington*, Revolutionary War Series, II: 95.

But the vital information Col. Arnold's copy of Montresor's journal was missing included how to find the mountain stream. The rebels' copy of the journal read, "Our course was [blank space]. After walking about [blank space] we came to a very beautiful lake about seven hundred yards in length and two hundred and seventy in breadth. The brook which falls into [blank space] passes through it."[4] Montresor's journal went on to explain that the route gently descended from the Height of Land onto a large grassy area (the Great Meadow) that led to a small river (today's Arnold River) which drained into Lake Megantic (also known at the time as Chaudière Pond). Lake Megantic was the source of the Chaudière River, which flowed north into the St. Lawrence River near Quebec. Uunbeknownst to Washington and Arnold, however, there was a desolate swampy area bordering the south end of Lake Megantic with numerous dead-end streams and ponds that had to be crossed to reach the lake. This was the section of the route that the Indians had purposely taken Montresor through at night. Thus, relying on Montresor's journal and map could turn the area into a deathtrap.

The 180-mile route from Fort Western to Quebec was estimated to take 20 days of hard traveling to complete. The Kennebec River had been explored by Colburn and others as far as the Great Carry, and conditions along this 90-mile stretch of waterway were known to be treacherous, requiring a number of portages around rapids and waterfalls. The rest of the route was believed to be easy going—despite the fact that no one, except Montresor, was known to have explored it.

The timing of the campaign was critical. Winter came early to Canada, and Arnold had to reach Quebec before snow blocked his route. There was also the fear that the British would reinforce Quebec before Arnold's Kennebec Corps could reach it. Once underway, the expedition would have to move quickly through the Maine wilderness. Therefore, it could not take any artillery along to breach the perimeter wall protecting the land approaches to Quebec. The patriot soldiers would have no naval support once they reached the deep waters of the St. Lawrence River. And there was no time to send advance parties to establish food depots that the expedition could draw upon; the Kennebec Corps itself would have to carry everything needed to complete the journey and attack Quebec. Local river men, guides, and boat repair crews were recruited in

4 *Journal of Lt. John Montresor, 1761* in Kenneth Roberts, *March to Quebec* (Garden City, New York: Doubleday & Company, Inc., 1940), 21.

Maine by Colburn to accompany the troops. But in the end, the success of the mission depended on the element of surprise and the accuracy of reports that Quebec was lightly defended and its population sympathetic to the patriot cause.

Washington authorized Arnold to raise an independent corps from the army for his "incursion into Canada" consisting of 1,150 officers and men. Everyone going on the expedition would be a volunteer, and men skilled in handling boats were given preference. Arnold selected his officers with the help of Washington and his staff. The officers going on the mission had to be experienced leaders who could be relied upon, especially in the event of an ambush in the forest by the British and their Native American allies.

Arnold was able to select his officers from a large pool of eager candidates, including men who had fought conspicuously at the Battle of Bunker Hill. The enthusiastic turnout was due in part to the monotony of the siege of Boston and a desire to see action before the war ended. The officers chosen to go on the expedition were allowed to pick the enlisted men for the campaign, and they tended to select men they knew from their former commands.

Despite efforts to keep the expedition a secret, Washington might just as well have paraded Arnold's Kennebec Corps through the streets of Boston. General Gage was informed early on of the unusual activity in the rebel camp by British spies and paid informers who included Dr. Benjamin Church, a member of the Massachusetts Committee of Safety. Gage's informants believed that Colonel Arnold's objective was the Royal Navy base at Halifax, Nova Scotia, which accounted for the detachments heading north to the ships awaiting them at Newburyport. To get more information, Gen. Gage had a young British soldier named John Hall pose as a deserter and volunteer for the expedition. At the same time, Gage alerted the Royal Navy to the insurgents' activities at Newburyport and requested that warships be dispatched to capture or sink their task force at sea.

The Arnold Expedition departed Cambridge quietly in small detachments starting on September 11, 1775. Using different roads, they travelled without incident to Newburyport, where they boarded a fleet of unarmed merchant ships. The rebel flotilla then sailed along the Maine coast and up the Kennebec River to Fort Western still without incident—an almost unbelievable feat considering that even a lone Royal Navy sloop could have sunk or scattered Arnold's unarmed merchant ships as they sailed up the New England coast. But the Royal Navy failed to take action to destroy the rebel fleet at sea due to the slow response and incompetence of its local commander, Vice Admiral Samuel Graves.

As planned, Arnold's ships offloaded the expedition's estimated 100 tons of provisions and equipment at Fort Western and transferred them to Colburn's bateaux. The selection of this type of boat is often cited as a serious mistake, perhaps a money-making scam perpetrated on Washington and Arnold by Reuben Colburn. The claim is made that the Arnold Expedition should have used light-weight Indian canoes instead of clumsy, 200-pound bateaux. But Washington and Arnold were no fools; they opted for bateaux because they knew they were the best boats for the job.[5] Working quickly, the Arnold Expedition started up the Kennebec River for Quebec on September 14, 1775. Washington made his decision to attack Quebec in mid-August, and Arnold's corps started its ascent of the Kennebec a month later. It was an amazing achievement for the fledgling Continental Army.

The overall appearance of the Kennebec Corps as it left Fort Western was of young men wearing civilian clothing and armed with a variety of weapons. Uniforms were uncommon in the Continental Army during this early period of the war. However, there probably were some pre-war militia uniforms on the Arnold Expedition, mainly worn by its officers while in camp. Other than that, everyone, including Arnold, probably donned civilian garb once underway, to save their uniforms for their anticipated triumphal entry into Quebec. Weapons were mostly the personal property of the men who joined the expedition, which means there was a hodgepodge of different sized and caliber muskets, swords, axes, and hatchets. The bateaux transported the provisions, ammunition, and

5 Indian canoes were fragile vessels made from thin birch bark and required experienced craftsmen to build. Heavily laden canoes sat low in the water and were vulnerable to being torn apart by the sharp rocks and other obstructions that littered the upper Kennebec River. In addition, canoes were time-consuming to build and prone to tip over if not skillfully handled. Ungainly bateaux, by comparison, were economical, easy to build using unskilled labor, and extremely seaworthy. They could carry a heavy cargo and their thick-timbered bottoms could withstand the jagged obstacles lurking below the surface of the water; in the same rough conditions, the hulls of birchbark canoes would be ripped apart. There also prevails the idea that there was a unique type of bateau being used on the Kennebec River. This is not correct. Bateaux were popular throughout the inland waterways of colonial America and they were all constructed using a common, simple design: pointed on both ends with a flat bottom. Bateaux could be made in any size, including the large ones built by Schuyler's Northern Army to transport their heavy artillery and equipment on Lake Champlain. In another example, the gunboats that Arnold later commanded at Valcour Bay were hastily built gondolas, of construction similar to that of the bateaux but large enough to carry sails and be armed with cannon. Lefkowitz, *Benedict Arnold's Army*, 105-106.

tents while the men carried their personal possessions with them, including their blankets, canteens, and some spare clothing. They carried these articles in a variety of knapsacks, haversacks, and belts. Despite their lack of military appearance, the men on the Arnold Expedition were a dangerous lot. Similarly dressed and armed Americans had dealt the British Army a crippling blow at Bunker Hill.

The Arnold Expedition traveled between Cambridge and Fort Western divided into two infantry battalions armed with muskets and three companies of riflemen. A lieutenant colonel was in command of each infantry battalion. The three rifle companies each had its own commander, with the rank of captain. There was no senior officer in charge of the rifle companies.

Arnold reorganized his army into four divisions at Fort Western. As far as Lake Megantic they travelled a day or two apart to avoid bottlenecks at the portages and make use of the campsites prepared by the lead division. The first division departed Fort Western on September 25, 1775. It consisted of three companies of riflemen recruited from men living in back-country communities such as Winchester, Virginia, and Lancaster, Pennsylvania. One of the companies was a Virginia outfit commanded by Captain Daniel Morgan. Although he was of equal rank to the other rifle company officers, Morgan became the unofficial senior captain and leader of Arnold's first division. He assumed this role because of his dynamic personality, courage, and imposing physical presence.

Dan Morgan was one of the most important and interesting officers on the Arnold Expedition. His birthplace is a matter of some speculation, but he was probably born in northwestern New Jersey, a region of rugged terrain and poor soil. His parents were poor immigrants from Ireland who settled in the area because it was the only land they could afford. Young Morgan ran away from home when he was a teenager and worked his way to Virginia's Shenandoah Valley, which at that time constituted the American frontier. After a series of adventures, including working for the British Army as a teamster, Morgan finally settled down with his common-law wife and prospered as a farmer. He was also active in the local militia, which was preparing for a possible war with Britain.

Morgan narrates what happened next in a sketch he wrote describing his military career: "I was appointed a captain by Congress on the 22nd of June, 1775, to raise a company of riflemen, and march with haste to Boston. In a few days, I raised ninety-six men and set out for Boston—reaching that place in twenty-one days from the time I marched, bad weather included, nor did I leave a man behind."[6]

Morgan's rifle company was the first of the ten authorized by Congress on June 14, 1775, to arrive in Cambridge. After reaching the rebel camp, they put on an impressive exhibition of marksmanship with their rifled guns for their Yankee brethren. But the riflemen were an independent and restless group unaccustomed to the strict discipline that General Washington demanded of his army. Bored with inactivity, they amused themselves by taking long-range shots at British sentries or getting into fights with the New England troops who composed the bulk of the army.

Six rifle companies had arrived in Cambridge when Washington organized the Arnold Expedition, and he ordered three of them to go on the secret mission. He was anxious to see them leave Cambridge, as much to rid himself of some of these wild men as to give Arnold a number of troops accustomed to the rugged wilderness and experienced in fighting Indians. All of the rifle companies in camp wanted to go with Arnold. To avoid a riot, Washington used the accepted custom of drawing lots to decide which companies would make the trip. Morgan's Virginians won the contest, along with two Pennsylvania units. Morgan made no reference to the competition when he described the organizational phase of the Arnold Expedition: "[We] remained at that place [Cambridge] inactive for six weeks, as the enemy was shut up in Boston; when, with my own consent [volunteered], detached to Quebec with the [unofficial] command of three rifle companies, viz; my own, and two from Pennsylvania, under the command of Captains Smith and Hendricks."[7]

The other two rifle company captains mentioned by Morgan were Matthew Smith[8] and William Hendricks. Smith's company had been raised in Lancaster County and Hendricks' company in Cumberland County. The Pennsylvania

6 James Graham, *The Life of General Daniel Morgan* (New York: Derby & Jackson, 1856), 464.

7 *Ibid.*

8 During Pontiac's Rebellion (1763), Matthew Smith helped organize the infamous Paxton Boys on what was then the Pennsylvania frontier. Their armed rebellion was in response to the colony's inattention to their demands for protection against Indian attacks. It is believed that Smith organized the brutal massacre of a small community of peaceful Conestoga Indians living in Lancaster County. In January 1764, the Paxton Boys marched toward Philadelphia to press their demands. Smith was their spokesman when they met with Benjamin Franklin and other civic leaders who intercepted them en route and agreed to address their grievances. Kevin Kenny, *Peaceable Kingdom Lost: The Paxton Boys and the Destruction of William Penn's Holy Experiment* (New York: Oxford University Press, 2009), 237.

captains were experienced woodsmen who competed with Morgan's Virginia company to be in the van (lead) of the expedition. The three rifle companies, comprising Arnold's first division, started up the Kennebec from Fort Western with a 45-day supply of food packed in casks and barrels.

Isaac Senter, the expedition's doctor, recorded the departure of the expedition's second division, which left one day after the riflemen: "September 26th, this morning at 10, left F. Western in company with Lieut. Col. Greene, Mr. Burr, and several other gentlemen."[9] The Lieutenant Colonel Greene mentioned was Christopher Greene from Rhode Island. His second division consisted of three companies of musketmen. Greene was the cousin of Gen. Nathanael Greene, one of Washington's most competent officers, who achieved great fame later in the war.

Christopher Greene was 38 years old when he volunteered for the Arnold Expedition. He was born in Warwick, Rhode Island, the son of a judge and a descendant of John Greene, a surgeon from England who settled in Rhode Island in 1637. There is no known record of Greene's schooling; he may have been tutored at home, a common practice at the time. In any case, he must have been a person of some education, as he represented Kent County in the 1771 and 1772 sessions of the Rhode Island legislature. He was also politically well-connected, in part through his marriage to the daughter of Samuel Ward, the three-term governor of Rhode Island and delegate from that colony to the First and Second Continental Congresses.

Greene helped run his family's thriving ironworks and sawmills prior to the war. He was also active in Rhode Island's militia, serving as a lieutenant in the colony's elite Kentish Guards which rushed to Cambridge following the

9 Isaac Senter was 22 years old when he volunteered for the Arnold Expedition. He was born and raised in Londonderry, New Hampshire. Young Senter studied medicine in Newport, Rhode Island, as a student of Dr. Thomas Moffat, who was described as a "Scotch physician of eminence." Senter interrupted his studies to join the Rhode Island troops who responded to the Lexington Alarm and accompanied them to Cambridge as a surgeon. Senter's original hand-written journal lay forgotten in Philadelphia until Dr. Lewis Roper, a Philadelphia autograph collector, was looking for a good specimen of the handwriting of Benedict Arnold. He was told that there was a note written by Arnold to Senter, the original of which Dr. Senter had tucked into his journal. Roper was shown the journal and immediately recognized its historical significance. He arranged for it to be published by the Historical Society of Pennsylvania in 1846. The journal was published with Arnold's note to Senter, as Dr. Roper had the good sense not to add it to his collection. Isaac Senter, *The Journal of Isaac Senter On A Secret Expedition Against Quebec* (Philadelphia: Historical Society of Pennsylvania, 1846), 7. For biographical information about Senter, see *ibid.*, 1. For the story of how Dr. Lewis Roper obtained the Senter Journal, see *ibid.*, Notice Page.

Lexington Alarm. Some historians place Greene at the Battle of Bunker Hill, but fail to provide sources to support their claim. They point out that Greene was promoted to major a few weeks after Bunker Hill in tribute to his heroism in the battle. But the facts are that no Rhode Island troops are known to have fought at Bunker Hill, and Greene was promoted to major in the newly organized Rhode Island Regiment on May 3, 1775, over a month before the Battle of Bunker Hill (June 17, 1775). Greene volunteered for the Arnold Expedition and was selected to go, with the rank of lieutenant colonel. He survived the arduous campaign, only to be hacked to death later in the war by DeLancey's Refugees (a Loyalist corps) when he refused to surrender.

The "Mr. Burr" cited by Dr. Senter was Aaron Burr, who is best known as the man who mortally wounded his political rival Alexander Hamilton in a duel in 1804. Burr may have had a controversial career as a politician, but his frequently overlooked service in the American Revolution was commendable. Note that Dr. Senter refers to him as *Mr.* Burr, which indicates that he held no rank on the Arnold Expedition. This is correct. Burr was studying law in Litchfield, Connecticut, when the war started. He left law school to join the Patriot Army, arriving in Cambridge in August 1775. Burr was 19 years old when he obtained an interview with General Washington to ask for a commission as an officer in the Continental Army. Young Burr had impressive credentials, which included a venerable lineage, a degree from the College of New Jersey (today's Princeton University), and a letter of recommendation from John Hancock, the president of the Continental Congress. Washington told the eager Burr that there were many other impressive young men already in camp seeking commissions, so he could not accommodate his request. Burr sulked about the rebel camp until he heard that an independent corps was being recruited by a colonel named Benedict Arnold. Arnold agreed to allow Burr to join his secret expedition as a gentleman volunteer, a traditional arrangement that meant he was assigned to an officer as an assistant, without rank or pay. One young Revolutionary War gentleman volunteer accurately described his situation when he said "I am neither an Officer nor a Soldier."[10]

Burr accepted this position in the hope that he would favorably attract the attention of officers who would arrange for him to be commissioned due to his

10 The phrase appears in a May 1776 letter written by a gentleman volunteer named John Howard. Holly A. Mayer, *Belonging to the Army: Camp Followers and Community During the American Revolution* (Columbia, South Carolina: University of South Carolina Press, 1996), 183.

Gentleman Volunteer Aaron Burr on the Arnold Expedition. This illustration is based on a letter Burr wrote to his sister from Fort Western at the start of the campaign. In his letter, 19-year-old Burr described his clothing, weapons, and accouterments. Burr's face is based on his earliest known portrait painted by Gilbert Stuart in 1794. *Illustration by George C. Woodbridge, Author's Collection*

diligence, his heroism in combat, or the promotion, death, or resignation of an existing junior officer. Burr was Lt. Col. Greene's volunteer aide on the Arnold Expedition. The other gentleman volunteer attached to Greene's division was Mathias Ogden, who ended his military career as a general. Volunteers David Hopkins and Charles Porterfield accompanied Morgan's first division. Porterfield, who later became a lieutenant colonel, was killed while leading his regiment at the 1780 Battle of Camden, South Carolina. The other gentlemen volunteers on the expedition were John McGuire and Matthew Duncan.

Major Timothy Bigelow was second in command of Greene's division. He was working as a blacksmith in his home town of Worcester, Massachusetts, when the war started. Despite little formal education, Bigelow had a talent for writing and speaking combined with a passionate hatred of what he viewed as British oppression. His enthusiasm got him appointed to Worcester's Committee of Correspondence and an officer's berth in the town's militia. Bigelow was elected commander of Worcester's Minute Company.

Understanding the role of the Minute Company in colonial America is critical to appreciating the high regard in which men such as Bigelow were held in their communities. The English colonists had a long history of self-defense. Every able-bodied man was required to join the militia (citizen army), which could be activated in an emergency. Some men were selected from the ranks of the Massachusetts militia to be trained for rapid deployment. They were called Minute Men and their detachments were called Minute Companies. Young men were selected to be Minute Men based on their strength, enthusiasm, and reliability. Their officers were the elite members of the militia and respected members of their communities.

Following the Lexington Alarm, Bigelow marched his impressive Worcester Minute Company to Cambridge, where he was soon appointed a major in the Provisional Army of Observation. He was given the same rank when the Continental Army was organized following the arrival of Gen. Washington at Cambridge. Major Bigelow was selected to go on the Arnold Expedition. He was 36 years old at the time, the married father of five children. The Bigelow mountain range in Maine is named in his honor.

Thus, the chain of command in Greene's second division of the Arnold Expedition was Lt. Col. Christopher Greene, then Maj. Timothy Bigelow, followed by the commanding officers of Greene's three musket companies. These company commanders were Captains Simeon Thayer, John Topham, and Jonas Hubbard. Thayer had the most military experience of the three. He was born in Mendon, Massachusetts, in 1737 and apprenticed at an early age to a peruke (wig) maker in Providence, Rhode Island. He left his trade to fight in the French & Indian War, enlisting in a Rhode Island regiment in 1756. The following year he joined Col. Joseph Frye's Provincial regiment, which included one ranger company. Thayer joined Frye's Ranger company, which operated at times with Rogers' Corps of Rangers, the most famous of the ranger units. Rangers were used for dangerous reconnaissance patrols and partisan (guerilla) warfare, and some of their most famous exploits occurred in the rugged country bordering Lake George and Lake Champlain. They were a tough group, skilled at conducting ambushes, raids deep into French-held territory, and the capture of enemy soldiers for interrogation.

Thayer's ranger training included survival techniques. In one alleged incident, a ranger detachment was stranded and starving in the wilderness. They had several captive Indians with them, including a young, plump squaw. In order to survive they killed the woman and cut her up: "we then broiled and eat [sic] the most of her, and received great strength thereby."[11] There are other similar stories, but whether Thayer ever turned to cannibalism to survive during one of his ranger missions is unknown.

Thayer was stationed with his regiment at Fort William Henry in the summer of 1757 when a French army and its Indian allies laid siege to the fort, which capitulated on August 7, 1757. Under the terms of the surrender, the fort's garrison was allowed to withdraw to Fort Edward.[12]

11 Stephen Brumwell, *White Devil: A True Story of War, Savagery, and Vengeance in Colonial America* (Cambridge, Massachusetts: DaCapo Press, 2004), 230. The original story appeared in *Memoirs of Robert Kirk*, published in 1775. Only a single copy of Kirk's 1775 *Memoirs* survives. There is an authoritatively edited edition: Ian McCulloch and Tim J. Todish, *Through So Many Dangers: The Memoirs and Adventures of Robert Kirk, Late of the Royal Highland Regiment* (Purple Mountain Press, 2004).

12 The members of the garrison of Fort William Henry marched out of their fortifications following their surrender and began moving south. An eyewitness described what happened next: "The morning after the capitulation was signed, as soon as day broke, the whole garrison, now consisting of about two thousand men, besides women and children, were drawn up within the lines, and on the point of marching off, when great numbers of the Indians gathered about and began to plunder. [The situation got more dangerous as the defenseless garrison marched south toward Fort Edward.]. . . . By this time the war whoop was given, and the Indians began to murder those that were nearest to them without distinction. It is not in the power of words to give any tolerable idea of the horrid scene that now ensued; men, women and children were dispatched in the most wanton and cruel manner, and immediately scalped. Many of these savages drank the blood of their victims, as it flowed warm from the fatal wound." Edwin Martin Stone, ed., *The Invasion of Canada in 1775: Including the Journal of Captain Simeon Thayer* (Providence, Rhode Island: Knowles, Anthony & Co., 1867), appendix, 72-73.

Thayer recounted that he was stripped of all his clothes by the Indians on the march from Fort William Henry. He described how the Indians became ever more hostile as the retreat of the fallen garrison continued. One of the Indians grabbed the unarmed Thayer and dragged him to the side of the trail. His captor held a tomahawk and a scalping knife in one hand and Thayer with the other. Thayer managed to break loose and escape by running into the forest. Later in the day he met a fellow soldier, and the two of them continued in the woods toward Fort Edward. But they were spotted by a hostile Indian, who pursued them with a tomahawk. Thayer and his friend ran for their lives until a large fallen tree trunk blocked their path. Thayer decided to crawl under the obstacle while his friend endeavored to leap over it. When his friend was in mid-air he was struck and killed by the tomahawk, which the Indian threw with great skill. Thayer managed to escape and reach Fort Edward—exhausted, naked, and starving, but feeling lucky to be alive. He left the army soon after and returned to Providence, where he got married and resumed making wigs.

But Thayer remained active in the militia, and was appointed captain of the Providence Grenadiers due to his military experience and "his zeal for the public welfare and the reputation he had acquired as a friend to liberty."[13] His unit responded to the Lexington Alarm and became part of the Patriot Army surrounding Boston. Thayer volunteered for the Arnold Expedition and joined Greene's second division as a company captain.

Another of Greene's company captains was Jonas Hubbard from Worcester, Massachusetts. One of the few sources of information about Hubbard is a letter that he wrote to his wife from Fort Western, which read in part: "I know not if I shall ever see you again. The weather grows severe cold, and the woods, they say, are terrible to pass. But I do not value life or property, as much as securing liberty for my children."[14] Hubbard was killed leading his company during the attack on Quebec.

John Topham was the third captain in Greene's division. He was farming in Newport County, Rhode Island, when the war started. He joined the army shortly after the Lexington Alarm and was appointed a captain in the Rhode

The account of the attack on the Fort William Henry garrison was written by Captain Jonathan Carver, a native of Connecticut, who commanded a company of Provincial troops in the French and Indian War.

13 Stone, *The Journal of Captain Simeon Thayer*, appendix, 72-73.

14 *Ibid.*, 57.

Island regiment organized by Col. Thomas Church. Topham proved to be a tough, aggressive officer, which got him a post as one of the company commanders on the Arnold Expedition. He survived the campaign and ended the war as a colonel in the 1st Rhode Island State Regiment.

The third division of the Arnold Expedition was commanded by Major Return Jonathan Meigs, who recorded his departure from Fort Western in his journal: "[September] 27th, At three o'clock, P.M., I embarked on board my battoe with the third division of the army, consisting of 4 companies of musketmen, with 45 days' provision, and proceeded up the river, hoping for the protection of a kind Providence."[15] Meigs commanded the largest division of the expedition, consisting of four companies of infantry. He was another pre-war militia officer who rose to high rank during his long and valuable service in the cause of American independence. Meigs had been a Connecticut businessman prior to the war. His father was a hatter, and Meigs is frequently associated with the same trade. The story of how he got the name Return Jonathan Meigs and the exploits of his brother Josiah's grandson Gen. Montgomery C. Meigs are classic stories in American history.[16] Meigs' story is typical of the patriotic militia officers who marched to Cambridge following the Lexington Alarm.

The four company captains under his command on the Arnold Expedition were Henry Dearborn, Samuel Ward Jr., William Goodrich, and Oliver Hanchet. Henry Dearborn is the best known today of Meigs' officers. He was

15 *A Journal of Occurrences Within The Observation of Return Jonathan Meigs*, in Kenneth Roberts, *March to Quebec* (New York: Doubleday & Company, Inc., 1940), 175.

16 The traditional legend of how Major Meigs got his name is that his father was in love with a beautiful young woman who told him, "I respect thee much, but I cannot marry thee." Meigs was persistent but eventually decided that his quest was hopeless. He was mounting his horse to depart her home for the last time when the young woman called to him, "Return Jonathan, Return Jonathan." Meigs remembered those beautiful words, and he vowed that if he had a son he would name him Return Jonathan Meigs. Brigadier General Montgomery C. Meigs (1816-1892) was the Quartermaster General of the U.S. Army during the Civil War. He recommended that a Virginia estate near Washington, D.C., called Arlington, should be confiscated by the federal government for use as a military cemetery. Meigs chose this site because it was the pre-war home of Mary Custis Lee and her husband Robert E. Lee. Arlington National Cemetery was created in 1864 from the Lee estate in retribution for Robert E. Lee resigning his U.S Army commission and joining the Confederate cause. For the story about Return Jonathan Meigs, see Dr. Henry B. Meigs, *Record of the Descendants of Vincent Meigs* (Privately Printed, 1901), 305. For the story about Civil War General Montgomery C. Meigs, see Robert M. Poole, *On Hallowed Ground: The Story of Arlington National Cemetery* (New York: Walker and Company, 2009), 60.

born in 1751 and was married and practicing medicine in his native town of Hampton, New Hampshire, at the outbreak of the Revolution. Dearborn responded to the Lexington Alarm by marching at the head of his militia company to Cambridge. He fought bravely alongside his men at Bunker Hill, which helped get him a post in Col. Arnold's secret mission. Typically, he asked men from his old militia unit to join him on the Arnold Expedition.

Dearborn's subsequent career included serving in Congress, as Secretary of War in Thomas Jefferson's cabinet, as a senior officer of the U.S. Army during the War of 1812, and then as American ambassador to Portugal. Dearborn, Michigan, is named in his honor.

Nineteen-year-old Samuel Ward, Jr., was another of Meigs' company captains. He was a graduate of the Rhode Island College (today's Brown University) and the son of Rhode Island Congressman Samuel Ward.

Tavern owner William Goodrich, from Stockbridge, Massachusetts, commanded another of Meigs' companies. At the start of the war Goodrich commanded a company of the Berkshire County (Massachusetts) militia, and he marched at the head of his 27-man company to Cambridge. In fact, the news of the Lexington Alarm reached the Berkshires on the afternoon of April 20, and the following morning at sunrise Goodrich's company was on its way to Cambridge, "completely equipped in arms and generally in uniform."[17] Following the arrival of Goodrich's unit in the rebel camp, it was designated a ranger company and given dangerous assignments which required its members to be "almost continuously on the alert . . . and many times marching thro the whole night."[18] Their bravery and combat experience earned them a place on

17 Rev. Chester Dewey, *A History of the County of Berkshire, Part I* (Pittsfield, Massachusetts: Samuel W. Bush, 1829), 118-199.

18 Affidavit of Fenner Foote (1754-1847, Connecticut), *Revolutionary War Pension and Land Bounty Records*, National Archives, Record series M805, Roll 328, File S42170. Foote's 1832 pension application is an interesting account of the beginning of the American Revolution by a common soldier. His petition reads in part: "That on the 3d day of January A.D. 1775, I enlisted into the Company commanded by Capt William Goodrich of Stockbridge in the Regiment commanded by Colo Patterson. We were enrolled and drilled immediately, and continued in Stockbridge and Lee until the Twenty First or Second of April, when we marched to Cambridge. The reason of our March was that a post had arrived giving information of the Battle of Lexington. We went thro Springfield, Brookfield, and Worcester to Cambridge. We were then engaged as fatigue men and keeping guard and scouting. Capt Goodrich had obtained for his men the privilege of Rangers and we were almost continuously on the alert sometimes going across to Roxbury & Dorchester and many times marching thro the whole night." For information about Revolutionary War pensions, see J. Todd White and Charles H.

Col. Arnold's secret mission. Captain Goodrich was 36 years old and married at the time.

Meigs' other company commander was Capt. Oliver Hanchet (also spelled Hanchett, Hanchel, Hanchit, Hanchard, and Handchitt in various letters, documents, and pension applications). He was born in 1741 in the farming community of Suffield, Connecticut. His family was among the leading residents of the town, dating from the time Thomas Hanchet settled there around 1650. As a teenager, Oliver served in one of the Connecticut provincial regiments raised in 1760 to augment the British army expedition against the French-held city of Montreal.[19] Hanchet saw considerable action during this campaign and his military experience and family connections helped him get elected as a lieutenant in the pre-Revolutionary War Suffield militia. Following the Lexington Alarm his company marched to Cambridge, where he was appointed an ensign in the new Second Connecticut regiment. Hanchet was promoted to a captain in his regiment on May 1, 1775, and later volunteered for the Arnold Expedition.[20] He was married at the time to the former Rachel Gillet.[21]

Lieutenant Colonel Roger Enos commanded Arnold's fourth division, the rear guard, which consisted of three companies of infantry totaling 300 men. Enos was born in Simsbury, Connecticut, in 1729. At 46, he was probably the oldest and most experienced soldier on the expedition. As a young man Enos fought in several dangerous campaigns during the French & Indian War as an officer in Col. Phineas Lyman's Connecticut Provincial Regiment. He next participated in the 1762 British siege and capture of Havana, Cuba. In 1764, he was a captain commanding a company of Connecticut troops called out for Pontiac's War, an Indian uprising, and later was a member of an exploring party sent to survey bounty lands (property given to soldiers as rewards for their service) in what later became Natchez, Mississippi. He was also the

Lesser, eds., *Fighters for Independence: A Guide to Sources of Biographical Information on Soldiers and Sailors of the American Revolution* (Chicago: The University of Chicago Press, 1977).

19 *Celebration of the Two Hundred and Fiftieth Anniversary of the Settlement of Suffield, Connecticut* (Suffield, 1921), 116. Hanchet also served in a Connecticut provincial regiment in 1758 and 1759, according to Albert Bates, ed., *Rolls of Connecticut Men in the French and Indian War 1755-1762.*

20 Heitman, *Historical Register of the Officers of the Continental Army*, 271.

21 Esther Gillett Latham, *Genealogical Data Concerning the Families of Gillet-Gillett-Gillette* (Somerville, Massachusetts, 1953), 43, 46.

father-in-law of Ira Allen, Ethan Allen's brother. Enos was second in command of the Arnold Expedition and given responsibility for its important rear guard. His division also carried the corps' food reserve, since it would be following a trail established by the three divisions that preceded his. The town of Enosburgh, Vermont, is named in his honor.

There was also a small number of staff officers and civilians in the Kennebec Corps who reported directly to Arnold. They included the expedition's 29-year-old adjutant Christian Febiger. He was born in Denmark, where he attended a military academy before reuniting in the colonies with his uncle, the governor of the Danish Virgin Islands and a horse trader. Young Febiger toured the American colonies in 1772 trading lumber, fish, and horses up and down the coast. He eventually established a business in Boston, where he resided when the Revolutionary War began. Febiger joined the rebel cause and fought at Bunker Hill. Arnold was impressed with Febiger, who accepted an offer to join the secret expedition as its adjutant with the rank of major. Arnold's military family included the expedition's civilian physician, Dr. Isaac Senter, who was assisted by surgeon's mate Matthew Irving. Arnold's other staff members were Chaplain Samuel Spring and Arnold's friend and confidant Eleazer Oswald. Oswald served as Arnold's volunteer aide-de-camp during the expedition.

Arnold moved between the various divisions in a birchbark canoe manned by a few Indians recruited in Cambridge for the campaign. Arnold was able to travel quickly in Indian canoes because he and his boat crew were drawing provisions from the various divisions rather than carrying their own.

Once underway, a host of unexpected problems developed as the expedition pushed its way up the Kennebec into the uninhabited wilderness of upper Maine. The hastily built bateaux required frequent repairs by the team of artificers (skilled workers) who accompanied the expedition. Time was lost offloading the 200-pound boats and portaging them and their heavy cargos around waterfalls and rapids. Everything was packed in barrels, which could at least be rolled across the portages. Sometimes the men jumped into the cold water and pulled the boats with ropes through the rapids to save time. But the hastily prepared and packed provisions spoiled from exposure to water or were wasted by the men in an effort to lighten their load. Then the route across the Great Carry and beyond proved to be just as grueling and time-consuming as the great effort it took to get the bateaux up the Kennebec. The worst came when, following days of heavy rain, the normally tranquil Dead River became a raging torrent. The rising waters flooded the region, leaving men isolated on small islands, sweeping away barrels of provisions, smashing tree limbs carried by the fast-moving current into the remaining bateaux.

Perhaps the most dramatic episode during the march to Canada occurred when the exhausted and famished soldiers commanded by Morgan, Greene, and Meigs descended from the Height of Land to the Great Meadow. They were now in Canada and could see magnificent Lake Megantic across the great expanse of tall grass. The three divisions gathered on the edge of the Great Meadow following their harrowing trek over the Height of Land. They had abandoned their remaining bateaux before crossing the mountains, in accordance with Arnold's instructions.

The officers gathered shivering in the cold and made the decision to pool all their remaining food and divide it equally among their men. Everything was delivered up into a pile and distributed among all those present. There was so little meat to divide that the officers decided not to take any. Each man received the equivalent of one small meal. Then they gathered up their weapons and remaining possessions and started marching north toward Lake Megantic. Their one meal's worth of food would have to carry them over 100 miles of rough terrain, travelling on foot, before they would reach the closest French-Canadian settlement. The officers told their starving soldiers that it was now every man for himself, and no one was to stop to help a fallen comrade. Adding to their desperation was the tall grass bordering the south shore of Lake Megantic, hiding a labyrinth of streams and swamps. This was the section of the trail that the Indians had taken Montresor through at night. Finding the route through the maze added to the misery of Arnold's starving and exhausted men.

Enos' division had fallen far behind the other three, even though it had a trail to follow and established campsites to utilize at night. Enos' three companies camped along the flooded Dead River when their commander decided that the situation was hopeless. His men were sick, exhausted, and on the verge of starvation, with more than one hundred miles of inhospitable wilderness remaining to be crossed. Enos believed that he was responsible for the lives of his men, and he decided to save them while there was still time. Many people at the time agreed with Enos' decision, including historian William Gordon:

> [Enos'] return to camp [Cambridge] excited both astonishment and indignation. A court martial was ordered to sit upon him. . . . It was the unanimous opinion of the court, that Colonel Enos was under a necessity of returning and he has been acquitted with honor. A number of the officers of the best character are fully satisfied, and

persuaded that his conduct deserves applause rather than centure. Had he not returned, his whole division must have been starved.[22]

Enos resigned from the Continental Army soon after his court martial, but became a senior militia officer and served until the end of the war. Enos was no coward, based on his military experience in the French & Indian War. Clearly, his reason for turning back from the Dead River was to protect the soldiers under his command.

Arnold's attitude was different—and more dangerous to the well-being of the troops he commanded. He would never accept defeat, even if it meant endangering the lives of his men. Arnold was able to inspire his troops by his personal example; he was always out in front at the point of greatest danger and ready to face death rather than failure. He was particularly fortunate to have a number of courageous officers and enlisted men in the Kennebec Corps who shared his determination to carry out their mission regardless of the hardships. The dangers they faced by pushing on to Quebec are evidenced by the estimated 50 of Arnold's men who died from exhaustion and starvation during the expedition's final dash north along the shoreline of the Chaudière River.

Another result of Arnold's tenacity was that some of the men who survived the ordeal never regained their health. The best-known example of this tragic consequence of Arnold's resolve was Pennsylvania rifleman John Joseph Henry, who survived the campaign but returned home with "numerous disorders [which] invaded his frame." He was a robust sixteen years old when he volunteered for the Arnold Expedition but arrived back home lame and suffering from scurvy. He never fully recovered his health and died in 1812 following a life of "misfortune and vicissitude."[23]

Rifleman Henry had a particularly rough time in late October when the Dead River flooded. It was shortly after this natural disaster that Arnold sent a fast-moving party consisting of some of his best men ahead, beyond the swollen river. Arnold gave command of this critical relief party to Capt. Hanchet, who

22 Gordon, *The History of the Rise, Progress and Establishment, of the Independence of the United States*, II: 133.

23 John Joseph Henry, *An Accurate and Interesting Account of the Hardships and Sufferings of that Band of Heroes* (Lancaster, Pennsylvania: William Geer, 1812), 8, 10. Private Henry's narrative is considered one of the most important diaries of the American Revolution. However, it was actually dictated to his daughter, in 1812, during the last months of his life. It is speculated that Henry referred to some notes that he had made during the Arnold Expedition.

was given several of the expedition's remaining bateaux. Hanchet was one of Arnold's most reliable and experienced officers. His mission was to get to the French settlements and return with food. With an enormous effort, Hanchet's detachment got their bateaux over the mountains to Lake Megantic, where Arnold's small headquarters party, also moving in advance of the main column, overtook them. Apparently without a kind word of thanks or acknowledgement, Arnold commandeered all of Capt. Hanchet's boats and some of his strongest men for a desperate dash to the settlements. He left the captain and his remaining men at Lake Megantic with orders to walk downriver toward succor. Hanchet was livid over his ill treatment by his commander. Arnold had made another enemy—who would soon find an opportunity to get even.

Arnold's party was carrying hard currency (coins) and was able to buy food from the French-Canadian peasants on the upper Chaudière and rush back in time to save the bulk of the corps. Then Arnold and his so-called "famine-proof" veterans trekked through the French-Canadian villages and farms to the south shore of the St. Lawrence River across from Quebec.[24] It was early November when 650 of the original 1,150-man army were able to look across the St. Lawrence at Quebec. The hardy young men who had begun the trek in September were now skeletons.

Only the mile-wide St. Lawrence River separated them from their objective—but there were two Royal Navy frigates in the river in front of the city to contest their passage. Yet Arnold continued to challenge and beat the odds. He got his men across the St. Lawrence at night in Indian canoes, only to find that Quebec's small garrison and jittery militia had been reinforced just hours before his arrival at the outskirts of the city. His adversary was Col. Allan Maclean, a veteran soldier whose combat experience included service as a young officer in the redoubtable Scots brigade of the Dutch Army.

Arnold's lack of military training and experience became evident as Maclean duped him into retreating 20 miles from Quebec to the town of Pointe aux Trembles (modern Neuville). Arnold's inexperience is also evidenced by his imposition of food rationing only when his army was nearing starvation. He had

24 The name of the village where Arnold's corps camped on the south shore of the St. Lawrence, across from Quebec, has been spelled various ways throughout history. The spelling used by the French during the colonial period was Pointe-de-Lévis. Following the British conquest of Canada the common Anglophone spelling became Point Levy. The modern spelling by the French Canadians is Lévis.

"A View of Quebec From the East," by Joseph F.W. Des Barres, ca. 1781. *Library and Archives Canada/C080270*

been remiss earlier in allowing provisions to be wasted by his troops, who believed that they had an ample supply and wanted to lighten their loads as they rowed, poled, pushed, and pulled their heavily laden bateaux up the Kennebec. Arnold only ordered an inventory of the condition of his men's weapons and supply of gunpowder when he felt threatened by Maclean. The stock-taking revealed a shortage of serviceable weapons and powder, which precipitated his scurrying down the St. Lawrence to Pointe aux Trembles.

Everything changed for Arnold on the night of November 11 as the heroic men of his Kennebec Corps gathered at the riverfront carrying lighted torches in their hands. A boat approached from out of the darkness from a sloop anchored in the river. The boat bumped the shore and General Richard Montgomery stepped ashore to the huzzahs of Arnold's men, who were lined up in military formation to be reviewed by the conqueror of Montreal. Arnold relinquished command of his corps to Montgomery and happily accepted his role as the general's subordinate.

Richard Montgomery was a former captain in the British Army. He had fought in America during the French & Indian War and returned in 1773. He bought some land in New York and became a gentleman farmer. After settling down, he was introduced to Janet Livingston, whom he married just prior to the start of the Revolution. His marriage aligned him with the wealthy and influential Livingston clan, which was as close to being landed gentry as ever existed in America. Montgomery's brother-in-law was Robert Livingston, a New York delegate to the Continental Congress, who successfully lobbied for Richard to be commissioned as a brigadier general and appointed as Schuyler's second-in-command. When Schuyler became too ill to lead the main American thrust into Canada via Lake Champlain, Montgomery took over the field command. Despite being frustrated by squabbling officers and undisciplined common soldiers, Montgomery managed to capture Montreal.[25] Arnold's old enemy, John Brown, was a major in Montgomery's army and was responsible

25 One story about the frustration Montgomery experienced with his dissenting and faint-hearted New York officers describes how some of them ran away at the shake of a leaf. One of these was named Quackenboss [probably Captain Isaac Quackenboss of the 1st New York Regiment], who was very bold until some attack was determined on, then he so frequently entreated for leave of absence that General Montgomery said to someone passing by, "I think this quake-in-the-bush had best be gone altogether." *Biographical Notes Concerning General Richard Montgomery Together With Hitherto Unpublished Letters* (Privately published, 1876), 8.

for the fortuitous surrender of Fort Chambly, a British outpost near Montreal, which held a storehouse of gunpowder.

Many of Montgomery's troops returned home following Montreal's capture, leaving him with only 800 men. Of those who remained, 500 were assigned by Montgomery to garrison Montreal under the command of Brigadier Gen. David Wooster. Next to Montgomery, Wooster was the senior American officer in Canada. Montgomery took the remaining 300 troops and sailed down the St. Lawrence River in captured ships to rendezvous with Arnold's Kennebec Corps.

Arnold was happy that an experienced officer was on the scene to take command. He also tended to get along with men of wealth and power such as Philip Schuyler; and Montgomery, as a member of the Livingston clan, was one of the best-connected young men in America. Montgomery was also elated, as Arnold's force represented a tough, disciplined corps led by dedicated officers. Amid the rigors of the journey, the colonel had built a cohesive and competent force from what had been mostly inexperienced soldiers a few months earlier. Montgomery was impressed with Arnold's corps, calling it "an exceeding fine one, inured to fatigue, and well accustomed to cannon shot. There is a style of discipline among them, much superior to what I have been used to see this campaign."[26] Arnold and Montgomery admired and befriended each other, and together turned to the conquest of Quebec.

26 Gen. Montgomery to Gen. Schuyler, dated "Holland-House [Montgomery's headquarters], near the Heights of Abraham, December 5th, 1775" in Force, ed., *American Archives,* Fourth Series, IV: 189.

Chapter Three

Montgomery and Arnold at Quebec

"I find Colonel Arnold's corps an exceeding fine one,
inured to fatigue, and well accustomed to cannon shot."

—*Richard Montgomery to Philip Schuyler*

Colonel Benedict Arnold watched the fortress city of Quebec from across the frozen Plains of Abraham, calculating how to terrify its garrison into surrendering. It was December 1775, and Col. Arnold wanted to be called the "Conqueror of Quebec" in addition to being known as "the American Hannibal."[1] The latter name came from his recent exploit of leading the Arnold Expedition over the Appalachian Mountains to Quebec.

Standing beside Arnold as he gazed out at Quebec was his commander and friend, Gen. Richard Montgomery. The General seemed less anxious for glory than his subordinate, as he had already made his mark in the world as a British Army officer. Montgomery sided with the colonists, and he reluctantly came out of retirement to accept a post as an American brigadier general. He was

1 Congressman Joseph Hewes penned an account of the expedition to a friend on January 8, 1776, in which he compared Arnold's march to Hannibal's: ". . . that extraordinary March is thought to equal Hanibals [sic] over the Alps." Paul H. Smith, ed., *Letters of Delegates to Congress, 1774-1789*, 26 vols. (Washington, D.C.: U.S. Government Printing Office, 1976-2000), III: 58. Hewes was not the first person to compare Hannibal to Arnold. Writing to Samuel Adams on December 5, 1775, James Warren, then president of the Massachusetts Provincial Congress, compared Arnold's achievement "with Hannibal's over the Alps."

looked upon as a rising star in the rebel army because of his impressive combat record during the French & Indian War, his engaging personality, and his humility in joining the rebel army without insisting upon high rank.

Montgomery and Arnold were both courageous combat officers who led by example. However, Montgomery was more calculating and sagacious than Arnold, who tended to be reckless and petulant. But these two aggressive patriot officers made a great team when they joined forces in early December 1775 to take Quebec, the last British stronghold in Canada. Yet they faced serious problems, including too few soldiers for the mission (their combined force was an estimated 1,100 men, some with expiring enlistments), frigid winter weather, inadequate artillery, and illness (especially smallpox).

Perhaps the biggest obstacle to their capture of Quebec was their opponent, Gen. Guy Carleton, the royal governor of Canada. Carleton was an experienced soldier who managed to escape from Montreal just prior to its capitulation and reach Quebec, where he assumed command of the city's defense. Carleton proved to be a determined and resourceful adversary. He ignored efforts by Montgomery and Arnold to bait him into coming out to fight on the open pastureland known as the Planes of Abraham, west of the city's perimeter wall. Instead the Governor was content to stay inside Quebec, warm and snug with his long-range artillery, awaiting reinforcements that he confidently expected would arrive in the spring.

Montgomery laid siege to Quebec. He received some reinforcements during his investment, including Maj. John Brown's Massachusetts detachment. Brown discovered Capt. Hanchet's hatred of Arnold, and Brown instigated a plot that would discredit Arnold while advancing his own career. Brown wanted to be promoted to Lt. Colonel. One way to get Montgomery to grant him a promotion was to command more troops. Brown got Hanchet to conspire with two of Arnold's other company commanders, Captains Hubbard and Goodrich, to insist that their units be transferred to Brown's command. The three company commanders went to see Montgomery with their demand in the midst of the siege. Montgomery's response was immediate and supportive of Arnold. He ordered Arnold's Kennebec Corps to assemble and made a passionate speech to them stating his confidence in Arnold. Brown's plot was wrecked—but, as we shall see, he continued to seek opportunities to embarrass and discredit Arnold. It is fascinating to realize that Arnold probably had never met Brown prior to their brief association during the attack on Fort Ticonderoga. Arnold's behavior at the time must have been imperious to have fostered such hostility from Brown.

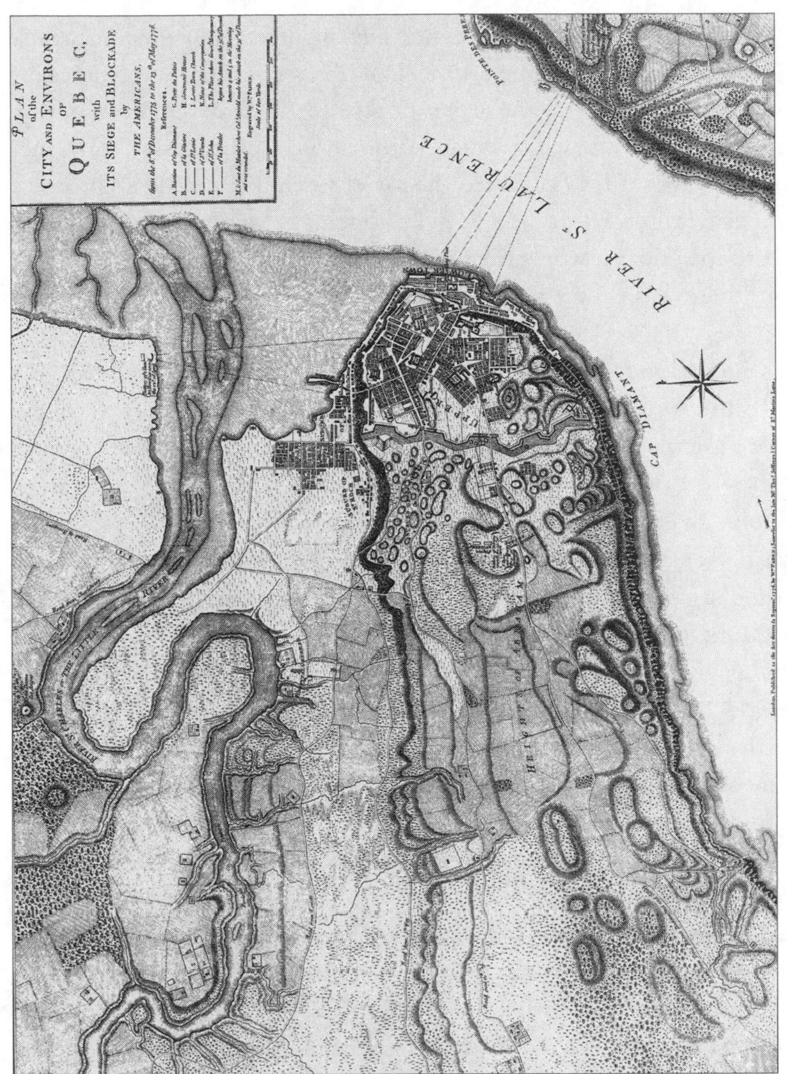

"Plan of the City and Environs of Quebec with Its Siege and Blockade by The Americans" (London, September, 1776), by William Faden. *Author's Collection*

By late December, time was running out for Montgomery. The enlistments of Arnold's corps, representing the bulk of Montgomery's army, would expire on January 1, 1776, and the cold, hungry, sick, and exhausted men were determined to go home. Reinforcing their attitude was Congress' concept of a citizen army serving short-term, voluntary enlistments. Arnold's men felt that they had done their duty and other patriots should take their place in the entrenchments surrounding Quebec.

Realizing that they had no chance of intimidating Carleton into fighting or surrendering, Montgomery and Arnold decided to storm the city with their infantry. The Americans had the presumed advantage of launching a surprise attack, at a time and place of their choosing. They could also avoid scaling Quebec's walls by striking at the city's poorly fortified commercial sector, known as the lower town, which hugged the shoreline of the St. Lawrence River. However, even if they captured the lower town they would still have to fight their way up a cliff to the heavily defended upper town. All land approaches to the upper town were protected by thick walls lined with cannon. In addition, there was only a single street connecting the lower town to the upper town.

Montgomery decided to gamble on a thrust aimed at the lower town. His plan was to capture it by a surprise attack and then race up the road to the upper town before Carleton could respond in force. He waited for a blizzard to help hide his army's movements. To further confuse the enemy, Montgomery ordered a noisy diversionary demonstration outside the walls of the upper town by Brown's detachment and a newly formed regiment of locals recruited from the region and organized by Col. James Livingston, designated the 1st Canadian Regiment. Montgomery and Arnold hoped that Carleton would focus on the diversion while they led the bulk of the Americans against the lower town from two directions. The general personally led one of the columns, consisting of 300 New York troops, while Col. Arnold attacked at the head of his 450 Kennebec veterans and 40 artillerymen commanded by Capt. John Lamb.

The Americans carried out their plan during a blizzard on the night of December 30, 1775. But Governor Carleton assumed that the rebels would attack during a blizzard, and when the storm struck he ordered his men to increase their vigilance. Carleton quickly concluded that the rebel gunfire aimed at the upper town was a feint and ordered reinforcements to the lower town, where sentries had already spotted the rebels. The American attack started to fall apart when Montgomery and a number of his men were killed assaulting a fortified house blocking their route. Colonel Donald Campbell took command of Montgomery's column and ordered a shameful retreat; meanwhile, at the other end of the lower town, Arnold's troops attempted to fight their way through a narrow main street called the Sault-au-Matelot, unaware of Montgomery's fate. Arnold was wounded in his left leg early in this assault and began bleeding badly. He was carried off to safety while Carleton's men poured into the lower town's barricades and houses. After desperate fighting, the veterans of the Arnold Expedition began surrendering in small groups. It is believed that Capt. Daniel Morgan was the last of these Americans to capitulate.

As the blizzard continued, rebel captives, including some badly wounded men, were rounded up and locked in makeshift jails. The elated but exhausted British defenders sought shelter from the storm, which pelted Quebec unabated through December 31, 1775, limiting visibility and muffling sounds.

The weather finally cleared during the night and the British ventured out the following morning, New Year's Day 1776, to inspect the sites where they had defeated the Americans and to retrieve the dead. At first they saw nothing unusual in the fresh snow that had fallen during the previous 48 hours. Then someone noticed a frozen arm protruding through the snow in the Pres de Ville, the site of the fortified house. When they shoveled the snow away, they uncovered the body of a rebel soldier. Additional probing and digging turned up a total of 13 frozen corpses. A similar grim scene was being repeated on the other side of the lower town, where many additional bodies were found. Some civilians came out to watch the gruesome scene as piles of frozen bodies, "their limbs distorted in various directions," were driven away in horse-drawn sleighs to the upper town. As the day wore on, Gov. Carleton left his headquarters to tour the battleground. Colonel Allan Maclean, whose "indefatigable diligence during the siege acquired him infinite honor," accompanied the governor. They looked on as their men probed and shoveled away snow to find many frozen rebel corpses littering the area around the Sault-au-Matelot.[2] Even so, some of the bodies remained undiscovered until the spring thaw melted the deep snow.

The British were searching for the dead when they found the badly wounded Capt. John Lamb in a cooper's shop in the lower town. His fine clothing had been stripped from his body by looters and he was barely alive. Lamb was carried away and a British army surgeon managed to save his life, but Lamb lost his left eye and his face was permanently disfigured.

One corpse was found lying on its back with its arms extended. A bloody fur cap was found nearby marked with the initials "R.M." An elegant ivory-hilted sword with a silver dog's-head pommel was also found near the crumpled body.[3] Captain John Marr, General Carleton's chief engineer, knew Richard

2 Henry, *An Accurate and Interesting Account . . . in the Campaign Against Quebec*, 134; Charles Stedman, *History of the American War*, 2 vols. (London, 1794), I:139; Sheldon S. Cohen, ed., *Canada Preserved: The Journal of Capt. Ainslie* (The Copp Clark Publishing Company, 1968), 39.

3 Montgomery's sword was obtained by James Thompson, who was the Brigade-Major (an officer appointed to assist a general in the management of his command) of Quebec at the time. Thompson described how he got the weapon. After finding Montgomery's frozen corpse, Thompson said, "Montgomery's sword was close by his side, and as soon as it was discovered,

Montgomery, the rebel general and commander, from their earlier service together in the British army.[4] Marr inspected the frozen corpse and felt sure that it was Montgomery's. Carleton ordered the body removed to a house on St. Louis Street, in the upper town, where its identity was further established by an old woman named Mrs. Prentice who had also known Montgomery when he was a young officer in the British army. Final confirmation came from a captured American officer who agreed to view the corpse.

Carleton insisted upon a modest burial for the fallen general, whom he deemed to be a traitor to England. Despite his feelings, he allowed Montgomery's body to be laid out in a decent coffin and buried with a brief ceremony. The interment took place at sundown on January 4, 1776. Montgomery's aides-de-camp, Captains John MacPherson and Jacob Cheeseman, who were killed with the general during the attack, received no coffins and were buried beside their commander in the clothes they died in. The three rebel officers were interred in a hollow in the frozen ground that was laboriously enlarged with pickaxes. The bodies of the other Americans who died in the assault on the blockhouse were consigned to another shallow grave located just inside the city near St. John's Gate.

With his usual keenness for reporting folklore as fact, historian John Codman said that Montgomery's pet spaniel lay whimpering over his master's grave for eight days without food, until the dog was removed by a kindhearted British officer.[5] Rifleman John Joseph Henry, who was taken prisoner during

---

which was first by a drummer-boy, who made a snatch of it on the spur of the moment, and no doubt considered it as his lawful prize, but I immediately made him deliver it up to me, and sometime after I made him a present of seven shillings and sixpence, by way of prize money. As it was lighter and shorter than my own sword, I adopted it and wore it in lieu. Having some business at the "Seminaire," where there was a number of American officers, prisoners of war of General Arnold's division, I had occasion to be much vexed with myself for having it with me, for the instant they observed it they knew it to have been their General's and they were very much affected by the recollections that it seemed to bring back to their minds, indeed, several of them wept audibly! The sword has been in my possession to the present day (16th Aug. 1828)." J. M. LeMonie, *The Sword of Brigadier-General Richard Montgomery: A Memoir* (Quebec: Middleton & Dawson, 1870), 26-27.

4 Capt. John Marr commanded the Royal Engineers at Quebec from 1769 to 1779 – Smith, *Our Struggle for the Fourteenth Colony*, II:79. His fellow engineer Archibald Robertson identified him as John Mar. Harry Miller Lydenberg, ed., *Archibald Robertson, His Diaries and Sketches in America 1762-1780* (New York: The New York Public Library, 1930), 5.

5 John Codman II, *Arnold's Expedition to Quebec* (New York: The Macmillan Company, 1901), 253.

the attack, visited the gravesite months later and said that he could see the edge of Montgomery's coffin in its shallow pit. Montgomery did not live long enough to learn that the Continental Congress had promoted him to the rank of major general in the army of the United Colonies on December 9, 1775, in appreciation of his accomplishments and the conviction that he would soon be the master of Quebec.[6]

6 Congress also rewarded Capt. John MacPherson [spelled Macpherson in *The Papers of George Washington*), on January 9, 1776, by promoting him to major. MacPherson's promotion included his being transferred to a line regiment (commanding troops in combat). Congress' resolution read: "That General Schuyler be directed to appoint Mr. J[John] M'Pherson, a Major in one of the battalions ordered to be raised out of the troops in Canada." Ford, ed., *Journal of the Continental Congress*, IV: 44. On the same day, Congress also promoted John Lamb from captain to major and appointed him commander of the artillery in Schuyler's Northern Department.

Chapter Four

A Winter of Despair

"I am heartily chagrined to think we have lost in one month
all the immortal Montgomery was a whole campaign in gaining."

— *Benedict Arnold to Horatio Gates*

Although seriously wounded in the failed attack on Quebec, Arnold took command of the remaining American troops from his hospital bed and continued the semblance of a siege. But with Montgomery dead, there was no one to restrain Arnold, and he quickly resumed his confrontational and egocentric ways.

In the hours following the attack, Arnold had no news of the fate of his Kennebec Corps. He only knew that Montgomery had been killed and that the New York troops under his command had retreated on the orders of Col. Donald Campbell, Montgomery's second-in-command. There was no sound of gunfire from the direction of Quebec City, but Arnold was hopeful that the members of his redoubtable corps had barricaded themselves inside the lower town and would fight their way out.

Although he lay immobile in a hospital bed in great pain, Arnold's mind was alert and thinking about a possible counterattack by the British from inside the city. In preparation for that possibility, he ordered every available man (five companies from the 1st New York Regiment, 92 men from the Massachusetts detachment commanded by Maj. John Brown, and the Canadian partisans led by Col. James Livingston) to establish a defensive line on the Plains of Abraham. He also instructed any man in the hospital who could hold a gun or a sword to arm himself and be ready to defend the building. As always, Arnold set the example: he lay in his bed with two loaded pistols and a sword. Having done everything possible with his meager resources, Arnold waited for news from his Kennebec Corps.[1]

New Year's Day, 1776, passed with no information about the fate of his men. Finally, on January 2, one of the Arnold Expedition officers, Maj. Return Jonathan Meigs, walked into the rebel camp from the walled city. Meigs explained that he was a British prisoner of war who had sworn on his honor to return to captivity after retrieving the personal belongings of his fellow captured officers. Meigs went to Arnold's bedside, where he told his commander everything that had happened after the colonel was carried off the field.

Despite his painful wound, Arnold listenened while Meigs described the details of the battle. Meigs confirmed his belief that every man belonging to Arnold's celebrated command had been killed or captured, and that the British claimed to have killed or captured 426 rebels.[2] One hundred of those captured were wounded, including Capt. Jonas Hubbard, one of Arnold's company commanders, who was not expected to live.[3]

1 "Journal of Col. Rudolphus Ritzema, August 8, 1775-March 30th, 1776," *Magazine of American History*, February, 1877, 103.

2 Cohen, ed., *Journal of Capt. Ainslie*, 37. Although Ainslie says that *426 Taken*, a careful reading of his diary entry shows that he included dead and wounded rebels in his calculation. Ainslie's figure is relatively close to two other creditable sources. One is the journal kept by Joseph Ware, which includes a detailed prisoner list. Ware was a common soldier on the Arnold Expedition captured during the attack. He says that Kennebec Corps losses in the attack were 440 officers and enlisted men, including 35 killed and 33 wounded. Ware gives a separate figure for the "York forces" (Montgomery's column), which was 13 killed and one wounded. Ware's total is 454. Roberts, *March to Quebec*, 40. The other important source for information on American losses was the journal of Capt. Dearborn, who was also captured in the attack. His lengthy entry for December 31, 1775, included: ". . . kill'd & wounded according to the best accounts I could obtain, Amounted to a bout one Hundred men, the number kill'd on the Spot, about 40." Dearborn also listed the names of 34 officers from the Arnold Expedition taken prisoner, to which he added, "The Number of Serg.[sergeants] and Corpor. & Privates Taken, but not wounded, are about 300." Dearborn's total is 474. Brown and Peckham, eds., *Revolutionary War Journals of Henry Dearborn*, 74-77. For a detailed list of American officers captured at Quebec, see Force, ed., *American Archives*, Fourth Series, IV: 708-709. This list is particularly interesting because it includes the names of all the junior-grade officers and volunteers taken prisoner at Quebec. I believe Private Ware's figure of 454 American losses during the December 31, 1775, attack is the most accurate figure, based on his detailed list and the number of men involved.

3 Capt. Jonas Hubbard (sometimes spelled Hurlbert) was from Worcester, Massachusetts. According to Thayer's journal, he was wounded at the outset of the attack as Arnold's column

The British believed that 60 insurgents had been killed in the attack. They did not have an exact number because they were still searching for bodies in the snow. The dead included three of Arnold's best officers: Pennsylvania Capt. William Hendricks, who was mortally wounded while taking aim with his rifle from an upper story window in the Sault-au-Matelot; Lt. John Humphries, a promising young lieutenant in Morgan's Virginia rifle company, killed trying to scale a barrier; and Lt. Samuel Cooper, from Hanchet's Connecticut company, shot dead in his attempt to retake a barricade from the enemy.[4]

Carleton's captives included the Arnold Expedition's senior officers: Lt. Col. Christopher Greene, the already-mentioned Maj. Return Jonathan Meigs, Maj. Timothy Bigelow, Capt. Daniel Morgan of the Virginia rifle company, and the company captains of the New England musket companies—Simeon Thayer, John Topham, Jonas Hubbard, Henry Dearborn, Samuel Ward, Oliver Hanchet, and William Goodrich. In addition, 15 of Arnold's lieutenants were taken prisoner, including Archibald Steele, who led Capt. Matthew Smith's Pennsylvania rifle company into the battle. Three of Steele's fingers were shot off during the fighting. Arnold's Danish-born adjutant, Christian Febiger, was also among the captured officers. Even the Expedition's quartermaster, Benjamin Chatlin, had participated in the fighting and was captured with the others. The British tally of rebel prisoners included 39 men from Lamb's artillery company. British Capt. Ainslie saw the captured Americans shortly after their surrender and called them "the Flower of the rebel army," noting that

was passing along Dog Lane. Thayer journal in Roberts, ed., *March to Quebec*, 275. Hubbard died in Quebec while a prisoner of the British. On June 17, 1776, the Massachusetts General Assembly passed a resolution: "That Mary Hubbard be paid the wages of her late husband, Captain Jonas Hubbard, who went on the expedition against Quebec and after his arrival there, Died." *Ibid.*, 573. Hubbard's death is confirmed by Ebenezer Wild, whose diary entries for January 1776 included the following: "Captain Hubbard died with the wound he received in coming in." Justin Winsor, ed., *Arnold's Expedition Against Quebec, 1775-1776, The Diary of Ebenezer Wild with a List of Such Diaries* (Cambridge, Massachusetts: John Wilson and Son, 1886), 10. Hubbard was a Minute Man who rushed to Cambridge following the outbreak of the war. He was appointed a captain in (Artemas) Ward's Massachusetts regiment in May 1775. Heitman states that Hubbard died of his wounds on January 1, 1776, while a British prisoner in Quebec. Heitman, *Historical Register of Officers of the Continental Army*, 305.

4 We know very little about Cooper other than he marched off to Cambridge at the start of the war and served as a lieutenant in a Connecticut regiment before volunteering for the Arnold Expedition. Heitman states Cooper was appointed a lieutenant in the 2nd Connecticut regiment (also known as Spencer's regiment) on May 1, 1775. *Ibid.*, 179; Wright, *The Continental Army*, 18.

they were all captured with slips of paper pinned to their hats reading "Liberty or Death."[5]

Eleazer Oswald, Benedict Arnold's volunteer secretary and pre-war friend, was also a British prisoner. Oswald was part of Arnold's "forlorn hope" (a detachment exposed to the greatest danger) of about twenty-five volunteers who led the attack against the lower town. Arnold wrote to his sister Hannah in January 1776 that their mutual friend Oswald "behaved gallantly, and gained much honor."[6] Similar compliments were paid to Oswald later in the war by Gen. Henry Knox, who described Oswald as "one of the best officers of the Army."[7]

The British found 13 dead and one wounded from Montgomery's column. The rest of the 300 New Yorkers who had followed Montgomery into the lower city were safely back on the Plains of Abraham, lamenting the death of their valiant general. Their officers wanted Arnold as their new commander instead of Campbell. But this compliment was of little consolation to Arnold, whose corps had been virtually wiped out in a single stroke.

Sitting at Arnold's bedside, Meigs continued his detailed account of what occurred after Arnold was carried away with his shattered leg oozing blood. As Meigs recalled it, the fighting at the first barricade on the Sault-au-Matelot began about 6:00 a.m. and the last man, reported to be Captain Morgan, finally surrendered near the second barricade three hours later, or about 9:00 a.m. Meigs remembered that Arnold's desperate men broke into the buildings facing the street during the fighting in a desperate search for safe and dry places to remove the wet powder and ball from their weapons and reload them with dry charges.

After finishing his unhappy story, Meigs reach in and removed a folded piece of cloth from his pocket, opened it, and carefully held out a pair of gentlemen's knee buckles for Arnold to see. Meigs told him that they had belonged to Montgomery, who was wearing them when he was killed. Meigs also showed Arnold a gold broach that had been found on Capt. Macpherson's body. These relics had been given to Meigs by a chivalrous British officer. Meigs

5 Cohen, ed., *Journal of Capt. Ainslie*, 38.

6 Force, ed., *American Archives*, Fourth Series, IV: 589-90.

7 Blanco, ed., *The American Revolution 1775-1783, An Encyclopedia*, 2 vols. (New York: Garland Publishing, Inc., 1993), II: 1268.

said he highly valued these mementoes, "for the sake of their late worthy owners."[8]

As their conversation ended, Arnold gave Meigs a generous amount of money from his personal funds, telling the major to use it to buy some small articles to ease the distress of his imprisoned men. Such generosity was typical of Arnold. In fact, Arnold had been using his own money or credit throughout the campaign to help supply his troops with food and clothing. Meigs thanked the colonel for his gift and left the room to gather up whatever clothing and personal articles he could find that belonged to his fellow officers. He then left the American camp and silently returned to captivity behind Quebec's walls.

When a tally was made of the dead, wounded, and captured in the gloomy American camp, Arnold discovered that a handful of his corps had survived the battle. Some of them were safe because they never participated in the attack. Dr. Isaac Senter, for example, had stayed behind to care for the wounded. John Pierce, the expedition's surveyor, had remained behind on the morning of the battle—with an advanced case of cannon fever (cowardice), it was rumored. Captain Smith, who commanded one of the Pennsylvania rifle companies, also never took part in the fighting. Private John Joseph Henry, who was in Smith's company, would only say that his captain was "absent from particular causes."[9] The implication is that Smith was too drunk to lead his men on the day of the battle.

Two officers, volunteer David Hopkins and Lt. Isaac Hull, participated in the assault and managed to escape the enemy encirclement. Hopkins was a Virginian and a gentleman volunteer in Daniel Morgan's company. He was a brave soldier who ended the war as a major in the Continental dragoons (horse soldiers). Lieutenant Hull was the only other officer who managed to escape.

8 Meigs journal, in Roberts, ed., *March to Quebec*, 193.

9 Henry, *An Accurate and Interesting Account . . . In the Campaign Against Quebec*, 114. Surprisingly, Roberts says that no one knows what happened to Smith and speculated that he died later in 1776 from smallpox. Roberts, ed., *March to Quebec*, 360-61 (footnote). However, Francis Heitman, that tireless investigator into the lives of Continental Army officers, gives a detailed biography of Smith's subsequent military career, stating that Smith retired from the army with the rank of Lt. Col. in February 1778 and died in 1794. Heitman, *Historical Register of Officers of the Continental Army*, 505-506. Heitman's book was published in 1914 and is usually accurate. I find it strange that Roberts did not refer to Heitman's important book. Another creditable source also acknowledges Smith's subsequent military career, stating that he served in the 9th Pennsylvania regiment until February 1778. W.W. Abbot, et al., eds., *The Papers of George Washington*, Revolutionary War Series, II: 43, footnote.

Doctor Senter had nicknamed Hull the "pretended pilot" after the young lieutenant led some of the Arnold Expedition's men into a marsh during their trek from Maine to Quebec.[10] Hull apparently did a better job of maneuvering himself out of Quebec's lower town than guiding his fellow soldiers around a swamp.

Another original member of the Arnold Expedition who survived the attack was feisty Aaron Burr. After joining the Expedition as an unpaid gentleman volunteer in hopes of receiving an officer's commission, as mentioned earlier, Burr performed superbly during the march and was commissioned as a captain and aide-de-camp to General Montgomery on Arnold's recommendation. Captain Burr claimed that he was standing next to the general when he was killed and was obligated to join the retreat of the New York troops from the lower town. Following the battle, Capt. Burr went to work for Arnold as an aide-de-camp.[11]

Matthias Ogden, Burr's childhood friend from New Jersey and another gentleman volunteer on the Arnold Expedition, also survived the fighting. He was wounded in the shoulder early in the attack and managed to stagger back to the hospital. There is a perplexing point about Ogden's rank on the day of the battle. He was mentioned as being a major at the time, even by Arnold, who identified him as "Major Ogden."[12] However, it is difficult to imagine how Ogden could have been promoted from gentleman volunteer to major in a matter of weeks. The answer to this riddle is found in a report of the attack by Col. Campbell, who identified Ogden as Brigadier Major Ogden.[13] This was an honorary title given to any person in the army assigned to temporary administrative duty; Ogden was probably still a volunteer on the morning of the battle, although he ended the Revolutionary War as a general.

10 Senter, *Journal of Isaac Senter*, 32.

11 Burr worked for Arnold until the end of May 1776, when he left Canada "on public business" and never returned. Mary-Jo Kline, ed., *Political Correspondence and Public Papers of Aaron Burr*, 2 vols. (Princeton, New Jersey: Princeton University Press, 1983), I: lxii.

12 Force, ed., *American Archives*, Fourth Series, IV: 482.

13 *Ibid.*, 480. The *Universal Military Dictionary* (1779) defines a brigade major as "an officer appointed by the brigadier [a general in charge of several regiments, which together make up a brigade] to assist him in the management of his brigade." Smith, *An Universal Military Dictionary*, (London: Printed for J. Millan, 1779), 36. Heitman identifies Ogden as "serving as a Brigade Major in the Expedition to Canada, and was wounded at Quebec, 31st December, 1775." Heitman, *Historical Register of Officers of the Continental Army*, 418.

Other than this handful of men, any other living Arnold Expedition veterans were either locked up in a British prison or lying prostrate in Dr.Senter's general hospital with smallpox, typhoid, influenza, dysentery, pneumonia, or "camp fever." The latter is known today as typhus, a disease spread by lice, especially in crowded, unsanitary living conditions.[14]

The total number of Americans surrounding Quebec City in early January 1776 was about 800.[15] But despite the unsteadiness of his little brigade, Arnold appeared determined to continue the siege, telling his sister Hannah in a letter, "I have no thoughts of leaving this proud town, until I first enter it in triumph."[16] However, Arnold was actually apprehensive as he tried to restore organization and morale following the staggering American defeat. Some of his remaining troops had lost heart and were deserting; smallpox continued to ravage the American camp; hard currency, so vital to maintaining the support of the French-Canadians, was running out; and only a mere trickle of provisions and equipment came in over the long supply line that began at Albany. In addition, the failed American attack made it difficult to recruit French-Canadians for his army.

Arnold acutely felt the loss of his friend Montgomery, to whom command had come so naturally. With Montgomery gone, Arnold quickly fell back into his former hostile ways. When, for example, his old antagonist Maj. John Brown insisted that Montgomery had promised him a promotion from major to

14 See David A. Relman, M.D., "Has Trench Fever Returned?", *The New England Journal of Medicine*, Vol. 332, No. 7, 1998, 463-64.

15 There is a return (a summary of a list of names (muster roll) in a detachment) for the American troops besieging Quebec dated February 10, 1776. This return gives us a good idea of the composition of Arnold's force in the weeks following Montgomery's failed attack. A total of 964 officers and men are reported to be "Present Fit For Duty & On Duty" and another 326 "Rank & File Sick, On Furlough, Etc." The bulk of the troops surrounding Quebec were from New York, plus James Livingston's Canadians (196 men, designated the 1st Canadian Regiment) and "Brown's det." [detachment] under the command of Maj. John Brown, consisting of 136 officers and enlisted men. Under the listing of "Arnold's det" there are 6 officers, 13 sergeants and corporals, and 95 common soldiers reported as fit for duty. Another 64 of Arnold's men are recorded as being unfit for duty, but their exact whereabouts (in the hospital?) is not clearly stated. This number is surprisingly high, considering that Arnold's entire corps took part in the December 31, 1775, attack on Quebec. The February number, however, probably includes Lt. Isaiah Wool's artillerymen and some scattered reinforcements who reached Quebec during January and early February 1776 and were assigned to Arnold. Charles H. Lesser, ed., *The Sinews of Independence: Monthly Strength Reports of the Continental Army* (Chicago: The University of Chicago Press, 1976), 17.

16 Force, ed., *American Archives*, Fourth Series, IV: 589-90.

colonel prior to his death, Arnold fired back that Montgomery had said that he would never promote Brown, whom he believed had stolen the personal property of captured British officers. With no one to mentor him, the impetuous Arnold sent an emotional missive to Congress claiming that Brown's promotion "would give great disgust to the Army."[17] This provoked Brown, who countered with attacks on Arnold's character; Brown's friend John Easton added his voice to the personal slurs reaching Congress from Canada, denouncing Arnold as a fraud.

Challenging both the enemy and his critics, bedridden and in constant pain from his wound, Arnold mustered all of his willpower to continue his paper-thin blockade of Quebec. Aaron Burr was there with him, struggling with the other resolute Americans to maintain their siege under such terrible conditions. Burr wrote to his sister Sally at the time that his comfortable pre-war law studies in Litchfield, Connecticut, seemed like "some ideal Region in the Moon, some place I have visited in Vision."[18]

While Arnold pondered his gloomy situation, Governor Carleton celebrated his lopsided victory. He had much to extol, with only five of his defenders killed, 13 wounded, and none captured.[19] Carleton was aware of the Americans' weakness following their unsuccessful attack, but he had plenty of food, artillery, and ammunition, and was content to remain behind Quebec's walls and await the arrival of reinforcements.

Meanwhile, Carleton segregated his captured American officers from the enlisted men. Both groups were imprisoned in the upper town. The officers were quartered in an upper story of the Seminary, while the enlisted men were kept in a building called the Récollets, which formerly housed a monastery.[20] The latter was used as Carleton's command post during the American siege of

17 *Ibid.*, 908.

18 Herbert S. Parmet and Marie B. Hecht, *Aaron Burr: Portrait of an Ambitious Man* (New York: The Macmillan Company, 1967), 24. The authors give their source as a manuscript letter from Aaron Burr to Mrs. Reeve (Sally Burr) dated February 2, 1776, in the Huntington Library, San Marino, California.

19 See Gen. Carleton to Gen. Howe, dated "Quebeck, January 12, 1776," in Force, ed., *American Archives*, Fourth Series, IV: 656. In this letter Carleton boasted that American losses (killed or captured) in the attack on Quebec were 700—an inflated number. A more accurate number of American losses during the assault is 454; see note 2, above.

20 The Récollets were the first missionaries sent to New France (Canada). They were eventually replaced by the Jesuits.

the city. Even as closely watched prisoners of war, Governor Carleton believed that Arnold's men were extremely dangerous. As events would prove, the governor was correct in his assessment.

From their makeshift prison inside Quebec, the Kennebec men attributed their humiliating rout in part to their inadequate weapons, which they claimed had misfired. The earliest known report of this problem appeared in Dr. Senter's journal for January 2, 1776. Senter got the story from Maj. Meigs when that worthy officer made his visit to the American camp on parole, saying that "for some time before they got into the city their guns were so foul, by reason of the inclement weather, as scarcely one of them could be discharged."[21] Private Henry told a similar story: "[O]ur guns were useless, because of the dampness."[22]

Captain Dearborn described the situation in greater detail in his journal, and the terminology he used indicates that the problem was genuine and serious. "I Clapt up my Piece [brought his gun to the firing position] which was Charged with a ball and Ten Buck shott. . . . Certainly to give him his due, but to my great mortification my Gun did not go off, I new prim'd her, and flushed and Try'd her again, but neither I, nor one in Ten of my men could get off our Guns they being so exceeding wet."[23] Damp conditions, which would have rendered black powder weapons impractical, were confirmed by one of the British defenders, who described the precipitation on the morning of the battle as a drizzling kind of snow.[24]

21 Senter, *Journal of Isaac Senter*, 54. Senter's journal has an incorrect date for the attack on Quebec. He says it took place on the night of December 31-January 1, whereas it took place on the night of December 30-31. However, Senter appears to be correct concerning the date of Meigs' visit to the American camp on parole, January 2, 1776. The confirmation is from the journal of Lt. William Humphrey, who was captured during the battle. Humphrey's entry for January 2, 1776, reads in part: "This day, the third of my imprisonment, Major Meigs was allowed by Genl. Carleton to go out and get in our baggage and to return on Friday [January 4]." Nathaniel N. Shipton and David Swain, eds., *Rhode Islanders Record the Revolution: The Journals of William Humphrey and Zuriel Waterman* (Providence: Rhode Island Publications Society, 1984), 35.

22 Henry, *An Interesting and Accurate Account . . . In the Campaign Against Quebec*, 116.

23 Brown and Peckham, eds., *Revolutionary War Journals of Henry Dearborn*, 69. Capt. Thayer also said his men were unable to fire their weapons because their powder was wet: "[W]e got some of our ladders up, but were oblig'd to retreat, our arms being wet, and scarcely one in ten would fire." Stone, ed., *The Journal of Captain Simeon Thayer*, 29.

24 Letter from Maj. Henry Caldwell to Gen. James Murray, dated "Sloop-of-War Hunter, June 15, 1776," in Commager and Morris, ed., *The Spirit of Seventy-Six*, I: 205.

It is difficult to know how the soldiers on the Arnold Expedition were loading their weapons. One Expedition diarist refers to the use of both cartridges and loose powder during the campaign, which is probably true because the Americans, especially early in the war, were using whatever they had.[25] Sometimes they increased the amount of lead fired. Dearborn, as noted above, said he loaded his musket with "a ball and Ten Buck shott" for the attack on Quebec.[26] This was a murderous load, which the British considered to be a savage act of cruelty contrary to the rules of warfare.

A wet charge in the barrel was a serious problem which required several minutes to clear the weapon and reload with a fresh charge. This accounts for the numerous references to the rebels going into buildings, which is exactly what Dearborn instructed his men to do when their weapons failed to fire: "I order'd my men to go into a lower room of an [sic] house, and new Prime their Guns, and prick dry Powder into the Touch-holes." In the process, Dearborn noted, "we Now found ourselves surrounded by Six to one and surrendered."[27] Dearborn's company surrendered at about 8 a.m. Meanwhile, up and down the Sault-au-Matelot, Arnold's other Kennebec men were desperately trying to clean and dry their fouled weapons and reload with fresh ammunition. They were also using the dry muskets that they seized from captured enemy troops;[28] the British defenders did not have to march for hours in the blizzard prior to fighting and had easier access to shelter to keep their weapons dry. The problems that the Americans experienced with their muskets during their attack on Quebec were repeated the following year when Washington's army attacked the Hessian garrison at Trenton, New Jersey, during a snowstorm. Their opponents experienced the same difficulty, as evidenced by one German

25 Dearborn mentioned cartridges in his journal entry for October 17: "[F]ound Colo. Arnold and Colo: Green with their Divisions, making up Cartridges." However, on the following day, his entry includes: "My men had their Powder-Horns filled with Powder." Brown and Peckham, eds., *Revolutionary War Journals of Henry Dearborn*, 46-47. The use of cartridges at the time of the Revolutionary War is often associated with muskets. However, experienced soldiers armed with muskets liked to also carry loose powder in horns as a backup, especially if they were operating in wet weather and/or in a small formation, where every shot counted. Riflemen carried loose powder and rifle balls.

26 *Ibid.*, 69.

27 *Ibid.*

28 Capt. Thayer wrote, "took them likewise Prisoners, and taking their dry arms for our own use, and laying ours up in order to dry them, being wet. . . ." Stone, ed., *The Journal of Captain Simeon Thayer*, 29.

soldier who commented following the battle, "Our muskets could not fire any more on account of the rain and snow and the rebels fired on us from, within the houses."[29]

As Arnold's Kennebec men sat in prison brooding about their weapons and cursing Col. Campbell and his New Yorkers for failing to support them, news of the American defeat at Quebec began to reach the outside world. Among the first reports was one written by Col. Campbell within hours of his shabby retreat. In his missive, addressed to Gen. David Wooster, who commanded the American garrison at Montreal, Campbell assumed that Arnold's Corps was still fighting in their sector of the lower town, "where they now maintain themselves, with between three and four hundred men; and it is extremely difficult to support them till dark, when I shall hope to draw them off."[30] Already aware that he was being accused of cowardice, Campbell blamed Arnold's Kennebec Corps for his actions, claiming that their expiring enlistments had forced Montgomery to execute a desperate, poorly planned attack on Quebec. Campbell also tried to cover up his embarrassing retreat by saying that his New York troops were unwilling to fight and insisted that he order a retreat.[31] The truth is that Campbell lost his nerve and ordered Montgomery's column to withdraw after viewing the bloody corpses of his fellow officers lying in the snow near the fortified house.

29 David Hackett Fischer, *Washington's Crossing* (New York: Oxford University Press, Inc., 2004), 249. The author gives some additional information about the Americans firing from inside houses and outbuildings during the Battle of Trenton on p. 246.

30 Col. Donald Campbell to Gen. Wooster, dated "At Holland House [Montgomery's headquarters], Saturday, December 31, 1775" in Force, ed., *American Archives*, Fourth Series, IV: 480-481.

31 *Ibid.* In his December 31, 1775, report to Wooster, Col. Campbell gave the time that he ordered a retreat. He claimed that his troops were unwilling to fight following Montgomery's death: "I found myself the disagreeable necessity of drawing off the troops (too ready to depart) at about seven o'clock [am]." Private Henry, who was taken prisoner by the British during Montgomery's attack on Quebec, had a lot to say about Campbell's actions on the morning of the battle: "Cowardice, or a want of good will towards our cause, left us to our miserable fate. A junction, though we might not conquer the fortress, would enable us to make an honorable retreat, though with the loss of many valuable lives. Campbell, who was ever after considered as a poltroon in grain [like saying a pig in clover], retreated, leaving the bodies of the general, M'Pherson and Cheeseman, to be devoured by the dogs. The disgust caused among us, as to Campbell, was so great as to create the unchristian wish, that he might be hanged. In that desultory period, though he was tried, he was acquitted; that was also the case of colonel Enos, who deserted us on the Kennebec. There never were two men more worthy of punishment of the most exemplary kind." Henry, *An Accurate and Interesting Account... In the Campaign Against Quebec*, 131.

Unaware of what Campbell had written, Arnold composed his own report to Wooster of the attack on the afternoon of the battle. At the time, Arnold had no news from his Kennebec Corps, which he believed could still be fighting its way into the city. He could only speculate that they would "either carry the lower town, be made prisoners, or cut to pieces." He knew when he wrote his report that Montgomery was dead and that the New York troops had retreated. Based on the sketchy information he had, Arnold urged Wooster to send reinforcements as well as forward the news of their daring attack and Montgomery's death to General Washington and Congress.[32]

The sealed reports from Campbell and Arnold were carried to Montreal by Edward Antill, Montgomery's Canadian insurgent engineer, who arrived at Wooster's headquarters on the night of January 4. Antill also gave Wooster an eyewitness account of the attack, since he was with Montgomery's column and claimed to be near the general when he was killed.[33] On January 2, Arnold was able to write Wooster again with a detailed account of the failed American attack based on information supplied by Meigs. In his dispatch, Arnold seemed overwhelmed by the extent of the American disaster and entreated Wooster for help:

> For God's sake order as many men down as you can possibly spare, consistent with the safety of Montreal, and all the mortars, howitzers and shells, that you can possibly bring. I hope you will stop every rascal who has deserted from us, and bring him back again. I am in such excessive pain from my wound. . . . Many officers here appear dispirited; your presence [here] will be absolutely necessary.[34]

32 Force, ed., *American Archives*, Fourth Series, IV: 670-671. Col. Campbell also wrote to Wooster on January 2. The text of his routine letter complaining of shortages, expiring enlistments, etc., can be found in *Ibid.*, 670.

33 Colonel Donald Campbell to General Wooster dated "Holland-House, Saturday, December 31, 1775" in Force, ed., *American Archives*, Fourth Series, IV: 480-481. Although Arnold never accused Campbell of cowardice, he was tried by a court martial on charges brought against him by Gen. John Sullivan. The court martial ordered Campbell to be dismissed from the army, but its ruling was later overturned by Congress, which resolved that "Campbell be continued in his former pay and rank; that he be directed immediately to repair to the commissioners for auditing and settling the accounts of the northern army, and settle with them the accounts of his late department." Ford, ed., *Journals of Congress*, VII: 114. Col. Campbell, however, never returned to active duty. He spent the rest of the long war squabbling with a committee of Congress over the settlement of his quartermaster accounts.

34 Force, ed., *American Archives*, Fourth Series, IV: 671.

After reading the various reports from Arnold and Campbell, Wooster felt obliged to add his own assessment of the situation to Congress. When he was finished, he gave the parcel of dispatches to Antill to carry to General Schuyler's headquarters in Albany. Antill arrived there on January 13.[35] Within half an hour after receipt of the alarming reports from Canada, Schuyler was writing to Congress, appealing for reinforcements, money, and supplies. He also urged Congress to send a delegation to Canada to assess the situation for itself.[36] (This proposal would prove to be a bad idea: Schuyler did not have Washington's talent for dealing with congressional committees, as well as other political bodies.) After finishing his letter, Schuyler instructed Antill to proceed to Philadelphia as fast as a sailing ship could carry him down the Hudson River. Schuyler also had copies made of all of Antill's discouraging dispatches, which he rushed to General Washington in Cambridge with a brief cover letter that began, "[W]e have met with a severe Check, in an unsuccessful Attempt on Quebec."[37]

The members of Congress had no inkling in early January 1776 of the disaster that had befallen their army in Canada. In fact, they were in a confident mood as they awaited news that the brilliant young hero General Montgomery and the fearless Colonel Arnold had captured Quebec. Congress voted promotions for both officers: Montgomery from brigadier to major general, and Arnold from colonel to brigadier general. The delegates were especially thrilled with stories of Arnold's courageous march to Quebec. "Arnold's Expedition," delegate William Hooper wrote home on January 2, "has been marked with such scenes of misery, that it requires a stretch of faith to believe that human nature was equal to them."[38] Other delegates including Thomas Jefferson and Samuel Ward equated Arnold's achievement to that of the ancient Greek warrior Xenophon, who led his army to safety through hostile enemy territory. Ward, for example, said that "Arnold's March is considered as the

35 *Ibid.*, 582; William Nelson, *Edward Antill, A New York Merchant of the 17th Century* (Paterson, New Jersey: The Press Printing and Publishing Company, 1899), 20.

36 Force, ed., *American Archives*, Fourth Series, IV: 666-667. The portion of Schuyler's letter which proved to be a calamity for the American cause read: "Congress, undoubtedly, conceives it to be advantageous to the cause of America to sit at Philadelphia, but they will be good enough to permit me to suggest the necessity of a full-empowered Committee immediately to repair to this place."

37 W.W. Abbot, et al. eds., *The Papers of Washington*, Revolutionary War Series, III: 78.

38 Smith, ed., *Letters of Delegates to Congress*, III: 18.

greatest Action done this War. Some say it equals Xenophon's Retreat from Persia, others that nothing greater has been done since the Days of Alexander."[39]

On the morning of January 17, Congress was occupied in a tedious debate concerning foreign trade. As the humdrum session wore on, the delegates were easily distracted to indulge in whispered conversations and paper shuffling. Suddenly it was announced that Mr. Edward Antill was waiting outside with important news from Canada.[40] The mundane business under discussion was abruptly halted by the anxious delegates, who ushered Antill into their presence with his packet of dispatches from Canada. Surely this was the news they had been waiting for—that their armies had taken Quebec and Canada was theirs! Excitement filled the room as the seal on the first dispatch was opened by Charles Thomson, the Secretary to Congress, as Antill sat silently nearby. The first report read was probably from General Schuyler, who was the senior officer in the Northern army. The delegates sat in rapt silence as Secretary Thomson began reading Schuyler's report in a strong voice: "To the Honorable members of Congress, my amiable and gallant friend, General Montgomery, is no more; he fell in an unsuccessful attack on Quebec. . . . My feelings on this unhappy occasion are too poignant to admit of expression. May Heaven avert any further evils."[41]

As Thomson continued to read the dispatches from Canada, the faces of the delegates turned ashen as they began to comprehend the enormity of the disaster.[42] Rhode Island delegate Samuel Ward was particularly alarmed by the

39 Samuel Ward to Deborah Ward (his daughter), dated "Phila. 24th Decr. 1775," in *Ibid.*, II: 518.

40 Delegate Richard Smith's diary for Wednesday, January 17, 1776, in *Ibid.*, III: 108. Apparently Moses Hazen accompanied Edward Antill, as evidenced by a letter from Delegate Josiah Bartlett, dated "Philadelphia, Feby 3d 1776," which includes, "Capt Hazzen of Canada who came here with the news of the fate of poor Montgomery is appointed Col of a regiment of Canadians and is returned to raise them." *Ibid.*, III: 189.

41 Force, ed., *American Archives*, Fourth Series, IV: 666.

42 Ford, ed. *Journals of the Continental Congress*, IV: 64. Congress appointed Antill a lieutenant colonel in the newly formed 2nd Canadian regiment (better known as Hazen's regiment). He was taken prisoner during an American raid on British-held Staten Island on August 22, 1777, and exchanged on November 2, 1780. He resigned from the Continental Army on January 1, 1783, after which he opened a law office in New York City at No. 25 Water Street. But he returned to Canada, where he died on May 21, 1789, at the age of 47. Antill married fourteen-year-old Charlotte Riverain in Quebec in 1767. Nelson, *Edward Antill*, 20-22.

tragic news from Canada because his son, Capt. Samuel Ward Jr., and son-in-law, Lt. Col. Christopher Greene, were both officers on the Arnold Expedition. Congressman Ward had received no news from his kinsmen since Arnold's Corps departed from Fort Western in Maine for Quebec the previous September. Antill later told Ward that he had seen his son hours before the battle and that his son-in-law had assumed command of the Kennebec Corps after Arnold was wounded. Ward was somewhat relieved when a preliminary list of American prisoners taken at Quebec included his relatives.[43]

Antill returned to Congress the following day and stood by while the dispatches he had brought from Arnold, Campbell, Wooster, and Schuyler were read aloud again. He then spent the next two hours answering questions from the delegates.[44] The shocking news from Canada drove home the sobering reality that the Americans faced a long war against a determined enemy who was reported to be transporting cold-hearted mercenaries from the German principalities to help quash the rebellion.

Congress had already voted to raise eight regiments for service in Canada and the news of Montgomery's defeat accelerated their establishment. New

43 Smith, ed., *Letters of Delegates to Congress*, III: 128. The list of American prisoners was included in Arnold's dispatch from Quebec dated January 2, 1776. It was prepared based on information provided by Maj. Meigs.

44 Richard Smith's diary entry for Thursday, January 18, 1776, in Ibid, 112-13. The interesting text in Smith's diary entry for January 18 concerning the war in Canada reads, "The Letters recd. Yesterday concerng. the Storm of Quebec were again read and Mr. Antill, Son of the late Hon. Mr. Antill of N Jersey [note that Antill held no military rank at this time and was therefore addressed as Mr.], who brought the Packet, was called in & examined for 2 Hours, he gave a very clear Account of every Circumstance, he was with Gen. Montgy. when he fell. Before this Gentn. came in, Hooper [a delegate from North Carolina] moved in a florid Speech that the Delegates may wear Mourning (a Crape round the left Arm) for One Month for Montgomery & that Mr. Duché be desired to preach a Sermon, to which Lynch [a delegate from South Carolina] added that a Public Monument be erected to his Memory, the Motions were objected to by Govr. Ward [Samuel Ward, who was also governor of Rhode Island] and others on the Ground that no Mourning is ever worn by any Courts on such Accounts & that the General is already embalmed in the Heart of every good American and that such Proceeding may cause too much alarm, at such a critical Junction. These reasons had their intended Weight." Following Antill's interview, John Hancock, the president of Congress, wrote to Gen. Washington on January 20, 1776: "I would just observe that by Mr. Antill's examination it appears our loss is greater than what is set forth in the dispatches he brought, a copy of which is transmitted to you. Almost the whole of General Arnolds gallant detachment are taken prisoners having after four hours resistance been obliged to surrender at discretion. However we have the satisfaction to hear that the prisoners are treated with humanity." In the same letter Hancock asked Washington to recommend a general to replace Montgomery as American commander in Canada. *Ibid.*, 123.

Jersey and Pennsylvania had agreed to raise one regiment each for service in Canada. On January 19, just two days after Antill's arrival in Philadelphia, Congress ordered that "Colonels Bull [John Bull from Pennsylvania] and Maxwell [William Maxwell from New Jersey], do, without delay, march such of the companies of their battalions [regiments] as are now ready, to General Schuyler."[45] New Hampshire's militia was also called out in the emergency and asked to race to Quebec. Congress further moved to organize two regiments of Canadians, designated the 1st and 2nd Canadian regiments. Command of the 1st and 2nd Canadian Regiments was given, respectively, to James Livingston and Moses Hazen, the latter a retired Provincial officer who had been aiding the insurgents.[46] Antill was appointed Hazen's second-in-command.

On the advice of General Schuyler, Congress also voted to send a delegation to Canada. The three Congressmen selected for the mission were the

45 Ford, ed., *Journals of the Continental Congress*, IV: 70. Col. Bull resigned in late January 1776 and command of his Pennsylvania regiment was given to Col. Philip De Haas. In a *Return of the Troops before Quebeck, in the service of the United Colonies, March 30, 1776*, Col. De Haas' regiment is listed as 235 effectives, with no men sick. Maxwell's had 216 at Quebec, with none listed as sick. Force, ed., *American Archives*, Fourth Series, V: 550.

46 Moses Hazen (1733-1803) was an interesting and colorful character from the American Revolution. He eventually became one of Benedict Arnold's most vocal enemies. Hazen was a native of Massachusetts who served as an officer in the rangers during the French & Indian War. These elite military detachments were used for scouting and reconnaissance missions. Hazen subsequently purchased a lieutenant's commission in the British 44th Regiment. But the conflict ended soon after he joined his new regiment, forcing him into retirement as a half-pay British officer. Hazen next purchased a valuable tract of land in the Richelieu River Valley and married a French-Canadian. He built a fine home on his land and settled down to a life as a respectable landowner—until the start of the Revolutionary War. His home and land adjoined the British outpost of St. Johns, whose garrison withstood a long siege from Gen. Montgomery's army. At first, Hazen sided with the British, then he began to secretly aid the Americans, and finally joined the rebel cause following Montgomery's impressive victories at St. Johns and Fort Chambly. On January 20, 1776, Congress resolved "That, exclusive of Colonel Livingston and his regiment, already determined upon [designated the 1st Canadian regiment], there be one thousand Canadians more raised, for one year, or during the present disputes." Ford, ed., *Journals of the Continental Congress*, IV: 75. Two days later, Congress unanimously elected Hazen as colonel and commanding officer of the new 2nd Canadian regiment and Edward Antill as the regiment's lieutenant colonel. Congress also resolved "That the United Colonies will indemnify Colonel Hazen for any loss of half pay [a reference to Hazen's pension as an inactive British officer] which he may sustain in consequence of his entering into the service of America." *Ibid.*, 78. Hazen continued to command the 2nd Canadian regiment (also called Congress' Own) until June 1783. He was brevetted a brigadier general on June 29, 1781. Antill served as the regiment's second-in-command until May 1, 1782, although he was taken prisoner on Staten Island on August 22, 1777, and exchanged on November 2, 1780. Antill died in 1789.

Philadelphian Benjamin Franklin, and Samuel Chase and Charles Carroll of Carrollton, Maryland. The latter was a good choice because he was Catholic. The other urgent plea from Canada was for hard cash. But Congress, with no specie to send, continued to finance the war with paper money.

In comparison to the vigorous efforts by the rebels to maintain their siege of Quebec, conditions inside the city remained calm. Other than a shortage of firewood the city was well supplied, and Carleton was satisfied to remain behind Quebec's strong defenses, sallying out only to gather firewood from the wrecked buildings in the suburbs that surrounded the city. Arnold continued to send emissaries to parley with the governor, who instructed his officers that "no flag will be received, unless it comes to implore the mercy of the King."[47]

Governor Carleton, however, was actively trying to increase the size of his garrison by encouraging rebel soldiers to desert and conscripting his prisoners. Carleton focused his recruiting efforts on his English- and Irish-born captives. These prisoners were particularly vulnerable to threats of being shipped back to England in irons to be tried and hanged as traitors. Perhaps, Carleton reasoned, they would prefer to fight for their mother country rather than face the possibility of being executed. The governor had the perfect regiment in which to place any prisoner who agreed to switch sides: Col. Maclean's Royal Highland Emigrants.

On January 4, 1776, Col. Maclean, accompanied by several other British officers, interviewed each prisoner, asking him where he was born. Those who confessed to British or Irish birth were told that they must serve His Majesty in the Royal Highland Emigrants or face the prospect of being returned to England where they would be tried as traitors. To sweeten the offer, Maclean offered land bounties and money to those prisoners who agreed to fight for Great Britain. Maclean's threats and bribes worked: 78 men from the Arnold Expedition and 16 from Lamb's artillery company joined his regiment. After taking an oath of allegiance to serve the King, they were issued uniforms and weapons and absorbed into the Royal Highland Emigrants.

Major Lamb (promoted from captain by Congress in January 1776) and Lt. Steele were particularly vocal in denouncing the backsliders who deserted to the enemy, prompting Maclean to write to them as follows:

47 Codman, *Arnold's Expedition to Quebec*, 288.

Quebec, January 30, 1776

To Messrs. Lamb and Steele

Gen. Carleton is very much surprised to hear, that you make use of improper language, respecting the unfortunate disputes between the Mother Country and her Colonies; particularly, your upbraiding some of the poor, unfortunate deluded people, who were taken prisoners with you, on the 31st December, in finding fault with their conduct, for their having now engaged to serve their King and Country.
I will venture to say, that it will give Gen. Carleton, and those under his command, great pleasure to show you all the marks of good nature, and humanity, that the situation of the garrison will admit of; but it will be out of his power to do that, if you, gentlemen, shall persist in holding a language, that is both indecent, and improper, in your present situation. . . .[48]

Lamb and Steele need not have worried, because the American prisoners who joined Col. Maclean's corps intended to run for freedom as soon as they could. The story of two of Maclean's converts is typical of the outcome of the colonel's machinations. Edward Cavenaugh and Timothy Conner were both riflemen in Capt. Smith's Pennsylvania company.[49] They decided that their oath of fidelity to King George III was not binding and they would escape at the first opportunity. Their chance came toward the end of January when both men were on sentry duty as part of a detachment guarding the Palace gate. The gate was closed and the surrounding walls were forty feet high, but there were deep snow drifts against the outside wall, perhaps 20 feet high. The two Americans decided to jump from the top of the rampart into a deep snow drift, which they hoped would cushion their fall. The problem was that they might sink too deeply into the snow, which might swallow them up and bury them alive. They decided to take their chances and make the leap.

However, they first had to dispose of a fellow sentry who was standing guard duty with them nearby with a loaded musket. It was a bitterly cold night and Conner had a bottle of rum with him, from which he offered a friendly swig

48 Isaac Q. Leake, *Memoir of the Life and Times of General John Lamb* (Albany, New York: Joel Munsell, 1850), 138-139.

49 See Henry, *An Interesting and Accurate Account . . . In the Campaign Against Quebec*, 135-136. Edward Cavenaugh (also spelled Edward Cavener) and Timothy Conner appear on a list of members of Capt. Smith's company who enlisted in the King's service in Roberts, ed., *March to Quebec*, 33.

to his fellow sentry. The man took the bottle and began to drink. While he was distracted Cavenaugh hit him with the butt of his musket, dropping him unconscious to the ground. They grabbed the senseless man's gun and threw it over the parapet. Then they tossed their own weapons over the rampart and, without a moment's hesitation, leaped from the top of the 40-foot wall into a snow bank. The plan worked perfectly: they survived their perilous jump with no broken bones or even bruises, got on their feet, grabbed the weapons, and started running toward the American lines. But they were spotted by some of the other guards, who started shooting at the two dark figures running across the white snow. The garrison was alerted and cannon opened fire, hurling artillery shells at the two deserters racing through the wrecked suburb of St. Roch. But the two men made it safely to the rebel works with their fine British muskets and warm clothing.

After a few similar episodes, the British rounded up all the remaining prisoners who had enlisted in Maclean's regiment. After confiscating their weapons and uniforms, a disgusted Maclean threw them back into prison, where they were reunited with their old messmates amid cheering and back slapping.[50] Captain Ainslie wrote a marvelous summary of Maclean's failed experiment in his diary:

> February 16th [1776]. Six of the penitent rebels again repenting left Col. McLean's corps: two of them knock'd down & disarm'd a sentry & six escaped over the wall behind the artillery barracks. This morning the remaining eighty four were shut up. It appears that they all intend to run away. We took them in arms, they are rebels still in appearance, yet if there is one among them who wishes not to return to the Rebels it is hard on him to be confin'd—but as we cannot read their hearts, prudence says keep them close.[51]

Carleton's problems were minor in comparison to those of his antagonist Arnold, whose vexations persisted throughout the bitterly cold winter. Now a brigadier general, Arnold described his situation in a letter to Silas Deane. Writing on March 30, 1776, Arnold confided that he was perplexed with a

50 For the complete story of Cavenaugh's and Conner's escape, see Henry, *An Interesting and Accurate Account . . . In the Campaign Against Quebec*, 135-138.

51 Cohen, ed., *Journal of Capt. Ainslie*, 50-51, and John F. Roche, ed., "Quebec Under Siege, 1775-1776: The Memorandums of Jacob Danford" in *The Canadian Historical Review*, volume L, Number 1 (March 1969), 76.

multiplicity of affairs beginning with his insufficient number of troops to maintain the siege: "From the 1st of January to the 1st of March," Arnold wrote, "we have never had more than seven hundred effective men on the ground, and frequently not more than five hundred." With this force, Arnold said, he had to blockade a 26-mile perimeter around Quebec.

On paper, Arnold's numbers were much higher, but many of his troops were sick with smallpox. This included numerous men who had inoculated themselves in the hopes of contracting a mild case of the dreaded disease, but whose self-inoculation resulted in their being bedridden, on the average, between three and four weeks. General Arnold included a chart with his letter to Deane to illustrate how self-inoculation had depleted his forces. Titled "A Return of the Troops before Quebec, in the service of the United Colonies, March 30, 1776," it lists 2,505 American troops besieging Quebec (Arnold received some reinforcements in March), but only 1,719 of whom were fit for service. The strength of each regiment or company under Arnold's command was reported in the Return, including Colonel Warner's militia regiment, which showed that out of a total of 373 men, 271were listed as being sick with smallpox by inoculation. A similar situation applied to Maj. Cady's detachment, which consisted of 132 men, 50 of whom were in the hospital after inoculating themselves. Arnold explained that the New England militiamen who had rushed to Quebec had agreed to serve for only 90 days, but not a quarter of them were fit for duty, "so that the publick will incur an expense of at least twenty pounds for each of those people, who will not on an average, have done ten day's service to the 15th April to which time they are engaged."

Arnold's list of problems also included a need for an experienced engineer, inadequate provisions, and only paper money with which to make purchases and pay the troops. He pleaded with Deane for a "well furnished military chest (which gives life and spirits to any army). . . . For to tell you the truth, our credit extends no farther than our arms." Arnold tried to end his long letter to Deane on a positive note by describing how he was expecting additional reinforcements, erecting artillery batteries, and preparing a fire ship that he planned to sail into Quebec harbor to burn the warships wintering there before they could be refitted.[52]

52 General Arnold to Silas Deane, dated "Camp before Quebeck, March 30, 1776," in Force, ed., *American Archives*, Fourth Series, V: 549-550.

Arnold had a handful of good men upon whom he could depend, including Lt. Isaiah Wool of Lamb's artillery, whom Arnold called a "spirited good officer."[53] Wool survived the December 31 attack and, with only twenty artillerymen, "very few of whom know their duty," periodically fired shells into Quebec during the winter siege. Although Wool's cannon did little damage, the sound of American artillery gave comfort to the men imprisoned inside the city and assured them that friends were nearby.

Perhaps the only good news Arnold had during the winter was from Dr. Senter, who told him that his shattered leg was healing nicely and would not have to be amputated. Hobbling about, Arnold realized that the situation at Quebec required a more experienced commander with extensive administrative and logistical skills. He begged General Wooster to come to Quebec, but that officer insisted on staying in Montreal to fend of suspected British sympathizers within the city and several small enemy garrisons in the west who were inciting the Indians. Arnold next turned to General Washington for help, asking the commander-in-chief to send "some Experienced Officer" to take command at Quebec, as "the Service requires a Person of greater Abilities, and experience, than I can pretend to."[54]

But the decision of who should command at Quebec rested with Congress. Heeding Arnold's request, and impatient for a victory in Canada, Congress appointed Gen. John Thomas on March 6, 1776, as Montgomery's successor.[55]

53 General Arnold to Samuel Chase, dated "Sorel, May 15, 1776," in *Ibid.*, Fourth Series, VI: 580. Wool was promoted to captain in January 1777. Heitman erroneously states that Wool was taken prisoner at Quebec during Montgomery's December 31, 1775, attack.

54 Arnold to Washington, dated "Camp Before Quebec, Feby 27th 1776" in W.W. Abbot, et al., eds., *Papers of Washington*, Revolutionary War Series, III: 382.

55 Ford, ed., *Journals of Congress*, IV: 186. Congress' resolution read: "That Brigadier General Thomas be appointed to command the forces in Canada, and that General Washington be directed to order him immediately to repair to that province." On the same date (March 6, 1776), Congress also promoted Thomas from brigadier to major general. Gen. Charles Lee was originally ordered by Congress on February 17, 1776, to take command of the army in Canada. Lee was a former British officer who had served in Canada during the French & Indian War. He also spoke French. However, Congress altered its decision on March 1, ordering Lee to help defend the southern colonies and appointing Thomas in his place. After being informed of Congress' decision, Washington wrote to Gen. Lee on March 14, 1776: "I was just about to congratulate you on your appointment to the Command in Canada, when I receiv'd the Account that your destination was altered—As a Virginian I must rejoice at the Change, but as an American I think you would have done more essential Service to the common Cause in Canada—for besides the advantage of 'speaking and thinking in French'[,] An Officer who is acquainted with their manners and Customs & has travell'd in their Country, must certainly take

Thomas was a Massachusetts doctor who had served with the British army in Canada during the French & Indian War. Washington approved of Congress' choice, calling Thomas "a brave and good officer."[56]

Having committed additional troops and an experienced commander, Congress was confident that Quebec would fall before British reinforcements could reach the city. However, the delegates would have been less optimistic about capturing Quebec if they could have read a February 1, 1776, letter from Lord George Germain, the British secretary of state for the American department, to Gen. William Howe in Boston, who had replaced General Gage as commander-in-chief of the British Army in America. It explained that Quebec was the government's highest priority: "The unfortunate events which have happened in Canada [the rebel capture of Montreal and siege of Quebec] make it necessary that we should exert every endeavor for the relief of Quebeck as early as possible." Germain continued that "His Majesty has thought fit that Major-General Burgoyne [John Burgoyne] should act as second in command to General Carleton in Canada, and that he should proceed thither with the eight regiments from Ireland," which Germain expected would sail for Quebec on March 20.[57]

The British reinforcements bound for Canada sailed nearly on schedule, according to a secret report sent to Paris by a French spy in London dated March 22, 1776:

> The first reinforcements destined for Canada sailed on board the warship *Isis* and five transports. They carried 15 hundred troops. Each ship will be on her own, crowding

---

the strongest Hold of their Affection and confidence." W.W. Abbot, et al., eds., *Papers of Washington*, Revolutionary War Series, III: 468. Thomas replaced Montgomery while Schuyler, who remained too ill to leave his Albany mansion, continued as the senior major general and commanding officer of the Northern Department. John Hancock, acting in his official capacity as president of the Continental Congress, wrote to Schuyler on March 7, 1776, explaining the chain of command in Canada following Thomas' appointment: "With regard to Canada, the Congress have . . . promoted Brigadr. General Thomas to the Rank of a Major General, & order'd him to Repair to the Province of Canada & Take the Command of the Continental Forces there. But still they Rely greatly on your Efforts for perfecting the work so conspicuously begun & so well Conducted under your orders last Campaign. The Generals under you will Receive & Execute your orders. . . ." Smith, ed., *Letters of Delegates to Congress*, III: 351.

56 W. W. Abbot, et al., eds., *Papers of Washington*, Revolutionary War Series, III: 423.

57 Force, ed., *American Archives*, Fourth Series, IV: 902.

> on all sail, to see which one will get there first. [It is reported that] [n]ot a single moment must be lost in trying to save Quebec, if there is still time.[58]

Ignorant of American efforts to get enough men and artillery to Quebec to storm the city before British reinforcements arrived, the imprisoned Arnold Expedition men began plotting desperate escape plans. The 37 American officers captured during the December 31 attack represented a small group. Their escape schemes were modest, focusing on bribing guards, chipping away at doors, and making ropes from bed sheets. But the 350 enlisted men had bolder ideas in mind, including staging a massive prison break and capturing the city.

It all started when Arnold's enlisted men were moved from the Récollets Seminary to another building in the upper town called the Dauphine Barracks. Their new prison was part of the fortifications built by the French in 1712 to defend Quebec. Called the Redoute [Redoubt] Dauphine by the French, the complex originally consisted of a strong artillery emplacement whose gun crews lived in the adjoining five-story barracks. Arnold's men occupied the barracks building, which was the only section of the original French redoubt still standing in 1776. The reason for the move was that a large number of guards were required to watch the American prisoners at the Récollet, which was a large, rectangular building enclosing almost half an acre of gardens and shrubbery. Although Arnold's enlisted men were confined to a small section of this rambling edifice, the building was never designed to be a prison, and Carleton needed the soldiers who were guarding the prisoners to help defend the city against the growing threat of a fresh rebel attack. He wanted to move the enlisted men to a smaller, more secure place where they could be guarded by militiamen. Thus, Carleton ordered the enlisted prisoners moved sometime in January 1776 to the Dauphine Barracks.

The windowless back of the barracks building faced toward Quebec's ramparts and gun emplacements, while the front of the structure, with numerous barred windows and locked wooden doors, opened onto a courtyard surrounded by a 20-foot stone wall. These features indicated that the building may have been modified by the French or British for use as a prison. However, it is just as likely that the building was constructed with barred windows and a

58 Clark, ed., *Naval Documents of the American Revolution*, IV: 987.

Dauphine Barracks as it looks today. *Amy Lawrence*

courtyard wall to keep its garrison from sneaking off at night to mingle with the city's civilian population.

The barracks looked formidable enough, but upon close inspection Arnold's men found it to be dilapidated: the iron bars covering the windows were loose in their sockets, the hardware holding the doors was rusted and easily pried open, and the seemingly solid high wall that surrounded the courtyard was crumpling and pockmarked with holes. Along certain parts of the wall, ten-foot snow drifts made a potential escape even easier. The old building was also in tempting proximity to St. Johns Gate, with open ground between the building and the gate.

The interior of the barracks consisted of large, unconnected rooms which housed the rebel prisoners in rows of wooden bunks. There was a single door to each room which could be locked from the outside. Arnold's men occupied rooms of their own choosing. For example, Morgan's Virginia rifle company bunked together in a room on the second floor of the jail. Referred to by one of the prisoners as "beautiful boys who knew how to handle and aim the rifle," the Virginians' ranks had been severely thinned by mishaps during the trek to Canada, battle casualties, and disease. Of the original 90 men in the company (including officers and gentleman volunteers) who left Cambridge in September, only 30 of Morgan's enlisted men were alive in April 1776.[59]

Arnold's enlisted men had been guarded by disciplined soldiers and sailors at the Récollets. That changed when they were moved to the barracks, where their guards were replaced by old men and boys serving in the militia.[60] The prisoners noticed that their new jailers tended to stay outside the prison walls, assuming that the impressive-looking barracks with their locked doors and surrounding wall were sufficient safeguards against trouble. The freezing weather further motivated the militiamen to spend their time in a warm house located about 40 yards from the prison, which they had commandeered for their guardhouse, rather than patrol the drafty prison corridors. Inside their cozy guardhouse, the carefree militiamen played cards and gossiped while Arnold's desperate men sat shivering nearby—discussing how to murder their guards and seize St. Johns Gate.

Realizing that their proposed mass prison break should be organized as a military exercise, the enlisted prisoners elected certain of their number to act as officers. Thus, sergeants and corporals were renamed as a council of generals and colonels. They commanded the prisoners' clandestine army, which consisted of 350 violent men who were secretly organizing and arming themselves into a dangerous fighting force.

The prisoners observed the routine of their jailers, who made infrequent visits to the prison during the day. Of greater interest to the rebel prisoners was what occurred inside the guardhouse at night. Illuminated by candles and lanterns that burned through the nighttime, the guardhouse was in full view of the prisoners from their barred windows, and they could see that their sentries remained in the building all night. The rebels detected no movement from the guardhouse during the coldest hours of the night, convincing them that all their jailers were asleep. Assiduous observation by the prisoners also showed that the front door of the guardhouse was kept unlocked, and that most of the guards' weapons were stored in a room on the second floor of the building. The prisoners' council calculated that it would take less than a minute for some of their agile comrades to scale the crumbling prison wall, run into the unlocked guardhouse past the slumbering sentries, climb the flight of steps to the second floor, and grab some muskets and swords.

59 Henry, *An Interesting and Accurate Account . . . In the Campaign Against Quebec*, 144.

60 Roch, ed., "Memorandums of Jacob Danford," 79.

The continued observation of the guardhouse was only part of the prisoners' nocturnal activities. While their sentries were relaxing at night in their guardhouse, the prisoners were hard at work nearby, having transformed their jail into a nighttime weapons factory. By carefully prying open locks to forgotten storerooms and attic spaces, Arnold's men found old scythes, barrel hoops, and scraps of discarded iron which they twisted and sharpened into knives and swords. Handles for their weapons were made from pieces of wood. The prisoners were also given one small axe by the guards to cut firewood; they hid the tool and told the guards it was lost. The unsuspecting guards gave them another axe, which they immediately added to their arsenal of weapons. This game went on, cautiously and plausibly, until Arnold's men had accumulated several axes.

Most of the militia guards entered the prison only once each day, escorting the Officer of the Day, who made a brief inspection tour of the prison before departing to continue his rounds of the city. The prisoners posted lookouts to watch for the approach of the daily inspection and any random visits by the guards. When the whispered alarm was sounded, everyone hid any weapons they were making in the false bottoms they had built into their bunks. Then they covered their beds with jumbles of clothing and blankets and fell limp on them, feigning disinterest in their guards.

In time, Arnold's men could covertly open every lock inside the barracks, including one that led to a trap door in the roof. At night, some of them lifted the trap door to peer out at St. Johns Gate, which was only 300 yards away. They observed that there were always 30 to 40 soldiers manning the gate, with two loaded cannon and extra ammunition nearby should the rebel besiegers attempt a surprise attack. A lit slow-match (a long piece of slowly burning braided rope attached to a pole called a linstock) was kept near each cannon; the cannon could be fired by touching the match to the priming powder that spilled from a hole in the rear of the weapon. Continued observation of the gate convinced the council that they had enough men to overpower its defenders, capture the cannon, and hold the gate long enough for the Americans besieging the city to rush to their aid.

John Hall, who had joined the Arnold Expedition posing as a British Army deserter, was confined in the jail with the other enlisted men. He observed his supposed comrades, and listened with growing alarm as they plotted their escape and the conquest of Quebec. Hall watched as the council divided the men into three detachments of unequal size for their nighttime breakout. One group, under the command of a sergeant named Boyd from Smith's rifle company, was assigned to climb over the prison wall, overpower the guardhouse, and seize the guards' muskets and ammunition. Another detachment, under the command of Sergeant Aston of Lamb's artillery company, would escape onto the street and surprise the men defending St. Johns Gate. This important detachment consisted of the 39 prisoners from Lamb's artillery company and 150 men from the Arnold Expedition. After seizing the portal, the Kennebec men would swing it wide open while Lamb's artillerymen turned the two loaded cannons around and fired into the city. The third and smallest detachment was assigned to run to three nearby buildings, which they would set on fire to create as much confusion as possible.

Lamb's artillerymen explained to the council that they had to carry their own match, just in case the British troops defending St. Johns Gate managed to destroy or carry off the ones they kept at their post; it was common for artillerymen to carry off their match if their position was in danger of being overrun. Lamb's men knew the recipes for making artillery slow-match, one of which was to boil a piece of rope or hemp in water, then remove the length of hot rope from the kettle and sprinkle it with a mixture of crushed gunpowder mixed with some wine or other spirits. After drying, the rope was ready for use as a match.[61]

Getting some gunpowder for Lamb's men was a problem, but the prisoners obtained it nonetheless—by inventing a game for their jailers. They befriended some of the youngest guards, those who seemed most susceptible to flattery and humor. The prisoners even pretended to learn French to gain the confidence of their young jailers. Having made friends with the guards, the prisoners showed them some toy cannons they had made from scraps of wood and folds of paper. The guards marveled at these miniature guns and gave the prisoners tiny amounts of gunpowder to try out their toys. The little cannons worked, and the prisoners were soon putting on mock battles for the guards, who were giving them larger amounts of powder, some of which was hidden by the prisoners during their elaborate performances. These silly war games continued until the Americans had accumulated enough gunpowder for Lamb's men to make artillery matches.

61 A good explanation of how an 18th-century cannon was loaded and fired, including the function of the match, appears in Harold L. Peterson, *Round Shot and Rammers* (Bonanza Books, 1969), 30. For recipes for making slow-match, see Smith, *An Universal Military Dictionary*, 161.

The council members decided they would carry out their plan in the predawn hours of April 1. Critical to the plan's success was notifying Arnold of their intentions and telling him to be ready to rush American troops to their assistance the moment they swung open St. Johns Gate. The council knew the American prisoners could hold the portal for only a short time before British reinforcements arrived to retake it. But getting information to Arnold presented a serious problem for his Kennebec veterans, who were locked in a prison in a city under siege. The council decided that one of their fellow prisoners had to escape and get to Arnold with the necessary information, including a prearranged signal that they had control of St. Johns Gate. Reaching the American lines meant not only breaking out of the barracks but also vaulting Quebec's formidable perimeter wall. There also had to be some signal from Arnold back to the prisoners that their courier had safely reached the American camp and that Arnold was ready to cooperate.

A prisoner named John Martin from Lamb's artillery company volunteered for the dangerous mission. On the afternoon of March 25, Martin dressed himself in warm clothing and joined the others for some exercise in the prison yard. One or two of them meandered to a corner near the wall. The weather was very cold, and the few guards on duty were more interested in keeping themselves warm than in watching their prisoners. At dusk, the Kennebec men were ordered inside for the night. Everyone filed into the building except Martin, who hid in the same dark corner that had been briefly visited earlier by his comrades, where he found the special articles of clothing they had hidden there for his escape. These items were white overalls, jacket, cap, shoes, and gloves which he put on over his regular clothing. Martin now blended in with the drifts of snow that covered the edges of the prison yard. He waited for darkness before climbing over the prison wall. Undetected in his camouflage gear, he cautiously made his way to the ramparts surrounding the city and leaped into a deep snow drift facing the outside wall. Martin's greatest fear at the time was that he would drop too deeply into the snow bank and not be able to pull himself out, but he made the leap safely and quickly vanished into the night. Martin reached Arnold's headquarters and told him about the intended April 1 jail break and plan to open St. Johns Gate.

Watching from their secret trapdoor vantage point, the prisoners saw a flag flying from the American lines that the wind seemed to have twisted into a knot. The prisoners rejoiced, for what looked like an accident of nature to anyone else looking on, the twisted flag was the signal from Martin that he had successfully escaped and Arnold was ready to help them. They were also relieved to see that

Martin's absence was not noticed by the guards, who had become lax in their duties in the cold weather.

The rebel prisoners were now ready to pry open the cellar door they had selected for their mass breakout. They needed this portal to get their men out of the building quickly. The door had been chosen by the ringleaders after several nighttime inspections of the building. What they found was that the Dauphine barracks were built on the slope of a hill, so part of the building's first floor was below ground level. Arnold's men found a secluded door that led to the outside from this subterranean section of the building. The door was bolted shut from the outside, but its hinges were rusted and reachable from the inside. However, parts of the door, including the hinges, were covered with a thick layer of ice, which the prisoners decided they would have to remove when they were ready to escape so they could open the door without making any noise.

While the council discussed how to deal with the ice covering the hinges (which included the possibility of melting it away with heat), Pvt. John Hall decided that the situation had become serious and he had to inform Governor Carleton of his fellow prisoners' dangerous plot. Hall believed that his life would be in danger if he even attempted to report the dangerous plot secretly. He knew from first-hand experience that his fellow Arnold Expedition prisoners were a formidable lot who would hunt down and kill anyone in their ranks who betrayed them. Hall could not give his information to the militia guards, who were a bunch of ignorant conscripts under the sway of the prisoners.

Hall made his move on March 31, just hours before the mass breakout was scheduled to take place. The provost marshal (the commander of the military police) was in the building with an armed guard of regular troops following a report that noises had been heard coming from a cellar door.[62] The prisoners were busy insisting that nothing unusual had taken place when Private Hall brashly stepped forward to announce that he had some knowledge of the incident. The private was quickly surrounded by the soldiers accompanying the provost marshal and ushered away. A short time later all hell broke loose in the barracks. A detachment of veteran soldiers arrived and locked all the prisoners

62 *An Universal Military Dictionary* described the duties of a provost marshal in the British army: "an officer appointed to secure deserters, and all other criminals: he is often to go round the army, hinder the soldiers from pillaging, indict offenders, execute the sentence pronounced, and regulate the weights and measures used in the army when in the field. He is attended by a lieutenant's guard, has a clerk, and an executioner." *Ibid.*, 218.

in manacles and leg irons. These troopers knew exactly where the prisoners had hidden their weapons and confiscated the lot. They also grabbed the ringleaders of the plot, who were hustled away to headquarters for interrogation.

Hall was never seen again, but his former fellow soldiers never forgot him. Private Abner Stocking called him "a vile traitor," and remembered that Hall had claimed that he was a deserter from the British army back at Cambridge.[63] Rifleman John Joseph Henry wrote about Hall in his journal, calling him a traitor and "vile informer." Henry recalled that when the leaders of the plot were taken to Governor Carleton, "they found that the wretch [Hall] had evidenced all our proceedings minutely." After being questioned, Sergeant Boyd, one of the council members, was returned to jail in chains, "where he shed the tears of excruciating anguish...deploring our adverse fate. We had vowed to each other to be free or die, and to be thus foolishly baulked, caused the most heartrending grief."[64]

Now familiar with every detail of the prisoners' plan, Governor Carleton decided to stage a masquerade to trick Arnold into sending his troops into an ambush. Carleton arranged for it to look as though Arnold's men had gained control of St. Johns Gate. The governor ordered the show to start at the prescribed time of 2:00 a.m. Firewood, previously piled near three buildings bordering the portal, was set ablaze to make it look as if the buildings were burning. Some British troops simultaneously began firing, creating a racket to imitate a fight for the gate. Carleton, meanwhile, had almost the entire garrison hidden nearby, ready to man the ramparts and unleash a barrage of artillery and volleys of musket fire when Arnold took the bait and neared the gate with his troops.

Everything occurred on schedule as Arnold watched from across the Plains of Abraham. He saw fires blazing behind the walls near St. Johns Gate, and heard the sounds of musket fire and men screaming in the night. The spectacle continued with "voices calling out Liberty" from St. Johns Gate, followed closely by the sounds of two six-pounders firing into the city.[65] Carleton's

63 "Journal of Abner Stocking" in Roberts, ed., *March to Quebec*, 567.

64 Henry, *An Accurate and Interesting Account . . . In the Campaign Against Quebec*, 161-162.

65 Danford's journal includes an excellent description of this incident: "1st April, This morning about ½ after 1 o'clock the Garrison being under arms at their alarm Posts, His Excellency gave orders to set fire to the 2 piles of wood, the Invalid Company [made up of soldiers too old or wounded to perform regular duty] to fire Musquetry near the prison in small parties, and a party was likewise sent to St. Johns Gate to keep a constant fire with Musquetry

staged musket and cannon fire continued while his troops silently waited for Arnold to support his brave comrades—who were actually chained and handcuffed in the Dauphine Barracks. But Arnold never budged. He sensed that something was amiss, and decided not to attack.[66] Carleton continued his performance for Arnold's benefit, with the two cannon at St. Johns Gate firing blanks into the city until 3:00 a.m., when he ordered the gate shut and everyone to return to their regular duties.

Sometime later, Colonel Maclean ordered all of Arnold's enlisted men paraded into the yard in their chains and assembled in a military formation. The colonel walked along the ranks of the shackled prisoners accompanied by some of the officers of the garrison. As he walked along, Maclean stopped in front of particular prisoners, saying, "This is General such-a-one—that is Colonel such-a-one," and in this manner pointed out the ringleaders of the plot.[67]

Coincidentally, just hours after the enlisted men's failed jail break, General Wooster arrived unannounced from Montreal. He was a 60-year-old Connecticut officer who had seen considerable combat during the French & Indian War. However, he owed his high rank as much to the politics of the time as to military experience. The pompous and supercilious Wooster toured Arnold's 26 miles of siege lines on horseback wearing an enormous periwig. He criticized everything that Arnold had done with his slim resources since the December 31 attack.[68] Effectively, Wooster engineered a swap: he ordered Arnold to take charge of Montreal while he handled the "very disagreeable

---

and to give 3 Cheers calling out Liberty every 8 or 10 minutes." Roche, ed., "Memorandums of Jacob Danford,", 81.

66 Arnold paraded his army in anticipation of the prisoner breakout, but there was a full moon that night and something that caught his attention made him decide against rushing St. John's Gate. Smith, *Our Struggle for the Fourteenth Colony*, II: 290.

67 Henry, *An Accurate and Interesting Account . . . In the Campaign Against Quebec*, 170.

68 Wooster had already made it clear that he, and not Schuyler, commanded the American troops in Canada. Writing to Schuyler from Montreal on February 11, 1776, the pretentious Wooster lectured his superior: "You will give me leave to inform you, that the commanding officer who is with this Army [a jab at Schuyler who was in his Albany mansion] is to give out orders, and is the only competent judge of what is proper, and what not, for the internal regulation of the Army, and for the immediate safety of the country. Since the death of the worthy and brave General Montgomery (with whom I had the happiness to serve in the strictest harmony and friendship, and who ever treated me like a gentleman,) the command devolves [sic] upon me, and I shall give out such orders as appear to me necessary for the publick good. . . ." See Force, ed., *American Archives*, Fourth Series, IV: 1218.

situation at Quebec."[69] Arnold obeyed; he rode away from the walled city on April 12, 1776, and never saw the place again.

The Arnold Expedition's enlisted men remained in chains in the Dauphine Barracks throughout April, so that Carleton could focus his energies on the growing rebel threat facing his beleaguered city. But across town in the seminary, several of Arnold's officers were busily cutting their way through a door in preparation for a jail break. Of the 37 American officers held prisoner in Quebec, 35 were from the Arnold Expedition. The British officers who talked to them were amazed at their undistinguished backgrounds. Major Caldwell described them in a letter:

> You can have no conception what kind of men composed the officers. Of those we took, one major was a blacksmith [Timothy Bigelow], another a hatter [a reference to Return Jonathan Meigs, who was a merchant but whose father was a hatter]; of their captains, there was a butcher, a tanner, a shoemaker, a tavern-keeper [William Goodrich], etc., yet they all pretended to be gentlemen.[70]

The two other American officers being held as prisoners of war in Quebec were artillerymen, Samuel Lockwood and Capt. John Lamb, both of whom had been captured with Arnold's men. Lamb had survived the serious wounds he sustained during the attack, although he lost one eye and his face was badly scarred. Lockwood is of particular interest because he was involved in several schemes with Arnold's officers to escape from prison and rejoin the American forces surrounding Quebec. He was sometimes referred to as "captain," but the title related to his being a civilian ship's captain prior to the war. He is also mentioned by several of the diarists as "Mr. Lockwood," which indicates he was a civilian.[71] Lockwood is presumed to have been an expert on the positioning and aiming of cannon because he was listed as an "assistant engineer" in Lamb's artillery company.[72]

69 General Wooster to President of Congress, dated "Holland-House, before Quebeck, April 10, 1776," in *Ibid.*, Fourth Series, V: 845.

70 Arthur Lefkowitz, *Benedict Arnold's Army* (New York: Savas-Beatie, LLC, 2008), 267-68.

71 Stone, ed., *The Journal of Captain Simeon Thayer*, 34.

72 Heitman, *Historical Register of Officers of the Continental Army*, 355. Further evidence that Lockwood was ranked as a lieutenant and functioned as an assistant engineer appears in the resolutions of the Continental Congress, dated November 21, 1776: "To Lieutenant Samuel

Lockwood and the other imprisoned American officers began to think seriously about escaping from the seminary when they realized that Governor Carleton had no intention of paroling them. Parole was a system that offered prisoners of war limited freedom based upon their word of honor that they would remain within a specified area as noncombatants until they were exchanged or otherwise absolved from their parole. General Schuyler, for example, paroled the British officers captured by Montgomery in Canada. However, Governor Carleton did not return the favor.[73]

Once paroled, officers hoped that they would be exchanged. Enlisted men, who were not considered gentlemen, were rarely paroled, but were still eligible for repatriation. Prisoner exchanges had to be negotiated informally between the Americans and the British during the Revolutionary War because the British government refused to recognize the legitimacy of the Continental Congress or the Continental Army. This frequently overlooked aspect of the American Revolution is important because it helps explain why it took so long to exchange the Arnold Expedition men. British policy concerning exchanges was stated in February 1, 1776, instructions from Lord Germain to General Howe. Germain's letter was prompted by the capture of several rebel naval officers who were being sent to Howe in Boston:

> It is hoped that the possession of these prisoners will enable you to procure the release of such of His Majesty's officers and loyal subjects as are in the disgraceful situation of being prisoners to the Rebels; for although it cannot be that you should enter into any treaty or agreement with Rebels for a regular cartel for exchange of prisoners, yet I doubt not but your own discretion will suggest to you the means of effecting such

---

Lockwood, for his pay as assistant engineer in the army in Canada, from the 5 November, 1775 to the 18 May, 1776 at 20 dollars per month...from the 19 May, to 5 November, at 30 dollars per month . . ." Ford, ed., *Journals of Congress*, VI: 971. Lockwood was 38 years old at the time of his capture at Quebec. He was from Greenwich, Connecticut. Lockwood returned to the Continental Army following his repatriation. He served as a captain in John Lamb's 2nd Continental Artillery regiment, then resigned his commission in 1779. Lockwood died in 1807.

73 Paroling of the British officers in Canada is evidenced by Gen. Schuyler's orders to Col. Wynkoop dated Albany, January 2, 1776: "Sir: Captain Billings will deliver to you the officers that were made prisoners in Canada. . . . You will be so good as to forward the officers and their baggage to Trenton [New Jersey], together with the baggage of the St. Johns garrison, the officers' servants, and four or five men [probably captured British enlisted men] to take care of the baggage. . . . The officers are now on their parole of honour; but, when you take them in charge, you will request them to renew their parole, agreeable to my former orders." Force, ed., *American Archives*, Fourth Series, IV: 542.

> exchange, without the King's dignity and honour being committed, or His Majesty's name used in any negotiation for that purpose.[74]

As a result of this policy, prisoner exchanges could only be negotiated according to the sentiment of the British commanding officer on the scene. Carleton was not interested in negotiating exchanges with the rebels, whom he considered to be traitors, nor was he willing to parole the American officers he held captive at Quebec, especially with the enemy laying siege to the city. Carleton's rigorous attitude toward parole and repatriation forced the rebel officers resort to escape as their only hope. Captain Thayer, for example, wrote that "after being confined in Quebec for months continuing in this lamentable situation for some time, and seeing no hopes of relief [parole or exchange], we unanimously resolv'd to make our escape if possible."[75] A breakout was particularly tempting to the Arnold Expedition prisoners because the Continental Army was only a short distance away.

Thayer, who was 38 at the time, had been toughened by his service in the French & Indian War, which included escaping the massacre of the garrison of Fort William Henry and surviving dangerous reconnaissance missions as a soldier in Rogers' Rangers. Breaking out of a Quebec prison was just another challenge to a man of Thayer's experience and daring.

74 Lord George Germain to Major General Howe, dated "Whitehall, February 1, 1776," in Ibid, 903. Some British officers were opposed to exchanging any prisoners with the rebels, including Lt. Frederick Mackenzie from the Royal Welch Fusiliers. Writing from Long Island on September 5, 1776, Mackenzie explained why he was against the practice. Note that he considers the warring Americans to be rebels, not constituting a legitimate army: "An exchange of prisoners is talked of. The measure may be right and politic; but it appears rather extraordinary that under the present circumstances we should treat with them as if on an equality; and for the sake of releasing a few of our officers and Soldiers, give up some of the principal actors in the Rebellion. Rebels taken in arms forfeit their lives by the laws of all Countries. The keeping all Rebel prisoners taken in arms, without any immediate hope of release, and in a state of uncertainty with respect to their fate, would certainly strike great terror into their army; whereas now, captivity has nothing dreadful in it; and it rather encourages them to continue their opposition to the utmost extremity, when they find, contrary to every expectation that capital punishment has not been inflicted on any of those who have fallen into our hands. . . . We act thus either from an apprehension that they might retaliate upon our prisoners in their hands, or from a desire to bring them back to a sense of their duty by an extraordinary degree of lenity." Frederick Mackenzie, *Diary of Frederick Mackenzie*, 2 vols. (Cambridge, Massachusetts: Harvard University Press, 1930), I: 39.

75 Stone, ed., *The Journal of Captain Simeon Thayer*, 32.

Any attempt to escape was a challenge, as Governor Carleton had all the rebel officers locked up and closely guarded in two rooms on the top floor of the seminary. Despite these handicaps, Thayer devised a plan to escape with the help of a guard he identified simply as "Joe." The guard's real name is unknown, and Thayer would only say that he "was of our party," meaning that he sympathized with the rebel cause. "Joe" was also paid a bribe to ensure his fidelity to the cause of liberty.[76]

Thayer had two fellow conspirators in his escape plot, Capt. Hanchet and Mr. Lockwood. Thayer's daring scheme called for escaping from their fourth-story prison at night by climbing down a rope made by tying blankets together. In an effort to avoid being seen descending on a line suspended from the side of the seminary, Joe would signal them from the ground when it was safe for them to lower themselves down on their improvised rope. Joe's signal would be his seemingly innocent slapping of his hand against the metal lock (firing mechanism) of his musket three times. Joe had clubs hidden for the three officers to use as weapons, and agreed to provide them with the countersign, which might help them if they were approached by an enemy patrol. However, once on the ground Thayer, Hanchet, and Lockwood would be on their own to get past the city's perimeter defenses and make it to the safety of the distant American lines.

On a dark February night, the three rebel officers listened intently from their chamber window for Joe's signal that it was safe to drop their improvised rope and begin their perilous descent. They heard the first distinctive metallic tap cutting through the still night and got ready to throw their rope out the window. The second tap followed and the three Americans braced themselves for their dangerous climb. But the third sound never came, and they quickly untied the string of blankets and silently returned to their bunks. Joe later explained that a patrol had suddenly come into view as he was about to give the final signal. The plan was attempted on two subsequent nights, but each time it had to be aborted. As a result, the plotters decided to abandon their scheme—especially when Joe told them that he had discovered an alternative.

The new plan was to get to the ground from a garret that lay above the prisoners' rooms. The route was not easy, and ended with a 14-foot jump into the seminary garden. Joe promised to be waiting there with weapons. But on April 26, 1776, a guard found Captain Thayer rummaging in the garret above

76 *Ibid.*, 33.

the fourth floor of the seminary. The captain had become too engrossed with some final escape preparations, and thus failed to hear the warning signal from Lockwood that someone was approaching. The sentry saw Thayer and called for his comrades, who held him for questioning by the provost marshal. An inspection of the garret door revealed that Thayer had gotten into the locked room by carefully wiggling loose the numerous nails that fastened several door slats to the door frame, allowing him to squeeze through the door. He could remove and replace the nails at will.

The provost marshal decided that Thayer was not working alone, to which Thayer replied "that there were none but myself, and that my sole motive was only to go up to the garret to view the town and forces around it."[77] Not believing him, the provost marshal assembled all the prisoners in one room for further questioning by Col. Maclean, who arrived accompanied by several other officers of the garrison. Thayer repeated his story to these investigators, stating emphatically that he had acted alone and was only harmlessly looking at the city from the garret. Maclean did not buy Thayer's story either, and ordered him removed to a schooner in the harbor, where he was locked in the cable room in leg chains and handcuffs. He was joined a few days later by Hanchet and Lockwood, who had been overheard talking intimately with one of the guards (Joe) about Thayer's whereabouts. Under intense questioning, Joe admitted to the provost marshal that Thayer, Hanchet, and Lockwood had been plotting to escape, with his help. Joe was removed and eventually sent to England to stand trial (and probably hanged), while Hanchet and Lockwood joined Thayer in the schooner, where they remained in a most lamentable situation.[78]

It is uncertain whether the Americans inside Quebec knew that General Thomas had reached the American camp on May 1 to take charge of the siege. Their hopes of being liberated would have soared had they known that Thomas had brought five hundred fresh troops with him and that several thousand

77 *Ibid.*, 34-35.

78 Captain Ainslie said the Americans had two conspirators helping them: "30TH [April 1776]. Two soldiers flush of money were question'd of their sergeants; after many contradictory tales they were threaten'd with confinement if they wou'd not immediately reveal how they had got so many dollars. They at last confess'd that they had been brib'd by some of the Rebel Officers to assist them in making their escape—the plan was laid & to be put in execution of the first time they were on guard at the Seminary, if unhappily any one shou'd be found in their way they were to have been dispatched without mercy. . . . On the charge of these men, 2 of the Rebel Officers were sent on board Capt La forces arm'd schooner." Cohen, ed., *Journal of Capt. Ainslie*, 85.

additional Continentals commanded by Gen. John Sullivan followed with more artillery. But the prisoners' hopes would have been dashed if they could have read the following excerpt from a report sent by Thomas:

> Immediately on my arrival at the Camp before Quebec . . . I examined into the state of the army and found by the returns there were 1,900 men. Only one thousand fit for duty, including officers. The rest were invalids, chiefly with the small pox. Three hundred of those effective [able-bodied men] were soldiers whose inlistments expired the 15th [of May], many of whom refused duty, and all were very importunate to return home. There were several posts to be supported with this small number, at such distances from each other, that not more than 300 men could be rallied to the relief of any one, should it be attacked by the whole force of the enemy, by means of rivers and other obstructions. In all our magazines there were but about one hundred & fifty pounds of powder & six days provisions, the French inhabitants much disaffected so that supplies of any kind were obtained with a great difficulty from them.[79]

The saving grace was that American reinforcements were en route. However, within days after his arrival, General Thomas realized that he had lost the race to capture Quebec.

General Thomas' trepidation began on the evening of May 5 when he heard some rumbling sounds emanating from down river. The sounds grew louder during the night and were identified as cannon being fired. At about 6 a.m. on May 6, a ship appeared off Pointe-de-Lévis. To Thomas' mortification, she was identified as a warship flying the Union Jack (the British flag). The Americans watched as a blue pennant was hoisted from the tallest flagpole in the city. This unusual flag was the prearranged signal that the British were still in possession of Quebec, and the big warship drew closer to the city. The news of her arrival quickly spread through the besieged city to the inconceivable joy of its residents, who ran down to the waterfront to view the spectacle. As she drew closer, the warship fired a broadside to salute the town, which was returned by an artillery battery and wild cheering from the people lining the docks. All the church bells in the city rang as Governor Carleton appeared with his staff.

The friendly warship was identified as the 50-gun frigate HMS *Surprise.* She tied up at the Royal Navy dock and began to immediately disembark marines and redcoats (British soldiers) from the 29th Regiment. Soon the frigate *Isis* and

79 Manuscript letter dated "Hd Qrs [Headquarters] Pointe de deshambeaux [Deschambault], 7 May, 1776." Philip Schuyler Papers, New York Public Library.

sloop *Martin* came into view, docked, and unloaded more troops. The three ships had brought only a small contingent of soldiers—amounting to 200—but Captain Lindsay, commander of the *Surprise*, warmly assured Governor Carleton that they were only the vanguard, and that more warships and transports would soon arrive with additional men.

Thayer, Hanchet, and Lockwood were eyewitnesses to the spectacle through the cable hole in their shipboard prison cell. They heard the drums of the garrison beat a call to arms and watched as Governor Carleton mustered his troops, including newly arrived reinforcements, in preparation for marching out to fight the invaders. Up in their fourth-story prison in the seminary, the other Arnold Expedition officers strained to get a look at the celebration taking place on the city's waterfront. Their jailers gleefully told them that powerful reinforcements had arrived from England. Upon hearing the terrible news, Captain Dearborn wrote in his journal that "we now gave over all hopes of being retaken [by the American besiegers], and consequently of seeing our families again until we had first taken a Voyage to England and there Tryed for rebels, as we have often been told by the officers of the Garrison."[80]

Lieutenant Colonel Greene stood nearby listening to the cheers and triumphant strains of martial music coming from the waterfront. He turned to his comrades and swore that if he ever got out of prison he would continue to fight, but "I will never again be taken prisoner alive."[81] Sadly, Greene kept his promise. When he was cornered by a party of British Tories later in the war, he fought rather than submit; his attackers hacked him to death.

On the other side of the Plains of Abraham, General Thomas hurriedly ordered a council of war. Informed by scouts and partisans of the size of the British relief expedition, Thomas and his officers decided to end their siege immediately and withdraw toward Montreal.[82] According to British accounts of the day's events, the Americans retreated with such precipitation that they left everything behind, including Thomas' dinner and his regimental coat; the Americans later claimed that their retreat was orderly. Whatever the case, at about noon on May 6, Governor Carleton ventured out from his long winter

80 Brown and Peckham, eds., *Revolutionary War Journals of Henry Dearborn*, 82.

81 Codman, *Arnold's Expedition to Quebec*, 301.

82 John Marshall (historian and future Chief Justice of the Supreme Court), *The Life of George Washington, Commander in Chief of the American Forces . . .*, 5 vols. (Philadelphia: C.P. Wayne, 1804-1807), II: 354-355.

hibernation to find that the Americans were gone, leaving behind tons of valuable equipment and supplies and hundreds of sick soldiers who were too weak to be moved. The British also picked up some stragglers, including two New Jersey soldiers who were found hiding in the woods with fruit-filled pieces of dough in their haversacks and coat pockets. The stragglers were transported to Quebec and thrown into the Dauphin prison with Arnold's enlisted men, who dubbed the new arrivals the "Jersey dumpling eaters."[83] And so the rebel siege of Quebec was lifted, and Capt. John Ainslie, an officer in the Quebec militia, proudly wrote in his journal, "Thus was the country round Quebec freed from a swarm of misguided people."[84]

The end of the siege brought some small relief to the Arnold Expedition prisoners. With the American besiegers gone, Capt. Thayer and his coconspirators were released from their shipboard prison and allowed to rejoin their fellow officers on the top floor of the seminary. The officers were also given the freedom to walk in the garden each day. Over at the Dauphin jail, conditions were also relaxed in the days following the arrival of the British reinforcements. The enlisted men had their chains removed and Private Henry and two of his friends were even allowed the freedom of the city for several hours each day. This favor was arranged by an officer named Capt. Prentiss, who knew Henry's family back in Pennsylvania.[85] It was on one of these walks that Henry found Montgomery's shallow grave near St. Johns Gate.

Some of Henry's fellow prisoners were invited to work for wages aboard the ships in the harbor. Among those who accepted the offer was Private Fobes, who said he was put to work aboard a British warship with three or four other prisoners. Fobes escaped with two of his comrades and eventually reached Maine by retracing the route they had followed with Col. Arnold. Fobes said they passed the corpses of some of the members of the expedition who had perished the previous year. They also found useable gear abandoned by the expedition and a serviceable bateau in the Chain of Ponds region, which they used to hasten their return home.

83 Andrew A. Melvin, ed., *The Journal of James Melvin Private Soldier in Arnold's Expedition Against Quebec in the Year 1775* (Portland, Maine: Hubbard W. Bryant, 1902), 75. Melvin told the story as follows: "[May] 10 [1776], . . . two Jersey dumpling eaters were brought in; they were found among the bushes, not having tried to make their escape, being too heavy laden with dumplings and pork, having forty pounds of pork, a knapsack full of dumplings, and a quantity of flour."

84 Cohen, ed., *Journal of Capt. Ainslie*, 91.

85 Andrew Melvin, ed., *James Melvin's Journal*, 75, footnote.

The end of the American siege of Quebec also allowed fresh food to come into the city. Carleton proved to be a humane jailer who arranged for his prisoners to get some fresh meat, bread, and vegetables. Many of Arnold's enlisted men were suffering from scurvy and the improved diet helped restore their health. Arnold's officers had fared better than the enlisted men. When Carleton learned that sixteen of them had never had smallpox, he allowed them to go through the variolation procedure to become inoculated. Once infected, they were moved to separate, comfortable quarters where they were cared for until the disease had run its course.[86] In addition, the officers either had money or could borrow some from the local merchants on credit, which enabled them to buy additional food and other sundries. There is, for example, a receipt for money given to a number of Arnold's officers while in prison, including a sum given to Lieutenant Colonel Greene, "for the use of Sick Soldiers belonging to the New England Colonies."[87] There are even references to washerwomen and servants attending the officers while they were being held captive.

Captain Dearborn was the first of Arnold's officers to be paroled. It happened through the intervention of Judge Peter Livius, an influential Tory who had fled his Portsmouth, New Hampshire, home at the start of the war for the safety of British-held Quebec. Livius left his family behind in his haste to get away and wanted Dearborn, a resident of New Hampshire, to return home and make arrangements for the judge's family to safely travel through rebel-held territory to Quebec.

Livius had become one of Governor Carleton's closest advisors and friends. He approached the governor with a deal to give Dearborn his parole in exchange for helping the judge's family. Carleton agreed to help his friend and approved the arrangement. Dearborn noted the exact time in his journal that Livius arrived at the seminary bearing the marvelous news: "[May] 16 At one O Clock P:M: Mr. Levius Came to see me & to my great Joy inform'd me that the Gen had given his Consent for me to go home, on Parole. . . ."[88] Governor Carleton also decided to parole Maj. Meigs, who had become sickly from his long imprisonment. Both men appeared before Quebec's Lt. Gov. Hector Cramahé and swore not to take up arms against the King until such time as they

86 "Diary of William Heth," *Annual Papers of Winchester Virginia Historical Society* (Winchester, Virginia, 1931), 39.

87 W.W. Abbot, et al., eds., *Papers of Washington, Revolutionary* War Series, VI: 484.

88 Brown and Peckham, eds., *Revolutionary War Journals of Henry Dearborn*, 84.

were exchanged. They were afterwards invited to meet with Governor Carleton, who wished them a safe voyage home and said that he planned to parole the other American officers that he was holding prisoner. Then the town major (the chief administrative officer of a municipality under military rule) escorted Dearborn and Meigs to the docks with their scanty baggage and put them aboard a schooner bound for Halifax. They sailed from Quebec early the next morning, May 17.

En route they passed 32 transports headed for Quebec, carrying 6,000 troops under the command of Gen. John Burgoyne. The British planned to win back all of Canada with this force and then advance south across Lake Champlain into New York to reclaim Crown Point and Fort Ticonderoga.

Dearborn and Meigs arrived at Halifax on May 30, where they found a number of other paroled American officers waiting for a ship to convey them back to New England. Their number included several officers whom the British had captured the previous June at the Battle of Bunker Hill. Meigs and Dearborn were local celebrities who dined with General Howe during their stay in Halifax. As a military man, Howe wanted to meet the two rebel officers who had survived the famous march through the Maine wilderness.

While Meigs and Dearborn were being entertained in Halifax, General Thomas was foraging for food at Sorel. Since quitting Quebec on May 6, Thomas' starving, smallpox-plagued army had been slowly retreating toward Montreal. On May 17, it reached Sorel, where Montgomery had scored an important victory against the British the previous year. Located at the mouth of the Richelieu River, the town was at the end of the tenuous American supply line that extended north through Albany, Fort Ticonderoga, St. Johns, and Fort Chambly. Thomas was desperately in need of provisions and reinforcements, and Sorel offered his best hope for immediate succor. The two regiments that Congress had ordered to Canada in January (Maxwell's New Jersey and DeHaas' Pennsylvania regiments) were already with Thomas, and six additional regiments, under the command of Gen. John Sullivan, were on their way from New York City. Because of the urgency to reinforce Thomas, General Sullivan told his officers to move their men in company-sized detachments as quickly as they could arm and provision them for the journey.

A Congressional delegation was also in Canada: the aforementioned blue-ribbon commission composed of delegates Franklin, Chase, and Carroll. They came on a fact-finding mission proposed in January by General Schuyler. But they arrived in Canada to a calamity in the making: Congress was sending young American soldiers into combat without the supporting logistical organization to supply them with weapons, gunpowder, transportation, food, clothing, housing, and medicine. Chase lectured his fellow Congressman, Richard Henry Lee, on the subject in a May 17, 1776, letter:

> We have now 4,000 Troops in Canada & not a Mouthful of food. . . . Our affairs here are almost desperate. For the Love of your Country cease the keen Encounter of your Tongues, discard your Tongue Artillery [merely talking about sending artillery] and send Us some field [artillery] or We are undone. My God, an Army of 10,000 [the total number of troops Congress had committed to Canada] without provisions or powder![89]

The Congressional delegation reached Montreal on April 29, where it was met by General Arnold, who was in command of the city. The general mustered as much ceremony as possible in an effort to welcome the Congressmen and to impress the city's population with the resolution of the Americans to remain in Canada. On the following day, Congressman Carroll had the opportunity to talk at length with Arnold and get a detailed account of his march from Cambridge to Quebec. Carroll came away from the meeting impressed, saying that the expedition across Maine "does him great honor and called him a man with a cool head and a warm heart."[90]

Congressman Franklin had become ill following the long and difficult journey to Montreal, and started for home on May 1 after just two days in Montreal. Chase and Carroll remained behind—and were soon meddling in army business, despite their lack of military experience. On May 21, they went to see General Thomas at Sorel, where they found a destitute, smallpox-ravaged army led by an ailing, overworked general who had finally conceded to the mass inoculation of his troops.[91] Thomas had no immunity to smallpox but was too busy to go through the month-long process of inoculation and recovery. Not surprisingly, within hours of his May 21 meeting with Chase and Carroll,

89 Smith, ed., *Letters of Delegates to Congress*, IV: 21-22.

90 Manuscript letter, "Charles Carroll of Carrollton to Papa [his father, Charles Carroll of Annapolis]," dated "30 April 1776, Montreal," in the *Charles Carroll Papers*, Maryland Historical Society.

91 A letter from the Commissioners to Canada to John Hancock, dated Montreal, May 27, 1776, includes the following: "Your Army in Canada does not exceed 4000. Above 400 are sick with different disorders. 3/4ths of the Army have not had the small Pox. The greater part of Greaton's Bonds, & Burrall's Regts. have been lately inoculated." Force, ed., *American Archives*, Fourth Series, VI: 590.

General Thomas was himself diagnosed with smallpox. He was transported to Chambly, where Congressman Chase visited him on May 31. After seeing him, Chase wrote home, "It is a Million to a Shilling that General Thomas will die."[92] Unfortunately, Chase was right: General Thomas, the great hope of reviving American fortunes in Canada, died on June 2. With Thomas' death, the command of the Canadian army fell to General Sullivan, who inherited a force described as "scattered and confused."[93] Fortunately for Sullivan, Governor Carleton remained cautious, and other than capturing the St. Lawrence River town of Trois Rivières (Three Rivers) in late May, he halted his advance toward Montreal for the moment.

92 Samuel Chase to Philip Schuyler dated "Chambly May 31st. 1776" in Smith, ed., *Letters of Delegates to Congress*, IV: 105. Commenting on the subject, historian David Ramsay wrote, "Thomas, the commander in chief in Canada, was seized with the small pox and died; having forbidden his men to inoculate, he conformed to his own rule, and refused to avail himself of that precaution."

93 Comments by Alexander Scammel, the Deputy Adjutant-General of the Northern Department, in Force, ed., *American Archives*, Fourth Series, VI: 915. Additional important information about the situation in Canada is included in a letter General Sullivan wrote to John Hancock dated St. Johns, June 1, 1776: "I must beg Leave to Inform Congress that I arrived here Last Evening with my Brigade except Col. Draytons [Elias Dayton's 3rd New Jersey regiment] & part of Col. Waines Regiment [Anthony Wayne's 4th Pennsylvania]. . . . [U]pon my arrival I was Informed that General Thomas was Down with the Small Pox without the Least prospect of a Recovery. General Worster [Wooster] is here with his Baggage Returning to Conecticut [sic] by means of which the Command Devolves upon me [the Congressional delegation sent to Canada dismissed Wooster]. I have done Every thing I possibly could in the time to get Information of the true State of affairs—and can in a word Inform you that no one thing is Right. Ever thing is in the utmost Confusion & almost Every one Frightened at they know not what. . . . Every kind of fraud [illegible] the Regiments Sent here are Torn & Divided into Numerous parts Scattered from one End of the Country to another." Otis G. Hammond, ed., *Letters and Papers of Major-General John Sullivan*, 3 vols. (Concord, New Hampshire: New Hampshire Historical Society, 1930), I: 212-213. Wooster returned to Connecticut following his dismissal. He was killed in April 1777 leading Connecticut militia during the British raid on the American supply depot at Danbury, Connecticut. In his scathing history of the Revolutionary War, Thomas Jones (who was a Tory) said that Wooster "lost his life fighting in a bad cause. . . . He was between 70 and 80 years of age at the time of his death [actually 67], and though he had accustomed himself during the greatest part of his life to swallow daily large potations of flip [hot spiced wine whipped up with egg] he was a healthy, hearty, strong man to the last." Thomas Jones, *History of New York During the Revolutionary War*, 2 vols. (New York: Printed for the New York Historical Society, 1879), I: 179-180. John Sullivan (1740-1795) was a New Hampshire lawyer who embraced the American patriot cause early. He represented New Hampshire at the Second Continental Congress, and when the war started he lobbied for a senior command. His fellow Congressmen named Sullivan a brigadier general, and he joined the army in Cambridge on July 10, 1775. One of Sullivan's most important qualities was his loyalty to Gen. Washington, which helped his military career throughout the war.

However, a small but aggressive detachment of British troops supported by Indian allies was threatening Montreal from the west. Arnold called a council of his officers at Montreal to decide how to deal with the menace. As usual, Arnold advocated action, in the form of an immediate attack on the enemy. Colonel Moses Hazen attended the council. Arnold considered Hazen his friend and supporter, and expected him to endorse any plan that Arnold proposed. However, Hazen argued against an attack, and Arnold struck back at his comrade by insulting him so vehemently in front of his fellow officers that their friendship was ruined beyond repair. Thus, Arnold created another dangerous enemy due to his belief that his judgment was superior to all others. In any case, any plans to attack the enemy from Montreal soon ended as a result of a failed American attack by Sullivan's army against Three Rivers, giving Arnold no option but to abandon the city.

The proposal for the ill-fated American attack on Three Rivers had originated with Congressmen Chase and Carroll, who incorrectly attributed Carleton's halt in his movement toward Montreal to a weakness in numbers. Chase and Carroll advised General Sullivan to attack Carleton's force at Three Rivers, and he followed their advice. He dispatched 2,000 troops on June 6 to attack the place, which they did two days later—only to find it defended by a large enemy force that repulsed them, killing about 30 Americans and capturing 200. Carleton, it turned out, had an army of 13,000, which resumed offensive operations aimed at Montreal following the American defeat at Three Rivers. Under pressure from the British advance, Sullivan abandoned Sorel on June 14 and retreated south to Chambly and St. Johns. With no alternative, Arnold abandoned Montreal the following day—while Congressmen Chase and Carroll went home.

A young American officer named James Wilkinson (1757-1825) recorded the rebel army's retreat from Canada. Background information about Wilkinson is important not only because he left a vivid account of the precipitous retreat, but also because a number of historians have incorrectly stated that he was a gentleman volunteer on the 1775 Arnold Expedition.[94]

94 See, for example, Mark Boatner, *Encyclopedia of the American Revolution* (New York: David McKay Company, Inc., 1976), 1205: "As a volunteer in Thompson's Pa. Bn, 9 Sept. '75 - March. '76, he and Aaron Burr took part in Arnold's march to Quebec. (An interesting collection of scoundrels, but their performance in this expedition was creditable.) Wilkinson remained with Arnold until Dec.'76." Another reference to Wilkinson being on the Arnold Expedition is Richard M. Ketchum, *Saratoga: Turning Point of America's Revolutionary War* (New

Wilkinson was in New York City in the spring of 1776 when the American retreat from Quebec began. According to his autobiography, titled *Memoirs of My Own Time*, published in 1816, Wilkinson was a captain at the time in the 2nd Continental Regiment (a New Hampshire outfit) commanded by Col. James Reed.

Wilkinson's autobiography is an important eyewitness account of the American Revolution. The book has much valuable information, despite the fact that it is a self-aggrandizing and sometimes distorted account of the war. Historians have not treated Wilkinson kindly, including Thomas Fleming, who described him as a "cash-hungry soldier who did not have a moral bone in his body."[95]

Wilkinson was a native of Maryland and was privately tutored at home before going to Philadelphia, where he studied medicine for two years (1773-1775). After completing his medical studies, he returned to Maryland "and sat down to the practice of medicine" just as the Revolution was beginning.[96] Writing in his memoirs that he was fired with patriotic zeal following the news of the Battle of Bunker Hill, young Dr. Wilkinson rushed to Cambridge in September 1775, where he accepted a post in Col. William Thompson's Pennsylvania rifle corps as a gentleman volunteer. Historians deduced that Wilkinson was a gentlemen volunteer in one of the two Pennsylvania rifle companies on the Arnold Expedition, but this is not correct: Wilkinson remained in Cambridge until March 1776, when he was commissioned as captain in Reed's 2nd New Hampshire Continental regiment. Captain Wilkinson next accepted an appointment as an aide-de-camp to General Nathanael Greene. He accompanied Greene from Boston to New York City in April 1776 as part of the main army (the troops under General Washington's immediate command) then moving to defend that important

York: Henry Holt and Company, 1997), 352, footnote. Also see Brendan Morrissey, *Quebec 1775* (Oxford, United Kingdom: Osprey Publishing, Ltd., 2003), 56, which reads in part: "As villains of the Revolution, Wilkinson and Burr barely rank below Arnold (post-betrayal) and are remarkable only for their ability to survive some highly dubious acts. Yet strangely both showed considerable fortitude and bravery during Arnold's expedition and the attack on Quebec. Wilkinson was born in Maryland, studied medicine, and joined Thompson's Pennsylvania rifle battalion on the outbreak of war. He befriended Burr on the march through Maine and, after being promoted to captain, replaced Burr as Arnold's aide-de-camp."

95 Thomas Fleming, *Duel* (New York: Basic Books, 1999), 141.

96 (General) James Wilkinson, *Memoirs of My Own Times*, 3 vols. (Philadelphia: Printed by Abraham Small, 1816), I: 14.

coastal city. Upon arriving in New York, Wilkinson learned that Gen. John Sullivan was preparing to leave the city with reinforcements for Quebec. Sullivan's troops included Reed's 2nd New Hampshire regiment, in which Wilkinson had previously been commissioned as captain. Anxious to see combat, Wilkinson resigned from Greene's staff and returned to Reed's regiment, where he was given command of a company.

In an effort to move quickly, Sullivan ordered every unit under his command to leave for Canada as soon as it was ready, and to rendezvous at St. Johns. Captain Wilkinson took the lead, arriving at St. Johns with his company on May 22, 1776. His memoirs give a vivid picture of the chaotic conditions he found at St. Johns. He described how groups of disheartened, dirty, sick, and hungry American troops were converging on the place, "without garrison or commandant, but infested by numbers of stragglers from the army, who could give no satisfactory account of themselves." Despite having no orders to proceed beyond St. Johns, the zealous young Wilkinson yielded "to the general impulse of my breast" and determined to reinforce the weakest point. Accordingly, "having taken under my command every man who acknowledged himself to be a soldier," Wilkinson took it upon himself to reinforce Arnold, who was nearby at Montreal.[97]

As Wilkinson worked alongside Arnold in the days that followed, the general became impressed with the 19-year-old, and invited him to become his aide-de-camp. Wilkinson accepted the post and was appointed Arnold's aide on June 2, 1776.

As Arnold's confidant, Wilkinson knew of the general's order to seize valuable provisions and other goods from Montreal merchants for use by the army. Prior to evacuating Montreal, Arnold ordered the merchandise confiscated from several Montreal merchants to be escorted by a detachment of troops and delivered to Colonel Hazen, who was in St. Johns with the retreating army. When Arnold arrived there, he found the valuable goods had been left unguarded and ransacked by Sullivan's troops as they fled south. Arnold was livid, and accused Hazen of disobeying orders. After assessing the situation, Arnold wrote to General Sullivan, explaining that the commandeered goods were "to be delivered to Colonel Hazen, to be stored. He refused receiving or taking any care of them. . . . [T]he goods have been opened and plundered. . . .

97 *Ibid.*, 40.

This is not the first or last order Colonel Hazen has disobeyed."[98] Arnold demanded that Sullivan immediately court martial Hazen for his insubordination.

Recalling the incident years later, Wilkinson accused Arnold of being a thief. He said that Arnold had ordered him to seize the valuable civilian-owned merchandise in Montreal as the British were closing in on the city. Arnold claimed that he wanted the food and clothing for his impoverished troops, but Wilkinson alleged that "the booty was transported to Albany, where it was sold, General Arnold pocketing the proceeds."[99] Wilkinson blamed Arnold's unscrupulous action on his shady background and previous unprincipled behavior as a "half-bred apothecary" and horse dealer.[100]

What Arnold also found at St. Johns was more serious than the missing merchandise from Montreal. The place held the remnants of a once-proud army, men who were little more than a filthy, disorganized, smallpox-infested, defeated lot that resembled a mob more than an organized military force. Looking back on recent events, Arnold wrote, "I am heartily chagrined to think we have lost in one month all the immortal Montgomery was a whole campaign in gaining."[101]

Wilkinson described how Arnold ordered the remaining troops at St. Johns to board boats and withdraw south across Lake Champlain to Fort Ticonderoga. However, the general ordered one boat to stay behind while he

98 Force, ed., *American Archives*, Fourth Series, VI: 1,105-1,106.

99 Wilkinson, *Memoirs of My Own Times*, I: 58. Wilkinson's *Memoirs* were published in 1816, but this story appears in earlier histories of the American Revolution. For example, David Ramsay's *The History of the American Revolution*, originally published in 1789, includes the story with some interesting additional details. Ramsay participated in the Revolutionary War, including serving in the Continental Congress, and his history of the conflict is based upon his personal experiences and interviews with its leaders: "A short time before the Americans evacuted [sic] the province of Canada, general Arnold convened the merchants of Montreal, and proposed to them to furnish a quantity of specified articles, for the use of the army in the service of Congress. While they were deliberating on the subject, he placed sentinels at their shop doors, and made such arrangements, that what was at first only a request, operated as a command. A great quantity of goods were taken on pretense that they were wanted for the use of the American army, but in their number were many articles only serviceable to women, and to persons in civil life. His nephew soon after opened a store in Albany, and publicly disposed of goods which had been procured at Montreal." David Ramsay, *The History of the American Revolution*, 2 vols. (Trenton: James J. Wilson, 1811), I: 351.

100 *Ibid.*

101 Isaac N. Arnold, *Life of Benedict Arnold* (Chicago: Jansen, McClurg & Company, 1880), 96.

and Wilkinson went to reconnoiter. They had ridden about two miles when they spotted a long column of British troops advancing toward them. They watched the enemy for a few minutes, then galloped back to St. Johns, where, according to Wilkinson, "we stripped our horses, Arnold shot his own, and ordered me to follow his example, which I did with reluctance." General Arnold ordered all hands on board and, "resisting my proffers of service, pushed off the boat with his own hands giving him the distinction of being last American soldier to leave Canada."[102]

Colonel Hazen's court martial convened at Fort Ticonderoga on July 19, 1776. Its purpose was to decide whether Hazen had deliberately failed to protect the valuable merchandise assigned to him. Gen. Horatio Gates was the senior officer at the fort. Arnold wanted generals to be the judges in the case, but Gates appointed majors and lieutenant colonels instead. The judges turned out to be sympathetic toward Hazen, and his court martial became a venue for accusations of wrongdoing against Arnold. After days of threats and hostile arguing, Gates dissolved the proceedings, explaining that he needed Arnold for more important assignments.

While the Northern Army was retreating back to Fort Ticonderoga, the Arnold Expedition prisoners of war continued to languish in Quebec. Governor Carleton finally showed some interest in paroling them in June 1776. He offered to send them all home on parole if they promised never to take up arms again against his majesty King George III. The prisoners refused to agree to such terms, so the dull routine of prison life continued. Then, in August 1776, with the war going well for the British, Governor Carleton, in a humanitarian mood, decided to allow the Arnold Expedition survivors to return to their homes on parole. The Americans gave their parole, promising not to fight until such time as they were exchanged. Rifleman Henry gave the text of the parole he signed:

> We whose names are hereunder written, do solemnly promise and engage, to his excellency general Carleton, not to say or do, anything against his majesty's person or government; and to repair whenever required so to do by his excellency, or any of his

102 Wilkinson, *Memoirs of My Own Times*, I: 54-55. Eager to criticize Arnold at every opportunity in his *Memoirs*, Wilkinson's exact words describing this incident are: "General Arnold then ordered all hands on board, and resisting my proffers of service, pushed off the boat with his own hands, and thus indulged the vanity of being the last man who embarked from the shores of the enemy."

majesty's commanders in chief in America, doth please us direct; in testimony of which, we have hereunto set our hands this day at Quebec. August 7, 1776.[103]

The paroled Americans were loaded into four transports convoyed by the frigate *Pearl* and sailed for home. The departing rebels were generously supplied with food and wine by Governor Carleton. According to historian John Codman, the Bishop of Quebec also contributed gifts for their voyage home, including several pounds of tea. The rebels respectfully declined the tea, and the bishop sent coffee instead.[104]

The little convoy sailed from Quebec on August 11 bound for New York City.[105] The city and its surroundings were in rebel hands, but there was a large British fleet in the harbor preparing to launch an attack aimed at capturing New York. On September 12, the British convoy carrying the survivors of the Arnold Expedition sailed into New York harbor. Their arrival was noted by Ambrose Serle, the civilian secretary to a British admiral: "Thursday, 12th, Septr. This afternoon [Royal Navy] Capt. Wilkinson in the Pearl, a fine Frigate of 32 Guns, arrived from Quebec. . . . Capt. Wilkinson convoyed several Transports with upwards of 500 Rebel Prisoners on board, with whom we know not what to do."[106]

The convoy arrived to learn that General Howe's imposing army had already captured Staten Island and eastern Long Island and was about to launch an attack to seize New York City, which then took up only the lower end of Manhattan Island. With the big assault about to start, the British kept the paroled Kennebec men aboard their transports safely anchored in the harbor. Howe's attack to capture New York City began on the morning of September 15 when Royal troops came ashore at Kips Bay on Manhattan Island. Following the rout of the rebel army there, the British took possession of the city.

Arnold's men were still aboard the transports on the night of September 19 when they looked across the harbor to see New York City burst into flames.

103 Henry, *An Accurate and Interesting Account . . . In the Campaign Against Quebec*, 224. Henry claimed that he was exchanged for a British soldier captured at St. Johns. Private Jeremiah Greenman's diary contains the same oath, which he says he signed on August 6. Bray and Bushnell, eds., *Military Journal of Jeremiah Greenman*, 30.

104 *Ibid.*, 308.

105 Stocking journal, in Roberts, ed., *March to Quebec*, 567.

106 Edward H. Tatum, Jr., ed., *The American Journal of Ambrose Serle,* (San Marino, California: The Huntington Library, 1940), 98.

Rifleman Henry remembered that he was below decks when he heard a sentry yell that the city was burning. Everyone ran on deck to watch the spectacle. Henry recalled that it was a windy night, which fanned the flames, making for "a most beautiful and luminous, but baleful sight."[107] From their vantage point in the harbor, Henry and his comrades observed the eerie spectacle. They saw boatloads of sailors rowing quickly toward the city from all the ships in the harbor to help fight the fire. At one point Henry saw the steeple of a large church in the city burst into flames. He was too far away to see any details, but a British officer stationed in the burning city identified the building as Trinity Church. The officer said that the church's spire was built of a wooden frame covered with shingles: "a lofty Pyramid of fire appeared, and as soon as the Shingles were burnt away the frame appeared with every separate piece of timber burning, until the principal timbers were burnt through, when the whole fell with a great noise."[108]

The fire, which destroyed about a quarter of the city, probably began accidentally, although the British believed that the rebels had started it. Henry said that when the sailors returned to his ship from fighting the fire, they said that they saw one American accused of having started the fire hanging by his heels, dead with a mortal bayonet wound through his chest.[109]

On September 24, Howe allowed the paroled Arnold Expedition men to go ashore at American-held Elizabethtown Point, New Jersey. Rifleman Henry recalled the event, and how all the returning men were filled with emotion. Henry said that Capt. Morgan leaped from the boat that was rowing him ashore, fell upon the ground with arms outspread, and cried, "Oh my country!"[110] About 350 of the original 1,150 members of the Arnold Expedition returned home in 1776. They left behind in Quebec some of their comrades, who had died in prison from their wounds, and their beloved General Montgomery, who lay in a shallow, unmarked grave inside the fortress city he had come to conquer.

In death, Gen. Richard Montgomery became a symbol of the revolutionaries' ideal of valor and self-sacrifice. Mercy Otis Warren, an

107 Henry, *An Accurate and Interesting Account . . . In the Campaign Against Quebec*, 184-185.

108 *Diary of Frederick Mackenzie*, I: 60-61.

109 Henry, *An Accurate and Interesting Account . . . In the Campaign Against Quebec*, 185.

110 *Ibid.*, 186.

eyewitness chronicler of the Revolution, described him as "an early martyr in the cause of freedom," and Thomas Paine wrote a story in 1776 in which Montgomery's ghost comes to Philadelphia to persuade Congress that the time had come to declare independence.[111]

Janet Montgomery, the general's wife, was at the forefront of the effort to get her husband's remains returned to America. The United States struck a deal with Britain in 1818 to exchange the body of Montgomery for that of a young British Army officer named John André, who was executed as a spy by the Americans during the war. (André was involved in Arnold's treason plot, and his story will be told in a subsequent chapter.)

To exhume Montgomery's remains for reburial in New York City, the U.S. government sent a blue-ribbon delegation to Quebec. His body was unearthed from its shallow grave and placed in an elaborate black coffin. The casket was transported to Albany, New York, where it was paraded through the streets with great ceremony to the steamboat *Richmond*, which had been chartered to convey the general's remains to New York City for reburial.[112] Following

111 Mercy Otis Warren, *History of the Rise, Progress and Termination of the American Revolution*, 3 vols. (Boston: Printed by Manning and Loring, for E. Larkin, 1805), I: 267.

112 On January 25, 1776, Congress resolved that a monument be procured from Paris or other part of France, with a suitable inscription, to honor "their late general" Richard Montgomery. Congress' resolution was finally carried into execution under the direction of Benjamin Franklin following his arrival in Paris in December 1776 as the American envoy to France. Montgomery's monument was created by Jean-Jacques Caffiéri, the sculptor to the King of France. It was completed a year later and shown at the Paris Salon of 1777. Originally intended for what became Independence Hall in Philadelphia, after the war it was installed in November 1787 on the porch of St. Paul's Chapel in New York City, where it stands today. Given its early commission, this ten-foot-high, non-figurative, marble wall memorial with carved symbols of war, death, liberty, and regeneration, is America's first monument. The inscription reads: "This monument is erected by order of Congress 25th. Jnary. 1776 to transmit to posterity a grateful remembrance of the patriotism conduct enterprize & perseverance of Major General Richard Montgomery who after a series of successes amidst the most discouraging difficulties fell in the attack on Quebec. 31st. Decbr. 1775. Aged 37 years." E-mail communication from Ms. Sara Webster, Professor of American Art, Lehman College, City University of New York. Montgomery's remains were reburied beneath this monument in 1818. Beneath the original inscription is a later tablet which reads: "[T]he State of New York caused the remains of Maj. Gen. Richard Montgomery to be conveyed from Quebec and deposited beneath this monument the 8th day of July 1818." There was also an inscription on Montgomery's coffin, which read: "The State of New York, in honor of Gen. Richard Montgomery, who fell gloriously fighting for the Independence and Liberty of the United States before the walls of Quebec, the 31st day of December, 1775, caused these remains of this distinguished hero to be conveyed from Quebec and deposited, on the 8th of July, in St. Paul's church, in the city of New York, near the monument erected to his memory by the United States." Allen, "Account

patriotic music and several speeches dockside in Albany, the crowds watched in silence as Montgomery's coffin was carried to the deck of the *Richmond*.

Then the steamboat got underway and began its voyage down the Hudson River, with Montgomery's coffin visible on its deck, draped in the 20-star flag of the young nation. Minute guns were fired along the route, and aged Revolutionary War veterans turned out in the little river towns to stand at attention as Montgomery's coffin passed by.[113]

Janet Montgomery was still alive in 1818, and her deceased husband was never far from her thoughts and actions. There had been other suitors following Richard's death—including Gen. Horatio Gates, who proposed marriage to Janet in 1784—but she declined them all, calling her martyred husband "the angel sent us for a moment."[114] Janet was an intelligent woman, and she made a fortune after the Revolution investing in real estate on Manhattan's Lower East Side. She used most of her money to build a mansion near Rhinebeck, New York, which she named Montgomery Place. Finished in 1803, when Janet was 60 years old, the house sat on 300 acres of prime land that commanded a magnificent view of the Hudson River and Catskill Mountains. It was the kind of estate she and Richard had dreamed of owning during the two years they were married.

DeWitt Clinton, the governor of New York, gave Janet the exact time that the *Richmond* would sail past her home. Many well-wishers came to share the poignant experience with her. At the appointed hour, the steamboat could be seen in the distance sailing south down the majestic Hudson with the black coffin on its deck. As the *Richmond* neared Montgomery Place, a military band standing on the deck behind the sarcophagus began playing a funeral march. The mansion had a long balcony facing the river, and Janet asked her friends to allow her to be alone to watch her husband pass by. She stood on her balcony, an old woman wearing a beautiful black dress that she had carefully chosen for

of Arnold's Expedition" in *Maine Historical Collections*, 529. Montgomery is the third-most-popular place name in the United States, and probably every city, town, and village named Montgomery (Montgomery, Alabama, for example) is named in honor of Gen. Richard Montgomery.

113 *Biographical Notes Concerning General Richard Montgomery* (privately published), 28. Newspaper stories about Montgomery's disinterment in Quebec and reinterment in New York City appeared in the Rutland, Vermont, *Herald* on July 7, 14, and 21, 1818.

114 Charles A. Royster, *A Revolutionary People at War: The Continental Army and American Character, 1775-1783* (Chapel Hill: The University of North Carolina Press, 1979), 123.

This monument to Gen. Richard Montgomery was authorized by the Continental Congress in January 1776. The monument rests in the east facade of St. Paul's Chapel in New York City's busy financial district. It was sculpted in France under the direction of Benjamin Franklin and finally installed in St. Paul's in 1787. Montgomery's body was brought from Quebec and interred below the monument on July 8, 1818, following an imposing funeral with full military honors and choral music. *Author's Collection*

the occasion. The *Richmond* slowed as it passed Montgomery Place, while the band played louder and a uniformed honor guard came to attention and fired a volley from the ship. Then the *Richmond's* shrill steam whistle sounded a salute that vibrated throughout the Hudson River Valley that Richard Montgomery had loved so deeply. A moment later, the little spectacle was over; the *Richmond* picked up steam and continued downriver. When the ship was out of sight, Janet's guests returned to the balcony—where they found the old woman fainted, lying unconscious on the floor.

At the time of Montgomery's death, he was a rising star among the American patriots; had he lived, he probably would have risen in rank and prestige—and taken his friend Benedict Arnold along with him as protégé. Instead Arnold was left without Montgomery's firm counsel and vulnerable to his own old enemies. Ethan Allen had been captured by the British and was languishing in a British prison, but John Brown and James Easton continued to attack Arnold—while his own unchecked, abusive conduct added new names to his growing list of enemies, such as Col. Moses Hazen. However, Brown, Easton, and Hazen were minor players in comparison to the enemies that Arnold would create later in the war among men of great power and influence.

Chapter Five

Arnold's Men Return to the War

"In respect to the Officers that were on the Canada expedition, their behavior & merit, and the severities they have experienced, entitle them to a particular notice in my opinion."

— *George Washington to Governor Nicholas Cooke of Rhode Island, in a letter dated October 12, 1776*

The survivors of the Arnold Expedition returned home after a one-year absence to find that many changes had taken place since their ascent into the Maine wilderness. Perhaps the most obvious was that the 13 colonies were no longer fighting for a redress of grievances, but for outright independence from Great Britain. Another change was that the seat of war had moved from Boston to New York City. With its excellent harbor and strategic location, New York was the best place in the colonies for the British to use as headquarters for their army. Their interest in occupying the city indicated their commitment to fight, rather than negotiate a quick and amicable end to the war.

Arnold's veterans also observed a more subtle and alarming change that had taken place during their long absence: the growing difficulty in finding men willing to serve in the Continental Army. Back in April 1775, thousands of patriotic Americans had flocked to Cambridge to join the rebel army forces. The men who went on the Arnold Expedition came from this legion of dedicated, public-spirited citizens who were willing to make personal sacrifices to defend their liberties, for themselves and their children. But a couple of bloody battles and the realization that the war was not going to end quickly had sobered the patriotic zeal of many Americans and quelled their resolution to fight. The terrible beating Washington's troops sustained in their unsuccessful bid to defend New York City factored into many Americans' trepidation about joining the cause. The British campaign to seize the city began in June 1776, when British warships and transports started arriving in New York harbor with troops and equipment from Britain and the Royal Navy base at Halifax, Nova Scotia. Washington's troops were intimidated as hundreds of enemy ships sailed into the harbor with their lethal contents. Gen. William Howe commanded the Royal forces converging on New York. He made his first in a series of well-calculated moves in July 1776 by occupying Staten Island. This gave the British a secure base of operations from which to launch their attacks on rebel defensive positions located in what are today Brooklyn and Manhattan.

After patiently gathering a force of 34,000, Howe unleashed his offensive by landing troops on western Long Island. His splendid army fought the largely untested Continental Army at the Battle of Long Island on August 27, 1776. The engagement constituted a British victory, although Washington managed to avoid a complete disaster by evacuating his troops two days later across the East River, from today's Brooklyn to Manhattan. Howe followed his victory on Long Island with a textbook-perfect amphibious landing on September 15 at Kips Bay, an inlet facing the East River, in the weakly defended midsection of rebel-held Manhattan. The ensuing Battle of Kips Bay was another triumph for the British, ending in their occupation of New York City. This time Washington escaped with his remaining forces to the hilly northern end of Manhattan, where they positioned themselves in some strong defenses prepared during the summer.

The news Americans received from Canada was as dispiriting as the multiple defeats suffered around New York City. Reports came in that Gen. Schuyler's Northern Army had retreated south as far as Fort Ticonderoga. The path of the American exodus from Canada was littered with abandoned equipment and hundreds of sick soldiers who had to be left behind to the mercy of the advancing enemy. Fort Ticonderoga was the enemy's immediate objective; Carleton was massing troops and boats at St. Johns for an attack on the rebel-held fort.

General Horatio Gates, the commandant of Fort Ticonderoga, countered by building a fleet of warships to defend Lake Champlain and Fort Ticonderoga, eventually giving the difficult assignment to Arnold, his zealous subordinate and experienced sailor. Arnold applied his usual energy to the project, quickly building a fleet of gondolas (gunboats that carried both sails and oars) by utilizing the same simple design used a year earlier to build the bateaux for the Arnold Expedition: sharp bow and stern, flat bottom, and clinker-sided hull (constructed of overlapping lengths of wood). News of the construction of Arnold's warships, outfitted with cannon captured at Crown Point and Fort Ticonderoga, forced the cautious Carleton to halt his advance and enlarge his own fleet.

Although incomplete and manned by inexperienced crews, the vessels of Arnold's flotilla sailed north across Lake Champlain in late August 1776 to challenge Carleton's superior flotilla. Arnold ultimately placed his ships in an advantageous position and engaged the enemy fleet on October 11, 1776, in a fierce gun duel near Valcour Island. In this famous engagement, known as the Battle of Valcour Bay, the Americans put up a tremendous fight. Arnold was in the thick of the melee as usual, exposing himself to enemy gunfire in an effort to aim his gunboat's cannon.

Arnold conducted an almost suicidal defense, and American losses were high. Such combativeness was typical of Arnold, who seemed to be ready to accept any level of carnage and suffering among his own troops to win a victory. Although the Battle of Valcour Bay was considered a tactical British victory, the clash strategically benefited the Americans. By building an American navy on Lake Champlain as winter approached, Arnold and his men delayed Carleton long enough to discourage him from continuing south to attack Fort Ticonderoga, despite his commanding army.

Routed and disheartened on every battle front, many American soldiers talked of serving out their one-year enlistments and returning home. If any rebel soldiers had earned the right to sit out the rest of the war, it was the survivors of the Arnold Expedition. But many of Arnold's veterans wanted to get back into the fight. Their eagerness is understandable when one remembers that they were all volunteers who had been selected to go on the Quebec expedition from a host of eligible applicants. Even after the march to Quebec got underway, the fainthearted and sickly among them returned to Cambridge with Lt. Col. Enos. The men who completed the trek to Quebec—and managed to make it back alive—were relics of the American martial spirit and patriot virtue of self-sacrifice that had reigned during the opening months of the war. Gen. Washington desperately needed such men, those who were not only devoted patriots but alsoexperienced, disciplined soldiers possessing great fortitude and courage. Understanding the value of Arnold's men to the patriot cause,

Washington even reserved positions in the army for them.[1] Problematically, the Kennebec veterans returned to America on parole, and thus were under oath to abstain from fighting until they had been exchanged.

Soon after arriving in New Jersey on parole, the Arnold Expedition survivors learned that one of their comrades, feisty Aaron Burr, had distinguished himself during the Battle of Kips Bay. The story of Burr's Manhattan exploit started with his arrival outside Quebec as a gentleman volunteer on the Arnold Expedition. Following Montgomery's failed attack on Quebec, Burr served as Gen. Arnold's aide before being sent to Philadelphia by Arnold with dispatches for the Continental Congress. Burr remained in Philadelphia, where Arnold recommended him as a courageous young officer worthy of special distinction. This recommendation gained Burr a temporary position as an aide to General Washington. With his distinguished family background, college education, legal training, participation in the already-legendary Arnold Expedition, combat experience in Canada, and service as an aide-de-camp to the eulogized General Montgomery, Burr seemed like a logical recipient of a coveted, permanent appointment in Washington's military family. However, he was too untamed for the workaholic commander-in-chief, and he left headquarters by mutual consent after a few weeks for a more amicable post as an aide to the rustic Gen. Israel Putnam, who commanded the American troops occupying New York City.[2]

The colonial city of New York was located on Manhattan's southern tip; the rest of the island was blanketed with farmland and forests. While serving as Putnam's aide, Burr became familiar with the island's geography, including its rambling farm roads and country lanes. During the Battle of Kips Bay, several hundred American troops, including a detachment of Colonel Knox's artillery

1 Writing to Arnold on December 5, 1775, Washington assured Arnold that his officers and he would not be forgotten in the planned reorganization of the Continental Army: "I was not unmindful of you or them [Arnold's officers] in the Establishment of a new army—One out of 26 Regiments (likely Genl. Putnams) you are appointed to the Command of, and I have Ordered all the Officers with you, to the one or the other of these Regiments, in the Rank they now bear. . . ." W.W. Abbot, et al., eds., *The Papers of George Washington*, Revolutionary War Series, II: 494.

2 Burr's friendly biographers often twisted this story to read that he joined Washington's military family until a more suitable appointment could be procured for him. See, for example, Samuel L. Knapp, *Life of Aaron Burr* (New York: Wiley & Long, 1835), 81. The idea of Burr marking time at headquarters is silly because the most desirable and prestigious post for an aide-de-camp was on Washington's personal staff.

company, remained steadfast in an earthen fort on Bayard's Hill (located on modern Grand Street in lower Manhattan), believing they were trapped. From their position, the rebels could see the British enveloping the island north of their position. At that moment, Captain Burr arrived at the fort at a full gallop and told its desperate garrison that he knew the terrain and there was still time for them to escape to the northern end of the island. General Putnam, the senior officer present, quickly gathered all the other units stranded in the city, and the whole column moved up the island under Burr's direction to Monument Lane (today's Greenwich Avenue in Greenwich Village), then onto a country byway that skirted the west side of the island. The American column followed this circuitous route to a road (later called Abington Road, paralleling modern Eighth Avenue) that ran north to Harlem Heights. American officers on horseback reconnoitering the retreating column's right flank reported that enemy troops were approaching. To keep from being seen, Burr told the column to leave the road and follow him through the woods. They had been given up for lost when, at dusk, Burr led them into Washington's camp on Harlem Heights, to the cheers of the army.[3]

Burr continued to serve Putnam, whose troops were ordered to defend Westchester County, New York, against a possible British attack. Burr remained in the region during the critical days of November – December 1776, which saw Howe's forces turn south and overrun Fort Washington, a big American fortress located on upper Manhattan near Harlem Heights. The surrender of Fort Washington was another rebel disaster; 2,700 American soldiers were killed, wounded or captured in what they had believed to be their impregnable hilltop redoubt.

At least one veteran from the Arnold Expedition was among Fort Washington's defenders. He was Matthew Duncan, a gentleman volunteer on the march to Quebec. Young Duncan was captured with the others, then emerged nine months later as a captain in the 5th Pennsylvania Regiment at

3 For an account of the American retreat from New York City, see Henry P. Johnston, *The Campaign of 1776 Around New York and Brooklyn* (Brooklyn, New York: The Long Island Historical Society, 1878), 237-239. There is an excellent folded map of colonial Manhattan Island, including the American and British troop positions during the Battle of Kips Bay, in the back of this book. The story of Burr's guiding the troops out of New York also appears in Christopher Ward, *The War of the Revolution*, 2 vols. (New York: The Macmillan Company, 1952), I: 243. Ward says that General Putnam "would have found himself hopelessly entrapped, had not young Aaron Burr, his aide-de-camp, guided him to an unfrequented road along the west side, close to the Hudson."

Fort Washington. Captain Duncan was taken captive when the fort surrendered on November 16, 1776.[4] Nothing further is known about him, and he may have died in British captivity.

After surrendering Fort Washington and abandoning Fort Lee (a New Jersey fortress across the Hudson River from Fort Washington which was overrun by the British on November 20), Washington's beleaguered main army retreated to the Delaware River town of Trenton, New Jersey. With few other options, it crossed the Delaware into Pennsylvania on the night of December 7-8, 1776. The British pursued Washington to Trenton but failed to follow his little army into Pennsylvania. The decision to end the chase of Washington's forces was made by General Howe, who felt that he had accomplished enough for 1776 and could finish off the amateur rebel army the following spring. After leaving troops at various towns in New Jersey, including a large garrison at Trenton, Howe returned to New York City to spend the winter.

The Arnold Expedition's officers and enlisted men could only observe the demoralizing string of American defeats in New York and New Jersey in late 1776 from the sidelines, still on parole. But their spirits soared along with other American patriots when they heard that General Washington had re-crossed the Delaware River and staged a spectacular surprise attack against the Royal troops defending Trenton. Attacking at dawn on December 26, 1776, the Americans scored a stunning victory at Trenton, which was soon followed by another triumph at Princeton on January 3, 1777. Then, in a well-planned maneuver, Washington rapidly marched his army, booty, and prisoners north from Princeton to the safety of the mountainous region around Morristown, New Jersey, where they camped for the remainder of the winter.

The Arnold Expedition men remained on parole during this dramatic period while efforts were underway to secure their exchange. Many of them waited at their homes for word that they had been exchanged while General Washington, from his winter headquarters at Morristown, was offering bounties to any man willing to join the Continental Army for a term of service

4 Supporting the story about Duncan being at Fort Washington is W. W. Abott, et al., eds., *The Papers of George Washington*, Revolutionary War Series, VI: 485, and Heitman, *Historical Register of Officers of the Continental Army*, 206. Although it is known that Duncan was taken prisoner by the British, his name does not appear on a list of American officers and volunteers who were British prisoners from the Arnold Expedition on May 18, 1776. Force, ed., *American Archives*, Fourth Series, IV: 708-709. Duncan was from Pennsylvania, and troops from that colony made up the bulk of the Fort Washington garrison.

stated as three years or the duration of the war. The commander-in- chief had also received approval from Congress to expand the number of regiments in the army, and he wanted to offer positions in some of the new regiments to Arnold's veteran officers.

Washington acknowledged his interest in having the Kennebec Corps veterans in his army in a letter to Governor Nicholas Cooke of Rhode Island. First Washington described the qualities he wanted in his officers: he desired men who had served with "reputation and bravery" and possessed "a warm attachment to their country. Such men," said Washington, "are fit for Office, and will use their best endeavours [sic] to introduce that discipline & subordination which are essential to good order, & inspire that confidence in the Men, which alone can give success. . . ." After explaining his standards, the General turned to the veteran officers from the Arnold Expedition, saying, "their behavior & merit, and the severities they have experienced, entitles them to a particular notice in my opinion."[5]

Captain Daniel Morgan was among the first of Arnold's officers to be exchanged. When he was first released on parole in New Jersey, Morgan went to his home in Frederick County, Virginia, where he was reunited with his wife and daughters. There he waited impatiently for news of his exchange. Washington, despite some discipline problems with the independent-minded Morgan at Cambridge at the start of the war, was impressed with favorable reports of the Virginian's participation in the Canadian campaign. The commander-in-chief recommended him for high command in a letter to John Hancock dated September 28, 1776, soon after Morgan returned to the colonies on parole. Washington's comments to Hancock are presented below in their entirety because they substantiate Morgan's reputation as a fighting officer and give valuable insights into the complicated process of prisoner exchanges. Note also how carefully Washington tread issues of seniority of rank among his officers. For example, although several men might hold the rank of captain, the first of them to be appointed was considered the senior officer, and he expected to be promoted before any other captain:

5 George Washington to Nicholas Cooke, letter dated "Head Qrs Harlem Heights [northern Manhattan Island] Octr 12, 1776" in W.W. Abbot, et al., eds., *The Papers of George Washington*, Revolutionary War Series, VI: 544-545.

As Col. Hugh Stephenson of the Rifle Regiment ordered lately to be raised, is dead, according to the information I have received, I would beg leave to recommend to the particular notice of Congress, Captn Daniel Morgan just returned among the prisoners from Canada as a fit and proper person to succeed to the vacancy occasioned by his death [Washington was recommending that Morgan be promoted from captain to colonel]. The present field Officers of the Regiment [a reference to other officers in Stephenson's new regiment, authorized on September 16, 1776, and designated the 11th Virginia Regiment] cannot claim any right in preference to him, because he [Morgan] ranked above them and as a Captain when he first entered the service. His conduct as an Officer on the expedition with Genl Arnold last fall; his intrepid behavior in the Assault upon Quebec when the brave Montgomery fell—the inflexible attachment he professed to our cause during his imprisonment and which he perseveres in; added to these his residence in the place Col. Stevenson came from & his interest and influence in the same circle and with such Men as are to compose such a Regiment, all in my opinion, entitle him to the favor of Congress and lead me to believe that in his promotion, the States will gain a good and valuable officer for the sort of Troops he is particularly recommended to command. . . . Should Congress be pleased to appoint Captn Morgan in the instance I have mentioned, I would still beg to suggest the propriety and necessity of keeping the matter close and not suffering It to transpire until he is exonerated from the parole he is under. His acceptance of a Commission under his present circumstances might be construed a violation of his Engagement, and if not, the difficulty attending his exchange might be encreased [sic]; the Enemy perhaps would consider him as a Field Officer [any rank above captain and beneath general], of which we have but very few in our hands and none that I recollect of that rank.[6]

General Arnold also expressed his high regard for Morgan in a letter to Washington written from Fort Ticonderoga on November 6, 1776. In his missive Arnold recommended that four of his officers should be among the first to be exchanged: Lamb, Lockwood, Oswald, and Morgan. "The two last,"

6 George Washington to John Hancock, dated "Head Quarters, Heights of Harlem [upper Manhattan Island] Septr 28 1776," in *Ibid.*, VI:421. Col. Hugh Stephenson was in Virginia at the time of his death recruiting a new rifle regiment for the Continental Army. He was reported to have died from "a return of camp fever." For additional information about Stephenson, see Danske Dandridge, *Historic Shepherdstown* (Charlottesville, Virginia: The Michie Company, 1910), 349.

Arnold said, "went with me from Cambridge; they have all distinguished themselves for their Bravery and Attachment to the Public Cause."[7]

Morgan was appointed the colonel of the new 11th Virginia rifle regiment by the Virginia General Assembly on November 12, 1776, while still on parole. He was finally exchanged on January 14, 1777, and immediately left home to join Washington's army wintering in Morristown.[8]

Colonel Morgan invited several of his fellow Arnold Expedition veterans to join his new regiment. Two of them, William Heth and Peter Bryan Bruin, had been lieutenants in his Virginia rifle company during the Canadian campaign. Both men joined Morgan's new regiment at a higher rank: Heth was promoted to major, and Bruin, who was 23 at the time, was appointed captain. Bruin had been a merchant in the Virginia backcountry prior to the war. Since most commodity transactions in the region were done by barter, Bruin must have had a quick mind to engage in this complicated business. Colonel Morgan also wanted Christian Febiger, his urbane Danish friend from the Arnold Expedition, to join his new 11th Virginia Regiment. Febiger had proved to be a courageous soldier during the Canadian campaign. One account of the Quebec attack cited Febiger's valor: "A Danish gentlemen, who holds a lieutenancy in the King of Denmark's service, behaved with all the resolution, calmness, and intrepidity, peculiar to an old veteran and an experienced officer."[9] Morgan and Febiger were an interesting pair; Febiger was educated and worldly while Morgan was a rough, unschooled, frontier brawler who read with difficulty, wrote almost illegibly, and was confused by the simplest arithmetic problem. But both men were dedicated American patriots and natural leaders, and they made a prodigious pair. Morgan arranged for Febiger to be appointed as a lieutenant colonel and second-in-command of his new regiment.

Morgan recruited men for his new regiment from the frontier settlements. Some enlisted men from his original rifle company joined his outfit, and he was proud to have them. Lieutenant Colonel Febiger arrived in Philadelphia on March 6, 1777, with the first company of Morgan's 11th Virginia Regiment. Interestingly, Febiger said that they were in Philadelphia to be inoculated against smallpox before reporting for active duty. Additional companies were

7 *Ibid.*, VII: 93.

8 *Ibid.*, VII: 245.

9 "Account of the Attempt on Quebeck", which appeared in the *New York Gazette* (no date given). Author is given as "A Soldier" in Force, ed., *American Archives*, Fourth Series, IV: 708.

en route to the city, including one detachment under Colonel Morgan's personal command.[10]

Washington had big ideas for using Morgan's abilities. Soon after arriving in Morristown, the commander-in-chief gave him command of an independent rifle corps composed of 500 men from the Pennsylvania, Maryland, and Virginia frontier, while Lieutenant Colonel Febiger took over command of the 11th Virginia Regiment. Washington called Morgan's new unit The Corps of Rangers (also called Morgan's Corps of Rifle Men), and he began to use them effectively in New Jersey for scouting and harassing the enemy. This work was dangerous; known then as *petite guerre* and today as guerilla warfare, it covered everything that took place in the area of ground separating the opposing military camps. Washington told his intrepid subordinate: "In case of any movement of the Enemy you are instantly to fall upon their flanks and gall them as much as possible, taking especial Care not to be surrounded, or have your Retreat to the Army cut off."[11]

Obtaining Morgan's exchange had been given high priority, and similar strong efforts were conducted to free many of the other Arnold Expedition men who remained on parole. For example, in a letter dated January 23, 1777, Connecticut's Governor Jonathan Trumbull wrote to Washington with a list of Connecticut officers on parole and specifically requested that Maj. Meigs and Captain Hanchett be exchanged as soon as possible.[12] In another example, General Washington wrote to Joshua Loring, the British commissioner of prisoners, on February 1, 1777, proposing to swap Captain Dearborn for a captive British officer. In the same letter Washington said that there were eight other Arnold Expedition officers (unnamed) that he wanted to be among the first to be exchanged for British officers being held by the Americans.[13]

10 Lieutenant Colonel Christian Febiger to Gen. George Washington, dated "Philadelphia, 6th of March 1777," in W.W. Abbot, et al., eds., *The Papers of George Washington*, Revolutionary War Series, VIII: 520-521.

11 George Washington to Colonel Daniel Morgan, dated "Middlebrook, N.J., 13 June 1777" in *Ibid.*, X: 31.

12 Jonathan Trumbull, Sr., to George Washington, dated "Lebanon [Connecticut], January 23rd, 1777" in *Ibid.*, VIII: 141.

13 George Washington to Joshua Loring, dated "Head Quarters Morris town 1st Feby 1777" in *Ibid.*, VIII: 217. Loring (1744-1789) was one of the most fascinating characters from the American Revolution. He was a Loyalist from Dorchester, Massachusetts, who fled Boston with the British army in 1776. Thomas Jones alleges in his *History of New York During the*

However, the British had the upper hand in these negotiations, since they were holding many rebel prisoners from the recent fighting around New York City. The Americans were mostly trading British officers and enlisted men who had surrendered to Montgomery the previous year at St. Johns and Sorel. Captain Dearborn was finally exchanged on March 24, 1777, and rejoined the Continental Army as a major in the 3rd New Hampshire Regiment.

Another Kennebec veteran who rejoined the army at Morristown was Pvt. Jeremiah Greenman. He was 17 years old when he volunteered for the Arnold Expedition as a common soldier in Ward's Rhode Island company, and was captured with the others during Montgomery's failed attack. Although their enlistments expired on January 1, 1777, Greenman and his comrades were held as prisoners of war in Quebec until they were paroled and returned to America. After being exchanged, Greenman re-enlisted in the army on February 23, 1777, as a sergeant in Col. Israel Angell's 2nd Rhode Island Regiment. Greenman began a diary during the Arnold Expedition which he kept up during his long military career. He participated in several major campaigns following his return to the army in 1777, and his diary will provide valuable information as the story of the war unfolds.

Lieutenant Colonel Christopher Greene was also exchanged in 1777. He was the subject of a February 9, 1777, letter from Gov. Nicholas Cooke of Rhode Island to General Washington. The governor wanted to know whether Greene was going to be exchanged soon, as the Rhode Island Assembly had nominated him to command the newly reorganized 1st Rhode Island Regiment.[14] Greene was exchanged in March 1777, received his promotion to the rank of colonel, and took command of his new regiment.

Thus, one by one the Arnold Expedition officers and enlisted men were traded during 1777. Capt. Simeon Thayer, for example, was not exchanged until July 1777, although he had been promoted to major and appointed to the 2nd Rhode Island Regiment almost five months earlier.[15]

Revolutionary War that Gen. William Howe gave Loring the lucrative post of commissary of prisoners because the general wanted Loring's beautiful wife, Elizabeth Lloyd Loring, as his mistress. In volume one, page 351of his book, Jones claimed that Joshua made no objections. "He fingered the cash, the General enjoyed madam."

14 *Ibid.*, VIII: 285; Wright, *The Continental Army*, 227.

15 Showman, et al., eds., *The Papers of General Nathanael Greene*, II: 15, footnote 3.

Major Return Jonathan Meigs was also freed of his parole in 1777. Following his exchange, Meigs was promoted to the rank of lieutenant colonel. He was among the first Arnold Expedition officers to go back into action when he led a raid on Sag Harbor, New York, on May 23, 1777. Meigs launched his daring raid from Connecticut with 170 troops in thirteen whaleboats escorted by two armed sloops. An unarmed sloop was brought along to carry away prisoners and valuables. The American flotilla crossed Long Island Sound undetected and landed on the north shore of Long Island near Sag Harbor, where the British had established a supply depot. Meigs waited for dark and then attacked with his raiding party. His troops believed they had secured the place when an armed Royal Navy schooner appeared offshore. According to a report of the raid made by Meigs' commander, Gen. Samuel Holden Parsons, the British schooner carried twelve guns and "began a fire upon our Troops which Continued without Cessation for About three Quarters of an Hour with Grape & round shott; but the Troop's with the Greatest Intrepidity returned the fire." While under fire from the enemy schooner, Meigs and his men rounded up 90 enemy soldiers and sailors, set fire to all the vessels in the harbor, burned 120 tons of valuable animal forage, and destroyed ten hogsheads of rum and "a large Quantity of Other Merchandize." Having completed his mission, Meigs eluded the schooner and managed to return to Connecticut, in Parsons' words, "having in 25 Hours; by land & Water transported his Men full Ninety Miles & Succeeded in his Attempt beyond my most Sanguine Expectations; without losing a Single Man either killed or Wounded."[16]

During that same spring of 1777, Washington marched his Main Army south from Morristown to a strong defensive position in the Watchung Mountains of central New Jersey. Opposing the entrenched rebels was the main British army commanded by Gen. Sir William Howe. His objective was Philadelphia, the largest city in America and the seat of the Continental Congress. The shortest route to Philadelphia from Howe's base at New Brunswick, New Jersey, was across the state to the Delaware River. But Howe would have to first defeat Washington's army or face the same debilitating *petite guerre* (ambushes and skirmishing on his flanks and supply lines) that his troops had endured during the previous winter.

16 Brigadier General Samuel Holden Parsons to George Washington, dated "N. Haven 25th, May. 1777" in W.W. Abbot, et al., eds., *The Papers of George Washington*, Revolutionary War Series, IX: 527-529.

Desiring a decisive battle with Washington but unable to bring about a general engagement, Howe withdrew his army to nearby Staten Island, New York, where a fleet of warships and transports were waiting. Howe and his army began boarding their ships on July 8 but delayed sailing until July 20. The fleet consisted of 260 vessels carrying an army of 18,000 enlisted men plus an additional 5,000 officers, servants, wives, and children.[17]

Their destination was unknown to the rebels. Howe could be sailing south to attack Philadelphia via the Delaware River, or even as far south as Charleston; or he could be going north up the deep-water Hudson River to support Gen. John Burgoyne, who was then marching south with 8,000 men and a large train of artillery from Montreal toward Albany. Burgoyne had been ordered by Germain to renew Carleton's offensive of the preceding year. A link-up between Burgoyne and Howe at Albany would be devastating to the rebel cause. It would give the British control of the Hudson River and isolate New England from the other rebelling states. With Howe's plans unknown and Burgoyne menacing New England, the rebels faced a crisis. The immediate threat was Burgoyne, so Washington ordered Arnold and several of his Kennebec Corps veterans into the fight to stop him. The ensuing campaign resulted in new and dangerous enemies for Arnold and marked the beginning of what Eleazer Oswald later called his friend's "vile prostitution of principle (treason)."[18]

Starting from Montreal in June 1777, Burgoyne's army followed the traditional inland water route south onto Lake Champlain. His army of 8,000 professionals and large train of artillery were opposed by General Philip Schuyler, who commanded the undermanned and poorly equipped Northern Army. Arnold's naval flotilla of the preceding year had not been rebuilt, so Burgoyne's progress down the lake went unimpeded. Schuyler committed his best troops and artillery to defending Fort Ticonderoga, where he planned to turn back Burgoyne's offensive.

Burgoyne anticipated a siege as his army approached Fort Ticonderoga in early July. But upon arriving on the scene, his artillery officers managed to drag cannon to the summit of Mount Defiance, which overlooked the American

17 Thomas J. McGuire, *The Philadelphia Campaign, Volume One: Brandywine and the Fall of Philadelphia* (Mechanicsburg, Pennsylvania: Stackpole Books, 2006), 71.

18 Eleazer Oswald to Col. John Lamb, dated "Philadelphia, 11th December, 1780" in Leake, *Memoir of the Life and Times of General John Lamb*, 266.

fortifications. This impressive feat by Burgoyne's army forced the Americans to abandon the place on the night of July 5-6 without a fight. The Royals chased some of the retreating Americans to Skenesboro, where Burgoyne decided to continue his advance to Albany by marching his army 23 miles overland to Fort Edward on the east side of the Hudson River. Once they crossed the Hudson, it was possible to reach Albany in just three days of hard marching.[19]

Arnold arrived at Fort Edward on July 22 to find Schuyler's troops working feverishly, destroying bridges and felling trees to slow Burgoyne's advance.[20] Despite Schuyler's efforts, the enemy broke through to Fort Edward on the east side of the Hudson on July 30 while the demoralized Northern Army retreated to a position perilously close to Albany.

Burgoyne's advance had been so rapid that he outran his long and tenuous supply line from Canada. With his army in high spirits, he halted at Fort Edward while he accumulated 30 days worth of provisions, the textbook minimum at the time for operating in the field, before resuming his army's seemingly unstoppable march to Albany.

Burgoyne suffered two serious setbacks while he waited for supplies. One was the defeat of a column of mostly German troops sent from Fort Edward to seize horses and provisions at Bennington, Vermont (known as the Battle of Bennington, on August 16, 1777). The second reversal was the retreat of a combined British and Indian force commanded by Col. Barry St. Leger that had swept east through New York's Mohawk Valley in support of Burgoyne's main thrust. St. Leger's corps laid siege to Fort Stanwix (on the site of modern Rome, New York), which blocked their route to Albany. Schuyler sent Arnold with about 900 troops to help the beleaguered American outpost. Arnold tricked St. Leger's capricious Indians into believing that a huge American relief column was approaching them. The Indians abandoned St. Leger, which left him with little choice other than to retreat while Arnold marched his detachment into Fort Stanwix.

19 Albany is about forty-five miles south of Fort Edward.

20 Washington explained his reasons for wanting to send Arnold north to support Schuyler in a letter to John Hancock dated "Morris Town, July 10th 1777." Washington wrote: "If General Arnold has settled his Affairs & can be spared from Philadelphia, I would recommend him for this business [rallying the local militia] & that he should immediately set out for the Northern department. He is active—judicious & brave, and an Officer in whom the Militia will repose great confidence." W.W. Abbot, et. al., eds., *The Papers of George Washington*, Revolutionary War Series, X: 240.

Burgoyne's delay at Fort Edward resulted in other dire consequences for his offensive. Mostly, it gave the rebels time to rush reinforcements to Schuyler from Washington's army, as well as for the state and county governments to order out militia drafts.

Schuyler's scorched-earth tactics and the buildup of his army were positive steps, but they came too late to offset the debacle of the loss of Fort Ticonderoga. The egalitarian Massachusetts delegates to Congress in particular disliked Schuyler for his aristocratic manners, and they wanted to replace him with Horatio Gates, a genial man who was a favorite among the New England militiamen. Schuyler's undoing was also due to his involvement in the bitter pre-war disputes between New England and New York over Vermont land claims. The maneuverings in Congress to remove him rivaled today's ruthless politics. Even more dramatically, the Revolutionary War bureaucrats could challenge their political opponents to a life-threatening duel. The case against Schuyler included wild accusations that he was bribed by Burgoyne into abandoning Fort Ticonderoga without a fight by the latter's firing silver cannon balls into the fortress which Schuyler's greedy subordinates picked up and shared with him. The anti-Schuyler faction in Congress persevered, and on August 4 the delegates voted to give Gates command of the Northern Army and reassign Schuyler to logistical support efforts from Albany.

Arnold returned from his foray to Fort Stanwix on August 30 to find Gates on the scene and in command of the Northern Army. Arnold got along with the aristocratic and self-assured Schuyler, but he had also campaigned with Gates the previous year and considered his new commander to be a friend.

Gates was a textbook officer who wanted to defeat Burgoyne with the least risk and fewest casualties to his army. His solution was to position his army behind strong fortifications rather than seek a pitched battle with the enemy. Gates implemented his strategy by sending his talented engineer Tadeusz Kosciuszko to find the best place to locate his defenses. Kosciuszko selected a range of hills called Bemis Heights that was 100-300 feet above the Hudson River. It was an excellent defensive position which dominated the surrounding countryside, including the key road that ran parallel to the Hudson River. Gates arrived at Bemis Heights on September 12, and immediately had his army assume positions along the ridge, and waited for Burgoyne's army to attack.

On the following day, September 13, Burgoyne's battalions began crossing the Hudson below Fort Edward on a pontoon bridge constructed under the supervision of Lt. John Schanks of the Royal Navy. They were now on the west side of the river and only 12 miles away from the heights where Gates' army awaited them. The nearby village of Saratoga (renamed Schuylerville in 1831), New York, inspired the name of the following weeks' maneuvering and fighting—the Battle of Saratoga.

Gates gave Arnold command of a large and important section of the American fortifications on the western side of Bemis Heights. Arnold's command consisted of two Continental brigades totaling 3,359 men and a 694-man elite corps, created by Gates, composed of light infantry and riflemen organized under a cohesive command. Henry Dearborn commanded the light infantrymen in Gates' special detachment. His journal entry for September 11, 1777, gives us some basic information about the new outfit: "I am appointed to the Command of 300 Light Infantry who are Draughted [drafted] from the Several Regements [sic] in the Northern army & to act in Conjunction with Colonel Morgan's Corps of Riflemen."[21] The story of this distinctive corps, which was organized for the Saratoga Campaign, is worth telling, especially since both Morgan and Dearborn were Arnold Expedition veterans who were campaigning at Saratoga alongside their old commander.

In his journal entry Dearborn described the troops he was appointed to command as light infantry. The term denotes infantrymen who were specially chosen, equipped, and trained for dangerous assignments. They were called light infantry because they generally carried less equipment and lighter-weight muskets than regular (line) troops. Light infantry detachments were expected to be capable of moving swiftly and operating independently of the main army. Their assignments included long-distance reconnaissance and raids against enemy positions. In a battle they could also be deployed as skirmishers, operating in loose formations in advance and to the flanks of an army, as well as using the terrain to their best advantage.

At the start of the American Revolution, British light infantry units were organized as one company in each regiment. But during campaign or battle situations, the British would brigade all of their regimental light infantry companies into a single battalion, or multiple battalions if it was a large army. Service in the light infantry was generally reserved for combat veterans of proven courage who could function independently under enemy fire. It is difficult to make generalizations about their appearance, but the ideal look included distinctive, cut-down uniforms (caps instead of hats, for example) and short muskets.

21 Brown and Peckham, eds., *Revolutionary War Journals of Henry Dearborn*, 104.

The command of light infantry troops was a great honor reserved for outstanding officers. Dearborn was selected for the coveted command of the American light infantry at Saratoga because of his heroic and extensive combat experience, which included Bunker Hill and the Arnold Expedition. He was also an ardent patriot whose inspired leadership was intended to help foster esprit-de-corps among the members of his elite corps, comprising 379 officers and men. James Wilkinson, Arnold's former aide-de-camp and now adjutant general to the Northern Department, said of Dearborn "that a more vigilant or determined soldier never wore a sword."[22]

Dearborn's light infantry unit was a temporary one, which would be disbanded at the end of the Saratoga campaign. It was made up of troops from the Continental Regiments attached to the Northern Army. The idea was not unique to the Battle of Saratoga, and the term "picked men" was generally used by the Americans to identify a makeshift corps of light infantry.[23] Because of its provisional nature, it is probable that detachments known as picked men or light infantry, including Dearborn's unit, had no distinctive uniforms or equipment. The emphasis was on using "the most able, active, spirited men" for the unit.[24]

The second component of Gates' elite unit was Morgan's Rifle Corps. At the start of the American Revolution, the colonists believed that their frontier riflemen were the equivalent of British light infantry. For example, in describing

22 Wilkinson, *Memoirs of My Own Times*, I: 230.

23 For example, in a September 20, 1775, letter to General Washington, Philip Schuyler described an attack on a British outpost as follows: "The sloop & Schooner and ten Batteaus [bateaux] with picked Men lay to in the River ready to attack the Enemy's Schooner. . . ." The *Papers of George Washington*, Revolutionary War Series, II: 20.

24 General Orders, 24 August, 1777, from the orderly book of John Patterson's brigade. A copy of the orderly book can be found in the collection of Saratoga National Historical Park, Historian's files. The original orderly book is in the collection of the New York Historical Society. The orderly book begins on August 21, 1777. The complete order reads as follows: "The Commanding Officers of Regiments are desir'd to recommend to the General one Officer, one Serjeant, one Corporal & fifteen Privates, each, of the most able, active, spirited Men in their respective Regiments. This Body is to be joined to, & do Duty with the Rifle Reg' commanded by Colonel Morgan. A Roll of the Rank, Names, Companies & Regiments of the Officers & men selected for this Service to be deliver'd to the Adjutant General [Lt. Col. James Wilkinson], tomorrow at Sun sett." Twenty-one Continental regiments took part in the Saratoga Campaign, and each regiment contributed men to Dearborn's Light Infantry. Seventeen officers and enlisted men per regiment plus Henry Dearborn equals 379 men in the Northern Army's Light Infantry Corps. No drummers, fifers, or staff to assist Dearborn were assigned.

the organization of the 1775 Arnold Expedition, Henry Dearborn's first entry in his journal included, "Said detachment [The Arnold Expedition] consisted of Eleven hundred Men, Two Battalians [battalions] of Musket-men, and three Companies of Rifle-men as Light-Infantry."[25] The Revolution's civilian leadership was particularly enthusiastic in their praise of American riflemen at the start of the war. Congressional delegate John Adams wrote to his wife Abigail from Philadelphia on June 17, 1775, describing riflemen as light infantry:

> They [The Continental Congress] have voted Ten Companies of Rifle Men to be sent from Pennsylvania, Maryland and Virginia, to join the Army before Boston. These are an excellent Species of Light Infantry. They use a peculiar Kind of gun called a Rifle—it has circular or cut Grooves within the Barrell [sic], and carries a Ball, with great Exactness to great Distances. They are the most accurate Marksmen in the World.[26]

The assumption made by Adams and others was that a frontiersman with a rifle was the equivalent of a light infantryman. But this was a misconception, as soon became evident. The disadvantages of the rifle as a weapon began with the fact that it took three to four times longer to load than did a smoothbore musket. Another serious problem was that the rifle's octagonal barrel could not hold a bayonet. Once the rifleman fired his single round, he was then vulnerable to attack until he could reload his weapon. The British exploited this drawback. Col. George Hanger of the British army, offered an example of how British light infantry learned to attack American riflemen: "He [The British officer] ordered his troops to charge [the riflemen] with the bayonet; not one man of them out of four, had time to fire, and those who did, had no time to load again; they did not stand three minutes; the light infantry not only dispersed them instantly, but drove them for miles over the country."[27]

25 Brown and Peckham, eds., *Revolutionary War Journals of Henry Dearborn*, 36.

26 Smith, ed., *Letters of Delegates to Congress*, I: 497.

27 British Col. George Hanger, quoted in Thomas J. McGuire, *The Philadelphia Campaign, Volume Two: Germantown and the Roads to Valley Forge* (Mechanicsburg, Pennsylvania: Stackpole Books, 2007), 251. Another excellent contemporary story about the problems with rifles concerns a 1776 proposal by Maryland to raise a rifle company for the Continental Army. The Board of War replied that if muskets were given them instead of rifles the service would be more benefitted, as there was a superabundance of riflemen in the Army. Were it in the power

Another drawback to employing riflemen was their independent and restless nature. They were, to put it mildly, very difficult to control and would obey only their own officers. General Washington understood this problem. When he organized his rifle corps in New Jersey in June 1777, Washington put it under the command of Col. Daniel Morgan, a tough and dominating officer who knew how to control his rowdy men. Morgan's legendary reputation included receiving 500 lashes for brawling with a British soldier and being shot through the mouth by an Indian. As previously noted, Washington was careful in his assignments and instructions to Morgan's units, aiming to take full advantage of the range and accuracy of the men's rifles without jeopardizing their lives.

As Burgoyne's Canadian Army advanced south, the New England members of Congress were clamoring for Washington to send Morgan's celebrated rifle corps to support the Northern Army. They wanted the rural riflemen on the scene to fight the Indians attached to Burgoyne's army. The British general had warned the colonists early on—in a theatrical proclamation (Burgoyne was an accomplished playwright)—that they must cooperate with his army or "the messengers of justice and wrath [his Indians] await them in the field, and devastation, famine, and every concomitant horror that a reluctant but indispensable prosecution of military duty must exercise."[28] Most of Burgoyne's Indian auxiliaries were from the eastern tribes, who could be controlled with gifts and the promise of caring for their families. However, a smaller group of about 150 warriors from the western Great Lakes tribes joined Burgoyne's army on July 20. They were a rapacious lot who brutally murdered and scalped their victims. The Continental troops and patriot militia were unskilled at fighting these natives. Small parties of soldiers were favorite prey for their skillfully executed ambushes and raids.

The terrorized soldiers and frightened settlers begged for help, and Washington acquiesced to Congress' demand by sending Morgan's Rifle Corps. Morgan was in Trenton, New Jersey, with his men when he received Washington's August 16 order to march as soon as possible to reinforce the

---

of Congress to supply muskets, it would speedily reduce the number of rifles and replace them with the former, as they were more easily kept in order, could be fired oftener, and had the advantage of fitting bayonets. Harold L. Peterson, *The Book of the Continental Soldier* (Harrisburg, Pennsylvania: Stackpole Books, 1968), 43.

28 James M. Hadden, *A Journal Kept in Canada and Upon Burgoyne's Campaign* (Albany, New York: Joel Munsell's Sons, 1884), 61.

Northern Army. The fact that Morgan's Corps of Riflemen was initially detached from the Main Army to fight Indians is evidenced by a letter that Washington wrote to Congress at the time stating that he had ordered Morgan's corps north with the hope that "they will be of material service, particularly in opposing the Savage part of Gen. Burgoyn's [sic] Force, which from every account spreads a General alarm among the Inhabitants."[29] Gates was anxious for Morgan to arrive, and when the Virginian reached the Northern Army on August 30 with 451 frontier riflemen, he was received with every mark of favor, including a fine dinner with the General and his headquarters staff.

Gates, however, had his own ideas for using Morgan's detachment, especially since many of Burgoyne's Indians had abandoned him when they sensed that the campaign was not going as well as promised. Gates created a detachment composed of Morgan's Rifle Corps and Dearborn's light infantry. Morgan's riflemen could fire accurately at long range while being protected by Dearborn's light infantrymen, who were armed with muskets and bayonets and were able to keep pace with the fast-moving, lightly equipped riflemen. The unit gave Gates a strong, combat-experienced detachment which could go after the enemy "acting in concert" while his main army remained behind their extensive fortifications.[30] Morgan was given command of the new elite outfit, which was called Morgan's Corps (as opposed to Morgan's Rifle Corps), with Dearborn as his second-in-command. Since the Corps was part of Arnold's wing of the army, it fell under his command.

The last time Arnold, Morgan, and Dearborn had been together was at Quebec when they stormed the city's lower town. Dearborn wrote of the desperate gamble they assumed that day, fighting on that bleak and frigid December morning at Quebec. His company, he explained, came "under a brisk fire from the walls and pickets [sentries], but it being very dark and stormy" the Americans were able to advance unscathed. But Quebec's defenders . . .

29 George Washington to John Hancock, dated "Neshamini Camp August 17th 1777" in W. W. Abott, et. al., eds., *The Papers of George Washington*, Revolutionary War Series, X: 649.

30 Henry Dearborn, "A Narrative of the Saratoga Campaign" (Fort Ticonderoga Bulletin, Vol. 1, No. 5, January 1929), 2-12 (individual pages unnumbered). Dearborn wrote a memoir (letter) of his experience during the Saratoga campaign to General James Wilkinson, dated Boston, Dec. 20, 1815, in response to an inquiry from the General for information for his book *Memoirs of My Own Time.*

> sent out two hundred men, who took possession of some houses which we had to pass. . . . I heard a shout in Town, which made me think that our people had got possession of the Same. I was just about to Hail them, when one of them hailed me, he asked who I was. I answered a friend, he asked me who I was friend to. I answered to liberty, he replied then God-damn you . . . and fired very briskly upon us.[31]

Hopelessly surrounded, Dearborn had no choice by to surrender with his company. Now, less than two years later, Arnold, Morgan, and Dearborn were going into combat again—but this time they had the advantage in both manpower and terrain.

A battle was inevitable as Burgoyne's army continued its cautious advance toward the American lines. By September 15, only eight miles separated the two armies. Reports reached Gates' headquarters of intense activity in the enemy's camp, in obvious preparation for driving the insurgents off Bemis Heights to open the road to Albany. The Royal army continued to advance in the days ahead, and by the morning of September 19 it was just three miles north of Bemis Heights. The area between the two armies was heavily wooded with ravines and small clearings hacked out by the local farmers to plant their crops. Having been abandoned by most of his Indians and with the woods swarming with rebel skirmishers, Burgoyne had little information about the position and strength of the rebel army facing him; but he knew that he wanted to turn its left flank, which meant that he wanted to attack the western-most section of Gates' defense line and get behind the Americans' fortifications.

The early morning of September 19 was cold and foggy. As the sun burned away the mist, scouts reported to Gates' headquarters that Burgoyne's army was on the move and advancing toward the American lines. At Arnold's urging, Gates ordered him to deploy Morgan's Corps into the woods to harass the British. The Corps moved out across a wide front in loose formation, looking for the enemy. Behind Morgan's Corps was Gates' army on Bemis Heights. Its ranks had swelled to 8,100, with additional troops harassing the enemy's supply line from Canada. In comparison, Burgoyne's army at the time had an estimated 8,500. These figures include camp followers, boatmen, teamsters, hospital staff, and patients. There are no reliable figures for the number of effective fighting men in either army.

31 Brown and Peckham, eds., *Revolutionary War Journals of Henry Dearborn*, 68-69.

The fighting started at about noon when Morgan's Corps ran into enemy pickets (perimeter guards) in a field on the Freeman Farm. Heavy fighting ensued during the afternoon as Gates reluctantly committed additional troops to the battle, which became known as the First Battle of Saratoga, or the Battle of Freeman's Farm. Morgan and Dearborn fought valiantly and were engaged in some of the heaviest fighting of the day. The fighting around Freeman's Farm lasted into the night. Dearborn recorded that "the enemy retired when it became so dark that we had no other visible object but the flash of their pieces [muskets]."[32] Dearborn further described the fighting in his journal:

> 19th [September], Hearing this morning that the Enemy were advancing, the Rifle & Light Infantry [Morgan's Corp] turned out to meet the Enemy. . . . The Enemy brought almost their whole force against us, together with 8 Pieces of Artillery. But we who had something more at Stake than fighting for six Pence per Day and we kept our ground til Night. . . . [Dearborn concluded,] [O]n this Day has Been fought one of the Greatest Battles that Ever was fought in America, & I Trust we have Convinced the British Butchers that the Cowardly Yankees Can & when there is a Call for it, will, fight.[33]

Dearborn's journal entry failed to mention that his light infantry was separated from Morgan's riflemen during most of the day-long battle. One of Dearborn's officers acknowledged the situation when he wrote that "the riflemen being ahead of us, the Enemy discovered them & gave them a shot."[34] Recalling the battle years later, Dearborn admitted that his men were defending the left of the American line in the woods facing the British, while Morgan's corps "was on the extreme right."[35] Morgan and Dearborn would have to learn to operate in concert, and they did so as the campaign continued. Their

32 Dearborn, "A Narrative of the Saratoga Campaign," 2-12 (individual pages unnumbered).

33 Brown and Peckham, eds., *Revolutionary War Journals of Henry Dearborn*, 105-107.

34 Joseph Lee Boyle, ed., "From Saratoga to Valley Forge: The Diary of Lt. Samuel Armstrong," *The Pennsylvania Magazine of History and Biography*, Vol. CXXI, No, 3 (July 1997), 245.

35 Dearborn, "A Narrative of the Saratoga Campaign," 2-12.

effectiveness was further increased by the addition of about 100 Oneida Indians to their elite corps.[36]

Arnold's whereabouts during the Battle of Freeman's Farm is a matter of controversy. One alleged eyewitness account says that "Arnold rushed into the thickest of the fight with his usual recklessness, and at times acted like a madman."[37] It is probable that he left the American defenses on Bemis Heights at some point during the day and got close to the firing line. When the guns finally fell silent, the British occupied the ground around Freeman's Farm—but it was a hollow victory. Not only did they never get close to Bemis Heights, but they sustained terrible casualties.

Following the fighting on September 19, Burgoyne fortified his camp in a fashion similar to Gates, but otherwise remained strangely quiet. Meanwhile, his escape route to Fort Ticonderoga was becoming less tenable by the day and his exhausted soldiers were consuming their remaining provisions. Burgoyne's inaction was based on a brief message that managed to reach him through the American lines that Gen. Sir Henry Clinton was sailing up the Hudson River from New York City with warships and transports carrying two thousand troops in a desperate move to create a diversion that would force Gates to rush part of his army south to defend Albany and the lower Hudson River. The message was inaccurate, however: Clinton did not have the ships or troops to attempt to reach Burgoyne's beleaguered army.

Meanwhile, in the American camp, tensions were on the rise between Gates and Arnold. The apparent cause of the rupture was Arnold's learning second-hand that Gates' report to Congress describing the September 19 Battle of Freeman's Farm gave no credit to Arnold nor noted that the troops that fought there were under his command. Adding to the hostility was Gates' order,

36 Boyle, ed., "The Diary of Lt. Samuel Armstrong," 246. Armstrong wrote: "Saturday [September] 20th: There came from Albany about 120 Indians and in the Afternoon the Rifle and Infantry Battalions were ordered out with them—but could not discover anything of the Enemy." Dearborn also mentioned the addition of the Oneidas to Morgan's Corps in his journal: "[September] 23rd about 100 Onyda Indians who Joined us the Next Day after the Battle [Freeman's Farm], have Brought in more or Less Prisoners Every Day." Brown and Peckham, eds., *Revolutionary War Journals of Henry Dearborn*, 107.

37 Frank Moore, *Diary of the American Revolution*, 2 vols. (New York: Charles Scribner, 1860), I: 497-498. The quote is attributed to General Enoch Poor. The authenticity of this so-called eyewitness account is questionable. Adding to the suspicion is that the original letter could not be found in its reported depository, which is the Jared Sparks Collection at Harvard University's Widener Library.

dated September 22, which put Morgan's Corps under his direct control. Prior to Gates' clarifying edict, Arnold had assumed that Morgan's Corps was part of his command, since it was posted in his section of Bemis Heights. Arnold took the directive as an insult and stalked over to Gates' farmhouse headquarters in a fury to protest. With his usual hot temper and lack of diplomacy, Arnold's years of friendship with Gates evaporated in a heated argument which ended with Arnold storming out of the farmhouse in a rage. He returned to his quarters, where he wrote a letter to Gates repeating his grievances and requesting that he be given a pass to go to Philadelphia, "where I propose to join General Washington, and may possibly have it in my power to serve my country although I am thought of no consequence in this Department [the Northern Army]."[38]

Gates responded the following morning by sending Arnold a note giving him permission to leave. Gates also wrote to Arnold that, as General Benjamin Lincoln was expected in camp in a few days, the Northern Army would have no further need for Arnold's services. But Arnold had never expected Gates to call his bluff and actually let him leave, with Burgoyne just three miles away and still full of fight. Arnold chose to remain in camp and brood.

Unbeknownst to Arnold, his altercation with Gates had been encouraged by officers sympathetic to Schuyler, and included one of Arnold's own aides-de-camp. Of all the tactless things Arnold could have done following his arrival at the Northern Army, his selection of Maj. Henry Brockholst Livingston as one of his staff officers was a whopper. Livingston had excellent pedigree. He was a graduate of the College of New Jersey and a member of the powerful Livingston clan whose members included his father William Livingston, the wartime governor of New Jersey and Washington's ally and friend. However, Brockholst had served as Schuyler's aide-de-camp and was known to be devoted to his former boss, including reporting every bit of camp gossip to Schuyler that might injure Gates' career. Young Livingston was known for his hot temper, and years later he responded to a humiliating "snouting" by shooting his antagonist in the groin.[39]

38 John F. Luzader, *Saratoga: A Military History of the Decisive Campaign of the American Revolution* (New York: Savas-Beatie, 2008), 262.

39 A snouting was a nose tweaking in public. The display was a traditional gesture of contempt used by political rivals. It sent a powerful message that frequently resulted in an affair of honor (a duel). In post-war America, Livingston was a dedicated and active Republican (Jeffersonian).

Livingston was also friendly with Lt. Col. Richard Varick, who was another former Schuyler staff member and admirer. Varick was a competent officer who was Gates' deputy muster master general, responsible for reviewing the troops and receiving and inspecting muster rolls, as well as a volunteer (also called a supernumerary) aide-de-camp to Arnold.[40] Varick worked at headquarters and kept Schuyler updated on Gates' activities. In one letter, Varick told Schuyler, "I wish to God we had a Commander who could see a little Distance before him without Spectacles." More compelling is Varick's September 22 missive to Schuyler describing the Battle of Freeman's Farm, which exaggerated Arnold's participation in the fighting, claimed that Gates, meanwhile, "was in Dr. Potts tent backbiting his neighbors," and stated that, " it is evident to me, he [Gates] never intended to fight Burgoyne, till Arnold, urged, begged & entreated him to do it."[41]

Gates' toady, Lt. Col. James Wilkinson, was aware of Livingston and Varick's hatred of Gates and reported everything he heard about them to his boss. Arnold, by his association with young Livingston and Varick, was considered part of the Schuyler clique, although he tried to stay clear of politics. It was Varick and Livingston who did much to incite Arnold following the Battle of Freeman's Farm in an effort to embarrass and discredit Gates.

Consequently, Arnold remained in camp with no active command. He continued to be ignored by Gates, yet was unwilling to leave and face Congress,

---

He wrote an article for *The New York Argus* newspaper in 1798 critical of the opposition Federalist Party. A New York merchant named James Jones was offended by Livingston's article. He confronted the author in The Battery (lower Manhattan) and gave him a snouting. Livingston responded by challenging Jones to a duel. Livingston was familiar with firearms from his days as an army officer and deliberately shot Jones in the groin. Jones died from the hideous wound. Livingston was one of the best and most expensive lawyers in postwar New York City. He shared the city's top clients with his fellow Revolutionary War veterans and lawyers Aaron Burr and Alexander Hamilton. President Jefferson appointed Livingston to the New York Supreme Court and later nominated him for the United States Supreme Court. His appointment was confirmed by the Senate and Livingston served as an associate Supreme Court justice until his death in 1823.

40 As a general officer in the Continental Army, Benedict Arnold was authorized by Congress to have two aides-de-camp. They held the rank of major in their position as aides. Henry Brockholst Livingston served as one of Arnold's aides, but he was actually still Schuyler's aide, on temporary assignment to Arnold's staff. Arnold's other authorized, official aide was Matthew Clarkson from Massachusetts, who was Livingston's first cousin. Both were teenagers at the time. Varick served as a volunteer aide to Arnold. He was identified as a "supernumerary Aid-de-camp" to Arnold.

41 Luzader, *Saratoga*, 265.

considering his several previous threats to resign his commission. Arnold also knew that General Washington would not appreciate his deserting the field with a restless British army nearby.

Days passed with no movement from the Royal army's fortified camp. Burgoyne was isolated; he had no news of Sir Henry Clinton's supposed diversionary sortie up the Hudson, but was still hopeful that help was on the way. The beleaguered general went so far as to order flares fired into the sky at night to show Clinton his position. Whether Burgoyne actually believed that Clinton was nearby or the display was an effort to boost the morale of his beleaguered troops is unknown. With no news from Clinton, and after meeting with some of his generals, Burgoyne decided to order out a strong reconnaissance party to test the enemy's western defense line to see if he could punch his way through. The British also used the opportunity to forage for food for their famished men and horses.

Wilkinson claims that he saw the movement of the British on October 7. He returned and reported to Gates, who asked him what the intentions of the enemy appeared to be. "They are foraging," Wilkinson said, "and endeavoring to reconnoiter your left; and I think Sir, they offer you battle." To which, according to Wilkinson, Gates gave a reply that became famous: "Well then, order on Morgan to begin the game."[42] The British reconnaissance on October 7 escalated into the Second Battle of Saratoga, or the Battle of Bemis Heights, as both sides committed additional troops to the fight. By the time of the Battle of Bemis Heights, the total number in Gates' army is estimated to have increased to 12,500 versus only 7,900 for Burgoyne. Once again, however, the actual number of combat troops fit for duty in each army is unknown.

Morgan's Corps was heavily engaged in the second battle, as were a number of other brigades and regiments. Arnold's role in the early phase of the battle is ambiguous; the picture was later complicated by storytellers whose tall tales have been given credibility by historians. What probably happened was that Arnold, unable to stew in his tent any longer, late in the day mounted his horse on his own initiative and rode to the scene of the fighting. He arrived in time to lead elements of General Enoch Poor's brigade against the British light infantry (at Balcarres Redoubt), then followed up by galloping over to participate in an attack on a German-held position (called Breymann's post, known today as Breymann's Redoubt). Putting himself at the head of some spirited men,

42 Wilkinson, *Memoirs of My Own Times*, I: 207-208.

Arnold attacked the rear of the enemy works. He was the first man to enter the redoubt.[43] The Germans gave way, but as they retreated they fired some scattered shots, one of which hit Arnold in his left leg while another killed the sorrel mare he was riding. Writing years later, Dearborn said he saw Arnold fall and described the scene in vivid detail. Dearborn's complete account of the attack on Breymann's Redoubt is included here because it is the best description we have of the event:

> The assault was commenced by the advance of Arnold with about 200 men through a copse of wood which covered the Enemies right, the appearance of Arnold on the right was the signal for us to advance and assault the front. The whole was executed in the most spirited and prompt manner and as soon as the Enemy had give us one fire, he fall back from his works to his line of tents, and as we entered he gave way and retreated in confusion. When Arnold entered on the right he ordered the Enemy to lay down their arms. A platoon fired upon him, killed his horse and wounded the General in the same leg that was shattered at Quebec. His horse fell upon the other leg, and as we entered at the same moment, seeing his situation, I assisted in extricating from it by removing his horse. I asked him if he was badly wounded. He replied, in the same leg, and wished the ball had passed his heart. . . . It being dark, the action of the 7th of October now ended, and as we thought highly honorable to our Army and country. I saw no General officers in either of the actions [Freeman Farm and Bemis Heights], except General Arnold and General Poor.[44]

An American militiaman named Oliver Boardman also claimed he saw Arnold go down: "[O]ur Genrl [Arnold] Little thought of Danger and forced his way through & spared none till a ball Break [sic] his leg & Kill'd his horse."[45]

43 Letter dated "Camp Jany 22d 1778," written by Lt. Col. Richard Butler. He served as second-in-command of Morgan's Corps during the Saratoga campaign. Butler described the attack on Breymann's Redoubt: "A storm of their works. General Arnold was the first who Enterd, one Major Morris with About 12 of the Rifle men followd him on the Rear of their Right flank while I led up the Rest of the Riflemen in front. I was the 3d officer in & had the Brave Gen Arnold sent off the field With his leg broke his horse being shot under him when he Recd his wound. . . ." Manuscript letter, Gratz Collection, Case 4, Box 11, Historical Society of Pennsylvania.

44 "Bulletin of the Fort Ticonderoga Museum", volume one, number five, 2-12.

45 Transcribed excerpts from the "Journal of Oliver Boardman From Col. Thaddeus Cook's Battalion of Connecticut Militia," manuscript in the Collection of Saratoga National Historical Park. For the story of Arnold's horse falling on his previously wounded leg, see Hoffman

Yet Arnold's heroics at Breymann's Redoubt unnecessarily endangered the lives of the American soldiers who charged into the enemy's works behind him: the capture of the nearby Balcarres Redoubt made Breymann's Redoubt untenable, forcing its defenders to either surrender or attempt to retreat under heavy rebel gunfire.

Among the units that took part in the fighting on October 7 was the 15th Massachusetts Regiment commanded by Col. Timothy Bigelow. He had been second-in-command of Lt. Col. Christopher Greene's second division on the Arnold Expedition. During the bleakest moment of the trek, when they were in the inhospitable forests of upper Maine and on the verge of starvation, Bigelow had written to his wife: "We are in a wilderness, nearly one hundred miles from any inhabitants. . . . If the French [Canadians] are our enemies, it will go hard with us for we have no retreat left. In that case, there will be no alternative between the sword and famine."

Bigelow was captured in the attack on Quebec and held captive inside the city. He was appointed a major in the 21st Continental Regiment in early 1776 while he was still a prisoner in Quebec. Bigelow was exchanged in May 1776, by which time the slot in the regiment had been filled. Instead, the popular and audacious Bigelow was appointed colonel and commander of the 15th Massachusetts Infantry on New Year's Day, January 1, 1777, and his regiment was ordered to march north by General Washington later that year. On October 4 on Bemis Heights, Bigelow led his troops as part of General Glover's brigade.[46]

Having failed in his second effort to defeat General Gates' army, General Burgoyne retreated about eight miles to Saratoga, where he entrenched his army. Surrounded by the Americans and almost out of food, Burgoyne surrendered his army at Saratoga on October 17, 1777. After capitulating, Burgoyne is claimed to have said that Morgan "commanded the finest corps in the world."[47]

Nickerson, *The Turning Point of the Revolution* (Boston: Houghton Mifflin Company, 1928), 366-376.

46 McAuliffe, "Timothy Bigelow", 12. Bigelow's arrival at Saratoga is mentioned in a letter he wrote dated "Camp Stillwater October 7, 1777, I arrived in Camp last Saturday [October 4], nothing of importance has turned up since. . . ."

47 Alexander Garden, *Anecdotes of the Revolutionary War in America with Sketches of Character of Persons The Most Distinguished, in the Southern States, For Civil and Military Service* (Charleston, South Carolina: Printed for the Author by A.E. Miller, 1822), 58-59.

Gates gave Wilkinson the honor of carrying the official report of the British surrender to Congress. His account acknowledged Benedict Arnold's participation in the fighting, but the badly wounded Arnold felt insulted and snubbed by Gates, who was being celebrated as the hero of Saratoga. While Gates was being thus applauded, Arnold lay in a hospital bed in Albany, New York.

In 1801, almost a quarter-century after General Burgoyne surrendered his army, President Thomas Jefferson appointed Henry Dearborn as his secretary of war. James Wilkinson was a brigadier general at the time and commander- in-chief of the small American army, most of which was stationed in scattered frontier outposts. Revenge is a dish best served cold, and Dearborn had a long memory. He regarded Wilkinson as little more than a smooth-talking scoundrel who had betrayed his brave former commander, Benedict Arnold, during the Saratoga Campaign. As a result, Dearborn used his political position as secretary of war to harass Wilkinson by cutting his expense budget, appointing a committee of officers to scrutinize his orders, and sending him on long and miserable assignments on the rugged frontier. It had taken decades to achieve, but Dearborn enjoyed the satisfaction of getting even with at least one of the men who had exploited Arnold's weaknesses.[48]

48 Andro Linklater, *An Artist in Treason: The Extraordinary Double Life of General James Wilkinson* (New York: Walker Publishing Co., 2009), 196.

Chapter Six

Arnold's Men Fight On

"Nothing under Heaven can save us but the enemy's
[Gen. Howe] going to the southward."

—*Connecticut Governor Jonathan Trumbull*[1]

General Sir William Howe seemed to have no conception of time. While Burgoyne was aggressively moving south from Canada in the spring of 1777, Howe dawdled the season away in New Jersey trying to lure Washington's army into a general engagement. Gaining control of the state was the first step in (the recently knighted) Sir William's plan; he intended to capture Philadelphia by approaching it from New Jersey. But Washington would not commit his army to a fight; he remained holed up with his troops in the Watchung Mountains of central New Jersey. Howe knew from experience that Washington would send detachments off his mountain stronghold to raid British supply lines and attack isolated detachments of Royal troops. After weeks of maneuvering, Howe gave up trying to lure Washington out of his mountain fastness. He ordered his army to evacuate New Jersey and withdraw to Staten Island, New York, where it began arriving on June 30, 1777. The futile campaign prompted one British officer to write home, "We have abandoned

1 Charles Francis Adams, *Studies Military and Diplomatic, 1775-1865* (New York: The Macmillan Company, 1911), 153.

the Jerseys, & left Genl. Washington to enjoy the satisfaction of having sent us to seek fortune elsewhere."[2]

Despite his setbacks in New Jersey, Gen. Howe was still determined to take Philadelphia in 1777. After returning to New York, he embarked his soldiers on a fleet of 260 ships that would transport them to a secure landing place where they could attack the rebel capital from the south. The British fleet was loaded and ready to sail on July 10, 1777, but Howe kept his ships in port. There was no explanation, but the delay in sailing was probably due to his decision to wait for what he anticipated would be positive news from Burgoyne's campaign before launching his own Philadelphia offensive. On July 13, Sir William received reliable information that Burgoyne's army had scored a major victory by capturing Fort Ticonderoga. Confident that the Canadian army was not only secure but well ahead of schedule, Howe ordered his convoy to set sail.[3]

But a further delay ensued as his ships waited for a favorable wind. Meanwhile, the men and animals in the overcrowded ships were suffering from the excessive summer heat and close confinement. On July 20, the armada finally put to sea. Learning enroute that the river approaches to Philadelphia were heavily fortified, the invasion fleet bypassed Delaware Bay entirely. It sailed further south into Chesapeake Bay, adding another three weeks to the journey.

Howe's ships at last reached Head of Elk, Maryland—the furthest point of navigation up the Elk River—on August 25, 1777. Ironically, when he landed his sickly army there, Howe was further from Philadelphia than he had been at

2 Thomas J. McGuire, The Philadelphia Campaign: Brandywine and the Fall of Philadelphia (Mechanicsburg, Pennsylvania: Stackpole Books, 2006), 61.

3 General Sir William Howe was secretive about his plans throughout the war, and his delay in starting his Philadelphia campaign is no exception. However, the diary of Captain Friedrich von Muenchhausen, who was one of Howe's aides-de-camp, indicated that the General delayed sailing from New York while waiting for positive news about Burgoyne's offensive. Von Muenchhausen wrote: "July 13 [1777] Rather reliable news makes us believe that Ticonderoga, 268 miles from New York, is in Burgoyne's possession. No one seems to be able to figure out why we are waiting here so long, considering the fact that everyone except Howe and a few officers, are aboard ship. Some malcontents have give some rather unfounded and unworthy reason for the delay. I for my part, am sure that we will depart when we get reliable information from Burgoyne. July 14, Some deserters have arrived and brought confirmation of the news of the capture of Ticonderoga and of the consequent restlessness of the rebels. We also received from these deserters, a Philadelphia newspaper of July 2, in which they report that the northern army had passed the Lakes and was on the march to Ticonderoga." Ernst Kipping and Samuel Stelle Smith, *At General Howe's Side 1776-1778* (Monmouth Beach, New Jersey: Philip Freneau Press, 1974), 21.

New Brunswick, New Jersey, in June. In addition, by the time Howe reached Head of Elk, his army was too far away to reinforce Burgoyne in a timely manner if it became necessary. Howe began a cautious advance northward toward the rebel capital.

When Howe's army was aboard ships in New York with their destination unknown, Connecticut's Governor Trumbull said, "Nothing under Heaven can save us but the enemy's [Howe] going to the southward." The lack of coordination between Howe and Burgoyne was probably the single biggest mistake the British made during the American Revolution. The underlying cause was that Britain attempted to administer the war from London instead of giving control to an officer or government official based in America. Britain's lack of brilliant, albeit capable, generals also contributed to its failure to suppress the rebellion.

Reliable news that a big enemy fleet had been sighted in Chesapeake Bay convinced Washington that Howe's objective was Philadelphia and not a ploy to put out to sea from New York and then turn around and sail up the Hudson River to support Burgoyne. With Howe's intentions now clear, Washington hastily abandoned his New Jersey positions and moved south to defend the rebel capital. The Continental Army marched through Philadelphia on August 24 and established a line of defense south of the city in the hills above Brandywine Creek, Pennsylvania. Washington concentrated his forces at Chadds Ford on the Brandywine and waited for Howe to attack.

His preparations included the establishment of a temporary corps of picked men to harass the enemy and slow down their advance. As stated in the previous chapter, Morgan's Corps of Riflemen had been deployed as light infantry earlier in the year in New Jersey, but they had been sent north to oppose Burgoyne' Indians.[4] In Morgan's absence, officers and men from each Continental Army brigade were selected to serve in the new light corps, consisting of 700 men under the command of Gen. William Maxwell. At least

4 The term "picked men" was used to identify a detachment of men selected for a specific duty, including operating as light infantry. Picked men were selected from their regiments for temporary duty. They probably wore no distinctive uniform or other identification and were armed with whatever weapons (e.g., flintlock muskets) they brought from their regiments. However, Washington's use of the term picked men as light infantry is clear from the General Orders dated "Head Quarters, Wilmington [Delaware] August 28th, 1777": "A corps of Light Infantry is to be formed; to consist of one Field Officer, two Captains, six Subalterns, eight Serjeants and 100 Rank & File from each brigade." W.W. Abbot, et. al., eds., *The Papers of George Washington*, Revolutionary War Series, XI: 82.

two Arnold Expedition veterans had the distinction of being among those selected to serve under Maxwell and lead detachments of picked men into battle: William Heth and Charles Porterfield. Both had served in Arnold's Kennebec Corps in Morgan's Rifle Company, Heth as a lieutenant and Porterfield as a gentleman volunteer. At the Brandywine, Heth was a lieutenant colonel, on detached duty from the 3rd Virginia Regiment, and Porterfield was a major, on loan to Maxwell from the 11th Virginia Regiment.

John Joseph Henry told a story about Heth, whom he called "Lt. Heath," in his narrative of the Arnold Expedition. Henry explained that Heth's commander, Capt. Morgan, was a very competitive officer who pushed his Virginians hard to keep them in the lead during the trek to Canada. One morning, rifleman Henry and his companions (who were from Pennsylvania) were poling their bateau when they saw Heth in a boat just ahead of them, "laboring like a slave" with some fellow Virginians to keep their boat in the lead. Henry's bateau raced alongside Heth's bateau and rammed it soundly, causing its occupants to lose their balance and allowing the Pennsylvanians' boat to pass them and take the lead. Henry remembered hearing Heth and his fellow Virginians curse the Pennsylvanians heartily as they scrambled to get moving again.[5]

Maxwell's elite corps was posted along the road to Chadds Ford in advance of Washington's Main Army. Detachments from the corps had been mauled in their earlier, initial encounters with the British. Heth, who had soldiered with outstanding combat officers Arnold and Morgan, was critical of Maxwell's generalship. He wrote to his old commander Morgan about the situation: "You have been greatly wished for since the Enemies [sic] Landing at the head of Elk. Maxwell's Corps it was expected would do great things—we had opportunities—and anybody but an old woman, would have availed themselves of them."[6]

The performance of Maxwell's picked men improved with experience. They were ready when a column of Royal troops commanded by German General von Knyphausen approached Chadds Ford on the morning of September 11. The British van skirmished with a detachment commanded by Maj. Porterfield. Using what Gen. Washington had earlier prescribed as

5 Henry, *An Accurate and Interesting Account . . . in the Campaign Against Quebec*, 61-62.

6 McGuire, *The Philadelphia Campaign: Brandywine and the Fall of Philadelphia*, 156-157.

"Indian-style" (hit-and-run) tactics, Porterfield joined Heth in harassing the enemy. Heth wrote of Porterfield's courage and leadership during the running battle: "His conduct through the whole day—was such, as has acquired him the greatest Honor—A great proportion of British Officers fell by a party under his command."[7]

A number of other Arnold Expedition veterans saw action at the Battle of the Brandywine, including Lt. Col. Febiger, who was the acting commander of the 11th Virginia Regiment at the time. He fought heroically in the battle and was rewarded with a promotion to colonel and permanent command of the 2nd Virginia Regiment. Other Arnold Expedition veterans who fought at the Brandywine included Maj. Francis Nichols, who commanded troops from the 9th Pennsylvania Regiment. Nichols had served as a lieutenant in Capt. Hendricks' Pennsylvania rifle company on the Arnold Expedition. He was standing next to Hendricks when a musket ball hit the captain in the chest while he was firing at the enemy from inside a building on the Sault-au-Matelot. Nichols said he watched in horror as the brave Hendricks staggered across the room to a bed, where he collapsed and died. Nichols took command of Hendricks' company, which fought on bravely for the rest of the battle, shooting at the enemy from inside buildings and shouting "We'll have revenge" for the death of their captain. His rifle company was among the last of the Americans to surrender at Quebec. Nichols was exchanged on October 10, 1776, and appointed a captain in the 9th Pennsylvania Regiment two months later. He was promoted to major in February 1777 and fought with his regiment until he resigned from the army in 1779. Nichols died on February 13, 1812.[8]

Despite the bravery of many American officers and men at the Brandywine, Howe outflanked Washington's lines and forced the rebels to retreat in disarray. Howe's success at the Brandywine opened the way for his army to occupy Philadelphia. But it was a hollow victory, since the members of the Continental Congress escaped to York, Pennsylvania, and Washington's army was left intact and encircling the city.

7 *Ibid.*, 176.

8 Heitman, *Historical Register of Officers of the Continental Army*, 51, 413; Robert Grant Crist, *Capt. William Hendricks and the March to Quebec, 1775* (Pennsylvania: The Hamilton Library and Historical Association of Cumberland County, 1960), 31-32; Wright, *The Continental Army*, 265-266.

Washington himself was still full of fight, and on October 4, 1777, he attacked Howe's troops defending Germantown, a town six miles north of Philadelphia. At Germantown, Col. Heth was leading his Virginia troops. Washington's battle plan—which Heth called "a grand enterprize, an inimitable plan"—proved to be too complicated for the young Continental Army, but the Americans put on an impressive fight. Following the muddled engagement, Heth wrote a letter describing the action to John Lamb, with whom he had shared close quarters for seven months in a Quebec prison:

> Before this reaches you, the news of our late action at German Town, no doubt will have come to hand. . . . [F]rom short marches and frequent halts it was near 6 [a.m.] before the first volley of small arms [muskets and rifles] were heard. . . . In the mean time [we] attempted to march in line of battle, till that order was found impracticable, which from the great number of post and rail fences, thickets and in short everything that could obstruct our march, threw us frequently into the greatest disorder. Tho we gave away a complete victory, we have learned this valuable truth: that we are able to beat them by vigorous exertion, and that we are far superior in point of swiftness.[9]

Another of Heth's fellow prisoners in Quebec was Lt. Peter Bryan Bruin. Bruin fought at Germantown as a captain, commanding a company of the 11th Virginia Regiment. In his 1818 pension application, Bruin gave a detailed account of his participation in the war, starting with his enlistment in the army in July 1775: "I was appointed a lieutenant in Capt. Daniel Morgan's company of riflemen, the first corps raised in Virginia that was placed on the Continental establishment [Continental Army]. So great was the enthusiasm of the moment that the difficulty did not depend on raising the number of men required, but in selecting those who would serve."[10] Bruin fought at Quebec, and recalled in his pension application how "Morgan's company led the attack. We planted ladders against the walls [barricades] in the face of a spirited opposition. We were roughly handled and at length were forced to surrender."[11]

Bruin was exchanged in September 1776. He next saw action as a captain in the 11th Virginia Regimen at Brandywine, where he was wounded: "I was

9 Commager and Morris, eds., T*he Spirit of Seventy-Six*, I: 629-630.

10 Affidavit of Peter Bryan Bruin (1754-1827, Virginia), *Revolutionary War Pension and Land Bounty Record*, Record series M-805, file S-42092.

11 *Ibid.*

struck by a spent ball [a musket or cannon ball which has slowed to a velocity insufficient to puncture the skin, but could still have the impact of a hammer], which for a time disabled me, and had it not been for a horseman belonging to Bland's Horse [1st Continental Light Dragoon Regiment, commanded by Theodorick Bland] who took me up behind him, I must (a second time) have fallen into the hands of the enemy." Bruin recovered from his injury in time to lead his company into battle at Germantown.

Following the fighting, Bruin was invited to become an aide-de-camp to Gen. John Sullivan. Bruin described the circumstances of his appointment in his pension application: "General Sullivan having lost both his aides (Col. White and Major Sherburne) [John White from Pennsylvania and Edward Sherburne from New Hampshire were both mortally wounded at Germantown], he requested General Scott [Charles Scott from Virginia] to point out to him, an officer in the Virginia Line, to fill the place of one of them. That gentleman recommended me and I joined his military family."[12]

Bruin was at Sullivan's side as the rebels continued to harass the British, especially by disrupting their supply line into Philadelphia. Although Howe had captured Philadelphia and driven back Washington's attack on Germantown, his problems continued because the Americans still controlled the Delaware River. While the Delaware appeared to be a wide river, the portion of its channel deep enough to accommodate large ships was narrow, and the insurgents exploited this situation by fortifying the waterway below Philadelphia. This forced the British to keep the city provisioned by wagon trains which were also preyed upon by Gen. Potter's Pennsylvania militia. General Howe had to open the Delaware River to ships before his army, as well as the civilian population of the city, ran out of food. His efforts to gain control of the river resulted in the involvement of a number of Arnold Expedition veterans, as they fought back tenaciously in the resulting battles.

The rebels had the Delaware blockaded at two strategic points. Approaching the city from the sea, the first rebel defense line was at a place called Billingsport on the New Jersey side of the river. The Americans built a fort at Billingsport to protect an ingenious row of obstructions strung across the channel called chevaux-de-frise. [13] These oddly named water obstacles were

12 *Ibid.*

13 A chevaux-de-frise is clearly described in the following diary passage: "This kind of chevaux de frise consists of large timbers, like the main mast of a ship at the top of which are three

unique to the American Revolution. They were prodigious, iron-tipped, wooden stakes projecting upward from stone-filled wooden boxes resting on the bottom of the river. Lying just below the surface of the water, these contraptions could tear gaping holes in the hulls of the wooden ships of the period. However, the British easily overran lightly defended Fort Billingsport on October 2, 1777, after which they destroyed enough of the chevaux-de-frise to allow their warships to proceed upriver.

There they encountered the second, and more formidable, rebel defense line. Located a few miles downriver from Philadelphia, the second barrier was composed of two unfinished forts lying directly across the river from one another: Fort Mercer (also called Fort Red Bank) on the New Jersey side and Fort Mifflin on the Pennsylvania side. These two posts defended a narrow channel obstructed with more chevaux-de-frise and a flotilla of gunboats that provided additional firepower to the forts. After consulting with his chief engineer, Gen. Howe decided to overwhelm Fort Mercer with an infantry assault and lay siege to Fort Mifflin with artillery. Howe's chief engineer at the time was Capt. John Montresor, the same British officer who in 1761 had surveyed the route followed by the Arnold Expedition in 1775.

Anticipating an attack on Fort Mercer, Washington needed a tough commander to defend the place. He gave the difficult assignment to Col. Christopher Greene from Rhode Island, the same fighting officer who had been second-in-command of the Arnold Expedition. Greene took charge of Fort Mercer with his 1st Rhode Island Regiment, whose officers included fellow Arnold Expedition veterans Maj. Samuel Ward, Jr., and Lt. Edward Slocum (from John Topham's company). Greene and his regiment arrived at Fort Mercer on Sunday, October 1, accompanied by Capt. Thomas-Antoine, Chevalier de Mauduit du Plessis, a French volunteer trained in artillery and engineering who was commissioned as a captain in the Continental Artillery.[14]

---

branches armed and pointed with iron, spreading out fanwise . . . fifteen feet asunder. The main beam is fixt at an elevation to the frame of a float or stage, composed of vast logs, bound together as fast as possible; then covered . . . and calked. When this machine is towed to its place, it is loaded with about thirty tons of stones, secured in cases, which, by taking the plugs out of the deck to admit the water into the float, sinks it down and keeps it firm and steady . . . the points of the branches about six or seven feet under the surface of the water." "Anonymous Diary Recording Howe's Military Operations in 1777," in *Ibid.*, 631-632.

14 Colonel Greene wrote to Washington shortly after arriving at Fort Mercer. Here is an excerpt from his letter: "Fort at Read [sic] Bank, 14th October 1777. I arrived here on Saturday last with my Regiment, they were much Fatigued with the March as I forced Thirty five Miles in

After inspecting the unfinished fort, Greene and du Plessis (as he was called at the time by the Americans) decided to concentrate their defenses in the strongest section of the post and abandon the rest. They constructed a traverse (defensive barrier) to defend the occupied section of the fort against an attack from the deserted sector.

Realizing that one regiment could not defend Fort Mercer, Washington sent Col. Israel Angell's 2nd Rhode Island Regiment to reinforce the place.[15] The arrival of Angell's regiment added four known heroes of the Arnold Expedition to the defense of Fort Mercer: Sgt. Jeremiah Greenman, Maj. Simeon Thayer, Capt. William Humphrey, and Capt. Sylvanus Shaw. The latter was a lieutenant in Samuel Ward's company on the trek to Canada. With the addition of Angell's regiment, Greene had 425 men supported by 14 pieces of artillery to defend his outpost.

On October 19, Gen. Howe ordered a land attack on Fort Mercer and gave the honor of commanding the assault to Col. Carl Emil Ulrich von Donop, one of the most distinguished officers among the German (Hessian) mercenaries. Von Donop was assigned a force of 1,200 Hessian troops to attack the rebel position, giving him a three-to-one advantage over the American defenders.

Von Donop approached Fort Mercer on October 22, with his Jägers (marksmen) leading the way. Realizing that he vastly outnumbered the American defenders, the self-assured von Donop paraded his imposing corps

one Day. . . . I have found it necessary to contract the Fort—but it's now too large for our Numbers, as we have very little to expect from the Militia." [Greene then mentions a meeting he had with New Jersey militia General Newcomb.] The General [Newcomb] thinks Your Excellency's Intentions were, for the Militia only to help compleat the Fort, after that to Fall on the rear of the Enemy in case of an Attack. . . . [C]ould your Excellency give us the Assistance of Colo. Angels Regiment [Col. Israel Angell's 2nd Rhode Island regiment]. I doubt not this point wou'd be secure with Dependance on Militia." W. W. Abbot, et al., eds., *The Papers of George Washington*, Revolutionary War Series, XI: 503-504. Israel Angell (1740-1832) was a cooper living and working in Providence, Rhode Island, before the war. For information about the French volunteer du Plessis, see Samuel Steele Smith, *Fight for the Delaware* (Monmouth Beach, New Jersey: Philip Freneau Press, 1979), 16. This French officer is also identified in McGuire, *The Philadelphia Campaign: Germantown and the Roads to Valley Forge*, 139.

15 Washington's order to Colonel Angell to reinforce Fort Mercer is dated October 16, 1777, and reads in part: "With the Regiment you command & what Baggage you think is absolutely necessary, you are immediately to proceed to Bristol [Pennsylvania] Cross the Delaware at that place & continue your Route to Red Bank, this March should be perform'd with the utmost Secrecy & under pretense of Covering [protecting] the Stores at Bristol until you arrive at the place as the Enemy might endeavor to Intercept you should your Route be known." W. W. Abbot, et.al., eds., *The Papers of George Washington*, Revolutionary War Series, XI: 524.

in front of the incomplete rebel works. Next an English-speaking officer approached the fort from von Donop's marshaled brigade, carrying a white flag and accompanied by a drummer beating the parley (from the French word *parler*, meaning to speak). The Royal officer demanded the unconditional surrender of the post, warning that von Donop's Hessians would give no quarter if the rebels persisted in defense. In response to the demand to surrender, Greene defiantly replied, "We shall not ask for nor expect any quarter, and mean to defend the fort to the last extremity."[16] Upon hearing Col. Greene's answer, von Donop immediately ordered his field artillery to open fire on the fort in preparation for an infantry assault. Sergeant Greenman recorded the sequence of events in his diary: "A flag came to Col. Green threatening to put the Garrison to death if he did not surrender immediately, Col. Green answered with disdain, that he would defend it 'till the last drop of his Blood—as soon as the Flag had returned they opened 7 field pieces and 2 Howitzers on the fort and played very smartly. . . ."[17]

Greene was uneasy about the morale of his troops in the face of overwhelming odds. To rally his men, he mounted the ramparts of the fort during the artillery barrage and walked calmly back and forth in front of his troops, as if he was inspecting his works. At another point in the cannonade, Greene coolly stood on top of the rampart and looked out at the Hessians with a glass (telescope). After observing the enemy, he jumped down from the wall and instructed his troops "to fire low men, they have a broad belt just above their hips—aim at that."[18]

The officers defending Fort Mercer—Greene, Ward, Thayer, Humphrey, and Shaw—were accustomed to overwhelming odds and hardened to privation and danger from their shared experience on the Arnold Expedition. Von Donop's blustering threats did not frighten men such as Samuel Ward, a veteran of the harrowing march to Canada. He had written home shortly after crossing the St. Lawrence River in November 1775:

> [W]e have gone up one of the most rapid rivers in the world where the water was so shoal that, moderately speaking, we have waded 100 miles. We were thirty days in a

16 John W. Jackson, *The Pennsylvania Navy 1775-1781: The Defense of the Delaware* (New Brunswick, New Jersey: Rutgers University Press, 1974), 178.

17 Bray and Bushnell, eds., *Military Journal of Jeremiah Greenman*, 82.

18 Jackson, *The Pennsylvania Navy*, 177.

> wilderness that none but savages ever attempted to pass. We marched 100 miles upon short, three days' provisions, waded over three rapid rivers, marched through snow and ice barefoot, and passed over the St. Lawrence where it was guarded by the enemy's frigates. . . . [W]e have a winter's campaign before us; but I trust we shall have the glory of taking Quebec![19]

Greene also had his men hang out their wash on the parapets of the fort prior to von Donop's arrival to give the Hessians the illusion that they had been caught by surprise. However, Greene, Ward, Thayer, and the others were indeed ready as the Hessians rushed the fort from three sides, with sappers and miners (military engineers, responsible for trenches and tunnels, respectively) leading each column. They easily breeched the post's low perimeter walls, which were undefended. Believing the insurgents to have scattered, the Germans waved their hats in the air, shouting of victory.

To encourage this premature confidence, Green had ordered his men to conceal themselves behind the fort's inner ramparts and to hold their fire until his command. When the Germans drew close, Greene yelled the order to open fire. A moment later the Hessian ranks were torn apart by a deadly volley of American musket fire and artillery grapeshot (small metal balls packed tightly into a canvas bag). The startled Germans reeled back in confusion, leaving many dead and wounded behind. They regrouped and charged again and again, only to face murderous volleys from the rebel gunners. At one point, von Donop personally led his men forward, but they had no ladders to scale the fort's inner walls.

The gruesome carnage went on for 45 minutes, at which point the few Hessian officers still standing ordered a retreat. Greene ordered his men to hold their positions to see whether the Hessians would renew their assault. When hours passed and nothing was heard outside the fort but the moans of the wounded Germans, Greene instructed Maj. Thayer to take a detachment to bring the injured into the fort. (Thayer had been the ringleader of the officers' plot to escape from the top floor of the seminary during their imprisonment at Quebec.) It was dark, so Thayer used a lantern to search among the German dead and wounded. He was looking for Col. von Donop, who had been seen in the thick of the fighting, but found no sign of him. Suddenly, from out of the darkness, two unarmed Hessian soldiers approached. Using gestures and

19 John Ward, *A Memoir of Lieut.-Colonel Samuel Ward* (New York: Privately Published, 1875), 8.

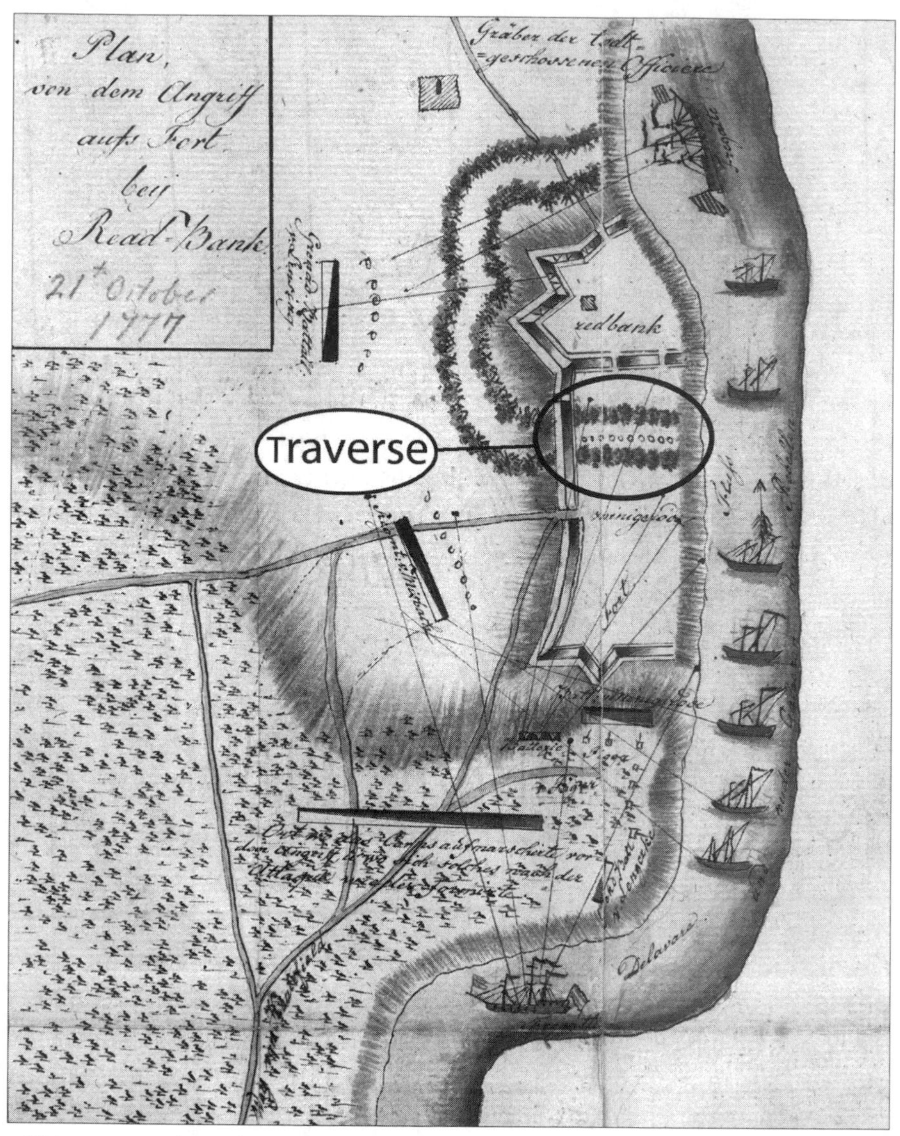

This map was drawn by Capt. Johann Ewald, a Hessian officer who participated in the ill-fated attack on Fort Mercer. His map shows the traverse constructed by the Americans which was the key to their successful defense of the fort. Despite its accurate details, Ewald shows the incorrect date of the Hessian attack. *Captain Johann Ewald Diary, Volume 1, Joseph P. Tustin Papers, Special Collections, Harvey A. Andruss Library, Bloomsburg University of Pennsylvania*

Remnants of the traverse constructed at Fort Mercer (Fort Red Bank), New Jersey. The traverse separated the large abandoned southern facing section of the fort (closest to the camera) from the heavily fortified northern portion occupied by Col. Christopher Greene and his garrison. Greene's strategy of concentrating his firepower was instrumental in defeating the Hessian attack on the fort. *Author's Collection*

repeating the words "Von Donop," the Germans were able to convey the message to Thayer that their commanding officer was nearby. Suspecting a trick, Thayer gathered a few of his soldiers before he followed the two Hessians. They led the Americans to their commander, who was propped up against a tree, badly wounded. Shining his lantern on the wounded officer, Thayer beheld a tall, blond, handsome man—one who had a notorious reputation for cruelty. In broken English, the 37-year-old von Donop asked the American standing over him whether he was an American officer, to which Thayer answered yes. Then von Donop, formal even in defeat, asked Thayer his rank, to which the American replied that he was a major. Satisfied with the response, the princely von Donop surrendered his sword to Simeon Thayer, the Rhode Island wigmaker-turned-soldier.

Thayer had von Donop gently placed in a blanket and carried into the fort, where he was tended by American surgeons. However, his wounds proved fatal and he died three days later. Greenman recorded von Donop's dying words, which became famous: "F. [Friday] 31[November 31, 1777] this day buried the

Hassan [Hessian] Colo. [von Donop] who said previous to his death I fall a Victim to my own ambition & to the avarice of my prince; but full of thankfulness for the good treatment I have received from my generous Enemy, he was buried with the Honors of War."[20]

Protected by the walls of the fort, the Americans suffered few casualties during the Hessian attack. One of the injured was Capt. Shaw, a veteran of the Arnold Expedition. He was shot through the neck during the fighting and died from his wound.

Greene gave Maj. Ward the honor of writing a dispatch to Gen. Washington to report the American victory. After describing how "Four Battalions of Germans . . . commanded by the Baron Donop" arrived in front of the fort, Ward related the details of the fighting:

> They began a Brisk Cannonade, and soon after advanced in two Columns to the Attack. They Passed the Abattis [entire cut trees, the branches of which are turned toward the enemy], gained the ditch & some few got over the Pickets [sharp stakes protruding from the ground], but the fire was so heavy that they soon were drove out again with considerable loss, and retreated precipitately towards Haddonfield [a New Jersey town near Fort Mercer].[21]

Congress voted Greene an elegant sword in appreciation for his courageous leadership in successfully defending Fort Mercer.[22]

Things were not going as well for the Americans across the river at Fort Mifflin. Lieutenant Colonel Samuel Smith was in command of the post with 400 men.[23] Smith, who was only 25 years old and educated for business, was

20 Bray and Bushnell, eds., *Military Journal of Jeremiah Greenman*, 83. The total number of Hessian casualties in the attack on Fort Mercer was probably 153 dead and 200 wounded. American losses were 14 killed, 23 wounded, and one captured.

21 Major Samuel Ward, Jr., to George Washington, dated "Red Bank 23d Octobr 1777," in W. W. Abbot, et al., eds., *The Papers of George Washington*, Revolutionary War Series, XI: 590-591.

22 Heitman, *Historical Register of Officers of the Continental Army*, 260.

23 Lieutenant Colonel Samuel Smith (1752-1839) was personally selected by General Washington to command at Ft. Mifflin—with good reason. His service record was impressive and worthy of note. Smith was in Europe when the war started. Upon returning home, he was appointed captain of the 6th company of Col. William Smallwood's famed Maryland regiment, which fought heroically at the Battle of Long Island (August 27, 1776), losing one-third of its men. Smith subsequently served with his regiment at the Battles of Harlem Heights (September 16, 1776) and White Plains (October 28, 1776) and in the retreat of the American army across

holding out against a host of experienced British officers and troops, including Capt. Montresor, the British engineer who had designed the fort in 1771 and knew its layout and weaknesses.[24] Acting under Gen. Howe's orders, Montresor surrounded the island fort with gun batteries and floating artillery platforms that pounded away at the American outpost around the clock. Smith stubbornly fought back with his few working cannon and refused to surrender. Following the failed Hessian attack on Fort Mercer, some Rhode Island troops stationed there volunteered to cross the river to reinforce Fort Mifflin. They were led by Maj. Thayer. According to Sgt. Greenman, the Rhode Islanders arrived at Fort Mifflin on November 12, at which time Maj. Thayer assumed command of the post.

> Col. Smith was wounded and went out of the fort with the old Garrison, being relieved by Major Thayer with some of our men, the Enemy now began to doubt the promises of their Engineer Montresor who had constructed the Fort & had boasted at the beginning that he would reduce it in few days.[25]

The beleaguered little fort took a terrible beating, yet Thayer and his Rhode Islanders held out for three more days. But the British were desperate to open the channel and get their ships to Philadelphia, so on November 15 they increased their artillery barrage, aiming at what had become mere mounds of mud and heaps of splintered debris. Montresor described the final attack: "As

---

New Jersey in late 1776. He was promoted to major in late 1776 and lieutenant colonel in early 1777, at which rank he fought at the Battle of the Brandywine (September 11, 1777). General Washington then asked Smith to take command of Fort Mifflin, which he successfully defended from September 26 to November 11, when he was severely wounded, evacuated, and replaced by Maj. Simeon Thayer. Although still not entirely recovered from his wounds, Smith rejoined the army at Valley Forge and participated in the Battle of Monmouth. Illness forced him to resign from active duty after the Battle of Monmouth, but he continued to serve as colonel and commander of the Baltimore militia until the end of the war. Following the war, Smith served several terms as a representative to Congress, U. S. senator, and mayor of Baltimore. He returned to active service during the War of 1812 and was put in charge of Baltimore's defenses. Smith proudly watched Fort McHenry, in Baltimore harbor, defiantly hold off a British bombardment with the same stubbornness he had shown 35 years earlier at Fort Mifflin.

24 In 1771, Montresor was selected by Pennsylvania Governor John Penn to prepare plans for fortifying the waterborne approaches to Philadelphia. Montresor chose Mud Island because it offered protection to both the Schuylkill and Delaware Rivers; work began on the fort in 1772. When the rebels occupied it, they named it Fort Mifflin.

25 Bray and Bushnell, eds., *Military Journal of Jeremiah Greenman*, 84.

A manuscript map showing the location of Fort Mifflin in the Delaware River. Fort Mifflin has been circled on the map. This attractive manuscript map is signed: "Drawn by T. Wheeler, ensn., 40th regt." Ensign Thomas Wheeler of the 40th Regiment was apparently attached to the British Engineers as a draughtsman. *Library of Congress*

soon as the Fog was dispelled which was about 7 o'clock [in the morning] the four Batteries under my direction opened upon the rebel Fort. . . ."[26] The British had a total of 350 cannon aimed at Fort Mifflin from their shore batteries and warships, firing into the fort at a rate of 1,000 shots every 20 minutes. The attack was fierce, but Thayer refused to surrender and defiantly fought back with his single working cannon. During the course of the day's fighting, British warships sailed so close to the fort that they were lobbing cannon balls and grapeshot into it at point-blank range while marines in the rigging were throwing hand grenades into the post.

By nightfall the British had leveled the fort and Thayer's defenders had suffered terrible casualties. Realizing that further defense was hopeless, Thayer ordered everyone to evacuate the fort at midnight. They were taken away by boats sent from Fort Mercer. Major Thayer was the last man to leave Fort Mifflin, and he departed with the American flag still flying. Fort Mifflin never surrendered, and Thayer's stubborn defense of the post was one of the most heroic acts of the American Revolution. Such was the mettle of the stalwart men who had marched with Arnold to Quebec.

With the British finally settled in at Philadelphia for the winter, Washington decided that he would move his army into winter quarters and renew the conflict in the spring. After considering several locations, he decided to winter his army at Valley Forge, Pennsylvania, which lay in a strong defensive position 18 miles northwest of Philadelphia. Greene, Dearborn, Burr, Bigelow, and Greenman were among the Arnold Expedition veterans who wintered at Valley Forge. Morgan's Rifle Corps also spent the winter there. The latter had rushed south following the Saratoga Campaign and rejoined Washington's main army in early November.[27] Colonel Morgan, however, did not spend the entire winter with his troops. He was granted a furlough sometime in early January to leave for Virginia and did not return until late April or early May.

The winter of 1777-1778 at Valley Forge was not particularly cold, and while food was often rationed because of supply problems there is no evidence that anyone starved to death. One wonders how the veterans of the Arnold Expedition at Valley Forge reacted when they heard soldiers complaining about

26 G. D. Scull, ed., "Journals of Capt. John Montresor," in *Collections of the New York Historical Society*, 1882, 466.

27 Don Higginbotham, *Daniel Morgan, Revolutionary Rifleman* (Chapel Hill: The University of North Carolina Press, 1961), 79.

short rations and miserable living conditions. At least they had huts and firewood and could count on some food. A few winters earlier the Arnold Expedition men had marched and slept in the woods in the midst of the Canadian winter and were reduced to eating dogs, soap, and shoe leather. Colonel Greene must have remembered how close his men had come to starving to death. Greene's desperation is best described by an entry in Dr. Senter's journal dated October 24, 1775. Senter came across Greene's division camped in the wilderness along the swollen banks of the Dead River. "[U]pon enquiry I found them almost destitute of any eatable whatever, except a few candles, which were used for supper, and breakfast the next morning, by boiling them in water gruel."[28]

There are several stories about Col. Bigelow's experiences during the Valley Forge encampment. One of his biographers tells a story about how General Washington greeted Bigelow when he arrived at the encampment. The commander-in-chief took Bigelow by the hand and addressed the officers present:

> This gentleman is Colonel Bigelow and the 15th regiment of the Massachusetts line under his command. This gentleman . . . marched the first company of minutemen from Worcester, at the alarm from Lexington. He shared largely in the sufferings of the Campaign against Quebec, and was taken prisoner there. After his exchange, he raised a regiment in his own neighborhood, and joining the northern army under Gates, participated in the struggle with Burgoyne, and shares largely in the honor of that victory.[29]

In another of the stories, Colonel Bigelow was visited one night at Valley Forge by his officers, who griped about the wretched living conditions in the winter encampment. Bigelow replied, "Gentlemen, I have heard all the remarks of discontentment offered here this evening, but as for me, I have long since come to the conclusion to stand by the American cause, come what will. . . . I expect to suffer with cold and with fatigue and, if need be, I expect to lay down my life for the liberty of these colonies."[30]

28 Senter, *Journal of Isaac Senter*, 26.

29 McAuliffe, "Timothy Bigelow," n.p.

30 *Ibid.*

On April 6, 1778, a British secret agent reported on the situation at Valley Forge: "No Reinforcements Come to Gen Washington's Camp though some on their Way from the Southward. One Regt in Particular of Blacks from Providence [Rhode Island] (Commanded by a Col Green [Greene] who Defended Red Bank Last fall) are on their Way and Expected any Day."[31] This April 1778 spy report introduces Col. Christopher Greene's so-called Black Regiment. By 1778, the American Revolution was in its third year, and it had become increasingly difficult to recruit men for the Continental Army. There were already numerous free blacks serving in the ranks in various regiments. But at Valley Forge, a group of Rhode Island officers, including Col. Christopher Greene, proposed the radical idea of enlisting slaves to fill the ranks of their state's depleted regiments.[32] Greene and other advocates of the scheme proposed the purchase of any slave willing to join the army and fight for the patriot cause.

Arming slaves was a controversial proposal, especially in the southern colonies, and Gen. Washington was too experienced a politician to give his opinion of the idea. On the other hand, he did not interfere with the project, even when Col. Greene announced that he was returning home to lobby the Rhode Island Assembly to enact a law to permit the enlistment of slaves. The exigencies of war got the plan approved on February 22, 1778, by the Rhode Island Assembly, which resolved that "every able-bodied Negro, mulatto or Indian man slave in this State may enlist . . . to serve during the continuance of the war with Great Britain; that every slave so enlisting shall, upon passing muster before Colonel Christopher Greene, be immediately discharged from

31 Manuscript letter, unsigned, Clinton Papers, "Codes Box," Clements Library, Ann Arbor, Michigan.

32 The earliest known reference to the idea of organizing a regiment of black troops in Rhode Island is a January 2, 1778, letter written to Washington by Gen. James Mitchell Varnum, the senior Rhode Island officer wintering at Valley Forge: "The Two Battalions; from the State of Rhode Island being small, & these being a Necessity of the State's furnishing an additional Number to make up their Proportion in the continental Army; The Field Officers have represented to me the Propriety of making one temporary Battalion from the two, so that one entire Core [sic] of Officers may repair to Rhode Island, in order to receive & prepare the Recruits for the Field. It is imagined that a Battalion of Negroes can be easily raised there. Should that Measure by adopted, or recruits obtained upon any other Principle [arming slaves], the Service will be advanced. The Field Officers who go upon this Command are Colo. Greene [Christopher Greene] Lt. Colo. Olney [Jeremiah Olney] and Major Ward [Samuel Ward, Jr.]: Seven Captains, Twelve Lieuts, six Ensigns, one Pay Master, one Surgeon & Mate, One Adjutant & one Chaplin." W. W. Abbot, et al., eds., *The Papers of George Washington*, Revolutionary War Series, XIII: 125.

the service of his master or mistress and be absolutely Free, as though he had never been encumbered with any kind of servitude or slavery."[33]

Colonel Greene immediately started recruiting slaves for the army. He was assisted by Maj. Samuel Ward Jr., who joined him in Rhode Island to help supervise the effort. Another Arnold Expedition veteran, Sgt. Jeremiah Greenman, also returned to Rhode Island to help train the new recruits. Greenman's journal entry for April 14, 1778, mentions that he "turned out our black troops."[34]

The new recruits reached Valley Forge on May 29, 1778.[35] Just prior to their arrival there was a reshuffling of men between the two undermanned Rhode Island regiments (the 1st and 2nd Rhode Island) wintering at Valley Forge. All the whites in the 1st Rhode Island were transferred to the 2nd Rhode Island, and the free blacks in the 2nd were moved to the 1st. Then the newly arrived black soldiers were put into the 1st Rhode Island to give the regiment a large black presence.[36] Although it is still frequently referred to as the Black Regiment, the 1st Rhode Island was actually a mixed outfit of about 350 men that included between 225 and 250 ex-slaves and free blacks.[37] Colonel Greene commanded the reorganized 1st Rhode Island.

33 "The Attempt of Rhode Island To Raise a Regiment of Slaves For Service in the War of the Revolution—The so-called Rhode Island Black Regiment of 1778," United States War Department, Office of the Chief of Staff, report prepared by the Historical Section, Army War College, September 3, 1924. A copy of the report is in the Archives Branch, U.S. Army Military History Institute, Carlisle, Pennsylvania.

34 Bray and Bushnell, *Military Journal of Jeremiah Greenman*, 114.

35 *Ibid.*, 119.

36 E-mail to the author from Joseph Lee Boyle. The information about the reshuffling of men between the 1st and 2nd Rhode Island regiments at Valley Forge during May 1778 is based on research by Mr. Boyle, who was the historian at Valley Forge National Historical Park.

37 Sidney Kaplan, *The Black Presence in the Era of the American Revolution* (New York: The New York Graphic Society, Ltd., in association with the Smithsonian Institution Press, 1973), 55, is an example of the use of the term Black regiment. While the total number of men in the 1st Rhode Island Regiment varied during its existence, 350 officers and enlisted men is a useful generalization. This number seems accurate based upon the *Return of the Continental Army Under the Command of His Excellency George Washington*, dated November 1, 1778. The *Return* lists the 1st Rhode Island under the command of Christopher Greene with "153 officers and rank & file [enlisted men] fit for duty; 197 rank & file sick, on furlough, etc;" three men who died in October and three men who deserted, for a total of 356. Lesser, *The Sinews of Independence*, 88. For the number of African-Americans serving in the 1st Rhode Island Regiment, see Charles Patrick Neimeyer, *America Goes to War: A Social History of the Continental Army* (New York: New York University Press, 1996), 75.

This regiment saw action in several engagements following the Valley Forge encampment. Then, in early 1781, Greene's regiment was given the assignment of guarding the dangerous neutral ground in Westchester County, New York. This contested "no-man's-land" lay between Manhattan Island, occupied by the British, and the Hudson River Highlands, held by the Americans. Col. Greene's regimental headquarters was in the Davenport House (which still stands) located on a strategic hilltop near the northern bank of the Croton River. The surrounding area was open farmland, giving Greene's detachment a broad view of the country surrounding the house.

The colonel had 28 battle-hardened men from his regiment protecting his headquarters, many of whom were ex-slaves and free blacks. During the night of May 14, 1781, about 300 members of a tough Loyalist mounted unit called DeLancey's Refugees stealthily crossed the Croton River at a remote ford and managed to surprise Greene's headquarters. They were attacking Greene in retaliation for a raid he had made on their headquarters. Although taken by surprise and heavily outnumbered, Greene and his bodyguards fought back. With most of his men dead or wounded, Greene retreated into the Davenport House and continued to fight. Even when cornered inside the building, he refused to surrender, so was brutally stabbed with bayonets and swords by the ruthless Refugees. Then they put the celebrated rebel colonel on a horse and rode him three-quarters of a mile before dumping him in the woods to bleed to death.[38]

Rivington's Royal Gazette boasted about the successful attack in its May 26, 1781, edition. It announced that the intrepid Lt. Col. James DeLancey, with about 100 cavalry and 200 foot soldiers marched from Morrisania (a section of

38 The most reliable account of Greene's brutal death is a letter written on the day of his death to his son, Job Greene, by Thomas Hughes, who was the paymaster of the 1st Rhode Island Regiment: "It is with pain I write you a subject that is so nearly and closely connected to you as a parent. I must my dear friend inform you of the unhappy fate that befell your father this morning. The enemy made an attack on the Lines (which was a complete surprise), and he fell, a sacrifice to the cruel hand of tyranny, in defending himself against the strokes struck by Light Horsemen; he had his right wrist almost cut off in two places, his left in one; a severe cut in the left shoulder, a sword run through his body, a bayonet into his right side, and another through his body, his head cut to pieces in several places, his back and body cut and hacked in such a manner as gives me pain to inform you. He was carried about three-quarters of a mile from his quarters, where they left him to die or rather, through loss of blood and not strength to go forward, finished his days in the woods, and as they went by the houses informed the inhabitants, should there be any inquiry after the Colonel, that they had left him dead in the edge of the woods. This cruel and barbarous treatment was perpetrated by Delancey's Corps himself [Col. DeLancey, Jr.] at the head."

The Davenport House. In 1781, Col. Christopher Greene's 1st Rhode Island Regiment was ordered to protect northern Westchester County, New York. Greene made his headquarters at the Davenport House, located on high ground within view of the strategic Pines Bridge that spanned the Croton River. The detachment guarding the house was attacked by Loyalists on May 14, 1781. Greene retreated inside the house, where he was brutally assaulted when he refused to surrender. He died soon after from his multiple wounds. *Author's Collection*

modern Bronx, New York), penetrated about 32 miles into the country, and "commenced to attack the Rebel Colonel Greene with a number of Continental troops. The colonel was mortally wounded, and Major [Ebenezer] Flagg [Greene's second-in-command], with twelve privates, killed; one doctor, with twelve or thirteen men, were taken prisoners." DeLancey's corps stopped that night at the Odell Inn, about three miles below Tarrytown, New York, where they held a "high carnival" to celebrate their victory.[39]

39 "Colonel Christopher Greene," *The Magazine of History*, vol. XXIII, July, 1916, No. 1, 146-147. Washington informed Congress about DeLancey's raid and the death of Col. Greene in a May 17, 1781, report: "I am sorry to inform your Excellency [the president of Congress] that a part of our advanced troops were surprised on Monday Morning near Croton River, by about sixty Horse and two hundred foot under the command of Colonel DeLancey. Colo. Greene who commanded our party was mortally wounded in his quarters. The enemy attempted to carry him off, but he died upon the Road. Major Flagg was killed. The loss of these

Greene had declared several years earlier in his Quebec prison cell that he would never be captured again, and he stayed true to his word. He preferred to die fighting than surrender again to the British. When his body was found it was discovered that his left arm was cut off, his right cut to the bone in two wide gashes, his left shoulder severely mutilated, his stomach pierced by a sword, his right side shockingly lacerated by a bayonet, and his head mangled in several places.[40] Greene and the men who died with him were buried in Crompond, New York (modern Yorktown Heights). A monument marks their gravesite.

Greene was 44 when he was brutally killed by DeLancey's men. He left behind a wife, three sons, and four daughters. The sword that Congress voted Greene in 1777 for his gallant defense of Fort Mercer was posthumously presented to his oldest son, Job Greene, in 1786, with a letter from Gen. Henry Knox. The letter reads in part: "The circumstances of the war prevented obtaining and delivery of the sword previous to your father's being killed at Croton River, in 1780. On that catastrophe, his country mourned the sacrifice of a patriot and a soldier, and mingled its tears with those of his family."[41] Greene's regiment continued to serve until the end of the war, then was disbanded at Saratoga, New York, on June 13, 1783.[42]

Returning to 1778 and the Valley Forge encampment: France entered the war on the side of the Americans that year, forcing the British to redeploy their troops and ships to protect their valuable islands in the Caribbean against the French army and navy. General Howe resigned and was replaced by Gen. Sir Henry Clinton. With orders from London to send part of his army to defend British territory in the Caribbean, Clinton lacked enough troops to hold both New York City and Philadelphia. He abandoned Philadelphia in June 1778, sending Loyalists wishing to leave the city and his least reliable troops (many of

---

two Officers is to be regretted, especially the former, who had upon several occasions distinguished himself, particularly in the defence [sic] of the post of Red Bank [Fort Mercer] in 1777, when he defeated Count Donop. I enclose a Return of our loss upon the late occasion." John C. Fitzpatrick, ed., *The Writings of George Washington*, 39 vols. (Washington, D.C.: Government Printing Office, 1931-1944), XXII: 98. James DeLancey, a former sheriff of Westchester County, New York, commanded a regiment of light horse serving in his uncle Oliver DeLancey's Loyalist brigade.

40 Stone, ed., *The Invasion of Canada in 1775*, 55.

41 *Ibid.*, 56.

42 Lorenzo J. Greene, "Some Observations on the Black Regiment of Rhode Island in the American Revolution," *Journal of Negro History*, vol. 37, number 2, April 1952, 171.

them dispirited Hessians) to New York by ship. Clinton took his best regiments cross-country through New Jersey, looking for a decisive battle with Washington's army before he reached New York.

Washington committed militia and some Continentals, including Morgan's Rifle Corps, to harass Clinton's column as it crossed New Jersey. He later dispatched 5,000 men under the command of Gen. Charles Lee to attack the rear of Clinton's long column of troops and wagons as they were pulling out of the village of Monmouth Courthouse, New Jersey, on the morning of June 28, 1778. At the same time, Washington advanced with the rest of his army to provide support for Lee if it became necessary.

With no definitive news from Lee, Washington sent his aide Lt. Col. Robert Hanson Harrison to reconnoiter. Harrison rode forward and found Lee's force retreating in confusion. When Harrison came upon Col. Matthias Ogden, he asked him why Lee's troops were retreating, to which the Arnold Expedition veteran gave his famous reply, "By God! they are flying from a shadow."[43]

Washington managed to stop the retreat and organized a strong defensive line supported by artillery. The climax of the day-long battle was an American infantry charge in the late afternoon against a British battalion that was trying to outflank the rebel lines. Led by Col. Joseph Cilley, 350 picked troops marched across fields into the teeth of an equal number of British troops from the famed 42nd Royal Highland Regiment. Colonel Henry Dearborn was Cilley's second-in-command in what was one of the most dramatic moments in the American Revolution. Dearborn described the climax of the assault:

> [T]hey began a heavy fire upon us. We were Descending toward them in Open field, with Shoulder'd arms until we have got within 4 Rods of them when our men Dress'd very Cooly & we then gave them a very heavy fire from the whole Battalion. They had two Pieces of artillery across a small Run which Play'd with grape very briskly upon us but when they found we were determined to Push upon them they retreated....We Pursued until we got Possession of the field of Battle, where we found 300 Dead & a Considerable number of wounded. . . .[44]

43 *The Lee Papers*, 4 vols. (New York: New York Historical Society, 1871-74), III: 73.

44 Brown and Peckham, eds., *Revolutionary War Journals of Henry Dearborn*, 128.

The British fell back under the pressure of the heroic American charge. Watching the enemy retreat, Col. Cilley shouted, "Come, my boys, reload your pieces, and we will give them a send-off."[45]

Besides Dearborn, another Arnold Expedition veteran participated in Cilley's celebrated infantry charge at the Battle of Monmouth. He was Capt. Nathaniel Hutchins, a company commander in Cilley's 1st New Hampshire Regiment. Hutchins had been a lieutenant in Dearborn's company on the Arnold Expedition and was captured with the others during Montgomery's failed attack on Quebec. Other Arnold Expedition men who participated in the Monmouth campaign were Timothy Bigelow, Aaron Burr, Christian Febiger, Daniel Morgan, Simeon Thayer (who was wounded at the battle, losing an eye), and Eleazer Oswald, who particularly distinguished himself during the day-long fighting.

Oswald was a volunteer on the Arnold Expedition, serving as Arnold's aide-de-camp. He fought at Quebec, where he was taken prisoner and paroled; when exchanged, he was appointed to the Continental artillery. At the Battle of Monmouth, his detachment, consisting of four pieces of field artillery, was in the thick of the morning fighting. As the senior artillery officer with Lee, Oswald took charge of additional cannon during the morning, at times commanding up to ten guns. His artillery unit retreated with the others, "having suffered much in men and horses killed and by his men falling at their guns overcome by the heat."[46] Oswald handled his field artillery brilliantly during the retreat of Lee's troops, repeatedly unlimbering and firing on the enemy to slow their advance. Lieutenant Colonel Alexander Hamilton (later the first Secretary of the Treasury), who was present, said, "I was Spectator to Lt. Col. Oswald's behavior, who kept up a gallant fire from some pieces commanded by him."[47] Gen. Lee also praised Oswald's conduct at Monmouth in a letter to the *Trenton Gazette* following the battle: "I confess it is difficult to refrain from paying compliments to the artillery, from Gen. Knox, and Col. Oswald, down to the

45 The story of Cilley's charge at Monmouth is from Garry Wheeler Stone, Daniel M. Sivilich, and Mark Edward Lender, "A Deadly Minuet: The Advance of the New England Picked Men Against the Royal Highlanders at the Battle of Monmouth, 28 June 1778," in *The Brigade Dispatch, Journal of the Brigade of the American Revolution*, Summer 1996, 11-16.

46 William Stryker, *The Battle of Monmouth* (Princeton: Princeton University Press, 1927), 156.

47 *The Lee Papers*, II: 470.

very drivers [teamsters]."[48] Additional praise came from General Knox, who called Oswald "one of the best officers in the army."[49]

Oswald's appointment to the artillery corps was a result of his friendship with Capt. John Lamb, who arrived in Quebec with Montgomery. Lamb and Oswald fought side by side in the Sault-au-Matelot and were imprisoned together following their capture. Upon his return to the army in 1777, Lamb was promoted to colonel and given command of the newly organized 2nd Continental Artillery. He arranged for his friend Oswald to be promoted to lieutenant colonel and named his second-in-command. General Arnold was also helpful in getting Oswald promoted, and Lamb reciprocated by appointing Samuel Mansfield (the brother of Arnold's deceased wife) as a captain in his new regiment.[50]

The Battle of Monmouth was the high point of Oswald's military career. He resigned from the army soon after the battle when Washington refused to promote him. This decision was personal, based on Oswald's friendship with Gen. Lee, who was court-martialed for his conduct at Monmouth. Washington and his supporters blamed Lee for the failure of the Continental Army to win a clear-cut victory at Monmouth. Oswald was one of the few officers who defended Lee at his court martial. At one point during the proceedings, Gen. Lee (who was handling his own defense) asked Oswald, "Through the whole process of the day, and upon all occasions, was I not perfectly composed and tranquil and fully possessed of myself?"

Oswald's reply damaged his standing with Washington's powerful clique: "You appeared calm and intrepid, and seemed fully to be possessed of yourself."

Then Lee asked, "When the troops retreated, was I not one of the last that remained on the field?"

Oswald probably ruined his army career when he answered, "[Y]ou were."[51]

48 Leake, *Life of John Lamb*, 203.

49 *Ibid.*, 202.

50 *Ibid.*, 150.

51 *The Lee Papers*, III: 137, 139.

Denied a promotion, Oswald resigned and returned to the printing business. He remained loyal to his friend Lee, and was one of the two men present when Lee died in 1782.[52] Oswald was also Lee's executor and heir.

Following the Battle of Monmouth, the rest of 1778 was relatively quiet. Washington wintered that year at Middlebrook, New Jersey, where he organized a campaign against hostile Indians in which several Arnold Expedition veterans participated. Washington was alarmed by successful attacks against frontier settlements, and described the objective of the expedition in a March 6, 1779, letter to Gen. Horatio Gates: "The objects of this expedition will be effectually to chastise and intimidate the hostile nations, to countenance and encourage the friendly ones, and to relieve our frontiers from the depredations to which they would otherwise by exposed."[53]

Washington appointed Gen. John Sullivan, a pre-war lawyer from New Hampshire, to command the campaign, which duly became known as the Sullivan Expedition. This American military campaign was the only other in the Revolutionary War, besides Arnold's 1775 march to Quebec, to be called an "expedition." However, the two campaigns were similar in name only. It was evident from the methodical planning that went into the Sullivan Expedition that Washington had matured as a military leader since the hastily planned Arnold Expedition. Also, unlike the Arnold Expedition, whose goal was striking deep into enemy territory and holding a fortress city, the Sullivan Expedition was a rapid slash-and-burn campaign with the limited objective of destroying Indian villages and farms before returning to the main army. A number of Arnold Expedition veterans were on the Sullivan Expedition, including Peter Bryan Bruin, who served as Sullivan's aide-de-camp.

On August 26, 1779, Sullivan's force cautiously moved up the Chemung River, with the Indians fleeing before them. The Indians finally made a stand on August 29 on the left bank of the Chemung, about six miles southwest of the present-day city of Elmira, New York, and close to the Indian village of Newtown. Here the Indians and their British allies erected a long breastwork of logs that they artfully concealed in the forest. It was positioned alongside a trail that Sullivan's army would have to follow to reach Newtown. Hiding behind the

52 John Richard Alden, *General Charles Lee* (Baton Rouge: Louisiana State University Press, 1951), 298. The other person present when Lee died in a Philadelphia tavern on October 2 was his servant Guiseppe Minghini.

53 Fitzpatrick, ed., *Writings of Washington*, XIV: 199.

breastwork and silently waiting to ambush Sullivan's column were Capt. Walter N. Butler with two battalions of Loyalist Rangers, 200 Tory militia, a small detachment of the 8th British Regiment, and Chief Joseph Brant with about 500 Indians. The Americans, however, were advancing cautiously, with a detachment of picked men a mile in advance of the main column, with additional troops guarding the flanks against a surprise attack. The army's pack horses and artillery were in the center protected by the main column. Sullivan's van was commanded by Maj. James Parr with three companies of Morgan's riflemen.

The riflemen discovered the camouflaged breastwork. They warned the main column, which halted and formed a battle line. Artillery was deployed while troops under the command of Gen. Poor were sent through the woods to attack the enemy's rear. The maneuver forced the Indians to abandon their breastwork, but they struck back by trying to outflank a New Hampshire regiment. Arnold Expedition veteran Col. Henry Dearborn came to their rescue with his 3rd New Hampshire Regiment. A sharp fight followed until the Indians retreated under pressure from Dearborn's men. The Americans remained on the scene, destroying a nearby Indian village and crops before moving on to wreck additional Indian villages.

Lieutenant Thomas Boyd from the 1st Pennsylvania Regiment was another Arnold Expedition veteran with Sullivan. Boyd joined Morgan's rifle company as a sergeant at the start of the war, was captured during the attack on Quebec, was exchanged, returned to the army as a lieutenant in the 1st Pennsylvania, and later was assigned to the Sullivan Expedition. Gen. Sullivan sent the plucky Boyd on a reconnaissance mission to observe a big, hostile Indian town named Genesee Castle, New York.

Boyd and his party were ambushed by the Indians on September 13, 1779. In the fight that followed, the Indians killed twenty-two Americans and captured Boyd and another man. The two captives were taken to Little Beard's town, where they were tortured before being decapitated. Rifleman John Joseph Henry memorialized Boyd in his later narrative of the Arnold Expedition:

> Thomas Boyd, so often spoken of in the wilderness for his good humor, his activity, and the intensity of his sufferings, struggled gloriously for his life as a captain

[lieutenant], and died a dreadful death by the hands of the savages in 1779, in the expedition conducted by Gen. Sullivan against the Six nation Indians."[54]

By October 15, 1779, the Sullivan Expedition was back at Easton, Pennsylvania, while the Indians retreated to British-held Fort Niagara (near Niagara Falls, New York), which they used as a base to continue to attack American frontier settlements.

There was little military action in the northern colonies following the Sullivan Expedition. Washington wanted to retake New York City, but lacked sufficient troops and artillery to launch an attack against the heavily fortified city. Also, the British changed their strategy in 1779 by concentrating on retaking the southern states, which they perceived to be weakly defended. However, there was one military action in the north, along the Hudson River at Stony Point, which won additional fame and honor for several Arnold Expedition veterans.

Getting a wagon or livestock across a wide river such as the Hudson was no simple task in colonial America. Access to both shorelines via gently sloping solid ground was required at a place where the river was safe to cross on a flatboat. One such locale on the Hudson was called Kings Ferry. This strategic crossing lay about 12 miles south of West Point, where the Hudson was squeezed between two headlands called Verplanck's Point and Stony Point. Kings Ferry was held by the Americans until June 1779, when Gen. Sir Henry Clinton moved a large force upriver from Manhattan and captured the place. Clinton enlarged the American fortifications at Verplanck's Point and Stony Point. He stationed British troops at both sites before returning down the river.

54 *Henry, An Accurate and Interesting Account . . . In the Campaign Against Quebec*, 201. Henry added a gruesome footnote in his narrative describing the capture of Boyd which does not appear in Kenneth Roberts' *March to Quebec*. Henry said that when General Sullivan's army overran Little Beard's Town the men found a number of fresh scalps, stretched in the usual manner on small hoops and painted. The head of Boyd lay in one of the cabins, newly dissevered. His scalp was still moist and hooped and painted. Simpson [anther Arnold Expedition veteran with Sullivan] knew it by its long, brown, silky hair. The story gets more grisly and explicit as Henry quotes a letter from an officer who helped bury Lieutenant Boyd, which reads in part: "I spread a blanket on the ground beside him, we then turned the corpse over on it. I took the head of the deceased, and put it as near the neck as possible. I procured a needle and thread from one of the taylors [sic], and sewed the corpse up as well as I could. As to the head of Michael Parker [the other man captured by the Indians], it could not be found. All the flesh was cut out, from his shoulders downward and otherwise his body was most inhumanly mangled. We interred the corpses of both near the Genessee Castle . . . on the 14th day of September, 1779."

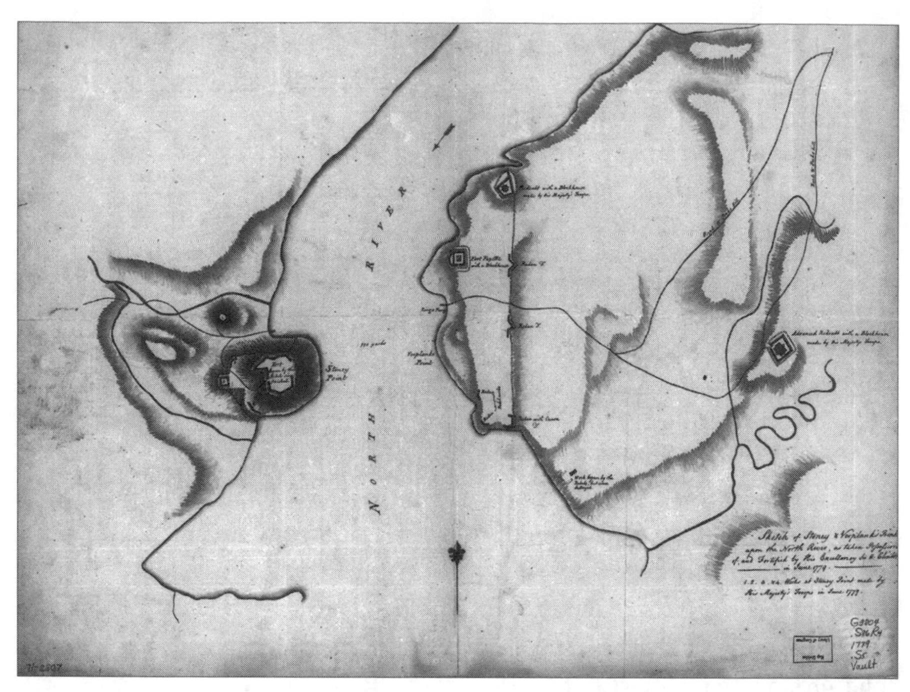

Manuscript map of Kings Ferry, New York. Kings Ferry was one of the important ferries on the lower Hudson River. General Washington planned the surprise American attack against Stony Point, which was on the western side of the crossing. The British army occupied the post when it was attacked by an American detachment led by Gen. Anthony Wayne. Arnold Expedition veteran Christian Febiger took command of the assault when Wayne fell wounded. *Library of Congress*

These two new British outposts gave Clinton control of the lower Hudson River and menaced the big American post at West Point.

General Washington received several reconnaissance reports concerning Stony Point that stated that the place was well defended but could be taken in a nighttime surprise attack. He decided to attack the fortress, which was defended by about 625 British troops under the command of Lt. Col. Henry Johnson. General Anthony Wayne (not called "Mad" Anthony Wayne until 1781), who was put in charge of the dangerous mission, promptly selected Col. Christian Febiger as his second-in-command. Another Arnold Expedition veteran, Col. Return Jonathan Meigs, was among the other experienced officers who were asked to participate in the dangerous mission. One thousand soldiers from a newly organized corps of light infantry were assigned to Wayne to carry out his assignment. This new corps was made up of some of the best soldiers from each regiment, who were given special training and put under the command of especially committed and courageous officers.

Wayne made his daring surprise attack on Stony Point on the night of July 16, 1779. The plan was to assault the post from two directions. The attack would start at midnight with Wayne, Febiger, and Meigs, leading 700 men, hitting the southern section of the British defenses. Another 300 men under the command of Col. Richard Butler were to attack the northern approach to the fort. Just as Montgomery had decreed at Quebec in 1775, every American at Stony Point prepared for the dark by pinning a white piece of paper to his hat to distinguish him from the enemy. According to Febiger, they approached Stony Point very "secretly, securing all the passes and preventing country people [the local civilian population] from going in [and warning the British]—and at dark were within one mile of the Fort where we lay till 12 o'clock at night," when they began to quietly move closer to start their assault.[55] To ensure surprise, Wayne ordered that his men attack with unloaded muskets; the Americans were going to use only bayonets and swords. Anyone disobeying this order was to be "instantly put to death by his proper officer."[56]

But the hopes of surprise were forlorn, as the sappers armed with axes were spotted by alert enemy pickets, who sounded the alarm. The light infantry responded by racing for the enemy lines amidst a torrent of British cannon balls, grapeshot, and musket fire. The fighting around the fort became a mêlée as the Americans rushed in, thrusting with their bayonets and swords and screaming "[T]he fort's our own!" Johnson and his men fought back tenaciously, but could not determine the direction of the main rebel attack. Wayne was wounded and Febiger, nicknamed the Old Quebecker from his days on the Arnold Expedition, assumed command from his fallen comrade. With Febiger in the lead, the bulk of the Americans attacked from the south. They overran the British gun emplacements, then turned the cannon around to fire on Johnson's men, who retreated to the hilltop that dominated the rocky peninsula. Outnumbered and surrounded, Johnson surrendered to Febiger some 25 harrowing minutes after the attack began.

55 Henry P. Johnston, *The Storming of Stony Point on the Hudson, Midnight, July 16, 1779* (New York: James T. White & Co, 1900), 187. Febiger married Elizabeth Carson, the daughter of a wealthy merchant, on August 14, 1777. They had one son whose name was Christian Carson Febiger. Colonel Febiger's grandson, John Carson Febiger (1821-1898), was a rear admiral in the U.S. Navy.

56 Ward, *The War of the Revolution*, II: 599.

Feeling lucky to be alive, Febiger wrote a letter to his wife Elizabeth soon after securing the fort:

> Stony Point, July 16, 1779.
>
> My Dear Girl:
>
> I have just borrowed pen, ink and paper to inform you that yesterday we march'd from Fort Montgomery [an American fort below West Point], and at 12 o'clock last night we stormed this Confounded place, and, with the loss of about fourteen killed and forty or fifty wounded, we carried it. I can give you no particulars as yet. A musquet [musket] ball scraped my nose. No other damage to "Old Denmark."
> God bless you.
> Febiger[57]

Febiger also wrote to his friend from the Arnold Expedition, Col.William Heth, describing the action and boasting that the British commander personally surrendered to him: "[M]y regiment which composed the front of the right column was in the works, and the Commandant, Colo. Johnson, surrendered to me."[58] Febiger helped spread the word of the American victory at Stony Point, including in a report to Gov. Thomas Jefferson of Virginia: "I have the happiness to say that every officer and soldier behaved with a fortitude and bravery peculiar to men who are determined to be free, and overcame every danger and difficulty without confusion or delay, far surpassing any enterprise in which I have had an active part."[59]

The Americans held Stony Point for only three days before retreating back to their own lines. The British cautiously returned, but soon abandoned the place as too exposed to the enemy. The heroic American assault helped boost the *esprit de corps* of the army and inspired the civilian population.

Washington's army remained relatively inactive for the balance of 1779 and went into winter quarters at Jockey Hollow, a farming region near Morristown, New Jersey. Record low temperatures and heavy snowstorms continued throughout the season. In fact, the winter of 1779-1780 is believed to be the

57 Johnston, *The Storming of Stony Point*, 186.

58 *Ibid.*, 189.

59 *Ibid.*, 188.

coldest winter in America during the 18th century. An anecdote which illustrates the severity of the weather is one that the Baron De Kalb wrote from Morristown: "It is so cold that the ink freezes on my pen, while I am sitting close to the fire."[60]

Much more serious than freezing ink was the fact that the army was starving because the deep snow and ice made it difficult to deliver provisions to the rural American encampment. The food shortage continued into the spring, aggravated by the country's exhausted credit abroad, which in turn was intensified by the depreciation of the continental dollar (Congress had printed mountains of paper money to finance the war). The crisis came when two half-starved Connecticut regiments at Jockey Hollow paraded (assembled) without their officers on May 25, 1780. James Thacher, a surgeon with the army, believed that the dissident troops had "the spirit of mutiny" and intended to march into the countryside to furnish "themselves with provisions at all hazards."[61]

The men's commander was Col. Return Jonathan Meigs, a soldier who had endured weeks of privation leading his division toward Quebec on the Arnold Expedition. In a narrative which was published in a popular edition titled *Private Yankee Doodle*, common soldier Joseph Plumb Martin described how Meigs handled the volatile situation. "The men were now exasperated beyond endurance," wrote Private Martin, "they could not stand it any longer. They saw no other alternative but to starve to death, or break up the army, give all up and go home." Martin and his grumbling comrades wanted other regiments to join their protest. Then Col. Meigs arrived on the scene, and "exerted himself to prevent his men from obtaining their arms [the rebellious troops still had their muskets racked]." Meigs said that "he had always considered himself the soldier's friend and thought the soldiers regarded him as such." Martin commented that "Colonel Meigs was truly an excellent man and a brave officer." As Meigs was entreating his men at dusk to be a little more patient, a shadowy figure approached him. A scuffle ensued, during which Meigs was wounded by a bayonet. Other officers arrived on the scene, and the shock of Meigs' injury sobered his troops, who continued to grumble and complain but disbanded and returned to their huts. Meigs recovered from his wound, and

60 Ward, *The War of the Revolution*, II: 613.

61 James Thacher, M.D., *Military Journal of the American Revolution* (Hartford, Connecticut: Hurlbut, Williams & Company, 1862), 197.

Martin reported that "[o]ur stir did us some good in the end, for we had provisions directly after, so we had no great cause for complaint for some time."[62]

While the relative quiet that would continue for the balance of the war in the northern colonies stretched on, the conflict proceeded in the southern states. With their change in strategy, the British now intended to subjugate Georgia, South Carolina, and North Carolina, then move north to conquer Virginia. Charleston, South Carolina, was the only major city in the south, and the key to controlling the surrounding region. In 1780, Gen. Sir Henry Clinton took advantage of the weakness of Washington's army in the north by moving his available forces south, where he successfully attacked Charleston.

Colonel William Heth was among the Americans defending Charleston in 1780. As a lieutenant on the Arnold Expedition, his exploits had included leading the reconnaissance party that crept up to Quebec's walls the night the Kennebec men crossed the St. Lawrence River.[63] At the siege of Charleston, Heth was a colonel and commander of the 3rd Virginia Regiment. He was among the Continental officers taken captive when the city surrendered on May 12, 1780, and remained a prisoner on parole until the end of the war.

Following the British victory at Charleston, Congress appointed Gen. Horatio Gates to take charge of the American war effort in the south. Once he arrived on the scene, Gates' officers included Arnold Expedition veteran Lt. Col. Charles Porterfield. This experienced combat veteran urged Gates to remain in rebel-controlled North Carolina, where he could build a strong army. But "Granny Gates," as he was called, was anxious to prove that he could be as tough a combat officer as Arnold and Wayne, so he marched his ragtag army into British-controlled South Carolina. Gates' objective was the enemy supply base at the crossroads town of Camden. But unknown to Gates at the time was that Gen. Charles Cornwallis had reached Camden with reinforcements to help defend the post.

The two armies met on August 16, 1780, on a road outside of Camden. The British routed Gates' army. The American general's vanity and execrable planning resulted in more than 600 American dead or wounded, including Charles Porterfield, who was mortally wounded and died in British captivity.

62 George E. Scheer, ed., *Private Yankee Doodle* (Boston: Little, Brown and Company, 1962), 182-187.

63 Higginbotham, *Daniel Morgan*, 37.

An eyewitness to the fighting mentioned his valor: "Lieutenant Colonel Porterfield, in whose bravery and judicious conduct great dependence was placed, received a mortal wound early in the battle. . . ."[64] Porterfield began his military career as a gentleman volunteer on the Arnold Expedition. He was one of the first men over the barricade at the Sault-au-Matelot, and was taken prisoner at Quebec with his comrades. Following his exchange in 1777, Porterfield rejoined the fight for independence and rose through the ranks. He commanded the Virginia State Regiment at the Battle of Camden.

Following Gates' thrashing at Camden, he was replaced by Gen. Nathanael Greene as American commander in the south. Greene made a daring decision: he divided his army in the face of a superior enemy force. This bold move was intended both to secure food for his troops and to confuse the opposition.

One wing of his army was given to Arnold Expedition veteran Daniel Morgan. It included: 320 regular troops from Maryland and Delaware; 200 Virginia riflemen; about 100 light dragoons commanded by Lt. Col. William Washington, a distant kinsman to the commander-in-chief; and some additional forces, for a total of about 890 men. Greene ordered Morgan to march to the interior of South Carolina, where he could threaten the rear of Cornwallis' army. Cornwallis countered by sending the resourceful and ruthless Lt. Col. Banastre Tarleton, whom the Americans called Bloody Ban, to catch and destroy Morgan's corps. Tarleton's force, numbering about 1,050 officers and men, was comprised of: the British Legion (a mixed force of cavalry and light infantry totaling 550 men); 200 troops from the Royal Fusilier Regiment; 200 men from the 71st Highland Regiment; 50 light dragoons; a detachment of artillery with two light pieces of field artillery; and a detachment of Tory militia. Morgan's force, including militia, was only slightly smaller (890 officers and men) than that of Tarleton (1,050), although the latter had better equipped and more experienced troops.

Tarleton's scouts discovered Morgan's position and a chase ensued. Morgan marched his force deeper into the interior of South Carolina until he reached a placed called Hannah's Cowpens, used by the locals to winter cattle, where he decided to make a stand. Morgan had become an expert at using his troops to their best advantage, and Cowpens was his masterpiece. For example,

64 "Narrative of Colonel Otho Williams," in Commager and Morris, eds., *The Spirit of Seventy-Six*, II: 1130. For information concerning Porterfield's military career, see Heitman, *Historical Register of Officers of the Continental Army*, 448.

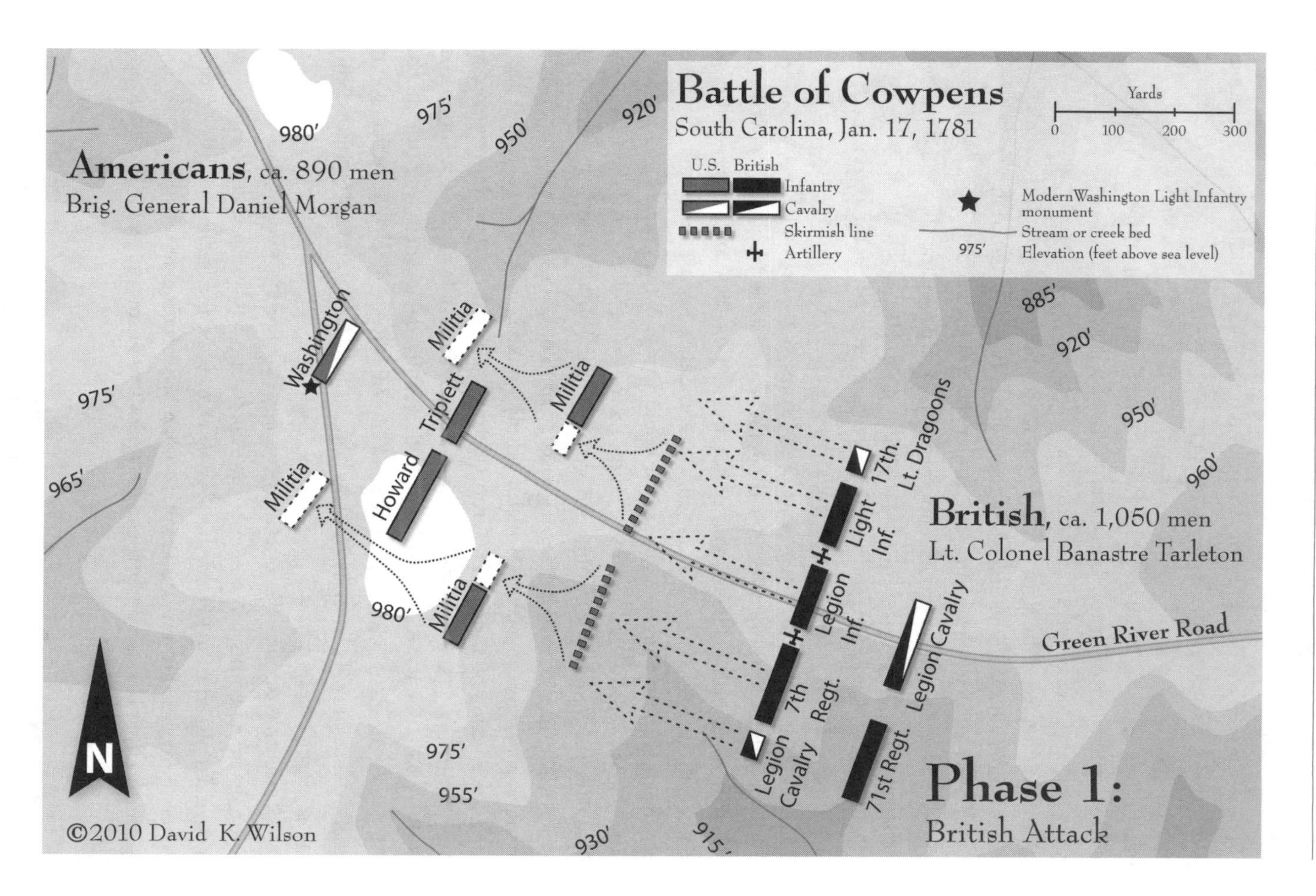

Battle of Cowpens
South Carolina, Jan. 17, 1781
Yards
0 100 200 300
U.S. British
Infantry
Cavalry
Skirmish line
Artillery
ModernWashington Light Infantry monument
Stream or creek bed
975'
Elevation (feet above sea level)
Americans, ca. 890 men
Brig. General Daniel Morgan
980'
975'
950'
920'
885'
920'
950'
960'
975'
965'
980'
975'
955'
930'
915'
Washington
Militia
Triplett
Militia
Militia
Howard
Militia
17th. Lt. Dragoons
Light Inf.
Legion Inf.
7th Regt.
Legion Cavalry
Legion Cavalry
71st Regt.
British, ca. 1,050 men
Lt. Colonel Banastre Tarleton
Green River Road
N
Phase 1:
British Attack
©2010 David K. Wilson

Cowpens Maps: Historian David K. Wilson created the maps on pages 190 and 192 to illustrate the opening phase of the Battle of Cowpens. They are based upon his outstanding research into the number of men engaged on both sides and their positions at the start of the battle. *David K. Wilson Collection. Copyright David K. Wilson*

many of the militiamen with Morgan at Cowpens were tough, reliable men with some combat experience. However, many of them had neither bayonets nor experience in maneuvering and firing as a unit. Knowing that his militiamen could not withstand an attack by Tarleton's men, Morgan asked them to fire two volleys, then run. He hoped their hasty retreat would convince Tarleton that he had broken American resistance when, in fact, his Continentals and dragoons were poised out of sight behind the militia.

Morgan visited the militia camp on the night before the battle, talking and joking with his men around their campfires. His voice was cheerful and his manner confident as he explained his battle plan and entreated the militiamen to "Just hold up your head boys, give them two fires [volleys] and you're free. And then, when you return to your homes, how the old folks will bless you and the girls kiss you for your gallant conduct!"[65] Then everyone in the American camp turned in for a good night's sleep, followed by a full breakfast early the next morning before forming their battle line.

Facing Morgan across the open ground the following morning, the Oxford-educated Tarleton got his troops into formation and, as was his custom, immediately charged the rebels. They promptly ran into Morgan's first line, which consisted of 120 Georgia and North Carolina militiamen armed with rifles and firing from behind trees. Morgan had divided them, with the Georgia men on one side of the skirmish line and the Carolina militia on the other. As the enemy approached, Morgan was alleged to have yelled, "Let me see which are most entitled to the credit of brave men, the boys of Carolina or those of Georgia."[66] Following Morgan's instructions, the skirmishers purposely shot as many of the officers as they could as they slowly fell back to join a line of 300 fellow militiamen standing 150 yards behind them.

The main body of militiamen held their fire until the enemy came within range, then, as agreed, fired two volleys "low and deliberate" before breaking

65 Graham, *The Life of General Daniel Morgan*, 293.

66 *Ibid.*, 297.

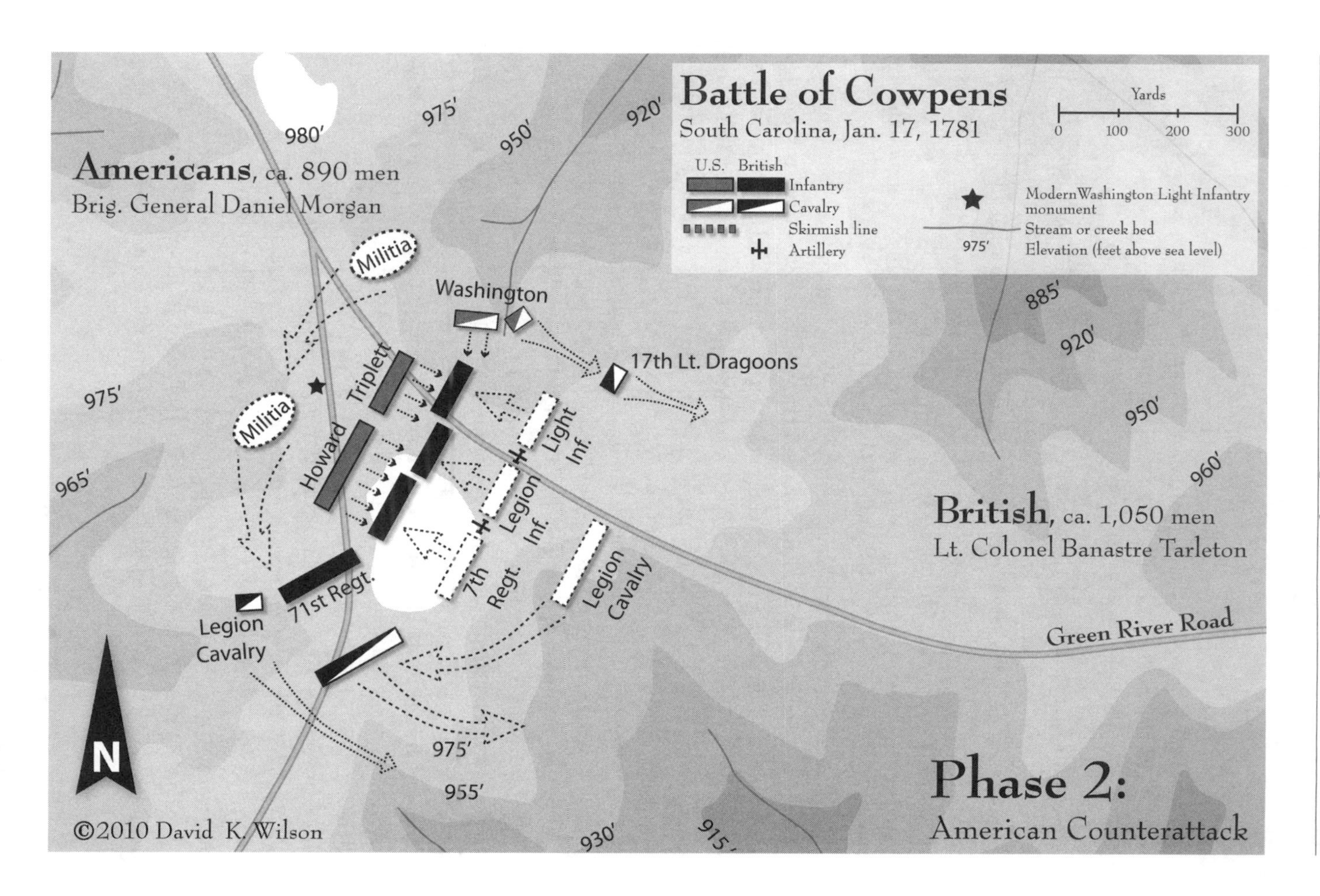

Battle of Cowpens
South Carolina, Jan. 17, 1781
Yards
0
100
200
300
U.S.
British
Infantry
Cavalry
Skirmish line
Artillery
Modern Washington Light Infantry monument
Stream or creek bed
975'
Elevation (feet above sea level)
Americans, ca. 890 men
Brig. General Daniel Morgan
British, ca. 1,050 men
Lt. Colonel Banastre Tarleton
Green River Road
Phase 2:
American Counterattack
Militia
Militia
Washington
17th Lt. Dragoons
Triplett
Howard
Light Inf.
Legion Inf.
7th Regt.
Legion Cavalry
71st Regt.
Legion Cavalry
980'
975'
950'
920'
885'
920'
950'
960'
975'
965'
975'
955'
930'
915'
N
©2010 David K. Wilson

ranks and running from the scene. Still according to plan, they gathered behind Morgan's next line, composed of his battle-tested Continental troops, whom Morgan had exhorted to "play well your parts for your honor and liberty."[67]

Tarleton's corps took some casualties from the militiamen, but the militia's retreat convinced the British that American resistance was collapsing. Tarleton's infantry was surprised to find the Continentals behind the militia, but they advanced against them as British mounted troops were dispatched to attack the retreating militia. The battle seemed to be going favorably for the British—until William Washington's cavalry emerged from behind a knoll and surprised the enemy horsemen.

Meanwhile, across the field, Tarleton's infantry, believing they had wrecked American resistance, broke ranks and went charging toward the Continentals—who stood fast, shooting low and firing volley after volley with deadly accuracy. The militia rallied, urged on by Morgan, who rode among them waving his sword and yelling, "Form, form, my brave fellows! Give them one more fire and the day is ours. Old Morgan was never beaten."[68]

Tarleton described what happened next: "An unexpected fire at this instant from the Americans [militia], who came about as they were retreating, stopped the British, and threw them into confusion. Exertions to make them advance were useless. The part of the cavalry which had not been engaged fell likewise into disorder, and an unaccountable panic extended itself along the whole line."[69]

The day ended with Washington's horsemen chasing down the remnants of Tarleton's troops, who were retreating back to Cornwallis' main army. Morgan scored a spectacular victory over the British at Cowpens, considered by many historians to be the best-fought battle of the American Revolution.

Following Tarleton's defeat at Cowpens, Cornwallis took up the pursuit and followed Morgan, who had returned to Greene's camp. A chase ensued, with Cornwallis determined to catch and destroy the rebel force. Years of strenuous campaigning and his long imprisonment in Quebec finally took their

67 John Buchanan, *The Road to Guilford Courthouse* (New York: John Wiley & Sons, Inc., 1997), 320.

68 Lawrence E. Babits, *A Devil of a Whipping: The Battle of Cowpens* (Chapel Hill: The University of North Carolina Press, 1998), 99.

69 Lieutenant-Colonel [Banastre] Tarleton, *A History of the Campaigns of 1780 and 1781, in the Southern Provinces of North America* (London: Printed For T. Cadell, 1787), 217.

toll on Morgan's health. Suffering with "rheumatic from head to feet" [probably what we know today as arthritis] and severe "piles" [hemorrhoids], Morgan was forced to return to his Virginia home.[70] On March 15, 1781, Greene finally clashed with Cornwallis at Guilford Courthouse, North Carolina, in what proved to be an indecisive battle.

However, in its aftermath, Cornwallis' exhausted army needed rest and fresh supplies, so he made the fateful decision to march north to Virginia, where he eventually fortified the river port of Yorktown. Here he hoped to make contact with the Royal Navy. But Washington, supported by the French, moved his army south in a great gamble that he could trap Cornwallis at Yorktown. The French Navy succeeded in driving off the British fleet, giving the combined American and French army the opportunity to lay siege to Cornwallis' now-isolated army.

The siege of Yorktown, Virginia, turned out to be the climax of the American Revolution. Several Arnold Expedition veterans were there, including Henry Dearborn, who was deputy quartermaster general of the Continental Army, and Capt. William Humphrey, who commanded a company of Rhode Island troops.[71]

The surrender of Cornwallis' army at Yorktown on October 19, 1781, did not end the war; sporadic fighting continued for two more years. This was a difficult period for Washington's army. It was impoverished, and officers were demanding back pay before they would follow orders, prompting a frustrated Gen. Washington to write to his virtuous fellow officer and friend Col. Febiger: "What can they expect from their soldiers, when they themselves strike at the Root of Authority and discipline? Do they think the remaining force of the enemy is to be crushed by Words or Blows?"[72]

The final scene of the American Revolution took place on December 23, 1783, when Washington resigned his commission as commander-in-chief of the American army. Washington had learned a great deal during his eight-year tenure at the head of the army. The failed Arnold Expedition, at the start of the

70 Higginbotham, *Daniel Morgan*, 152.

71 On January 1, 1781, the 1st and 2nd Rhode Island regiments of infantry were consolidated and designated as the Rhode Island Regiment. *Fred Anderson Berg, Encyclopedia of Continental Army Units* (Harrisburg, Pennsylvania: Stackpole Books, 1972), 105-106; Wright, *The Continental Army*, 227; Heitman, Historical Register of Officers of the Continental Army, 308.

72 Fitzpatrick, ed., *The Writings of George Washington*, XXII: 442-443.

war, had taught him to avoid reckless and expensive forays deep into enemy territory. It is no coincidence that he never staged a similarly impulsive campaign over the balance of the war.

Chapter Seven

The Last Roll Call

"And you will, by the dignity of your Conduct, afford occasion for Posterity to say, when speaking of the glorious example you have exhibited to Mankind, had this day been wanting, the World had never seen the last stage of perfection to which human nature is capable of attaining."

— *George Washington, "The Newburgh Address," January 2, 1783*

General Daniel Morgan was honored by Congress following his victory at Cowpens with a gold medal engraved with emblems and mottos descriptive of his conduct on that memorable day. His health returned sporadically, allowing him to occasionally return to the field during the closing years of the conflict. Following the war, Morgan retired to his Virginia estate. He was recalled to active duty in 1794 by President Washington to command the Virginia militia during the Whiskey Rebellion. Morgan's post-war career was also marked by his defeat in 1796 as a Federalist Party candidate for election to the 4th United States Congress. However, he won the next election and served one term in Congress (1797-1799). Morgan declined the nomination for a second term because of poor health and died after a long illness on July 6, 1802. He was buried with the honors of war; seven of the riflemen who were with him on the Arnold Expedition served as an honor guard at his funeral and fired their battle-scarred weapons in a final salute.[1]

1 Graham, *The Life of General Daniel Morgan*, 448.

Portrait of Henry Dearborn by Charles Willson Peale. This portrait of Dearborn was probably painted sometime in 1796 or 1797 when he was in Philadelphia serving in Congress. *Independence National Historical Park Collection*

Colonel Henry Dearborn settled in Maine after the war. His impressive postwar career included representing the District of Maine in the U.S. Congress from 1793-1797, serving as Secretary of War during the presidential administration of Thomas Jefferson, as collector of the port of Boston, as senior major general of the United States Army during the War of 1812, and as U.S. Minister to Portugal from 1822 to 1824. He died at his home in Kennebec

County, Maine, on June 6, 1829. Dearborn's dedication to the American cause was extraordinary. He served unselfishly throughout the conflict, compiling an impressive service record spanning eight years that included Bunker Hill, the Arnold Expedition, Saratoga, Monmouth, the Sullivan Expedition, and the siege of Yorktown. Dearborn, Michigan, is named in his honor.

Captured at Quebec, John Topham was exchanged in 1777, after which he rejoined the army and rose to the rank of colonel. He commanded the 1st Rhode Island State Regiment (state regiments were raised for local defense) from February 1778 until May 1780. He led his regiment into combat during the failed attempt to recapture Newport, Rhode Island, in 1778. Topham died on September 26, 1793, an honored combat veteran of the American Revolution.

Colonel Timothy Bigelow served as commander of the 15th Massachusetts Regiment until he resigned from the army at the end of 1780. Bigelow's mid-war resignation was a familiar and tragic pattern among long-serving American soldiers in the Revolutionary War, resulting from failing health or financial distress. In Bigelow's case, it was both. His health steadily declined as a result of his participation in the 1775 Arnold Expedition and siege of Quebec, as well as his long imprisonment in Quebec during 1776 and the 1777-78 winter encampment at Valley Forge. Bigelow was physically unable to continue to serve in the army by the end of 1780. At the time of his resignation, the young nation was in an economic crisis. Its credit had been exhausted by the long and costly war, and the army was being paid infrequently and in depressed paper currency, which left the families of many soldiers destitute and unable to provide for themselves. Bigelow returned home too ill to resume his blacksmith trade, and with his family deep in debt. In the end, he was unable to pay his creditors, so in February 1790 was sent to debtor's prison, where he died on March 31, 1790, at the age of 51.

Eleazer Oswald returned to his prewar printing career following his resignation from the army. He joined forces with William Goddard in 1779, and an announcement of their new Baltimore printing, book-selling, and stationery business appeared in the June 8, 1779, issue of the respected *Maryland Journal*.[2]

2 Joseph T. Wheeler, *The Maryland Press, 1777-1790* (Baltimore: The Maryland Historical Society, 1938), 29.

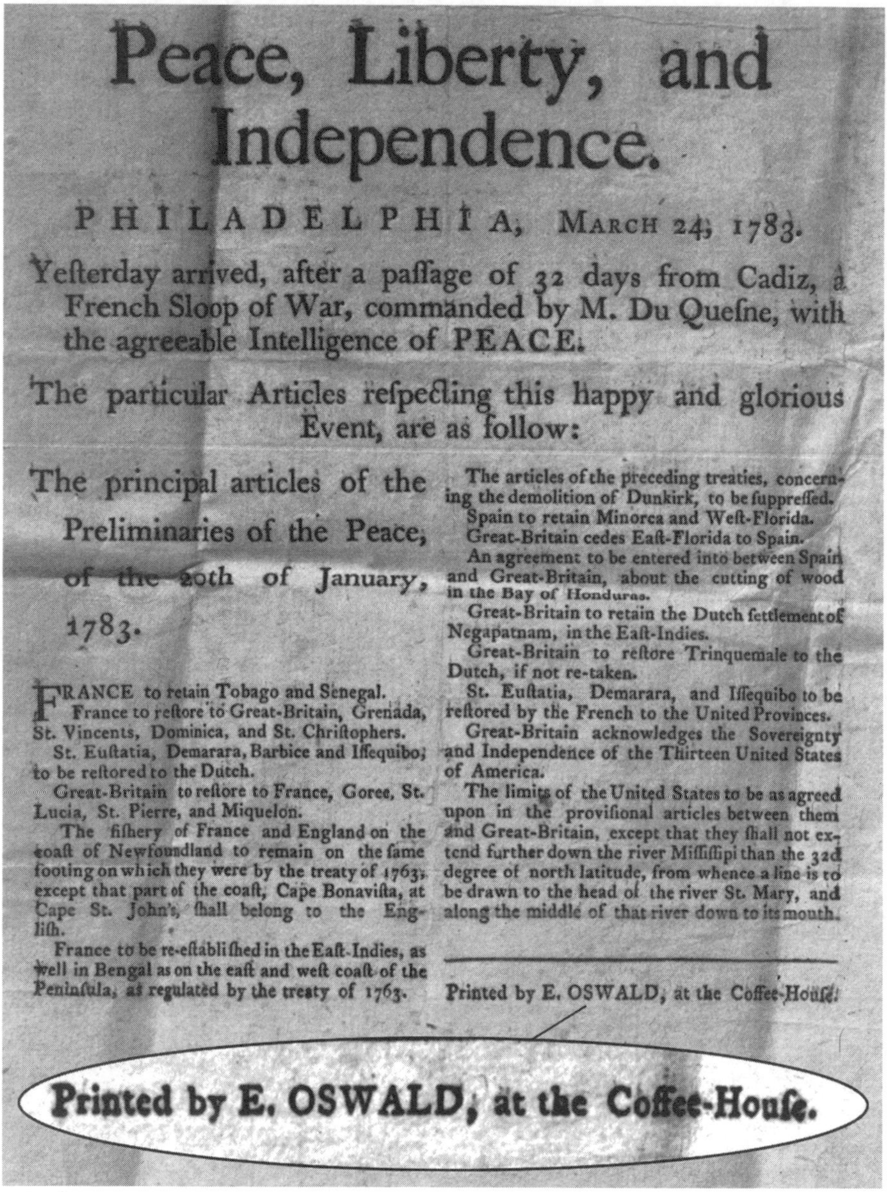

Peace, Liberty, and Independence.

PHILADELPHIA, MARCH 24, 1783.

Yeſterday arrived, after a paſſage of 32 days from Cadiz, a French Sloop of War, commanded by M. Du Queſne, with the agreeable Intelligence of PEACE.

The particular Articles reſpecting this happy and glorious Event, are as follow:

The principal articles of the Preliminaries of the Peace, of the 20th of January, 1783.

FRANCE to retain Tobago and Senegal.

France to reſtore to Great-Britain, Grenada, St. Vincents, Dominica, and St. Chriſtophers.

St. Euſtatia, Demarara, Barbice and Iſſequibo, to be reſtored to the Dutch.

Great-Britain to reſtore to France, Goree, St. Lucia, St. Pierre, and Miquelon.

The fiſhery of France and England on the coaſt of Newfoundland to remain on the ſame footing on which they were by the treaty of 1763, except that part of the coaſt, Cape Bonaviſta, at Cape St. John's, ſhall belong to the Engliſh.

France to be re-eſtabliſhed in the Eaſt-Indies, as well in Bengal as on the eaſt and weſt coaſt of the Peninſula, as regulated by the treaty of 1763.

The articles of the preceding treaties, concerning the demolition of Dunkirk, to be ſuppreſſed.

Spain to retain Minorca and Weſt-Florida.

Great-Britain cedes Eaſt-Florida to Spain.

An agreement to be entered into between Spain and Great-Britain, about the cutting of wood in the Bay of Honduras.

Great-Britain to retain the Dutch ſettlement of Negapatnam, in the Eaſt-Indies.

Great-Britain to reſtore Trinquemale to the Dutch, if not re-taken.

St. Euſtatia, Demarara, and Iſſequibo to be reſtored by the French to the United Provinces.

Great-Britain acknowledges the Sovereignty and Independence of the Thirteen United States of America.

The limits of the United States to be as agreed upon in the proviſional articles between them and Great-Britain, except that they ſhall not extend further down the river Miſſiſſipi than the 32d degree of north latitude, from whence a line is to be drawn to the head of the river St. Mary, and along the middle of that river down to its mouth.

Printed by E. OSWALD, at the Coffee-Houſe.

Printed by E. OSWALD, at the Coffee-Houſe.

Broadside announcing the end of the American Revolution printed by Eleazer Oswald. *The Library Company of Philadelphia*

The stunning news in 1780, when Benedict Arnold's treason was first uncovered, shocked his former friend. Oswald wrote: "I never knew, or heard of any Man who had acquired by his merit, so distinguished a Rank in Life, so totally lost to every honorable and virtuous Principle—to the World—to his Friends—and to himself."[3]

Oswald later moved to Philadelphia, where he started his own printing business and coffee house. He advertised his new enterprise by noting that "[a]ll the various newspapers, magazines, Etc, both foreign and domestic, will be regularly filed in the public rooms for the information and amusement of the curious."[4] He became an ardent Anti-Federalist and opposed the adoption of the Constitution, which he criticized in his Philadelphia newspaper, the *Independent Gazetteer*. The fearless Oswald did not hide behind pen names in his attacks opposing ratification. Backed by the anti-Constitution forces within the city, Oswald courageously penned a series of blistering articles under his own name. The savage struggle fought among the unbridled Philadelphia newspapers over the adoption of the Constitution prompted a visitor from Boston to write home with no little disgust, "The papers of this place are now the receptacles of obscenity and filth, the vehicles of scandal, and the instruments of the most infamous abuse."[5]

Oswald's defamatory political views and irascibility resulted in a series of dueling challenges and duels. Still resentful of Washington and his followers for denying his promotion during the Revolutionary War, Oswald challenged Col. Alexander Hamilton, a member of Washington's inner circle, to a duel over a personal quarrel that grew out of the fight over the ratification of the Constitution. When friends interceded, Oswald withdrew his challenge.

Oswald's other dueling challenges included Lt. Col. Samuel Smith, the Maryland officer who was wounded in 1777 defending Fort Mifflin, and the Philadelphia printer Mathew Carey. The story of Oswald's duel with Carey is an interesting window into Oswald's apparently truculent personality. Oswald was

3 *Ibid*, 22. Oswald and Arnold had drifted apart by the time of the latter's treason. The rift's circumstances concerned Arnold's failure to return valuable French mathematical instruments Oswald had left in his care. Oswald noted Arnold's treason again on another occasion: "Happy for him, and for his Friends, it had been, had the Ball which pierced his Leg at Saratoga, been directed thro' his Heart—He then would have finished his Career in Glory." *Ibid.*

4 *Ibid.*

5 Jeffrey L. Pasley, *The Tyranny of Printers: Newspaper Politics in the Early American Republic* (Charlottesville: University Press of Virginia, 2001), 40-41.

publishing his newspaper in Philadelphia when, in the spring of 1785, a newly arrived Irish immigrant named Mathew Carey announced that he would commence the publication of a rival paper, which he called the *Pennsylvania Evening Herald.* Carey was planning to buy a used printing press and printer's type that were coming up for auction in Philadelphia. On the appointed day of the sale, Oswald showed up and bid up the price of the press, forcing Carey to use up much of his limited capital for the purchase. Carey's newspaper prospered nonetheless, and Oswald, alarmed at his rival's success, began attacking him viciously in his own tabloid, even making fun of the fact that Carey walked with a limp. Carey replied in kind, which led to Oswald challenging his rival to a duel. Carey had no experience with firearms, while Col. Oswald was familiar with guns from his days as a soldier. In the ensuing duel, Carey's shot predictably went wild while Colonel Oswald took careful aim and shot Carey in the thigh of his already crippled leg.[6]

But the most interesting aspect of Oswald's postwar career was his participation in the French Revolution as a colonel in the French Republican Army. Oswald was one of only two American army officers known to have fought in both the American Revolution and the French Revolution. (The other patriot officer was Col. John Skey Eustace (1760-1805) from Georgia.)

Oswald got involved in the French Revolution while he was in England in 1792 to settle the estate of a relative. Fired with the noble ideas of the French cause, Oswald crossed the English Channel and offered his services to the revolutionary government, which welcomed him. He was appointed a colonel in the French Republican Army and put in command of a field artillery regiment. Oswald fought as a French artillery officer in several engagements, including the November 6, 1792, Battle of Jemappes (the name of a town in Belgium) in which the French defeated the Austrians. Oswald was experienced in the rapid deployment of horse-drawn field artillery, which he had performed successfully during the 1778 Battle of Monmouth. A contemporary account of the Battle of Jemappes mentioned an American artillery officer (an obvious reference to Oswald) with this expertise: "The French were strongly advised by an American, who had made a campaign with them in the Low Countries, and

6 James N. Green, *Mathew Carey, Publisher and Patriot* (Philadelphia: The Library Company of Philadelphia, 1985), 5-6.

was at the battle of Jemappe [sic], to bring a more than usual quantity of artillery into the field."[7]

Following the battle, Oswald returned to Paris, where there was talk of the Irish people revolting against the British and aligning themselves with the French. Oswald later recounted, "as I was an American and could go to Ireland with less suspicion than another person I was sent by the Minister LeBrun upon that business."[8] Excited at the prospect of an important mission, and asking only that his expenses be reimbursed, Oswald went to Ireland via Norway, but there was little he could do because England had just declared war on France. He returned to Paris, where his personal property, including a valuable horse, had been taken for use by the government, and his expense account was rejected. Disillusioned, he returned to America, where he delighted in taunting President Washington's administration for its neutrality in the war between England and France by wearing his French uniform and extolling the virtues of the French Revolution.

Colonel Oswald, who had so often faced death on the battlefields of the American Revolution, met his demise in a different sphere. He was living in New York when a yellow fever epidemic broke out in the city during the summer of 1795, causing many people to temporarily flee the city, including Oswald and his family. One of the epidemic's victims was Capt. Charles Tillinghast, Gen. John Lamb's son-in-law and Oswald's old friend. The aging general was too sick with gout (which he may have first contracted while a prisoner in Quebec) to help his son-in-law. Ignoring the pleas of his wife and family, Oswald hurried to the bedside of the dying young man. As a result of his lingering in the city to attend to Tillinghast, Oswald contracted yellow fever and died from the disease on September 30, 1795.[9] He was 40 years old at the time of his death. His old friend John Lamb died five years later, on May 31, 1800.

7 Leake, *The Life and Times of Gen. John Lamb*, 344; Wheeler, *The Maryland Press*, 35.

8 Wheeler, *The Maryland Press*, 35.

9 The most complete account of Oswald's death appears in Leake, *The Life of General John Lamb*, 350. This book was published in 1850, before the actual cause of yellow fever was known. The author, Isaac Q. Leake, incorrectly stated that Colonel Oswald's close contact with Tillinghast resulted in the colonel's death. There were a number of yellow fever epidemics in post-Revolutionary War America centered in Philadelphia and New York City. Focusing on one of the earliest and biggest yellow fever epidemics in America helps to understand the primitive state of medical knowledge of the time. In 1793, Philadelphia was America's largest and most cosmopolitan city. During the summer and fall of 1793, roughly a tenth of its

Christian Febiger was breveted brigadier general in the final months of the Revolution in recognition of his outstanding service. Following the war he settled in Philadelphia, where he resumed his pre-war business activities with great success. He was honored for his wartime service with an appointment as state treasurer of Pennsylvania in 1789. Febiger held this post until his death on September 20, 1796.

Dr. Isaac Senter retired from the Continental Army in 1779 and practiced medicine in Cranston, Rhode Island, in addition to serving as the surgeon-general of the Rhode Island militia. He was subsequently elected a member of the state's General Assembly and was lauded with honorary degrees from Harvard, Yale, and Brown, the latter of which also named him a trustee. Senter moved his medical practice to Newport, Rhode Island, where he died on December 20, 1799.

Major Simeon Thayer, the Rhode Island officer who fought with Greene at Fort Mercer and commanded at Fort Mifflin during the final days of its defense, was originally from Mendon, Massachusetts, and apprenticed as a boy to a wigmaker in Providence, Rhode Island. He resigned from the Continental

---

population, some 5,000 people, perished from yellow fever. The trouble began soon after French refugees from a bloody slave rebellion on Saint Domingue (now Haiti) arrived in Philadelphia. In addition to news of the rebellion, the refugees relayed stories of a mysterious pestilential fever decimating several islands in the West Indies. In July, the same disease broke out in Philadelphia. The first to fall were working-class people living along the Delaware River. They suffered high fevers and hemorrhages; their eyes and skin turned yellow; and they brought up black vomit. Many of them died from internal bleeding within days of becoming ill. Dr. Benjamin Rush, one of America's premier doctors, then in his late 40s, called the disease bilious remitting yellow fever, which was shortened to yellow fever. Rush and his fellow physicians concluded that the disease was contagious and spread by putrid vapors (bad air). This conformed to the prevailing theory that diseases were caused by impurities in the air, particularly vapors from decaying plant matter. Rush, for example, attributed the outbreak of yellow fever in Philadelphia to a shipload of coffee that had spoiled en route from the West Indies and lay abandoned and rotting on a wharf. People were told to breathe through cloths soaked with camphor or vinegar and to burn gunpowder to clear the air to prevent contracting yellow fever, while Rush and other doctors in the city advocated aggressive bloodletting as a cure. Yellow fever is now known to be a viral infection transmitted by female mosquitoes of the species *Aedes aegypti.* These mosquitoes arrived by ship to Philadelphia with the refugees from Saint Domingue. One of the victims of the 1793 Philadelphia yellow fever epidemic was John Todd, a lawyer who remained in Philadelphia to handle the surge of legal matters arising from the many deaths. Todd caught the fever and died. Within a year, his widow, Dolly, married Congressman James Madison. When Madison became the fourth U.S. president, his wife (Dolly Madison) became the First Lady.

Army in January 1781 and opened a public house (an establishment licensed to provide liquor, meals, and accommodations), which he named the Montgomery Hotel in honor of his old commander. Simeon Thayer died on October 14, 1800.[10]

Colonel William Heth, who was captured when Charleston surrendered in 1780, remained in British captivity until the end of the war. Following his release, he became a planter in Henrico County, Virginia. Heth also served on several Virginia commissions that reviewed wartime service records and recommended pensions and land grants. On February 21, 1788, Colonel Heth visited General Washington at Mount Vernon. The colonel wrote that he spent an agreeable day with his former commander talking about the war and their hopes that the new United States Constitution would be ratified by the states. Heth stayed overnight at Mount Vernon, and after breakfast the next morning Washington honored Heth by accompanying him on horseback for several miles. The two veterans bade farewell to each other on the road, never to meet again. Washington died in 1799 and Heth on April 15, 1808.[11]

After returning from Quebec, rifleman John Joseph Henry was invited to join Daniel Morgan's new regiment as a captain. Young Henry refused the honor because of the periodic recurrence of the scurvy he had contracted during the siege of Quebec. Henry was also lame as a result of two falls he took during the Quebec attack. The first happened when he slipped on the ice as he was running toward the first barricade in the lower town, and the second when he tripped over a ship's cable and fell down a ten-foot embankment in an unsuccessful bid to escape the British encirclement of the Sault-au-Matelot. After returning to civilian life, Henry became a lawyer and was appointed a

10 Heitman, *Historical Register of Officers of the Continental Army*, 538; Henry Lee, *Memoirs of the War In The Southern Department of the United States*, 2 vols. (Philadelphia: Bradford and Inskeep, 1812), I: 384-385.

11 Heth's diary, including an account of his visit to Mount Vernon, is available on the website *New River Valley Historical Notes.com.* The original diary is in the collection of the Virginia Historical Society. A biography of Heth is in Heitman, *Historical Register of Officers of the Continental Army*, 287.

judge by the governor of Pennsylvania in 1793. He died in 1810 at the age of 52.[12]

Captain Oliver Hanchet returned to his Suffield, Connecticut, home following his exchange in January 1777. He continued to command his old militia company, which was periodically called up for several months at a time during the war to support the Continental army. In one exploit, Hanchet's company was recalled for two months of active duty in the fall of 1777 when British troops under Gen. Clinton embarked in Royal Navy ships and sallied up the Hudson River from New York to try to relieve Burgoyne's army at Saratoga. Clinton's Redcoats burned Kingston, New York, on October 16. It was shortly after this that Hanchet led his men in the capture of a Royal Navy sloop, "armed with four swivels" [small cannon mounted on a rotating stand], which had run aground on the Hudson a few miles above Poughkeepsie.[13] Seizing the opportunity, the militiamen boarded the sloop and overpowered its crew and 15 soldiers.[14]

Their seizure of the enemy vessel was a victory for the patriot cause and a financial windfall for Hanchet and his men: the captured sloop was sold as a prize and the money split among the intrepid militiamen. Benjamin Warner, a private on the Arnold Expedition, and Rufus Gillet, a Continental army combat veteran, were members of Hanchet's militia company at the time. These combat veterans probably urged their less experienced fellow militiamen to attack the ship.[15] The presence of veteran soldiers such as Hanchet, Warner, and Gillet in militia companies helped to make them a tolerable fighting force in the final years of the American Revolution.

Little else is known about Hanchet's service for the balance of the war. Apparently he was a leader of his home town of Suffield, Connecticut, based on

12 William Allen, "Account of Arnold's Expedition," in *Maine Historical Society Collections*, Volume One (1831), 531.

13 Affidavit of Rufus Gillet (Connecticut), *Revolutionary War Pension and Land Bounty Records*, Record series M805, file W117948.

14 Affidavit of Benjamin Warner (1757-1846, Connecticut), *Ibid*, Record series 839, file S14798.

15 *Ibid.* Also affidavit of Rufus Gillet, Record series M805, file W17948.

newspaper accounts of his house being used for local meetings.[16] Hanchet died on May 26, 1816.

Edward Slocum enlisted in May 1775 in Capt. William Cook's company, which was part of a Rhode Island regiment raised in Bristol and Newport Counties by Thomas Church. He was 21 when he joined Church's regiment as an orderly sergeant (officer's assistant) and was quickly promoted to ensign (junior infantry officer).[17] Slocum volunteered for the Arnold Expedition on September 14, 1775, with the rank of lieutenant in John Topham's company. He was captured at Quebec and appeared on one list of prisoners as "Lt. Edward Sloakum" and on another as "Lieut Edw. Slocam, Tivertown [Tiverton], Rhode Island."[18] Following his exchange in 1777, Slocum returned to the army and was appointed a captain in the 1st Rhode Island Regiment, serving on active duty until he retired in November 1779. Slocum died on March 2, 1822.[19]

Col. Return Jonathan Meigs continued in active service until his resignation in June 1781. Following the war, he was a leader in the establishment of Marietta, Ohio, and was a federal agent to the Cherokee Indians. He was also the chief negotiator for Indian treaties involving the Chickasaws and Creeks. Just after he celebrated his 82nd birthday, Meigs gave up his comfortable quarters at the Hiwassee Cherokee Reservation (near modern Calhoun, Tennessee) to a visiting Indian chief and slept outdoors. In so doing he contracted pneumonia, from which he died on January 23, 1823.

16 *Impartial Herald,* September 20, 1797.

17 An ensign was the most junior officer in an infantry company. The rank existed in both the British and American armies at the time of the Revolutionary War. Smith's 1779 military dictionary includes some interesting additional information on the subject: "Ensign, or ensign-bearer, is an officer who carries the colours, being the lowest commissioned officer in a company of foot [infantry], subordinate to the captain and lieutenant. The word ensign is very ancient, being used both by the Greeks and Romans." Smith, *An Universal Military Dictionary*, 82-83.

18 The first prisoner list that mentions Slocum is Joseph Ware's journal in Roberts, ed., *March to Quebec*, 35. The second reference to Slocum's imprisonment in Quebec is Brown and Peckham, eds., *Revolutionary War Journals of Henry Dearborn,* 76.

19 Affidavit of Capt. Edward Slocum (1754-1822, Rhode Island), *Revolutionary War Pension and Land Bounty Records*, Record series 743, file S33682.

David Hopkins was a gentleman volunteer on the Arnold Expedition and one of the few men who escaped being captured during the attack on Quebec. It was Hopkins who went to Philadelphia in February 1776 with a dispatch from Arnold to Congress. Arnold mentioned Hopkins in his report: "His spirited conduct, both on the march and since our arrival in this country, merits my recommendation to your notice, of which I think him worthy."[20] Congress rewarded Hopkins by appointing him a captain in the new 4th Continental Light Dragoon Regiment, also known as Moylan's Horse after its commander Col. Stephen Moylan. Hopkins participated in several campaigns with Moylan's Regiment, including the 1777 Philadelphia Campaign and skirmishes with the enemy in New Jersey, New York, and Connecticut. He was promoted to major in 1780 and transferred to the 1st Continental Dragoons (Bland's Horse), with whom he served until the unit was disbanded in November 1783 at Winchester, Virginia. In his 1818 Revolutionary War pension application, Hopkins stated that he was living in Baltimore County, Maryland, and that he was married with two sons. He listed his occupation as shopkeeper.[21]

As part of his proof of military service in the Revolutionary War to obtain a pension, Hopkins included a personal letter he had received from Col. Return Jonathan Meigs, dated "Washington City, 15th March 1816." In his letter the colonel reminisced about their service together on the Arnold Expedition. Meigs began by writing, "I intended to write you a long letter to bring to recollection a number of incidents on our ascending the River Kennebec. We left the Army lying before Boston on the 9th of September 1775." The old soldier went on to recount their hardships during the trek to Canada, including an intriguing statement about the bateaux: "When we arrived at the head of the river [Moosehead Lake in the Chain of Ponds] one hundred and eighty of our Battoes were lost, or had become useless. We carried three or four over the Alleghanee Mountain [the Terrible Carry] to the head of the Chaudiere river, our march from that time was by land through a trackless wilderness." After describing how they crossed the St. Lawrence River and attacked Quebec with Montgomery, Meigs closed his heartfelt letter to his old comrade by writing:

20 Force, ed., *American Archives*, Fourth Series, IV: 908.

21 Affidavit of David Hopkins (Continental Maryland Troops), *Revolutionary War Pension and Land Bounty Records*, file S. 34925.

It is now forty years since that interesting event happened; time has silvered our heads. This daily reminds me that I am now an old man. I am now 75 years old, 15 years probably older than you. I hope we can both look back & forward, console ourselves that we have done our duty to our Country. Most of our companions are gone before us, a Kind & tender providence has sustained us— this ought to awaken in our hearts the finest sensibility. P.S. I recollect all the names of the Cadets [gentlemen volunteers] who voluntarily attached themselves to our little Army on that expedition. Besides yourself there were Matthias Ogden, Peter Grubb [an error: Grubb was not a gentleman volunteer on the Arnold Expedition], Eleazer Oswald, Matthew Duncan, and Aaron Burr, of which two only are living—yourself and Aaron Burr.[22]

Hopkins died in Baltimore on March 4, 1824.

Peter Bryan Bruin resigned his post as Gen. Sullivan's aide soon after the completion of the Sullivan Expedition into Indian country. Bruin returned to a combat command, serving as a major in the 7th Virginia Regiment until the end of the war. He afterward settled in the Mississippi Territory, where he owned a large plantation and also served as a judge from 1798 to 1810. Fellow Arnold Expedition veteran Col. Aaron Burr visited Judge Bruin at his estate near Natchez in 1807. The two aging veterans must have talked about their shared hardships on the march to Quebec and the many comrades they lost in the campaign, including the "lamented General Montgomery."[23] Bruin died at his mansion on January 27, 1827. The area around his home was known as Bruinsburg, which became famous in the Civil War as the place where General Grant landed his army in 1863 for the great campaign against Vicksburg.

22 Manuscript letter, Return J. Meigs to Major David Hopkins, March 15, 1816, in Ibid. This list should also include gentleman volunteer Charles Porterfield, who was killed during the war. Peter Grubb does not appear on any known records as being on the Arnold Expedition. There was a Lt. Peter Grubb who was an officer in Thompson's Pennsylvania Rifle Battalion, who is listed as having resigned on September 10, 1775. The next reference to him is being appointed a captain in Miles' Pennsylvania Rifle Regiment on March 12, 1776. Heitman, *Historical Register of Officers of the Continental Army*, 264. The missing timeframe (September 10, 1775-March 12, 1776) is intriguing; however, it is unlikely that Grubb would have agreed to resign as a lieutenant to accept a position as an unpaid gentleman volunteer. In addition, there is no Arnold Expedition soldier listed with this name reported as being taken prisoner by the British.

23 Affidavit of Peter Bryan Bruin, *Revolutionary War Pension and Land Bounty Warrant Application Files*, Record group M-805, file S-42092.

Matthew Irvine was the surgeon's mate in Morgan's company who was left in charge of the makeshift hospital that Arnold established at the Great Carrying place. He next appears in the annals of the American Revolution as a surgeon's mate in an independent corps of cavalry and infantry which was officially designated the 2nd Partisan Corps, but better known as Lee's Legion.[24] Commanded by Maj. "Light Horse" Harry Lee, the Legion's most famous exploit was a daring and successful raid on the British fort at Paulus (or Powles) Hook, New Jersey (modern Jersey City), on the night of August 18-19, 1779. Irvine was later named the Legion's surgeon and rode with Lee's intrepid corps to the end of the war. Although he was the Legion's doctor, Irvine was known to have fought with them in several campaigns, including the Battle of Monmouth and Gen. Nathanael Greene's southern campaign. Irvine settled in Georgetown, South Carolina, after the war, where he practiced medicine. He died there on August 31, 1827.

Sergeant Jeremiah Greenman was promoted to lieutenant in May, 1781. At the end of the war he returned to Rhode Island, where he married, then eventually purchased a farm in Ohio. Lieutenant Greenman died in his home on November 15, 1828, and was buried on a hilltop overlooking his farm. His grave was marked with a tombstone placed there by his children that can still be seen today. The inscription reads: "In memory of Jeremiah Greenman Esq an active officer in that army which bid defiance to Britain's power and established the independence of the United States."[25]

Captain Nathaniel Hutchins, who was a lieutenant in Dearborn's company on the Arnold Expedition, served as a captain in Col. Cilley's 1st New

24 A partisan corps is a body of special troops composed of infantry, cavalry, and sometimes artillery. They were organized for raiding and reconnaissance during the war, but evolved into shock troops in battle, where they were employed to hold a flank or an advanced post. On April 7, 1778, Capt. Henry Lee of the 1st Regiment of Light Dragoons was promoted to major and authorized to increase his force to two troops, which were to form an independent corps called Lee's Corps of Partisan Light Dragoons. Lee's command was reorganized and expanded during the war, and by January 1, 1781, it was called the 2nd Partisan Corps and consisted of three companies each of mounted troops and light infantry, with 50 men in each company. The unit was disbanded on November 15, 1783, at Winchester, Virginia. Lee Berg, *Encyclopedia of Continental Army Units*, 60-61; Wright, *The Continental Army*, 348.

25 Bray and Bushnell, eds., *Military Journal of Jeremiah Greenman*, xxxvi.

Hampshire Regiment until he resigned from the army in 1781. Hutchins died on January 10, 1832.[26]

Captain William Humphrey served until the end of the war, after which he returned to his native Rhode Island. He was elected to the Rhode Island General Assembly from 1802-1812 and served as an officer in the Rhode Island militia. Humphrey died on July 1, 1832.[27]

Samuel Ward, Jr., rose to the rank of lieutenant colonel during the war. Following the end of hostilities, he became a prosperous merchant in New York City (Samuel Ward and Brother). Ward was among the first Americans to open trade with China, arriving in Canton in 1788 aboard his merchant ship *George Washington.* Ward later moved his business to East Greenwich, Rhode Island, but returned to live in New York City, where he died on August 16, 1832.

Thus, one by one, the veterans of the Kennebec Corps died, and by 1836 there were only a few old men still alive who could say that they had marched to Quebec with Arnold in 1775. One of them was Aaron Burr.

John Lamb, Montgomery's artillery officer, first met Burr on the Plains of Abraham during the siege of Quebec. His initial reaction was that Burr was "juvenile in the extreme," and wondered what had possessed Gen. Montgomery to pick this boy to be his aide-de-camp. But greater familiarity showed Lamb that the 19-year-old Burr was a brave soldier who demonstrated such staunch coolness under fire that he declared him to be "no ordinary man."[28] Burr was called many things during his lifetime, including assassin, womanizer, traitor, scapegoat, and villain, but no one ever accused him of being dull.

26 Brown and Peckham, eds., *Revolutionary War Journals of Henry Dearborn*, 45, note 27; Heitman, *Historical Register of Officers of the Continental Army*, 312.

27 See Shipton and Swain, eds., "Humphrey Journal," in *Rhode Islanders Record the Revolution,* 9; Heitman, *Historical Register of Officers of the Continental Army*, 308.

28 Leake, *The Life of General John Lamb*, 125-26.

Burr's valuable military service during the American Revolution is perhaps the most overlooked aspect of his long and colorful career.[29] Besides the Arnold Expedition, his distinguished military record included the field command of a regiment (Malcolm's Additional Continentals) at the Battle of Monmouth.[30] He was only 22 at the time, the youngest lieutenant colonel in the

29 One of the most important sources of information about Burr's military service during the Revolutionary War was his 1828 pension application. As background, the first pension acts were passed during the Revolutionary War; however, they were limited to disabled veterans or widows and orphans of men killed during the war. This changed in 1818 when Congress offered a pension to any officer or enlisted man who had served at least nine months or until the end of the war and was in financial need. Burr did not apply for this pension. Then in 1828, with tender sentiments for the men who had fought in the Revolutionary War, Congress passed a broader and more generous pension act which granted full pay for life to those officers who had been entitled to half pay under the Continental Congress resolution of October 1780. Enlisted personnel who had served in the American Revolution and met certain criteria were also eligible for full pay for life. All applicants for this magnanimous pension were required to give a narrative deposition of their wartime service in a local court, which recorded and submitted their applications. The narrative was meant to prove military service during the Revolutionary War. Burr applied for the 1828 pension. The highlights of Burr's 1828 pension application are as follows: "For the purpose of obtaining the benefit of an act entitled 'An Act for the relief of certain Surviving officers and Soldiers of the army of the Revolution' approved on the 15th: day of May 1828. I, Aaron Burr native of New Jersey now residing in the City of New York in the State of New York do hereby declare, that I was an officer in the Continental line of the Army of the Revolution and served as such as follows: I entered the Continental Army during the Revolutionary war as a volunteer in the summer of the year 1775. In December following (in the same year) I was appointed Aid de Camp to Genl. Montgomery, and after his death continued to perform the same duties under Genl. Arnold and in the summer of 1776 was appointed aid de camp to Genl. Putnam in which capacity I served until the summer following [June 1777] when I received from General Washington the appointment of Lieut. Col. of Malcoms Regiment (one of the additional sixteen) that in the month of October 1778, my health being much impaired, I wrote to Genl. Washington requesting permission to resign." Burr continued by explaining that Washington offered him a furlough instead, which Burr declined. He continued in active service with Malcom's Regiment until November 1779, when Burr stated, "I was appointed to the command of the lines and advanced posts in Westchester County [Westchester County, New York, just above British-held Manhattan Island] on which duty I continued until the Spring following [1780] when I was compelled by the exhausted state of my health to request that some officer might be appointed to succeed me in the command." Burr left the army shortly thereafter, although he gave no specific date for his resignation. The actual date that Burr returned to civilian life remains confusing. Heitman gives his resignation date as March 3, 1779, which differs greatly from the information contained in Burr's pension application, which states that he remained on active duty until the spring of 1780. Kline, ed., *Political Correspondence and Public Papers of Aaron Burr*, I: 1193; Heitman, *Historical Register of Officers of the Continental Army*, 135. Surprisingly, Burr never mentioned in his pension application that he wintered with the army at Valley Forge (1777-1778) and fought at the Battle of Monmouth Courthouse in New Jersey (June 28, 1778).

30 Burr held the administrative rank of major while serving as General Putnam's aide-de-camp. On June 27, 1777, Burr was promoted to lieutenant colonel in the Continental Army and

American army. Despite their differences, Washington respected Burr's courage and dedication to the revolutionary cause, and following the Battle of Monmouth the commander gave Burr the important task of defending lower Westchester County, New York, which bordered on British-occupied Manhattan Island. Much of Westchester was a lawless no-man's-land, the scene of raids, ambushes, and skirmishes by soldiers, partisans, and bandits.

Recalling the situation years later, Samuel Youngs, one of Burr's officers at the time, recalled that "[p]arties of marauders assuming either character [British or American], or none as suited their convenience, indiscriminately assailed both Whigs and Tories. These calamities continued undiminished, until the arrival of Col. Burr, in the autumn of the year 1778." Burr brought order and discipline to the American soldiers patrolling the county. Youngs recalled one of Burr's techniques: "Between midnight & 2 o'clock in the morning, accompanied by two or three of his Corps of horsemen, he visited the quarters of all his Captains and their picket guards. You may judge of the severity of this duty, when I assure you that the distance which he thus rode, every night, must have been from 16 to 24 miles."[31]

Apparently Burr was able during this period to continue his affair with Mrs. Theodosia Bartow Prevost, the wife of British army Capt. James Mark Prevost,

---

named second-in-command of a new regiment commanded by Col. William Malcom. W. W. Abbot, et al., eds., *The Papers of George Washington,* Revolutionary War Series, X: 131, 133. Colonel Malcolm's Additional Continental Regiment, also called The Malcolms, was authorized on January 7, 1777, and assigned on June 27 of that year to the Highlands Department. Its commander, Col. William Malcolm, was a wealthy New York militia officer who left the operation of the regiment to Burr. The regiment was headquartered at Ramapo in northern New Jersey through September 1777, when it was assigned to the main army as part of the 3rd Pennsylvania Brigade for the defense of Philadelphia. It participated with this brigade during the June 28, 1778, Battle of Monmouth as part of the force under Washington's command that reinforced General Lee. The regiment returned to northern New Jersey following the battle. For the history of Malcolm's regiment, see Wright, *The Continental Army,* 100, 323; Berg, *Encyclopedia of Continental Army Units,* 63; Samuel Engle Burr, *The Aaron Burr Lectures* (Burr Publications, 1981), 66. For information about the regiment's participation in the Battle of Monmouth, see Brendan Morrissey, *Monmouth Courthouse 1778* (Oxford: Osprey Publishing, 2004), 88.

31 Samuel Youngs, "Aaron Burr As a Soldier, A Letter From Judge Youngs of West Chester County, N.Y., [dated] Mount Pleasant Jany 25, 1814," *Historical Magazine,* Vol. IX, Second Series (June, 1871), No. 6, 384-387.

who was stationed in Florida at the time.[32] She lived in northern New Jersey; Burr first met her while serving with Malcolm's Regiment. He became infatuated with Theodosia, even though she was ten years his senior and the mother of five children. Burr's political enemies later claimed that he quit the army in April 1779 to devote his full time to his tryst with the beautiful and intelligent Mrs. Prevost, but a more likely explanation was that he had to leave the army because of poor health from his several years of arduous soldiering.[33]

Back in civilian life, Burr resumed his legal studies and was admitted to the New York Bar in 1782. That same year he married Theodosia, whose husband had conveniently died in 1781 on the island of Jamaica. At first the happy couple lived in Albany, but when the war ended they moved to New York City, where there were greater opportunities for him to make money practicing law. The Burrs had one child, a daughter also named Theodosia, born in 1783. The high-spirited and prosperous Burr family enjoyed life in post-war New York City, where young Aaron competed with Col. Alexander Hamilton to be the city's most successful attorney. Problems, however, soon developed. Mrs. Burr was frequently in poor health, and she died in 1794. Also, while Burr was a big wage earner, he made speculative upstate New York land investments which failed. He also loaned generous sums of money to his friends which were never repaid.

Burr's political career was also a wild affair. Although he served for many years as an elected official, it is difficult to find a letter or speech in which he expressed his political ideas. The reason is that Burr had no political philosophy, so he latched on to whatever group seemed to offer him the best opportunity to reward his constituents and advance his own political career. What is sad about Burr is that he had the family lineage, education, and experience to have done better for himself and his country. What is scary about Burr was that he became so adept at political manipulation and influence peddling that he came close to

32 One historian gave an imaginative explanation for how Burr was able to visit Mrs. Prevost in New Jersey while continuing his demanding duties in New York: "[H]e rode horseback to the Hudson River. There, he secured the services of a boatman who rowed him across the river to the Jersey shore. There, he secured another horse and rode to "The Hermitage" [the Prevost homestead is still standing as a museum, but with many additions and alternations] at Paramus [modern Ho-Ho-Kus]. After an evening visit with Mrs. Prevost, he returned to White Plains. The chances are that he did not sleep at all on such a night." Burr, *The Aaron Burr Lectures*, 73. Among the problems with this fanciful story is that it was dangerous for anyone to be traveling in Westchester County, especially a lone American officer journeying at night.

33 John Ferling, *A Leap in the Dark* (New York: Oxford University Press, 2003), 457.

being elected President of the United States in 1800. He was the Vice President in 1804 during Jefferson's first administration, the same year that he lost a heated election for governor of New York.

Burr blamed Alexander Hamilton for orchestrating vindictive newspaper stories about him that allegedly resulted in his loss. Burr challenged Col. Hamilton to a duel, which took place on July 11, 1804, in Weehawken, New Jersey. It seems that Burr fired first, hitting Hamilton in the spine. As Hamilton fell, he fired his pistol wildly, leaving Burr unhurt. Hamilton died the next day, and in the minds of many Burr was a cold-blooded murderer. Warrants were issued for his arrest, but he fled to South Carolina, where dueling was tolerated and his son-in-law was a wealthy plantation owner.[34] Burr eventually returned to Washington to serve out his term as vice president, which proved to be the end of his political career.

In 1805, Burr organized a scheme to seize Spanish territory in the west.[35] Among his confederates was Gen. James Wilkinson, the same officer who had served as an aide-de-camp to Benedict Arnold in 1776 and adjutant under Horatio Gates during the 1777 Saratoga Campaign. Wilkinson became wary of Burr's plot and eventually informed President Jefferson of a "deep, dark, wicked and widespread conspiracy" that included the intent to annex parts of the Louisiana Purchase to create a new nation in the American West. Jefferson had Burr arrested and tried for treason, but Chief Justice John Marshall, who

34 Aaron Burr's son-in-law was Joseph Alston (1779-1816), a wealthy and cultured South Carolina rice planter. Alston's ancestral home, called The Oaks, was on the Waccamaw River near Georgetown. He married Burr's daughter Theodosia on February 2, 1801, at Richmond Hill, Burr's Manhattan mansion. Joseph and Theodosia accompanied Burr to Washington for his inauguration as vice president (March 4, 1801). The couple traveled to upstate New York that summer and became the first known newlyweds to visit Niagara Falls. Theodosia was lost at sea in 1812 while en route from South Carolina to visit her father in New York. Alston served one term as the governor of South Carolina (1812-1814).

35 Burr toured the American West in 1805 to stir interest in a jingoist filibustering expedition against Spanish possessions in the Southwest, possibly Mexico itself. He also approached Anthony Merry, the British minister to the United States at the time, to raise money for his scheme, the supposition being that what hurt Spain would help Britain. The British, however, were not interested in helping the former vice president. Burr managed to raise about 100 men with the help of Harmon Blennerhassett, a wealthy young Irishman living on an island (Blennerhassett's Island) in the Ohio River. The expedition, however, quickly disbanded. Here is a good appraisal of Burr's activities during this period: "As to what Burr had in mind, it may be exactly what the convoluted and voluminous records show: a vague set of contingency plans, laced with a large dose of desperation-tinged romanticism, all calculated to benefit Aaron Burr." R. Kent Newmyer, *John Marshall and the Heroic Age of the Supreme Court* (Baton Rouge: Louisiana State University Press, 2001), 181.

Illustration of the 1804 Burr-Hamilton Duel. *Author's Collection*

despised Jefferson, saved Burr by imposing a strict interpretation of the phrase "levying war" in the Constitution. Following his trial, Burr went to Europe, where he lived from 1808-1812 before returning to New York City to resume his law practice.

There are several accounts of the story of how Colonel Burr ran into his fellow Arnold Expedition veteran Chaplain Samuel Spring, who was walking with his son in New York years after the end of the Revolutionary War. As Spring and Burr chatted on the street, the minister's son found an opportune moment to whisper to his father not to associate with Col. Burr, who was regarded as a scoundrel by many genteel people in the city. The old clergyman replied that his image of young Burr during the march to Quebec was too vivid in his mind for him to follow his son's advice. The two old veterans met later in a restaurant where they talked amicably for hours, sharing their memories of their trek to Canada and Montgomery's desperate attack on Quebec.[36]

By 1836, Burr had become weak and paralyzed. He was moved to a room in the Port Richmond Hotel on what was then Staten Island, New York's fashionable north shore. There he lay immobile in bed, with no family or wartime comrades to comfort him. His best friend from childhood and the war—Matthias Ogden, who had wrapped his worn-out shoes in pieces of cloth during the trek into Canada—was among the first of Burr's friends from the Arnold Expedition to die.[37] Ogden, who retired from the army with the rank of brigadier general, expired at his home in Elizabeth, New Jersey, on March 31, 1791. Perhaps Burr could still recall that Ogden and he, after volunteering for the Arnold Expedition back in 1775, had overheard one of its officers declare, "A man that enlists in this service should not be afraid of dying."[38] Some of the other men Burr knew from the Arnold Expedition had never reached Canada or were killed in the heroic attack on Quebec. Still other comrades from the campaign, including Christopher Greene and Charles Porterfield, had been killed in the war. All the rest, including Morgan, Meigs, Bigelow, Febiger,

36 For accounts of the story of Colonel Burr meeting Chaplain Spring, see Henry Childs Merwin, *Aaron Burr* (Boston: Small, Maynard & Company, 1899), 27; Charles Burr Todd, *Life of Colonel Aaron Burr* (New York: S.W. Green, 1879), 84.

37 For the story of Ogden wrapping his shoes in flour bags, see Ward, *The War of the Revolution*, I: 179.

38 Anthony Walker, *So Few the Brave: Rhode Island Continentals 1775-1783* (Newport, Rhode Island: Seafield Press, 1981), 8. The quote is attributed to Capt. John Topham.

Dearborn, Ward, Thayer, and Oswald, were also dead by the time Burr was carried on a litter to a second-floor room in the Port Richmond Hotel to die.

One of the doctors who visited Burr at the time was Ephraim Clark, who wrote about his experience years later. Dr. Clark described Burr as a mere shadow of the glorious man he once was, but noted that the fire of genius blazed in him still. Clark recalled:

> Burr had a grand head—a splendid head—with the most brilliant eyes I ever saw, but below the head he was little more than a helpless skeleton. I never saw him stand up . . . always in his room he was laying upon his bed or couch. . . . All power of moving his lower extremities seemed to have been lost. But the first time I took his hand . . . thin, weak, wasted away it was like the claw of a bird and I could not help thinking of the deed that hand had done, and a strange feeling passed over me, not exactly a shudder, perhaps. Aaron Burr seemed to be all alone, horribly alone for a man who had been a Vice President of the United States and had held the social position that he once did.[39]

On June 17, 1836, the Tompkins Guards, a fashionable Staten Island militia company, was holding its annual banquet in the downstairs dining room of the Port Richmond Hotel to celebrate the anniversary of the Battle of Bunker Hill. During their festivities they learned that Col. Burr, a combat veteran from the American Revolution, was residing in an upstairs room. A young lieutenant named Mersereau was sent upstairs to invite the colonel to join the celebration. After knocking on the door, Lt. Mersereau opened it to find a frail old man lying in bed. The young lieutenant tendered his invitation to this relic of the Revolutionary War to join the festivities below. Burr whispered that he was too weak to leave his bed, but would be grateful if the company's officers would visit him. Mersereau returned downstairs and reported what had happened. Led by their commander, Captain Laforge, the company's officers went upstairs, where they talked for a long time with Col. Burr and listened to his reminiscences from the Revolutionary War. After returning to the banquet room, Laforge assembled his company outside, below Burr's window, where they serenaded the old soldier with patriotic songs and honored him with toasts and cheers.

39 "Memories of Aaron Burr, The Miserable Old Age and Death of a Once Great Man; Interview with Dr. Ephraim Clark," *The New York Times*, Wednesday, May 31, 1878, 5.

Burr died soon after, on September 14, 1836, on the anniversary of the order that more than 60 years earlier had launched the Arnold Expedition and started his military career:[40]

> Cambridge, September 14, 1775
>
> Instructions to Colonel Benedict Arnold
>
> By his Excellency George Washington Esqr. Commander in Chief of the Army of the United Colonies of North America.
>
> You are immediately . . . to take the Command of the Detachment from the Continental Army against Quebeck, & use all possible Expedition as the Winter Season is now Advancing . . .[41]

Based on Washington's order, 19-year-old Aaron Burr and more than 1,000 other young Americans set out with Arnold for Maine, convinced that they would snatch Quebec from the jaws of the sleeping British lion.

40 Following his death, Burr's body was brought to Princeton University, where it lay in state in Nassau Hall. Burr was buried on the university grounds alongside his father and grandfather, both of whom served as presidents of the college. His funeral service was conducted by Princeton's 9th president, James Carnahan, who took the opportunity to deliver a discourse on the evils of dueling.

41 W. W. Abbot, et. al., eds., *The Papers of George Washington,* Revolutionary War Series, I: 457.

Chapter Eight

Benedict Arnold: The American Traitor and British General

"There is no character in history, nor is there any in poetry or fiction, better calculated to teach and illustrate the beauty and the wisdom of fidelity, and the infamy and the folly of treachery than his."

— *Isaac N. Arnold, The Life of Benedict Arnold*[1]

Both the British and Americans used a variety of covert methods during the Revolutionary War to obtain military information or damage civilian morale. One of the techniques used by the British Army was to probe high-ranking American officers to see whether any of them would desert for money, or from dissatisfaction with the patriot cause and other personal grievances. Philip Schuyler, Ethan Allen, Daniel Morgan, Israel Putnam, and John Sullivan were among the Continental officers approached in this manner. No patriot officer was known to have negotiated with the enemy except for Maj. Gen. Benedict Arnold, who went beyond mere defection. Arnold, as history has recorded, not only defected but conspired with the British to capture West Point, the important American supply depot and fortress guarding the Hudson River.

1 As previously noted, Isaac N. Arnold was a distant relative of Benedict Arnold.

The story of Arnold's treason begins with the severe leg wound he suffered in the Battle of Bemis Heights while leading an American attack against Breymann's Redoubt. The assault was an act of courage by Arnold and the soldiers who charged into the breastwork behind him. However, as noted previously, Burgoyne's army was already beaten by the time Arnold stormed into the enemy position, and his reckless act needlessly endangered the lives of the men who followed him.

Arnold was taken to a field hospital, where he came close to losing his shattered leg for a second time. He was later moved to a hospital in Albany, where he lay in bed—with ample time to brood. Burgoyne made a desperate attempt to retreat back to Canada, but his army was hopelessly trapped as a result of Gates' methodical planning, and Burgoyne surrendered on October 19, 1777.

Saratoga was a great American victory, and Gates was proclaimed a military genius. However, Schuyler also deserved credit for his delaying tactics, as did Arnold for his brilliant leadership. It was Arnold who urged Gates to attack the British in the woods and fields facing Bemis Heights to prevent them from outflanking the American lines. But Arnold's bitter confrontations with Gates during the campaign wrecked any chance of his being praised by the hero of Saratoga. Gates grudgingly acknowledged Arnold's participation in the October 7 Battle of Bemis Heights in a letter to John Hancock: "[A]mongst the Latter [wounded on October 7] is the Gallant Major General Arnold, whose Leg was fractured by a Musket Ball, as he was Forcing the Enemy's Breast Work."[2] Other American officers on the scene were more solicitous toward Arnold. In response to reports that Arnold had been wounded in action at Saratoga, General Washington sent him a gift of a pair of epaulettes and an elegant sword knot (a cord attached to the guard of a sword that tied around the wrist). Washington's action may have been motivated in part by his concern for Gates' growing reputation and aloof behavior following his great victory, but it also reflected his admiration for Arnold.[3]

2 William M. Darlington, ed., *Christopher Gist's Journal with Historical, Geographical and Ethnological Notes and Biographies of His Contemporaries* (Pittsburgh: J. R. Weldin & Co., 1893), 279.

3 Commenting on Gates' victory at Saratoga, American General Nathanael Greene wrote to a fellow officer: "This Gentleman [Gates] is a mere child of fortune; the foundation of all the Northern successes was laid long before his arrival there; and Arnold and Lincoln [General Benjamin Lincoln] were the principal instruments in compleating [sic] the work." Richard K.

When he was well enough to travel, Arnold went to Valley Forge by wagon, where he rejoined the army and received a warm welcome from Gen. Washington. Lieutenant Colonel Henry Dearborn (promoted from major in January 1778) recorded his former commander's arrival in his journal: "May 21st . . . General Lee [Charles Lee] & General Arnold have both arivd [sic] in Camp to the great joy of the army."[4] Arnold was walking with the aid of a cane at the time and unable to ride a horse. Washington wanted him to take command of troops in the field, but he was still too weak to actively campaign.

Instead Washington appointed him the military governor of the Philadelphia region following the British evacuation of that city. The ransacked city was in chaos following seven months of British occupation, and Washington named Arnold to govern the city in cooperation with the civilian authorities. It seemed like a harmless enough assignment, but the belligerent and obstinate Arnold was a poor choice for the post. Commenting on Arnold's appointment as Philadelphia's military governor, historian Dave Palmer said, "One would be hard-pressed to find a worse personnel decision made by Washington in the entire war."[5] With the commander-in-chief away with the army in New Jersey and no one like Montgomery or Schuyler to mentor him, Arnold was on his own.

Philadelphia became the center of commerce in wartime America following the British flight. The city's commercial rival, New York, was in British hands, and despite rampant inflation there was money to be made in Philadelphia through various means, including smuggling, selling equipment left behind by the British, hoarding food and merchandise, trading with the enemy, and investing in privateers. (The latter were government-licensed, privately funded armed ships that were authorized to seize enemy vessels and sell the captured ships and their cargos.)[6] Arnold was an experienced merchant from his pre-war

---

Showman, et. al., eds. *The Papers of General Nathanael Greene*, 13 vols. (Chapel Hill: The University of North Carolina Press, 1976-2005), II: 260.

4 Brown and Peckham, eds., *Revolutionary War Journals of Henry Dearborn,* 121.

5 Dave R. Palmer, *George Washington and Benedict Arnold* (Washington, DC: Regnery Publishing, Inc., 2006), 280.

6 There were actually two categories of government-licensed, privately funded armed ships that were authorized to seize enemy vessels and sell the captured ships and their cargoes. A privateer was an armed civilian ship that operated under a privateering license, whose primary purpose was to patrol for enemy ships, engage them in combat, and capture them if possible, but take on portions of their cargo only as an auxiliary function. A so-called letter of marque

days in New Haven, and he became a player in the city's complicated wartime business activities, aided by his powerful position as military governor.

Arnold also quickly became immersed in the flourishing social scene in the newly liberated city. He used poor judgment in flaunting a lavish lifestyle in Philadelphia, which he financed mostly on credit. Anonymously authored newspaper stories published at the time included one that appeared in the *Pennsylvania Packet*, which read in part: "When I meet your carriage in the street, and think of the splendor in which you live . . . it is impossible to avoid the question, From whence have these riches flowed, if you did not plunder Montreal?"[7] Arnold enjoyed hosting elegant dinners and socializing with wealthy families who had entertained the British during their occupation of the city.

Among Arnold's new circle of Philadelphia acquaintances was Edward Shippen, a wealthy person suspected of being a Tory.[8] Arnold was particularly attracted to Shippen's youngest daughter, a lively teenage beauty named Margaret, or Peggy as she was called. With the popular Peggy clutching onto his arm, America's greatest combat officer mingled with the most important people in Philadelphia—some of whom were of questionable fidelity to the patriot cause.

Despite their age difference (he was 38 at the time and she was 18), Benedict and Peggy were attracted to each other. They were both intelligent and ambitious, and each loved living and entertaining in a grand style. Peggy had enjoyed a marvelous social life during the British occupation, and now the dashing, twice-wounded General Arnold had replaced her British Army

ship operated under a Letter of Marque and Reprisal, and was primarily a civilian merchant ship that armed itself with sufficient guns to protect itself and be of some danger to weaker combatants. Its primary purpose was to go about the business of carrying cargo for hire, but would engage in warfare as an auxiliary function, when forced to do so or as advantageous circumstances presented themselves. E-mail exchange with Robert C. Ayer, CAPT U.S. Coast Guard (ret.), former Professor of Maritime History, U.S. Coast Guard Academy, New London, CT, April 2012.

7 Brandt, *The Man in the Mirror*, 171.

8 Edward Shippen studied law in London. According to historian James Thomas Flexner, Shippen "lacked the dash necessary for a trial lawyer, but filled successfully his hereditary role as an officer of government." Shippen was simultaneously Judge of the Vice-Admiralty Court, town clerk, member and clerk of the Common Council, and protonotary [chief clerk] of the Supreme Court. He was remembered as a judge who lacked originality, but revealed "some talent," much "common sense," and a mind "of eminently practical cast." James Thomas Flexner, *The Traitor and the Spy* (New York: Harcourt, Brace and Company, 1953), 189-190.

admirers. Their shared visions of wealth and power blossomed into love, and the superficially dissimilar pair were married on April 18, 1779.

Arnold's marriage to the daughter of a suspected Loyalist attracted significant unwelcome attention. Congress was already hostile toward Arnold because of his persistent demands for both money and promotion. Arnold further antagonized Congress by demanding that it provide a pension for the wife and children of his friend and patriot martyr Dr. Joseph Warren. Warren was mortally wounded while treating American soldiers wounded in the fighting at Bunker Hill.

Pennsylvania officials became particularly angry with Arnold when he ordered all the shops and businesses operating in Philadelphia to be closed. According to Arnold, he issued the order so that their inventories could be inspected for contraband or stolen merchandise. However, many people claimed that Arnold had instituted this draconian measure for his own advantage: that he stole goods from the vacant shops and carted them away in army wagons.

Arnold's high living and altercations with Congress and various Pennsylvania functionaries attracted much unwanted attention. Admittedly, many other American officers were also trying to make as much mone as possible money while in office, but the costliness of Arnold's lifestyle aroused suspicions among government officials that he was using his position in Philadelphia for his own profit.

The Pennsylvania Supreme Executive Council finally took action, charging Arnold with four counts of corruption. The case was referred to Congress, which was happy to accommodate Arnold's demand for a military court martial to clear his name. The trial took place from January to April 1779 at Peter Dickerson's Tavern in Morristown, New Jersey, where the army was encamped for the winter. Arnold was found guilty of two of the four charges: using government wagons for his personal use and issuing a pass to a ship he later invested in. The court sentenced him to be publicly censured by the commander-in-chief. In his reprimand, Washington was as gentle as the circumstances would allow.

By this time, however, Washington's reprimand fell upon deaf ears. Arnold, constantly attacked in the press and desperately in need of money, had already turned to treason for both pecuniary rewards and revenge. According to Jared

Portrait of Benjamin Franklin, by Benjamin Wilson. The reputation of Maj. John André as an honorable gentleman and genteel officer is called into question based on the history of this painting. André lived in Franklin's home during the British occupation of Philadelphia (1777-1778). André looted the house when the British evacuated the city and his booty included this portrait of Franklin. The painting was returned to America 100 years later, and is now part of the White House art collection. *White House Historical Association (White House Collection): 981*

Sparks, Arnold's earliest biographer, "It only remained for him to settle in his mind the manner in which this could so be done, as to produce the greatest advantage to himself, and injury to the cause he was about to desert."[9]

9 Sparks, *The Life and Treason of Benedict Arnold*, 152.

Although Arnold had made the acquaintance of some residents of Philadelphia who were rumored to be sympathetic to the King, it was dangerous to approach any of them to discuss treason amid a conflict that was rampant with spies, double agents, and paid informers. If Arnold's disloyalty was exposed, he faced humiliation, imprisonment, or the gallows. Peggy Arnold was in on the plot from the outset, assuring her husband that she had a trustworthy, high-level connection in British-occupied New York. Peggy's contact was 29-year-old Captain John André, her friend and former suitor who had become warmly attached to her during the British occupation. André worked at the time at British Army headquarters as an aide-de-camp and confidant to Gen. Sir Henry Clinton, who commanded the British Army in America.

There remained only the selection of a secure means of contacting André to introduce him to Arnold's interest in switching sides, and seeing what kind of deal could be made. Once again, Peggy provided the answer in the person of a Philadelphia china (crockery) dealer named Joseph Stansbury. He was a 33-year-old English-born social climber who dressed as fashionably as a gentleman (defined at the time as someone who did not work for a living) and circulated in Philadelphia's best society. Stansbury had befriended the socially prominent Peggy and confided in her about his loyalty to the King. He was also a good candidate to get a message to André, since he had experience passing through the American lines to New York to arrange complicated business transactions concerning his imported dinnerware.

When Arnold sent a servant to request that Stansbury come to his home, the tradesman thought that the general wanted to place another order for cups and saucers. Stansbury arrived at Arnold's home on May 1, 1779, and was ushered into a secure room, or perhaps the garden, where the former horse dealer broached the subject of treason with the crockery salesman. Stansbury readily agreed to go to New York and contact André. And with this simple meeting the plot was hatched.

Stansbury met with André in New York on May 10, 1779. Peggy Arnold's connection with André was fortuitous, as Gen. Clinton had recently added the position of chief of intelligence to his talented aide's responsibilities. Arnold wanted a large sum of money to desert (£20,000—equal to more than one million dollars in today's money), and André told him that he had to do something hugely damaging to the patriot cause for such a big reward. Arnold's relatively insignificant assignment as military governor of Philadelphia put him in a weak position to get the money he wanted.

The negotiations dragged on for over a year, encouraged by Arnold, who provided André with enough information to keep him interested. Stansbury remained the courier, but he received assistance from André, who used a British secret agent named John Ratoon (code name Mercury) to help Stansbury slip through the American lines in New Jersey. The means of communication were innocent-looking letters which included text written between the lines in invisible ink. The ink used was not lemon juice, which could be easily detected, but the result of complicated chemical formulas known as sympathetic stain, which would evade scrutiny.[10]

As an additional security measure, the messages sent back and forth were encoded. The code used was simple but difficult to break. Words were represented by three numbers. The first number was the page in a specific book, the second number was the line on the page of the book, and the third number was the word on the line. The system was well known, but the difficult part for a cryptanalyst was to determine what book was being used to create the cipher. General Washington had clever volunteers working for him to break codes, including Massachusetts Congressman James Lovell. However, Arnold and André were very careful, and their negotiations were never uncovered by Washington's intelligence organization.

André proposed that Arnold get command of the group of Hudson River fortifications and military depots known as West Point, "the possession of which were supposed by many to hinge the fortunes of the war."[11] Arnold was assured that he would get a huge payment and a high rank in the Royal army if he could deliver West Point to Sir Henry Clinton.

Arnold manipulated his friendship with Washington to get command of the strategic fortress and its dependencies. In early August 1780, he arrived to

10 The use of invisible ink in the American Revolution is a fascinating story. While serving in Paris early in the war as an agent of the Committee of Secret Correspondence, Silas Deane is known to have used a heat-developing invisible ink for some of his intelligence reports. Deane's ink was a compound of cobalt chloride, glycerin, and water. He later used what was called a sympathetic stain created for secret communications by physician James Jay. Dr. Jay supplied his stain to Silas Deane and to George Washington. His stain required one chemical for writing a message and a second to develop it. Washington instructed his secret agents to write their intelligence reports in Jay's invisible ink in some blank area, or within the lines of text of an innocent-looking letter. He also suggested that messages could be written in invisible ink in any inexpensive pamphlet or book. However, despite all these precautions, the British were alert to the patriots' techniques and were able to intercept and read numerous American intelligence reports.

11 Washington Irving, *Life of George Washington*, IV: 107.

take charge of his new post, where he continued his correspondence with André using the code name Monk. André used the subterfuge of an identity as a New York City merchant named John Anderson who was interested in doing business with the Americans. The plan was for a Royal Navy flotilla to make a dash up the Hudson carrying troops who would seize West Point. Arnold would surrender the post when the enemy arrived. It only remained for Arnold to meet with an envoy of the British Army to prove that he was Maj. Gen. Benedict Arnold and make final arrangements for the British attack.

General Sir Henry Clinton was an unhappy, suspicious man who once described himself as a "shy bitch." But his relationship with André was different. Clinton was devoted to his handsome young aide, who was educated (André, for example, spoke English, French, and German fluently) as well as being a talented musician, artist, and poet. Clinton's relationship with André was not unlike Washington's affection for Lafayette.

In October 1779, Clinton rewarded André by appointing him the adjutant general of the army with the rank of major. André was ambitious and wanted the prestige of meeting with Arnold to finalize the spectacular plot to capture West Point. It was a dangerous mission, but when the arrangements seemed safe Clinton reluctantly agreed. The plan was for André to sail up the Hudson on the Royal Navy sloop *Vulture*. Once in position, he would be rowed ashore at night for a brief meeting with Arnold, then return to the sloop. For added security, André would wear his uniform throughout the mission, covered by a civilian greatcoat (overcoat). If he was apprehended in uniform he would be a prisoner of war; if he was captured wearing civilian clothing, however, he would be considered a spy under the rules of warfare and could be hanged.

The meeting with Arnold took place as planned on the night of September 20, 1780. But American shore artillery fired on the *Vulture*, forcing her to sail back downstream—leaving André stranded behind enemy lines. Rather than wait for the return of the *Vulture*, Arnold convinced André to change into civilian clothing, assume his disguise as John Anderson, and ride back to the British lines. As an added measure of security, Arnold wrote out a warrant for him: "Sept. 21, 1780, Permit Mr. John Anderson to pass the guards to the White Plains, or below, if he chuses. He being on public business by my direction. [signed] B. Arnold, M [Major] Gen."[12]

12 The original document is in the collections of the New York State Archives.

Thus André found himself alone and riding through the lawless Neutral Ground of Westchester County, New York, the scene of raids by maundering parties from both sides. As he approached the village of Tarrytown, a burly young man stepped out from the trees and leveled a musket at him. Then two other men, similarly armed, showed themselves. One of them grabbed the bit of the outlander's horse while John Paulding, the leader of the three, questioned the stranger. According to later testimony, the dialog between Paulding and the man on horseback went as follows:

"Gentlemen," the rider blurted out, "I hope you belong to our party."

"What party?" replied Paulding.

"The lower party." [The British, who occupied New York City.]

Paulding nodded, which encouraged the stranger to continue.

"I am glad to see you. I am an officer in the British service, and have now been on particular business in the country, and I hope you will not detain me. And for a token to let you know that I am a gentleman." [André showed the three men his expensive gold pocket watch to impress them.]

Paulding was indifferent, and ordered the traveler to dismount.

Sensing that he had made a terrible mistake, the stranger begin to laugh as he spoke. "My God, I must do anything to get along," and handed Paulding his pass signed by Arnold.

Unmoved, Paulding repeated his order.

After getting off his horse, the stranger told his antagonists, "You had best let me go, or you will bring yourselves in trouble, for, by your stopping me, you will detain the general's business."

Their suspicions aroused, the three young men herded their captive to some nearby underbrush, where they ordered him to undress. As each piece of clothing was removed, it was carefully searched until the man calling himself John Anderson was standing with only his britches and boots on. Paulding ordered him to take off his boots. After one boot was removed it was searched but nothing was found. Then one of the militiamen ran his hands along the stocking thus exposed and felt something between it and the bottom of the stranger's foot. André was ordered at gunpoint to remove his stocking, inside of which Paulding found three folded pieces of paper. After hastily scanning the documents, Paulding spoke the legendary words, "My God! He is a spy!"[13]

13 Flexner, *The Traitor and The Spy,* 357-359.

If this dialogue is true, then André had handled himself badly. Why didn't he show Arnold's pass when he was stopped? If he was safely within the British lines, there would have been no harm done. André's capture was attributed to luck. However, his apprehension was largely due to the fact that he was a stranger with a natural elegance and military bearing that attracted suspicion in a region of outlaws, farmers, and tradesmen.

As the senior officer in the lower Hudson River Valley, Arnold was quickly informed of the arrest of a civilian named John Anderson who was caught with vital information about West Point. Arnold knew it was only a matter of time before his role in the plot was discovered. He raced to reach the *Vulture* before he could be apprehended, and made it safely to New York.

Clinton, meanwhile, negotiated frantically to free his young adjutant. But the only deal Washington would accept was Arnold for André. Clinton refused the exchange; acquiescing would ruin any chance of getting other American officers to defect. Although the Americans, including Washington, were sympathetic toward André's plight, the fact remained that he was a spy and, on the recommendation of a military tribunal, the commander-in-chief sentenced him to be hanged. Both sides blamed Arnold for the youthful officer's ignominious death. With André dead, Arnold in New York, and West Point still safely in American hands, General Clinton wrote to his superiors in London, "Thus ended this proposed plan . . . which I had conceived such great hopes and from whence I imagined would be derived such great consequences."[14]

The capture of André was looked upon by many Americans as a sign of divine intervention in their cause. Gen. Nathanael Greene remarked that "[t]he providential train of circumstances which led to it [the discovery of the plot], affords the most convincing proofs that the liberties of America are the object of Divine protection."[15] The exposure of the dangerous plan gave the patriot cause a morale boost.

Meanwhile, the British went through the motions of warmly accepting Arnold into their ranks as a brigadier general of Provincial troops. Clinton

14 General Sir Henry Clinton to Lord George Germain, dated "11 October, New York" in K.G. Davies, ed., *Documents of the American Revolution 1770-1783 (Colonial Office Series),* 21 vols. (Shannon: Irish University Press, 1972-1981), XVIII: 184.

15 Showman, et al., eds., *The Papers of General Nathanael Greene*, VI: 314. Greene also commented that he attributed Arnold's courage on the battlefield to "imbibing strong liquor, even to intoxication." Theodore Thayer, *Nathanael Greene, Strategist of the American Revolution* (New York: Twayne Publishers, 1960), 278.

acknowledged this rank in an October 11, 1780, letter to Lord George Germain. The pertinent text reads: "As this very commendable step of General Arnold's [defecting to the British] is likely to produce great and good consequences I have thought it right to appoint him colonel of a regiment with the rank of brigadier-general of provincial forces."[16] This position was different from and less prestigious than the rank of brigadier general in the British Army. As a provincial (Loyalist) officer, Arnold was about equal in rank to a colonel in the British Army. Such distinctions are important to understand, especially as Arnold had constantly squabbled with Congress over his rank as an American officer. The date that an officer was promoted was also meaningful, since the officer whose commission came first was acknowledged as the senior officer in that rank, with all other officers of the same rank subordinate to him.

When Eleazer Oswald learned about Benedict Arnold's treason, he wrote the aforementioned passage to his friend Col. John Lamb: "[H]ad the ball which pierced his leg at Saratoga, been directed thro' his heart; he would have finished his career in glory."[17] Oswald's father-in-law, John Holt, published a poem about Arnold in his newspaper:

> Curses of ages shall attend his name;
> Traitors, alone shall glory in his fame
> Let Hell receive him, riveted in chains,
> Damn'd to the focus of its hottest flames.[18]

Besides being held responsible for the popular André's death, stories were soon spreading in New York City about Arnold's insensitive haggling with Clinton over the money that had been promised to him. The agreement with Clinton called for Arnold to be paid £20,000 if he switched sides and delivered West Point, and £6,000 if the plot failed. But Arnold told Clinton that at their meeting his now-dead adjutant had promised Arnold a larger sum just for switching sides—"he assured me though he was commissioned to promise me only six thousand pounds sterling he would use his influence and recommend it to your Excellency to allow the sum I proposed." Clinton was shocked by

16 Davies, ed., *Documents of the American Revolution,* Colonial Office Series, XVIII: 186.

17 Letter from Col. Eleazer Oswald to Col. John Lamb, dated "December 11th, 1780," in Leake, *The Life of General John Lamb*, 266.

18 John Holt's *New York Journal* newspaper, Poughkeepsie, New York, February 1781.

Arnold's insensitive quibbling, and paid him the £6,000 originally promised. It was an enormous amount of money for the time. For example, a family could live well at the time, including in a house, with servants and a coach, on an income of £500 per year.[19]

A consolation was Arnold's assurance to Clinton that he could raise a Loyalist regiment from the multitude of American deserters who would follow his example. With his usual zeal, Arnold began to recruit men for his new regiment, which he called the Loyal American Refugees. His recruiting efforts included an advertisement in the *Royal Gazette*, a New York City newspaper which circulated in the camps of the Continental Army. Arnold's notice in the *Gazette* ran from October 23 to December 6, 1780. Here is a portion of it:

> To the officers and soldiers of the continental army who have the real interest of their country at heart, and who are determined to be no longer the tools and dupes of Congress, or of France.
>
> His Excellency Sir Henry Clinton has authoriz'd me to raise a corps of cavalry and infantry, who are to be clothed, subsisted, and paid as the other troops are in the British service. . . . Great as these encouragements must appear to such as have suffered every distress of want of pay, hunger, and nakedness, from the neglect, contempt, and corruption of Congress, they are nothing to the motives which I expect will influence the brave and generous minds I hope to have the honor to command. . . . I only add my promise of the most affectionate welcome and attention to all who are disposed to join me . . . [20]

But Arnold's recruiting efforts failed to produce the promised results. By the end of December 1780, enlistments in the Refugees stood at eight officers, three sergeants, twenty-eight common soldiers, and one drummer. Those who joined were American deserters and fanatic Loyalists who were already in New York City, "prepared for any desperate or despicable service."[21] At its peak, Arnold's regiment totaled just 212 officers and men.

19 Jackson Turner Main, *The Social Structure of Revolutionary America* (Princeton: Princeton University Press, 1965), 123.

20 See "Regimental History, American Legion, Arnold's Proclamation" on the website *The On-Line Institute for Advanced Loyalist Studies.*

21 Irving, *Life of Washington*, IV: 161.

These men included Sgt. John Champe, a deserter from the Continental Army.[22] It was common for both sides to question deserters to check their stories and to discover information about the enemy. Champe was interrogated by Asst. Adj. Gen. George Beckwith when he arrived in New York on October 23, 1780. The young American explained that he had been a sergeant in Lee's Light Horse Corps, an elite Continental dragoon regiment (made up of horsemen specially armed and equipped for rapid deployment) stationed near Totowa, New Jersey. He told Beckwith that he deserted because "provisions were very irregular" and that he was "very much dissatisfied with the French (America's new ally)."[23] Champe described how he bolted on the night of October 20, 1780, and rode on horseback across northern New Jersey toward two Royal Navy frigates anchored near the coast. He said that he was pursued by a detachment of dragoons. Champe did not mention that the pursuit party was oddly delayed by Col. Henry Lee, the unit's commander. Upon reaching the New Jersey coast, Champe was observed by a British officer aboard one of the frigates, who watched him dismount and swim toward the ship. While in the water, he was being shot at from the shoreline by a party of American dragoons. The British officer concluded that the man was an American deserter who was swimming for his life to reach the British ship. An armed boat was dispatched to pick him up while a cannon aboard the frigate fired grapeshot to chase off his pursuers. Champe's account of his desertion was accepted by Beckwith, and he walked out of British headquarters, at 1 Broadway, a free man. He learned that Arnold was living next door in a mansion at 3 Broadway which had a back yard facing the Hudson River.

Champe seems to have accidently encountered Arnold on the street, and told him that Arnold's example had inspired him to desert. The new British general was impressed, and warmly welcomed the experienced sergeant into his Loyalist regiment. It was shortly after this that Champe had what looked like a casual conversation with a man on the street known only as Mr. Baldwin. But their meeting was no accident. Champe's desertion had been carefully staged, and Baldwin was an American secret agent operating in New York City. Both Champe and Baldwin were working under direct orders from General Washington to kidnap Arnold and deliver him to headquarters. The two

22 Brandt, *Man in the Mirror,* 23.

23 George F. Scheer, "The Sergeant Major's Strange Mission," in *American Heritage*, Volume VIII, Number 6 (October 1957), 26-29, 98.

conspirators soon had a plan to abduct the traitor. The plot was relayed to Washington's headquarters by Mr. Baldwin, and the General made the appropriate arrangements.

While Champe and Baldwin were hatching their plot, senior British officers went through the motions of cooperating with Arnold. But they were privately disgusted that he had sold his honor for money, and held him responsible for André's death. Junior officers were less tactful toward Arnold and refused to serve under him. General Clinton showed respect to Arnold in the hopes of coaxing other American officers to defect. He also wanted to use Arnold's talents as a combat officer, and gave him command of a campaign aimed at Virginia. Clinton expressed his thoughts in his narrative of his campaigns in America: "I was induced to select Brigadier General Arnold for this service [the Virginia campaign] from the very high estimation in which he was held among the enemy for active intrepidity [and] that the confidence I thus appeared to place in an officer who had acted against us might be a strong incitement to other able leaders of the rebel army to desert their cause."[24]

While Arnold was planning his foray into Virginia, Sergeant Champe was clandestinely loosening a row of slats from the wooden fence in Arnold's back yard. Champe and Baldwin had everything arranged to kidnap Arnold on the night of December 11, 1780. Their plan was to gag him and carry him between them, as if he was drunk, down to the waterfront to a waiting rowboat. They would take him across the Hudson for a rendezvous with Col. Lee's light dragoons. However, in an ironic twist of fate, Arnold's Loyalist regiment received orders earlier that same day to board a transport at once as part of the task force being sent to Virginia. Champe was lying in the hull of a ship bound for Virginia while Colonel Lee and his dragoons waited in vain all night on the Jersey shore for him to arrive with Arnold.

Clinton gave Arnold command of the Virginia expedition, but he sent two trusted lieutenant colonels, Thomas Dundas and John Graves Simcoe, along to watch him. To ensure that Arnold would work with Dundas and Simcoe, Clinton instructed him "that you will always consult those gentlemen previous to your undertaking any operation of consequence."[25] As an additional check

24 William B. Willcox, ed., *The American Rebellion, Sir Henry Clinton's Narrative of His Campaigns, 1775-1782* (New Haven: Yale University Press, 1954), 235-236.

25 Clinton to Arnold, orders dated "14 December, New York," in Davies, ed., *Documents of the American Revolution,* Colonial Office Series, XVIII: 256.

Westover Plantation, Virginia. Arnold used this mansion, located along the James River, as his headquarters during his 1780 Virginia raid which included the burning of Richmond. *Author's Collection*

on his new and untested general, Clinton gave Dundas and Simcoe, "officers of experience and much in my confidence," secret orders "authorizing them, if they suspected Arnold of sinister intent, to supersede him, and put him under arrest."[26]

Arnold landed his 1,200 troops in Virginia on December 30, 1780. Virginia was a good target, as most of her Continental troops had been sent south to reinforce the patriot forces fighting Cornwallis. The rich state was also supplying food and equipment to the patriots' southern army. Governor Thomas Jefferson called out the militia, but its members were slow to respond. With Arnold's encouragement, his corps advanced unopposed up the James River, leaving a path of looting and destruction behind it. On January 5, 1781, it attacked and burned Richmond, including large quantities of valuable tobacco. There is a story that Arnold asked a fellow officer at the time what he thought the Americans would do if they captured him. The soldier replied that he believed they would cut off Arnold's "patriot leg," which had been twice

26 John Graves Simcoe, *Simcoe's Military Journal* (New York: Bartlett & Welford, 1844), 325.

wounded in combat, bury it with honors—and hang the rest of him. In fact, Governor Jefferson offered a big reward for Arnold, dead or alive.

After burning Richmond and the Continental cannon works at Westham, Arnold retired with his booty-laden army to Portsmouth, Virginia, where he arrived on January 19, 1781, and dug in for the balance of the winter. During this time Champe made his escape back to the Continental Army. Washington arranged for him to be discharged from the army, since he was technically a deserter from both the American and British armies. Champe went to the back country of Virginia, where he sat out the remainder of the war.

Events moved quickly in Virginia for the balance of 1781, starting with the sending of 2,000 additional British troops to the state. They were commanded by Maj. Gen. William Phillips, who outranked Arnold. Arnold remained in Portsmouth under Phillips, who received an urgent order in early May from Gen. Cornwallis to rendezvous with him in Petersburg, Virginia. Phillips was instructed to bring provisions with him for Cornwallis' hungry and exhausted army, which was marching from North Carolina to meet him. Cornwallis' move into Virginia to replenish his army was in violation of Clinton's orders to remain in the Carolinas. Arnold rode into Petersburg on May 9. Phillips followed him in a carriage, as he was gravely ill with a fever, and dead by the time Cornwallis arrived on May 20, 1781.[27] Phillips' unfortunate death was a source of camp gossip that Arnold had poisoned him to regain command of the Virginia army. Another story involved Arnold's passion for plunder. The word was that he had become as rich as a nabob (defined at the time as a European who made a fortune in India) ransacking Virginia homes and warehouses.

When Cornwallis combined his forces with Phillips' corps, he had a formidable army. The Americans countered by sending Gen. Lafayette to the state with Continental troops—and orders from Gen. Washington to hang Arnold if he caught him. But Arnold was gone by the time Lafayette reached Virginia. He was recalled by Gen. Clinton and arrived in New York on June 10. Meanwhile, Cornwallis began considering a strong place in Virginia to move his army. He selected Yorktown on the York River, where he counted on protection from the Royal Navy.

27 Cornwallis wrote to Lord Rawdon, dated "Petersburgh, May 20th, 1781, I this day formed a junction with the corps under Phillips at this place." Charles Ross, ed., *Correspondence of Charles, First Marquis Cornwallis*, 3 vols. (London: John Murray, 1859), I: 98.

Back in New York, Arnold wanted another mission, and pestered Clinton with various proposals. Clinton was anxious to accommodate his new provincial general, especially since a destructive raid would help take the pressure off Cornwallis. A raid in force would also rattle Mr. Washington, who, Clinton knew, wanted to launch a campaign with the French to retake New York City. However, unknown to Clinton at the time was that the French viewed Cornwallis' army in Virginia and not New York City as the great opportunity to score a major victory in the war.

Arnold's proposal to raid New London, Connecticut, was approved by Clinton in September 1781. It was a good target for Arnold, who knew the town from his childhood years in nearby Norwich.

The facts of Arnold's New London raid have been interpreted to fit the patriot perception of him as a scheming buccaneer. Arnold had started the war in 1775 as a resourceful militia officer with great potential and became a leading officer in the American army. But he quarreled with almost everyone along the way, starting with the attack on Fort Ticonderoga, which led to his being branded as an arrogant dissenter. As the war went on, vicious stories about him were spread, resulting from his poor judgment, belligerent conduct, and lack of influential friends in government; all this was capped by his treason. His 1781 New London raid is a good example of how the public twisted the facts of an event to reinforce their perception of Arnold as a ruthless, greedy mercenary.

New London, Connecticut, was situated at the mouth of the Thames River, which emptied into Long Island Sound. The seaport town was a notorious haven for American privateers. In September 1781, there were 15 captured British ships (prizes) laden with valuable cargos anchored in New London's deepwater harbor, along with American privateers and other shipping. The town was protected by two forts. One was a small bastion on the western shore of the Thames River called Fort Trumbull. The other was an impressive stone fortress called Fort Griswold, which was well-situated on the eastern bank of the river (the site of the present-day town of Groton) at the crest of a long and steep hill. New London sat on the western bank of the Thames, just upriver from Fort Trumbull.

Arnold's flotilla of 24 armed schooners and sloops carrying 1,400 troops arrived at the entrance to the Thames River without warning at dawn on September 6, 1781. His task force was composed of three British Army regiments and three Provincial regiments, the Loyal Americans, the 3rd battalion of New Jersey Volunteers, and Arnold's own Loyal American Refugees.

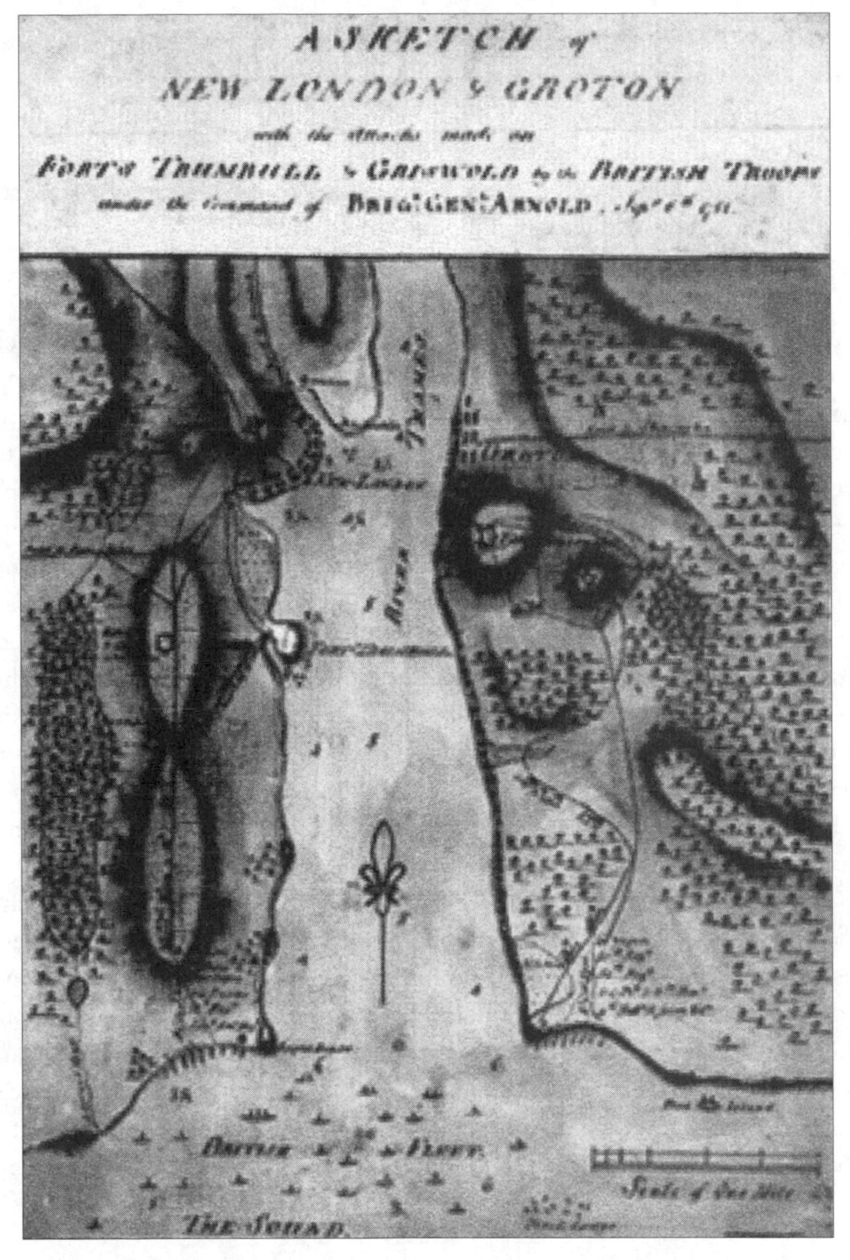

Map of New London, Connecticut. This manuscript map shows the American defenses of the town at the time of Arnold's raid. *Library of Congress*

New London was defended by local militia who would turn out at the sound of two consecutive cannon shots. Arnold planned his attack craftily. He knew the militia's warning signal, and when militia lookouts fired the two guns, Arnold ordered one of his warships to follow immediately with a third cannon blast to confuse the town's defenders. The firing of three successive artillery pieces was used by privateers to announce their arrival at New London with a valuable prize.

Arnold landed his troops quickly on both sides of the harbor in two almost equal divisions, which simultaneously attacked the rebel forts. His fast-moving columns gave the local rebel militiamen little time to man their fortifications. Arnold personally led the detachment that attacked Fort Trumbull, which was described as "a mere breast-work or water battery open from behind" meant to prevent enemy ships from entering the harbor.[28] Upon Arnold's approach, the members of the fort's small garrison abandoned their posts and rowed across the harbor to Fort Griswold. Arnold next marched into the unprotected town, where his troops seized valuable merchandise and military equipment.

Meanwhile, across the harbor British Army Lt. Col. Eyre was attacking Fort Griswold, whose hastily gathered defenders were ready to fight from behind the fort's 12-foot walls surrounded by a ditch. The rebel defenders, 178 militia officers and men commanded by Lt. Col. William Ledyard, a militia officer, faced 600 combat-hardened Redcoats. Lt. Col. Eyre called for a parley and, following the ancient ritual, demanded that the fort surrender or suffer no quarter—death to the entire garrison. Colonel Ledyard refused to yield.

The Redcoats charged up the hill from three directions simultaneously. Eyre came on leading a solid column of troops. Some of the rebel defenders were experienced in handling artillery from their service aboard privateers. One such gun crew expertly fired a cannon loaded with grapeshot at Eyre's column. The shot cleared a wide space among the British, leaving 20 men dead or wounded, including Eyre, who was killed. Major Montgomery, Eyre's second-in-command, was also dead, "having been thrust through the body, whilst in the act of scaling the walls."[29] The rebels repelled the initial attack and

28 "Narrative of Stephen Hempstead," in Charles Allyn, *The Battle of Groton Heights: A Collection of Narratives, Official Reports, Records, Inc. of the Storming of Fort Griswold* (New London, Connecticut: Privately printed, 1882), 47.

29 *Ibid.*

two others, leaving the hillside littered with British casualties. The rebel losses were trifling by comparison.

Fort Griswold fell silent following the third failed attack, leading the enraged Redcoats to believe that the fort had run low on ammunition. Encouraged by their remaining officers, they staged a fourth charge and finally succeeded in forcing their way into the fortress. Upon seeing the enemy within the fort, Lt. Col. Ledyard ordered his men to cease firing and lay down their arms. But the incensed British kept shooting and thrusting their bayonets, "even on those who were helplessly wounded and in the agonies of death."[30] Order was finally restored among the attackers, who counted over 150 dead and wounded comrades lying on the hill leading to the rebel citadel.

The senior living officer among the British was Maj. Stephen Bromfield from the 40th Regiment of Foot. According to an eyewitness account, Bromfield asked his captives, "Who commands this garrison?" The rebel commander, Lt. Col. Ledyard, stepped forward and answered, "I did sir, but you do now," and tendered his sword to the British officer hilt first, as was the custom. The point of the sword was now facing Ledyard.[31] Major Bromfield asked Ledyard, "Do you know the rules of war?" "Certainly," replied the rebel commander. "Then," said Bromfield, "you rebels prepare for death," and instantly plunged the sword into Ledyard's body, killing him.[32] This was the signal for a slaughter by the enraged Royal troops, who began their retaliation by dragging all the badly wounded insurgents to the parade ground. They laid them there, side by side on their backs, and brutally bayoneted them until all were dead. Then the British herded the remaining wounded rebels into a large ammunition wagon—which they rolled over the precipice. The wagon gained speed as it rolled down the steep hill and crashed into the stump of an apple tree, which violently threw some of the wounded to the ground. Only six Americans had been killed and 18 wounded during the four British attacks, but 85 defenders lay dead and 60 wounded following the rampage.[33] Then the remaining rebel defenders (about 40 men) were robbed of everything they had

30 *Ibid*, 53.

31 *Ibid*, 52.

32 "Narrative of Thomas Hertell," in Allyn, *The Battle of Groton Heights*, 72.

33 Benedict Arnold to Sir Henry Clinton, a report dated "[Long Island] Sound, off Plumb Island, September 8, 1781," *Ibid*, 105.

and marched almost naked down the hill to the waterfront, where they were loaded onto the waiting warships.

By the afternoon of the raid, New London's harbor must have been a ghastly scene: the wounded from Fort Griswold piercing the air with their screams, ships burning in the harbor, and New London in flames. The village of Groton, which was located on the waterfront near Fort Griswold, was also on fire. The inferno destroying New London had been started by Arnold's troops after they sacked the town. The General's orders were to carry off or burn anything of military value, but the fires started in the warehouses along the waterfront got out of control and spread to engulf the whole town. Adding to the horrific scene were periodic explosions of kegs of gunpowder stored in the torched warehouses, which showered the town with lethal fragments of burning wood.

By 4:00 p.m., the invaders were back on board their ships with their swag and prisoners. Arnold's flotilla sailed out of the harbor, leaving behind a scene of destruction that had few equals in the history of the American Revolution. Several days later a local newspaper reported that eight dead bodies had been found, washed up along the Connecticut shoreline. They were identified as wounded rebel prisoners who had died aboard Arnold's ships and been thrown overboard.[34]

Arnold was held personally responsible for the brutal raid on New London. In one exaggerated story, the infamous traitor Arnold stood in the steeple of a nearby church watching New London being engulfed in flames. He was compared to the despot Nero watching Rome burn. He was also condemned for the large number of Royal troops killed and wounded during the expedition, 48 and 145 respectively.

The attack on New London was so devastating that free land was given to the civilians of New London by the Connecticut legislature. The grant land, located in modern Ohio, was called the Firelands, the name by which the area is still known today.

British puff (propaganda) extolled the success of the New London raid, including in Rivington's *New York Gazette*. The newspaper's September 21, 1781, issue described Arnold's foray in glowing terms, concluding: "The breast of every honest loyalist cannot help emotions of joy on finding that the most detestable nest of pirates on the continent have as last attracted the notice of his

34 *Connecticut Gazette*, September 21, 1781, 21.

Excellency the commander-in-chief [Gen. Sir Henry Clinton]."[35] Clinton praised the victory in his General Orders: "Brigadier-General Arnold having reported to the commander-in-chief [Gen. Clinton] the success of the expedition under his direction, against New London on the 6th inst., His Excellency has the pleasure of signifying to the army the high sense he entertains of the very distinguished merit of the corps employed upon that service."[36]

Clinton continued to be outwardly supportive of Arnold, but he was actually infuriated with him. The cause of the rift was Arnold's doing: he showed his usual poor judgment by writing to Lord George Germain, Clinton's civilian boss, with his ideas for winning the war. Germain was Secretary of State for the American Department and responsible for managing the British war effort. Arnold wrote to Germain from New York City a few days after his arrival there to assure him of his loyalty, and promised "to devote my life and fortune to His Majesty's service and that I was intent to have demonstrated my zeal by an act which, had it succeeded [the capture of West Point] as intented, must have immediately terminated the unnatural convulsions that have so long distracted the empire." In the same letter Arnold recommended that Germain send commissioners with "decisive powers" to end the war by negotiation.[37] Obviously unable to contain himself, Arnold wrote to Germain again a few weeks later suggesting that Britain could end the war by promising to American soldiers that, "on their laying down their arms or joining the King's Army," they would receive the back pay due them from Congress or the states; half pay for seven years after the war's end; and free land in proportion to their rank.

But Clinton and every honest Loyalist were too preoccupied with events in Virginia to think about Arnold's New London raid. The compelling situation in Virginia began on September 5, 1781, just as Arnold's flotilla was approaching New London. On that date, French warships engaged a Royal Navy fleet off the coast of Virginia in what became known as the Battle of the Capes. Although the sea battle ended in a draw, the British admiral, Thomas Graves, departed Chesapeake Bay and sailed for New York to repair and refit his ships. Graves'

35 *Rivington's Royal Gazette,* September 21, 1781, 97.

36 Allyn, *Battle of Groton Heights,* 111.

37 Brigadier General Benedict Arnold to Lord George Germain, dated "7 October, New York" in Davies, ed., *Documents of the American Revolution,* Colonial Office Series, XVIII: 180, 182.

withdrawal left Gen. Cornwallis and his army of 8,000 isolated in Yorktown, Virginia, on the James River. On the same date, Continental troops began to board ships in Head of Elk, Maryland, for the short voyage to the Yorktown area, where patriot troops were already engaging Cornwallis' army. Cornwallis countered by fortifying his position at Yorktown to await the return of the Royal Navy. The British warships never came—but Gen. Washington did, with thousands of troops. These included a French army with siege guns (heavy artillery) under the command of Gen. Comte de Rochambeau. The allies slowly and methodically squeezed the enemy, and on October 19, 1781, Cornwallis surrendered his army.

The first rumors that Cornwallis had capitulated reached New York in late October. The British were devastated by the news, and even die-hard Loyalists believed that the war was lost. Arnold refused to accept the idea. Once he had changed sides, everything depended on the British winning the war to vindicate his actions. With so much at stake, Arnold wanted to go to London to press for the continuation of the war. He had a plan: the king and his ministers should give him command of the British army in America and continue the war.

Clinton was distraught over the disaster at Yorktown. This, coupled with Arnold's sadistic raid on New London and his writing directly to the King's ministers, meant that Clinton had had enough of Arnold, and was happy to ship him to England. Arnold sailed for England in December 1781, in a convoy of 150 ships. His wife and children were aboard one ship while Cornwallis and he were on another. Unknown to Arnold at the time, his military career had ended, and he would never see America again.

Arnold arrived in London with his wife and young children. His reputation preceded him—especially his supposed responsibility for Andre's execution and the alleged vicious nature of the New London raid. Referring to the attack, English statesman Edmund Burke, a foe of the war, called Arnold "a man whose conduct had been marked by glaring strokes of cruelty and perfidiousness [treachery]." Burke observed that "such a person could not be held by any laws to serve with strict fidelity, the people and the sovereign against whom he was before in arms."[38]

Questions were also raised about Arnold's ethics by Charles Fox, who had long opposed the war. He said, "[I]n the character of an American officer, Arnold had treacherously abandoned his command [West Point]; and now

38 Warren, *History of the American Revolution*, III: 91.

rewarded with an active military promotion in British service, he might probably proceed hereafter to similar transactions, and sacrifice for lucre [money] the troops of Britain."[39]

Many people in Britain treated Arnold coldly. King George III, however, was obliged by policy to take some notice of him, and was actually interested in talking to Arnold. George III wanted to continue the war in America, and was happy to have a general who shared his views. Arnold was seen in agitated conversation with the monarch and his supporters with schemes to win the war. But public opinion and the opposition in Parliament wanted peace following Cornwallis' defeat at Yorktown. Arnold was standing near King George when Parliament petitioned him for a bill authorizing peace negotiations with the Americans. Lord Lauderdale, who attended the gathering, was shocked to see Arnold standing next to the King. "My indignation could not but be highly excited," Lauderdale wrote, "as beholding his Majesty supported by a traitor."[40] In another instance, Lord Surrey rose to speak in the House of Lords when he observed Arnold, "the American deserter," in the gallery. Surrey sat down, pointed to Arnold and said, "I will not speak while that man is in the house."[41]

Of all the stories about Arnold's years in exile in England, the most compelling is the report of his visit to Westminster Abbey in London. Arnold and his wife were observed strolling through the vestry by Peter Van Shaack, an exiled American Loyalist. He observed the couple stopping at a cenotaph (a commemorative plaque) erected in the building in honor of Maj. John André. André was buried at the time near his place of execution. The exiled American watched as the couple read the inscription dedicated to the young man who, according to Van Shaack, "had gone to his death for his part in the plot that had made the name of Arnold odious to all who esteemed fidelity and honor."[42]

39 *Ibid.*, 90-91.

40 Sparks, *The Life and Treason of Benedict Arnold*, 331.

41 *Ibid.* The story of Lord Surrey refusing to speak with Arnold present also appeared in *Niles Weekly Register*, New Series #26, August 25, 1821, 404.

42 The first published account of this story appeared in Lorenzo Sabine, *The American Loyalists, or Biographical Sketches of Adherents to the British Crown in the War of the Revolution* (Boston: Charles C. Little & James Brown, 1847), 132. The memorial in Westminster Abbey reads: "Sacred to the memory of Major John André, who, raised by his merits at an early period of life to the rank of Adjutant-General of the British Forces in America, and employed in an important but hazardous enterprise, fell a sacrifice to his zeal for his King and County on the 2nd of October, AD 1780 Aged 29. Universally beloved and esteemed by the Army in which he served, and

Arnold was probably unemotional in his attitude toward the memorial and any role that he may have played in André's execution as a spy. As a twice-wounded combat officer who had seen scores of men die around him in battle, Arnold understood the risks involved in war. André had knowingly accepted the dangers associated with the mission, and his death was not Arnold's responsibility.

Arnold's obsession with money and active military service never ceased. He spent the rest of his life petitioning for reimbursement of expenses and losses of property, including his claims that he had paid to equip his American Legion regiment. Arnold also continued to press for the money which he claimed André had promised him.

Seeking a new life, Arnold immigrated to the Loyalist refugee colony at St. John's in New Brunswick, Canada, in 1785. There he resumed his merchant business and took a mistress, who bore him a son.[43] His wife and children remained in London for a time, but joined him in Canada in 1787. His sister Hannah arrived from Connecticut, bringing his three sons from his first marriage.

Arnold's years in New Brunswick were not happy. He was the target of vulgar stories encouraged by his treason and extravagant lifestyle. In one story, he burned down a warehouse full of goods that he owned in St. John's to collect the insurance money. In another, a local business partner accused Arnold of cheating him. The opposition to Arnold grew more violent when a mob appeared in front of his house burning an effigy of the general with a sign reading "Traitor." The situation in the small colony grew so hostile that Arnold sold his house and furnishings and took his family back to London in 1791. Some people at the time said that Arnold had been run out of town.

---

lamented even by his foes, His gracious Sovereign King George the Third has caused this Monument to be erected." A further inscription was added later that reads: "The Remains of Major John André were, on the 10th of August, 1821, removed from Tappan by James Buchanan, Esq. R, His Majesty's Consul at New York, Under instructions from His Royal Highness The Duke of York, and, with the permission of the Dean and Chapter, Finally deposited in a Grave Contiguous to his Monument On the 28th of November, 1821." The story of Van Schaak seeing the Arnolds in Westminster Abbey is told in greater detail in Milton Lomask, "Benedict Arnold: The Aftermath of Treason," *American Heritage*, Volume XVIII, Number 6 (October 1967), 17. The wooden chest in which André's remains were transported across the Atlantic in 1821 is also on display in Westminster Abbey.

43 *Ibid.*, 84-92.

Back in London, Arnold tried unsuccessfully to return to active military service when war broke out between England and France. He next turned to financing privateers to restore his family's dwindling fortunes. But his ships were unsuccessful, and his wife wrote at the time that her husband, "wishing to do something, without the health or power of acting he knows not which way to turn himself." Arnold's health grew progressively weaker, and he became delirious on June 10, 1801. He remained in that delirium for four days, then died on June 14.

The legends and stories of his final days are numerous. One story was that his death was brought on by the stress of humiliation. In one deathbed scene, Arnold asked to hold the gold epaulettes that General Washington had given him for his bravery at Saratoga. It was also reported that on his deathbed he relived his attack on Quebec with his devoted friend Montgomery, and shouted orders to his men as if he were again at Valcour Bay and Saratoga. In the end, Arnold died a sad and forgotten man. The European Magazine for July 1801 curtly reported his death: "June 14 In Gloucester Place Brigadier General Arnold, a person much noticed during the American War."[44]

His wife Peggy lived a few years longer, dying from cancer on August 24, 1804, at the age of 44.

44 J. G. Taylor, *Some New Light on the Later Life and Last Resting Place of Benedict Arnold and of His Wife Margaret Shippen* (London: George White, 1931), 26.

Chapter Nine

The Last Veterans of the Arnold Expedition

"Never surrender your liberties to a foreign invader or an aspiring demagogue."

— *Arnold Expedition veteran Benjamin Warner—advice to his son*[1]

By 1840, with the nation's attention focused on headline stories about the Republic of Texas and the newly established anti-slavery Liberty Party, the Arnold Expedition was a forgotten chapter in American history. Benedict Arnold, however, was known to every American as the Revolutionary War traitor who tried to sell West Point to the British. But there were a few men who still talked reverentially about the infamous turncoat. They were veterans of the 1775 Arnold Expedition, men who had traversed the Maine wilderness 65 years earlier under Arnold's courageous leadership in a bid to capture the British-held city of Quebec for the patriot cause.

Of the 1,150 infantry and riflemen who began the march to Quebec with Arnold, only five are known to have been alive in 1840: John Shackford, Ephraim Squier, Benjamin Warner, Fenner Foote, and James Dougherty. All had been common soldiers in 1775, and we are fortunate to have some of their recollections of the war as gathered through their pension applications, contemporary newspaper articles, and genealogical research conducted by their

1 A portion of a note found in the Revolutionary War knapsack of Arnold Expedition veteran Benjamin Warner. Fort Ticonderoga collection.

descendants. Of the five, Fenner Foote and James Dougherty are of particular interest, not only because of their diverse wartime experiences but because they were the last known members of Arnold's "famine-proof" army to die.

Each of these last five survivors of the Arnold Expedition lived long enough to apply for a pension offered by a grateful nation to its living Revolutionary War veterans. Official wartime records were scattered or destroyed, including a major loss when the British burned Washington, D.C. during the War of 1812. As a result, Congress decreed that men applying for a pension had to include, in lieu of discharge papers and government records, an affidavit describing their service in the war in as much detail as possible, including the names of their regiments, officers, and fellow soldiers. Although written by old men, these detailed affidavits provide us with valuable information.[2]

The roll call of the last survivors of the Arnold Expedition starts with John Shackford, from Newburyport, Massachusetts. Shackford enlisted in Capt. Ezra Lunt's company in the 17th Massachusetts Regiment of the Continental Line in July 1775, from which he volunteered to serve on Benedict Arnold's secret mission. He was 20 years old at the time. He was captured during the patriots' failed attack on Quebec and held prisoner in the city for nine months before being paroled. After being exchanged, Shackford rejoined his old Massachusetts regiment and served for six months in the Hudson Highlands region, where he was involved in the failed American assault in January 1777 to recapture Fort Independence (a fort built by the Americans and occupied by the British located in the Bronx, New York). Recalling the campaign, Shackford wrote, "I went on the advanced guard to reconnoiter Fort Independence and storm it. But we had no ladders and we returned to headquarters."[3] He eventually settled in Eastport, Maine, where he raised and commanded a militia company for local defense. Shackford was still the captain of the Eastport

2 The most comprehensive Revolutionary War pension was offered by the United States government in 1832. It provided benefits to any veteran of the war who had served for at least six months. A history of Revolutionary War pensions can be found in J. Todd White and Charles H. Lesser, *Fighters for Independence* (Chicago: The University of Chicago Press, 1977), 9-10; and John Resch, *Suffering Soldiers: Revolutionary War Veterans, Moral Sentiments, and Political Culture in the Early Republic* (Amherst: University of Massachusetts Press, 1999).

3 Affidavit of John Shackford (1755-1840, Massachusetts), Revolutionary War Pension and Land Bounty Records, Record series M805, roll 727, file W7179, National Archives and Records Administration, Washington, D.C. (hereafter National Archives).

militia when a Royal Navy squadron captured the town during the War of 1812. The British ordered the inhabitants to swear fidelity to the King. Shackford appeared before them wearing his old-fashioned Revolutionary War regimental coat and hat. He refused to submit to their demands, saying that he had fought under General Washington, and "that the British could take four horses and draw him to quarters, but never would he swear allegiance to the King of England." The old veteran was neither forced to take the oath, nor stripped of his property.[4] Shackford died in Eastport on December 25, 1840, at the age of 88.

Private Ephraim Squier was born in Ashford, Connecticut, on February 9, 1748, marched to Cambridge with his militia company at the start of the war, and fought at Bunker Hill. Squier volunteered for the Arnold Expedition on September 7, 1775. He was assigned to Col. Roger Enos' fourth division that turned back from the Dead River on October 5, 1775. While technically a member of the Arnold Expedition, Squier never reached Quebec. He died on August 19, 1841, at the age of 94.[5]

Arnold Expedition veteran Benjamin Warner's military service in the war provides an example of a young patriot who divided his time between fighting for independence and helping support his family. Warner first enlisted in Wooster's Connecticut regiment on May 8, 1775, shortly after the war began. He was stationed with his regiment at Cambridge the following September when, according to his pension application, "he volunteered for Canada at the beat of the drum for that expedition [the Arnold Expedition]."[6] Private Warner was 18 at the time. He made the trek to Canada in Capt. Hanchet's company. Warner recalled that Arnold's Corps was discovered by patrol boats while crossing the St. Lawrence, and "immediately the bells rung but we landed and marched off onto the Plains of Abraham. The next morning the enemy fired upon us from their fort [and we] retreated back a mile or two amongst the French." Warner also remembered Gen. Montgomery's arrival, "with supplies

4 George Thomas Little, *Genealogical and Family History of the State of Maine*, 3 vols. (New York: Lewis Historical Publishing Company, 1909), II: 837-838. For additional information about Shackford, see William T. Luck, "An Eastport, Maine, Legend and His Ties to the Arnold Expedition," in *The Arnold Expedition Historical Society Newsletter* (Pittston, Maine), Newsletter 94 (November 1999), 1-2.

5 Smith, *Arnold's March From Cambridge to Quebec*, 277, note.

6 Affidavit of Benjamin Warner (1757-1846, Connecticut), Revolutionary War Pension and Land Bounty Records, Record series M805, roll 839, file S14798, National Archives.

for our men and a British uniform for each of us which the General and his party took from the British at Sorel."[7] He was too ill at the time to participate in Montgomery's attack on Quebec, but served under Arnold at Quebec until mid-April 1776, when he was discharged and went home.

Warner returned to the army on August 6, 1776, in Col. G. S. Silliman's Connecticut State Regiment, with which he fought in the August 27, 1776, Battle of Long Island. This enlistment expired on or about December 1, 1776, at which time he returned home. He returned to active duty again in April 1777, serving for eight months in Maj. Atkinson's Connecticut militia. Warner was back on active duty in 1779 when he served for three months in Capt. William McClure's company in Col. Crane's Continental artillery.[8] His final known tour of duty was in the Hudson Highlands region around West Point, where he served from July to December 1780 in Lamb's Continental Artillery.

Warner died at Ticonderoga, New York, on January 30, 1846. His pride in helping to win American independence and fighting for the idea expressed in the Declaration of Independence that "all men are created equal" was summed up in the words on his tombstone: "Benjamin Warner, A Revolutionary Soldier and a Friend of the Slave." At the time of his death, Warner's modest possessions included a knapsack which he had carried throughout the American Revolution. When the knapsack was acquired by Fort Ticonderoga in 1929, the museum's curators found a note inside. Warner's note (its text standardized here for clarity) reads:

> This knapsack I carried through the War of the Revolution to achieve American Independence. I transmit it to my oldest son, Benjamin Warner, Jr., with directions to keep it and transmit it to his oldest son and so on to the latest posterity and while one shred of it shall remain never surrender your liberties to a foreign invader or an aspiring demagogue.[9]

If Warner carried his knapsack throughout the war, as he says, then he wore it on the Arnold Expedition. His knapsack survives to this day in the collection of Fort Ticonderoga as a relic of one of the greatest events in American military history.

7 *Ibid.*

8 *Ibid.*

9 Fort Ticonderoga Museum Collection.

The knapsack carried by Arnold Expedition veteran Benjamin Warner. Warner claimed that he wore this knapsack throughout the American Revolution. The note was found inside the knapsack when it was being prepared for exhibition. *Library of Congress Fort Ticonderoga Collection*

Privates Fenner Foote and James Dougherty died within months of each other in 1847. Besides their longevity, Foote and Dougherty are interesting because a study of their dissimilar wartime service helps explain how the infant Continental Army was able to win a prolonged eight-year-long war against the the most experienced and best-equipped army and navy in the world.

Fenner Foote was born in Colchester, Connecticut, in 1755. His family moved to Glass Works (today's Lee), Massachusetts, in 1770 where, on January 3, 1775, he enlisted as a private in the militia company commanded by Capt. William Goodrich, who owned a tavern in Stockbridge. Goodrich recruited his men from the vicinity of Glass Works and Stockbridge. Foote remembered that

The Jonathan Foote House. This house was built in 1778 by Jonathan Foote, the father of Arnold Expedition veteran Fenner Foote. The house is located in Lee, Massachusetts, and was probably built with the help of Fenner following his return from winter militia duty (1777-1778) at Fort Ticonderoga. Fenner lived in the house prior to his marriage to Sarah Wilcox in 1779. After their marriage, young Foote built his own house nearby, which no longer stands. The Jonathan Foote house is operated today as the 1778 House Bed & Breakfast. *Author's Collection*

he and his neighbors "were enrolled and drilled immediately."[10] Goodrich's unit was a Minute Company composed of 27 men who were equipped, trained, and ready should the Redcoats in Boston venture into the countryside.

According to Foote, a report of the Lexington Alarm reached Stockbridge around noon on April 20, 1775. Captain Goodrich's company responded quickly to the news, starting for Cambridge at sunrise the following morning. After joining the rebel army, Goodrich's Minute Company became part of Col. Patterson's provincial regiment and saw conspicuous action during the siege of Boston. Foote recalled that his unit was used as rangers, an indication of its fighting prowess.

10 Affidavit of Fenner Foote (1754-1847, Connecticut), Revolutionary War Pension and Land Bounty Records, Record series M805, roll 328, file S42170, National Archives.

In September 1775, Capt. Goodrich was given command of one of the companies on the Arnold Expedition. He recruited most of the men for his unit from his own Stockbridge company, including Foote, who volunteered to go on the secret mission. Years later Foote described his experiences: "We went up the Kennebec River in Batteaux as far as we could, then we had to carry them and our ammunition and our provisions across a carrying place of seven miles [a reference to the Great Carry] to another Stream [the Dead River]." Confirming the difficulty in attempting to calculate the actual, total distance travelled by Arnold's Corps, Foote said, "Sometimes we had to go back over these carrying places three or Four times to bring all our effects."[11]

Foote described how the suffering of the men on the march intensified as the expedition slowly advanced through the wilderness toward Quebec. Even years later, Foote could vividly recall how "[s]ome of our companions were taken ill and we could do no less than lay them down to die and go on and leave them, being ourselves so emaciated and worn that we could afford them no relief." When Foote arrived at the south shore of the St. Lawrence River, across from Quebec, he was sick and exhausted. However, he was able to join his comrades on the night of November 13, 1775, when "orders came whispered to us to be in readiness [to cross the St. Lawrence River in Indian canoes]. We soon were in Motion and took possession of the heights [the Plains of Abraham] where our whole army encamped that night."[12]

Private Foote then participated in the feeble siege of Quebec; however, probably because of illness, he was put on guard duty at Dr. Senter's hospital and did not participate in the failed December 31 attack on Quebec. He remained with the small force that continued the siege of the walled city under Arnold's command, then retreated all the way back to Fort Ticonderoga with his comrades when the British went on the offensive in Canada in the spring of 1776. Foote arrived back home in Lee on June 1, 1776, claiming that he never received a dollar for his service in the dreadful campaign.

By the time he returned home, Foote had arguably done more than his share of the fighting on behalf of the patriot cause. However, he continued to serve periodically as a member of his local militia company. He signed on to defend Fort Ticonderoga during the terrible winter of 1776-1777. Foote later

11 *Ibid.*

12 *Ibid.*

turned out again when New England was threatened by Gen. Burgoyne's offensive in 1777, although he saw no action.

During his service in the militia, Foote did not fit the traditional profile of the inexperienced, easily intimidated militiaman of the Revolutionary War. He was a tough trooper who had seen extensive combat prior to his service in the militia. There were many other former soldiers like Foote who helped make the American militia a useful auxiliary fighting force as the war continued. Foote lived to be 92 and died in Lee, Massachusetts, on April 27, 1847.[13]

James Dougherty's participation in the American Revolution represents a different type of patriotic contribution that helped to win the war. Unlike Foote, who joined the army several times for a specified number of months, Dougherty remained on active duty throughout most of the war. He exemplifies the core of experienced soldiers who sustained the Continental Army. Dougherty's campaign credits read like a history of the American Revolution: the siege of Boston, the Arnold Expedition, Trenton, Princeton, the Brandywine, Germantown, Monmouth, and Yorktown.

Dougherty, like many other soldiers, was motivated to serve for a variety of reasons that included political beliefs, adventure, hatred of Britain, bounty money, and the promise of pay and warm clothing. But whatever their motivations, the presence of these dependable soldiers—men who had the combat experience to stand and face a fierce bayonet attack—was critical to the success of the American Revolution. Dougherty is unique even among these hardcore veterans because in addition to his extended active duty in the Continental Army, he served as a member of General Washington's personal bodyguard.

Dougherty was born in County Antrim in Ulster Province, Ireland, on Christmas Day in 1749. He came from a family of tenant farmers who rented their land from the English and Irish noblemen who owned the property. In 1771, at age 22, he married 15-year-old Jane Lawson. Two years later, they immigrated to America and settled near the town of Lancaster, Pennsylvania, a favorite destination for Ulstermen. Lancaster, although often associated with the frontier, was actually an established town (the largest inland city in America

13 *Berkshire Star* (newspaper), June 10, 1847, obituary notice. Fenner Foote was the last veteran of the Arnold Expedition to die. The last living soldier of the American Revolution is believed to have been Daniel F. Bakeman, who died on April 5, 1869, at the age of 109. The last widow of a Revolutionary War soldier was Catherine S. Damon, who died on November 11, 1906, at the age of 92.

in 1775, in fact) surrounded by flourishing farms when the Doughertys arrived there. The first of their four children who survived to adulthood was born in Lancaster. The child, a boy named James, Jr., was born in 1775.

The Doughertys were among the estimated 250,000 people who left Ulster for America between 1715 (the start of a severe drought in Ireland) and 1775 in what became known as "The Great Migration." While the Dougherty (changed from O'Dougherty) clan converted to Protestantism in the 1500s, Ulstermen in America were generally called Scotch-Irish because many of their forefathers were originally from Scotland. These Protestant Scots had been encouraged to immigrate to Ireland during the reigns of Elizabeth I (1558-1603) and James I (1603-1625) to supplant the native-Irish Catholics. The transplanted Scots raised sheep and established a profitable woolens industry centered in Ulster.

However, their situation changed because of the drought; unanticipated increases in their rents (called rack-renting), which resulted in mass expulsions (the Antrim Evictions); and the passage of the Woolens Act (1699) by the British Parliament, which prohibited the exportation of Irish wool and cloth to Europe. These factors resulted in a mass migration of Ulstermen to America and a deep hatred of the British government. The so-called Scotch-Irish brought their abhorrence of England with them to America and overwhelmingly sided with the rebels during the American Revolution.[14]

On June 14, 1775, less than two months after the start of the war, the Continental Congress authorized the raising of eight rifle companies, two each from Virginia and Maryland and six from Pennsylvania. Two additional Pennsylvania rifle companies were approved a few weeks later. The bulk of the rifle companies were raised in the back country of Pennsylvania, the center of rifle-making in America and home to marksmen who knew how to effectively load and fire the weapon. The men who volunteered to serve in the rifle companies had to provide their own weapons, clothing, and accoutrements.

Matthew Smith, an American of Scotch-Irish ancestry, organized one of Pennsylvania's first units in the Lancaster area. The response for volunteers to serve in his Pennsylvania rifle company was overwhelming. James Dougherty is

14 The mass immigration of the Scots-Irish to America took place over a 58-year period between 1717 and 1775. The earliest Scots-Irish immigrants arriving in America settled in Philadelphia and along the Delaware River in Pennsylvania. Subsequent Scots-Irish immigrants tended to establish themselves in the backcountry of the various colonies, including Virginia and North Carolina. "Scots-Irish" is strictly an American term; in England and Ireland the same people are called "Ulster Scots."

listed as one of the 80 privates in the unit. Smith's company mustered at Lancaster on July 15, 1775, and rapidly marched cross country to Cambridge, arriving there on August 9.

Soon after reaching Cambridge, the men of Smith's company heard rumors of a secret mission being organized by Col. Benedict Arnold. By early September Arnold was recruiting men for his corps and Smith's company was one of the three rifle companies selected to go. Dougherty participated in the full drama of the Arnold Expedition: the march across Maine, the attack on Quebec, and capture and imprisonment for seven months inside the city. James, who apparently was illiterate, left no record of his experiences during the Arnold Expedition. However, he was mentioned in rifleman John Joseph Henry's published account of the expedition. In his narrative, Henry described how the riflemen preceded the main body of the little army, "both by land and water. The boats, which were heavily laden with baggage and provisions, took in no more men than were necessary to navigate them, that is, three to a boat." Henry identified Dougherty as one of his fellow boatmen.[15]

Dougherty was paroled on August 3, 1776, when he signed a promise to neither take up arms nor do anything injurious to his majesty King George Third until regularly exchanged. James and his fellow paroled Arnold Expedition comrades departed Quebec in British transports, which took them to New York harbor. There, on September 24, 1776, about 350 members of the original 1,150-man Arnold Expedition went ashore at American-held Elizabethtown Point in New Jersey. After reaching New Jersey, Dougherty started for home in western Pennsylvania, arriving there in early October 1776.

However, he remained at home for only a few weeks before re-enlisting in the Continental Army and serving on active duty until the end of the war. It is probable that Dougherty broke the parole he signed at Quebec by which he agreed not to serve in the army until he was exchanged. Thus, he risked being severely whipped or executed if he was caught in uniform by the British.

Dougherty's pension application narrative consisted largely of his recollection of the units in which he served during the war. We can piece together his service record based on what is known about the movements of his detachments during the time he served in them.

15 John Joseph Henry, *An Accurate and Interesting Account of the Hardships and Sufferings . . . of that Band of Heroes*, 55.

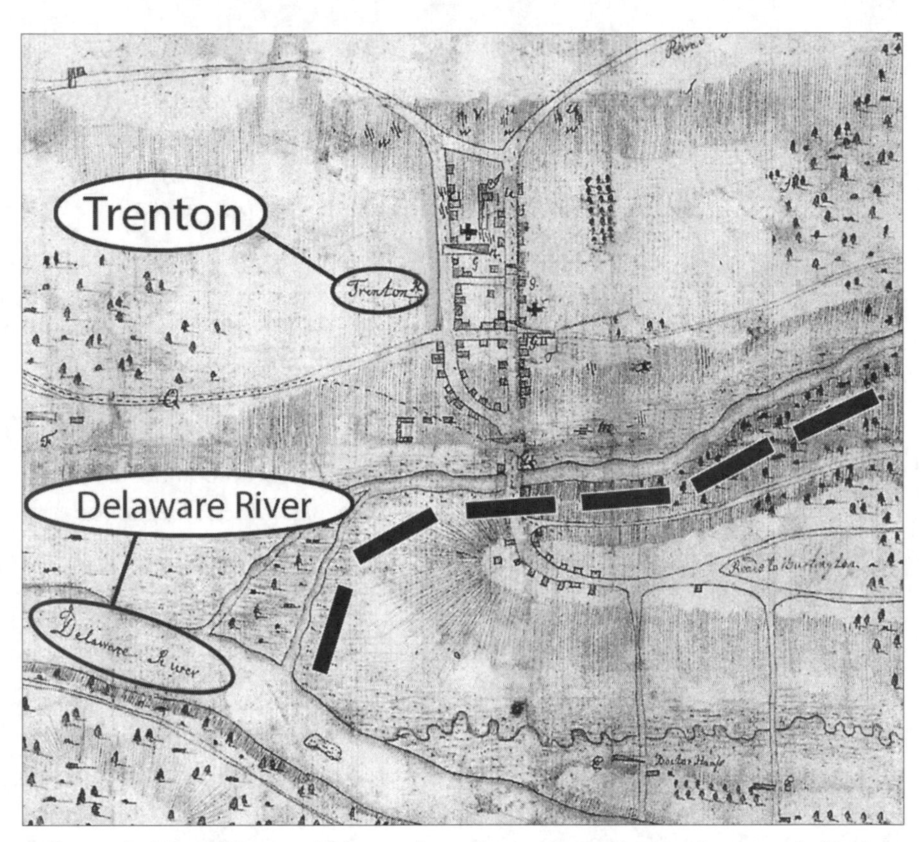

Manuscript Map of Trenton . This map shows the position of the American army during the January 2, 1777, Second Battle of Trenton. Private James Dougherty was present at this engagement and participated in the night march that followed and the attack on Princeton on the following morning. *Library of Congress*

James enlisted in the newly established 12th Pennsylvania Rifle Regiment soon after arriving back home. The unit was organized at Sunbury, Pennsylvania, and consisted of eight companies of riflemen under the command of Col. William Cooke. The regiment joined Washington's main army in late December 1776 and fought in the Second Battle of Trenton (January 2, 1777) and the Battle of Princeton on the following day. Following the spectacular American victory at Princeton, Cooke's regiment retreated with the rest of the army to Morristown, New Jersey, for the winter.

In the spring of 1777, the 12th Pennsylvania left Morristown and moved south with other troops to organize a strong defensive position along the ridge of New Jersey's Watchung Mountains. While stationed in the Watchungs, Dougherty transferred to Capt. Thomas Clark's field artillery company. Clark's company saw action in the important September 1777 battles of Brandywine and Germantown, both of which took place the following month.

Dougherty was a member of Clark's gun battery when the army established its winter encampment (1777-1778) at Valley Forge. Dougherty spent the winter at the legendary cantonment, but his status changed in March 1778, shortly after Baron Friedrich Wilhelm Augustin Ludolf Gerhard von Steuben arrived in camp.

Baron von Steuben had served in the much-admired Prussian army, and Washington asked him to train (drill) the members of his Continental Army so they could effectively move and fire their weapons in large formations. Von Steuben approached the difficult task by devising a simple drill that he would personally teach to a company of handpicked veterans, who could then act as drillmasters for the balance of the army.[16] The experiment began on the morning of March 19, 1778, on the parade ground at Valley Forge. James Dougherty was one of the 100 soldiers selected to be personally trained by von Steuben.

The orderly book of a Virginia regiment at Valley Forge stated the qualifications of the men who were recruited for von Steuben's model company. The specifications give us an idea of Dougherty's appearance at the time: "Size of the men from 5 feet Eight to five feet 10 Inches from 28 years to thirty [Dougherty was 29 years old at the time]—a Robust Constitution & Limbs well formed for strength & Activity & of an Established Character Sobriety & fidelity."[17] For administrative purposes, the troops in Von Steuben's model company were assigned to the Commander-in-Chief's Guard, or Life Guard as it was more commonly known. The elite unit's purpose was to protect General Washington. It consisted of 40 men at the time, all from Washington's home state of Virginia.

The Baron, who spoke almost no English, gave his instructions to his model company in German or French, which were translated into English by various multilingual officers and aides. When his students made a mistake, the Baron would curse them in his native German. At one point in the training, he

16 General Orders dated "Head-Quarters V. Forge March 17th 1778 Tuesday," in W. W. Abbot, et. al., eds., *The Papers of George Washington*, Revolutionary War Series, XIV: 205.

17 *Ibid.*, footnote 1.

General Baron von Steuben's Model Company at Valley Forge. The Model Company consisted of 100 hand-picked men organized to learn von Steuben's new drill. Private James Dougherty was a member of this elite detachment. *Library of Congress*

turned to his translator and exclaimed, "[C]ome and swear for me in English, these fellows won't do what I bid them."[18]

Dougherty continued to serve in the Life Guard for the balance of the war. His name appears on its records, and he likely fought as part of the unit in the 1778 Battle of Monmouth and the 1781 siege of Yorktown.

The Life Guard had been established in the army's General Orders dated Cambridge, March 11, 1776, which stated in part: "The General being desirous of selecting a particular number of men, as a Guard for himself, and baggage, His Excellency depends upon the Colonels [the commanding officers of each infantry regiment] for good Men, such as they can recommend for their sobriety, honesty and good behavior."[19] Washington used his Life Guard to provide perimeter protection for his headquarters against unauthorized entry (for example, by local farmers with a complaint who wanted to see Washington) or an enemy raid. The latter was a serious problem; the British are known to have made at least one attempt to kidnap the General from his headquarters

18 Lockhart, *The Drillmaster of Valley Forge*, 103.

19 W. W. Abbot, et. al., eds., *The Papers of George Washington*, Revolutionary War Series, III: 448- 449.

during the war.[20] The Life Guard was also responsible for safeguarding Washington's personal possessions (dinnerware, camp equipment, provisions, clothing, etc.) along with the property of his aides-de-camp. Finally, the General wanted the specially trained, distinctively uniformed and equipped Life Guard to help give his headquarters a professional military appearance. A French officer described Washington's headquarters as having "perfect order with the battalion of the General's guards encamped within the precincts of his house; nine wagons, destined to carry his baggage, ranged in his court."[21]

The other routine function of the Life Guard was to guard Washington's headquarters papers, which included copies of every order and letter issued from his office. We can thank Washington's Life Guard for their diligence, for today all of Washington's Revolutionary War headquarters records are in the Library of Congress. Washington wanted his records close by for reference if necessary, and the papers followed him throughout the war, stored in trunks and portable bookcases which accompanied the army in wagons protected by the Life Guard.

When he rode into battle, Washington did not use his Life Guard to surround and protect him. When he was in harm's way, the General rode with only a small number of men to avoid drawing attention to himself as well as to exhibit the personal courage that he expected from his troops. As an experienced Indian fighter, it is unreasonable to believe that Washington rode into combat accompanied by a headquarters flag and a retinue of guards that would have identified his person and revealed his position.

Washington's low-key movements in combat freed his Life Guard to fight with the army. After leaving enough men behind to guard the headquarters baggage and papers, the commander-in-chief deployed the Life Guard for combat. A good example of how the Life Guard was used in battle was its service during the 1778 Battle of Monmouth, an engagement in which Dougherty fought alongside Daniel Morgan, a fellow veteran of the Arnold

20 Eric Olsen, "A Raid to Capture General Washington" (unpublished article). Mr. Olsen is the National Park Service historian at Morristown National Historical Park, New Jersey. His article deals with an attempt to kidnap Washington from his winter headquarters at the Ford Mansion in Morristown during the winter of 1779-1780. The British attempt consisted of 500 mounted men who started out for Morristown from Paulus Hook, New Jersey. Cold weather and ice turned them back before they had a chance to test the security surrounding Washington's headquarters. A copy of Mr. Olsen's article is on file in the museum's library.

21 Marquis de Chastellux, *Travels in North-America, in the Years 1780, 1781, and 1782*, I: 140.

Expedition. Two officers and eighty enlisted men from the Life Guard joined Morgan's corps, whose mission was to harass the British army as it marched across New Jersey from Philadelphia to New York City. The Life Guard joined other picked troops armed with muskets and bayonets who were assigned to Morgan's Corps. Such troops were the solution to the vulnerability of riflemen; it will be recalled that Gates supported Morgan's rifle corps at Saratoga in a similar manner. The combined corps at Monmouth skirmished with the British and harassed their flanks as they marched across New Jersey. Although Morgan may have recognized Dougherty from the Arnold Expedition, the commander-in-chief discouraged fraternization between officers and enlisted men. With Washington close by, even the affable Col. Morgan probably forbore from friendly conversation with the rank and file.

Dougherty's service in the Life Guard included the 1781 siege of Yorktown, the final great campaign of the American Revolution. Washington established his headquarters in the fields surrounding Yorktown on September 29, 1781. He lived and operated from two large marquee tents: one for the general's personal use, and the other designated for dining and entertainment. There was also a baggage marquee which served a multitude of purposes, including storing the headquarters staff's personal property and the headquarters papers. Washington's aides pitched their tents nearby. Beyond the headquarters compound were the rows of tents belonging to the Life Guard and tents for the servants, grooms, cooks, and washerwomen who worked at headquarters.

As Washington required, the headquarters area had an orderly and professional military appearance to help maintain discipline and the dignity of his office. The members of the Life Guard added to the headquarters esprit-de-corps with their handsome uniforms of dark blue regimental coats with buff facings, buckskin breeches, and black hats bound with white tape. While Washington established his camp beyond the range of the British artillery defending Yorktown, the compound was still close enough to the enemy to be vulnerable to a surprise night attack or a daring raid to kidnap or kill the General. Therefore Washington's headquarters had to be heavily guarded by the Life Guard, augmented by additional troops on detached service. The Life Guard provided perimeter protection and patrolled within the compound to prevent anyone from committing theft or any outsider from disturbing Washington or his aides-de-camp. No one, not even a gentleman in fine clothing, could just walk up to Washington and engage him in conversation; a lengthy process was required for anyone who hoped to see him. That process started with his Life Guard.

As Washington and his staff lived and operated from their tents throughout the Yorktown campaign, members of the Life Guard were witnesses to the behind-the-scenes planning and progress of the siege. They saw high-ranking American and French officers coming and going from headquarters, and may have been witnesses on October 17 when Washington received the glorious news that Cornwallis was ready to negotiate terms of surrender. Cornwallis surrendered his army two days later, on October 19, 1781.

The siege of Yorktown proved to be the last major battle of the American Revolution; over the next two years, the conflict slowly wound down. Private Dougherty remained in the Life Guard during these final years of the war, then was discharged from the army on November 3, 1783.

Dougherty returned home at the end of the war to resume farming. Besides their son James, born in 1775, James the elder and his wife Jane had three other children, two boys and a girl, all of whom were born after the war. The family moved farther west in Pennsylvania before finally settling in Venango County. James died there on January 15, 1847, at the ripe old age of 97. Despite two generous Revolutionary War pensions and bounty land awarded for his wartime service, James died in poverty. Like so many Revolutionary War veterans, he probably sold his bounty land certificates to speculators for a fraction of their value, fearing that they would prove worthless. In an 1818 Revolutionary War pension application, Dougherty listed his assets at $59.15 and his debts at $139.24.[22] His list of assets included all of his household possessions, which consisted of "5 Chairs old, 1 sett cups & saucers, 5 plates, and 6 pewter table spoons." Dougherty's financial distress was a sad situation for a patriot soldier.

With the passage of time, the American Revolution became a fabled event in the history of the new republic. Veterans of the Revolutionary War were respected members of their community. They participated in 4th of July parades and were asked to recount their experiences to children who were reading history books about the war's great leaders and battles. It was typical for these old soldiers to embellish their wartime experiences, perhaps describing how they watched Gen. Burgoyne surrender at Saratoga or stood next to George Washington at Yorktown. By the 1840s, there were few of these old

22 Affidavit of James Dougherty (1749-1847), Revolutionary War Pension and Land Bounty Records, Record series M805, Roll 278, file S42170, National Archives.

soldiers around to tell their stories. But Fenner Foote and James Dougherty were alive, and the stories they told to eager youngsters were true. Experiences like wading chest-deep in the freezing swamps of northern Maine and crossing the St. Lawrence River at night between patrolling Royal Navy frigates whose cannon were loaded with deadly grapeshot are not easily forgotten, even by very old men.

At the start of the American Revolution in 1775, Foote and Dougherty had little to complain about. They paid minimal taxes and lived in the freest civilized society in the world at the time. Nonetheless, by 1775 many Americans shared Marylander Charles Carroll's conviction that "our dear-bought liberty stands on the brink of destruction." The colonists believed that King George and his corrupt ministry were conspiring to methodically abolish their rights, such as trial by jury, and imposing arbitrary taxes which would be enforced by a swarm of government-paid toadies, pimps, collectors, comptrollers, searchers, placemen, informers, and the army. The people's belief that their children would suffer the ultimate fate of this regular, systematic plan of oppression was at the heart of the Revolutionary movement. William Prescott, who fought at Bunker Hill, expressed the idea of the colonists' obligation to their children. "Our forefathers," he began, "passed the vast Atlantic, spent their blood and treasure, that they might enjoy their liberties . . . and transmit them to their posterity. . . . Now if we should give them up, can our children rise up [become adults] and call us blest?"

In 1775, the idea of going to war to protect the birthright of future generations was a simple and strong message that appealed to many Americans, from wealthy young college graduates such as Samuel Ward, Jr., third- and fourth-generation New England farmers such as Fenner Foote, and newly arrived immigrants such as James Dougherty. Fifteen months into the war, the colonists decided that independence from Britain was the best way to protect their liberties for themselves and their children.

Fenner Foote and his wife Sarah had nine children (five boys and four girls), each of whom married and lived in the towns of Stockbridge and Lee, Massachusetts, close to their parents' home. They were mostly farmers who prospered in the new nation which their father had helped to create. James Dougherty's children also thrived in the new United States of America. They had families and owned farms and businesses. Two of Dougherty's sons, James, Jr., and William, owned a successful hardware business in Steubenville, Ohio. Perhaps James Dougherty fought so long and hard for American independence because he had seen the oppression of tyrannical government as a youth in Ireland and he wanted a better life for his children and his children's children.

Postscript

The Legacy of the Arnold Expedition

"The rising generation—while they enjoy the blessings of liberty, may they never forget those who achieved it."

— *A toast offered at an 1820 banquet honoring Revolutionary War veterans*[1]

This work sets forth the fascinating story of the officers and men who served in the ill-fated Arnold Expedition. The book's contention is that these dedicated patriots gained valuable experience during the 1775 campaign to capture Quebec that they used later to help win the war for the American colonists.

The list of Arnold Expedition officers who contributed to the success of the American Revolution is long and impressive. Equally notable is the high military rank that many of these men reached in the years following their return, often as junior officers, from the expedition to Canada under Benedict Arnold's command. The Arnold Expedition officers who returned to the war included Timothy Bigelow, Aaron Burr, Henry Dearborn, Christian Febiger, Christopher Greene, Return Jonathan Meigs, Daniel Morgan, Charles Porterfield, Matthias Ogden, Eleazer Oswald, Simeon Thayer, John Topham,

1 The toast was offered at an 1820 banquet honoring Revolutionary War veterans held in Hartford, Connecticut, and was reported in the *Connecticut Mirror,* August 7, 1820. Hezekiah Niles, *Principles and Acts of the Revolution in America* (Baltimore: William Ogden Niles, 1822), 364.

and Samuel Ward. They all served the American cause with distinction and honor as front-line combat officers.

The wartime accomplishments of this large number of officers are too impressive to attribute exclusively to their service in Arnold's Kennebec Corps. Just as these officers were originally chosen for the Arnold Expedition for their dedication, courage, and leadership, it makes sense that they would continue in this mold when they returned to the army following their captivity in Quebec. However, Benedict Arnold should get credit for introducing them, during the 1775 campaign, to an impressive style of leadership which they then emulated and imparted to other American officers.

What made Arnold such an outstanding combat officer? To start with, he was courageous, and conspicuous in showing his bravery. He led by example, sharing in the dangers and hardships of his campaigns with his officers and men. These traits were evident when he fearlessly led his troops against Quebec, aimed cannon in the thick of the fighting at Valcour Bay, and stormed a redoubt at Saratoga. Arnold was smart, innovative, and ready to take risks to achieve success. And he was a positive thinker, with a natural talent for gaining the trust of his men and rallying them to perform incredible acts of bravery.

Sadly, Arnold's great abilities did not extend beyond the battlefield. He was a misguided, exploited officer who fell victim to the intrigues and jealousies of wartime America. Even the most venerated officers, including Washington, were subjected to the sectional interests, the diversity of ideas (for example, whether to fight with a regular army or militia), and the cliques that championed their favorite army officers. Besides his problems with the civilian government, Arnold faced criticism within the army because he was an egocentric loner incapable of accepting a subordinate role. His conduct during the Saratoga campaign was typical of his belief that he was smarter than everyone around him. Gates' judgment as a commander may have been flawed, but Arnold's defiance of him says a great deal about his character. Arnold was Gates' subordinate, and his behavior at Bemis Heights was disobedient and irresponsible. Gates got even with him by downplaying Arnold's contribution to the victory at Saratoga.

Arnold turned to treason out of anger and frustration. But his actions went beyond defecting to the British because of ill-treatment by the rebellion's leaders or his disenchantment with the entry of France into the war. He conspired with the British to plan a strategic blow to the Continental army at a time when the patriot cause was staggering from Gates' defeat at Camden and the financial collapse of the American economy. Fortunately for the patriots,

Arnold's perfidy was exposed due to André's inexperience as an undercover operative. André loved the theater, but his performance for the three militiamen on the Tarrytown Road was a flop. The drama ended with Arnold fleeing for his life and spending the rest of his days as a bitter outcast hated by the Americans and distrusted by the British.

Things probably would have turned out differently, and better, for Arnold if Gen. Richard Montgomery had lived. Montgomery was a rising star in the Continental Army in 1775 and he seemed to get along famously with Arnold, who was happy to serve as his subordinate. In the brief month that they worked together they made a great team; both men were courageous, with a fighting spirit, and skilled in motivating the troops under their command. Montgomery staggered into Canada early in the war herding a band of petulant officers and unruly men. Arnold and his disciplined, tough corps were a welcome change. Montgomery respected Arnold for his skill and audacity in bringing his expedition to the gates of Quebec. After they met, Montgomery protected Arnold and brought out the best in him. General Montgomery's death during the attack on Quebec ended what, in retrospect, was probably Arnold's best chance for success.

Arnold's need for a hands-on mentor and influential spokesperson becomes obvious upon taking a closer look at his relationship with Congress. The delegates created trouble for officers whose military accomplishments were questionable, notably Generals John Sullivan, Charles Lee, and Philip Schuyler. However, although Arnold was a winner, he was shunned by the members of Congress and only grudgingly promoted. George Washington admired Arnold's generalship and skill as a combat officer. But Washington was frequently too distant and preoccupied to prevent the ongoing altercations Arnold created with his fellow officers and politicians. Washington was careful to avoid confrontations with Congress over his subordinate's demands for higher rank and more money. In one example, Arnold wanted his promotion to major general to be made retroactive. Washington wrote to Congress on the subject in the summer of 1777, but avoided taking a strong position on Arnold's behalf. Instead Washington diplomatically wrote, "These considerations are not without their weight, though I pretend not to judge what motives may have influenced the conduct of Congress upon this occasion."[2] Montgomery, in

2 George Washington to John Hancock, dated "Morristown May 12th, 1777" in W. W. Abbot, et. al., eds., *The Papers of George Washington,* Revolutionary War Series, IX: 396-397.

contrast, probably would have served as the active mentor and influential patron Arnold desperately needed to prevent him from wrecking his career as an outstanding American combat officer.

The root of Arnold's troubles, as an officer in both the Continental and the British armies, was his inability to learn from his mistakes. This becomes evident when studying his role in the 1775 attack on Fort Ticonderoga, a brief campaign during which Arnold's belligerent conduct created dangerous enemies. However, he refused to change his style even after experiencing the fallout caused by his tactless behavior. He probably never realized that he was creating his own problems—and he had no teacher to enlighten him.

The stark realities of the Revolutionary War movement also worked against Arnold. Despite the speeches of Fourth of July orators, the American Revolution was not a total uprising of the American colonists united against Great Britain. In fact, the conflict can be characterized as a civil war, with enough of the people either supporting their mother country or attempting to remain neutral to give the war a factious character.

Even within the ranks of the patriot army there was much to be embarrassed about. Entire regiments mutinied during the war, and over 20 percent of the men who enlisted in the Continental Army deserted. Many of the officers came to their positions with little knowledge of what was expected of professional soldiers. Jealousies and intrigues over rank and promotion were common. Some of the officers turned out to be cowards, cheats, and troublemakers. Such men were pressured to resign or removed by court martial. Startlingly, 393 American officers are known to have been tried by court martial during the American Revolution. [3] The problems of the American officer corps prompted Henry Knox to describe them as "a parcel of stupid men who might make tolerable soldiers, but are bad officers. As the army now stands it is only a receptacle for ragamuffins."[4]

The civilian leaders of the Revolution also had much to be embarrassed about. For example, during the winter of 1779-1780 the army was living under horrible conditions at Morristown—while politicians and businessmen banqueted in Philadelphia. Corrupt government functionaries and other

3 James C. Neagles, *Summer Soldiers: A Survey & Index of Revolutionary War Courts-Martial* (Salt Lake City, Utah: Ancestry Incorporated, 1986), 29.

4 Noah Brooks, *Henry Knox, A Soldier of the Revolution* (New York, G.P. Putnam's Sons, 1900), 70-71.

civilians hoarded and stole army provisions and got rich from their deals—while the army suffered, wearing threadbare clothing and eating short rations.

What sustained the revolutionary movement, despite all this, and led to victory? George Washington stands as the great symbol of the patriot movement. He was dedicated to the cause of American independence and the creation of a professional army. Helping him were a cadre of devoted, experienced officers and men who stood by him throughout the eight-year conflict. The veteran officers and enlisted men from the 1775 Arnold Expedition stand tall among these fighting patriots. The Arnold Expedition came early in the war and proved to be a training ground for some of the best officers to emerge in the Continental Army. Their original teacher was Benedict Arnold, who showed them how to lead and fight. The men who survived the Arnold Expedition were experienced and tough, and they set an example for their fellow soldiers with their courage and determination.

The combat-hardened Americans who returned from Canada to resume the fight for independence were the positive ending to the saga of the Arnold Expedition and the flawed and traitorous man who led it. Their accomplishments contributed mightily to the success of the American Revolution. I am proud to have had this opportunity to honor them and tell their stories.

Bibliography

Manuscript Sources

Benedict Arnold's letter book and a journal of a tour from the St. Lawrence to the Kennebec (Montresor's journal). Maine Historical Society Collection.

The Papers of Aaron Burr. New York Historical Society.

The Emmet Collection. New York Public Library.

Philip J. Schuyler Papers. New York Public Library.

Reed Collection. Valley Forge National Historical Park.

Joseph Trumbull Papers. Connecticut Historical Society.

General Sir Henry Clinton Papers. Clements Library.

Revolutionary War Pension and Land Bounty Records. National Archives
- Clark, Jesse (1757-1837). Mass. Roll 188. File W1763
- Dougherty, James (1749-1847). Roll 278. File S42170
- Foote, Fenner (1754-1847). Mass. Roll 328. File S13065
- Percival, John (1754-?). Mass. Roll 644. File S11227
- Shackford, John (1755-1840). Mass. Roll 727. File W7179
- Slocum, Capt. Edward (1754-1822). RI. Roll 743. File S33682
- Squier, Ebenezer (1748-1841). Conn. Roll 764. File R10026
- Warner, Benjamin (1757-1846). Conn. Roll 839. File S14798

Published Primary Sources

Abbot, W. W., et al., eds. *The Papers of George Washington.* Revolutionary War Series. 18 vols. to date. Charlottesville, Virginia: University Press of Virginia, 1985–.

Allen, Ethan. *A Narrative of Col. Ethan Allen's Captivity.* Burlington, Vermont: Chauncey Goodrich, 1846. (originally published in 1779)

Baxter, James Phinney. *Documentary History of the State of Maine.* 2nd series, vol. 14. Portland: Lefavor-Tower Company, 1910.

Bray, Robert C., and Paul E. Bushnell, eds. *Diary of a Common Soldier in the American Revolution, 1775-1783: An Annotated Edition of the Military Journal of Jeremiah Greenman.* DeKalb, Illinois: Northern Illinois University Press, 1978.

Brown, Lloyd A., and Howard H. Peckham, eds. *Revolutionary War Journals of Henry Dearborn, 1775-1783.* Chicago: The Caxton Club, 1939.

Chastellux, Marquis de. *Travels in North-America, in the Years 1780, 1781 and 1782.* 2 vols. London: Printed for G. G. J. and J. Robinson, 1787.

Clark, William Bell, ed. N*aval Documents of the American Revolution.* 11 vols. to date. Washington, D.C.: U.S. Government Printing Office, 1964–.

Cohen, Sheldon S., ed. *Canada Preserved: The Journal of Captain Thomas Ainslie.* Canada: The Copp Clark Publishing Company, 1968.

Commager, Henry Steele, and Richard B. Morris, eds. *The Spirit of Seventy-Six.* 2 vols. Indianapolis and New York: The Bobbs-Merrill Company, Inc., 1967.

Corner, George W., ed. *The Autobiography of Benjamin Rush.* Princeton, New Jersey: Princeton University Press, 1948.

Davies, K.G., ed. *Documents of the American Revolution.* Colonial Office Series. 21 vols. Shannon: Irish University Press, 1972-1981.

Fitzpatrick, John C., ed. *The Writings of George Washington.* 39 vols. Washington, D.C.: Government Printing Office, 1934-44.

Foner, Eric, ed. *Thomas Paine Collected Writings.* New York: Literary Classics of the United States, Inc., 1995.

Force, Peter, ed. *American Archives: A Documentary History of the English Colonies in North America, From the King's Message to Parliament, of March 7, 1774, to the Declaration of Independence of the United States.* 6 vols. Fourth Series. Washington, D.C. M. St. Clair Clarke and Peter Force, 1843.

——. *A Documentary History of the Origin and Progress of the North American Colonies; of the Causes and Accomplishment] of the American Revolution: and of The Constitution of the Government For the United States to the Final Ratification Thereof.* 3 vols. Fifth Series. Washington, D.C. M. St. Clair Clarke and Peter Force, 1848.

Ford, Worthington C., et. al., eds. *The Journals of the Continental Congress, 1774-1789.* 34 vols. Washington, D.C.: Government Printing Office, 1904-37.

Greenwood, John. *A Young Patriot in the American Revolution.* Westvaco, 1981.

Henry, John Joseph. *An Accurate and Interesting Account of the Hardships and Sufferings of that Band of Heroes, Who Traversed the Wilderness in the Campaign Against Quebec in 1775.* Lancaster, Pennsylvania: William Greer, 1812.

Kalm, Peter. *Travels Into North America; Containing Its Natural History, and A Circumstantial Account of its Plantations and Agriculture in General.* 2 vols. London: Printed for T. Lowndes, 1772.

Kline, Mary-Jo, ed. *Political Correspondence and Public Papers of Aaron Burr.* 2 vols. Princeton, New Jersey: Princeton University Press, 1983.

Lee, Charles. *The Lee Papers.* 4 vols. New York: New York Historical Society, 1871-1874.

Lesser, Charles H., ed. *The Sinews of Independence: Monthly Strength Reports of the Continental Army.* Chicago: University of Chicago Press, 1976.

Meigs, Maj. *Return J. Journal of the Expedition Against Quebec, Under Command of Col. Benedict Arnold.* New York: privately printed, 1864.

Melvin, Andrew A., ed. *The Journal of James Melvin Private Soldier in Arnold's Expedition Against Quebec In the Year 1775.* Portland, Maine: Hubbard W. Bryant, 1902.

Montgomery, Mrs. Janet (Livingston). *Biographical Notes Concerning General Richard Montgomery Together with Hitherto Unpublished Letters.* 1876.

Officer of the Garrison (name unknown). "Journal of the Most Remarkable Occurrences in Quebec." *Collections of the New York Historical Society for the Year 1880.* New York: Printed for the Society, 1881.

Ogden, Matthias. "Journal of Major Matthias Ogden, 1775 In Arnold's Campaign Against Quebec." *Proceedings of the New Jersey Historical Society*, New Series, Vol. XIII (1928): 17-30.

Roberts, Kenneth. March to Quebec, *Journals of the Members of Arnold's Expedition Including the Lost Journal of John Pierce.* Garden City, New York: Doubleday & Company, Inc., 1940.

Rogers, Horatio, ed. Journal Kept in Canada and Upon Burgoyne's Campaign in 1776 and 1777 by Lieut. James M. Hadden. Albany, New York: Joel Munsell's Sons, 1884.

Ross, Charles, ed. *Correspondence of Charles, First Marquis Cornwallis.* 3 vols. London: John Murray, 1859.

Scull, G. D., ed., "Journals of Capt. John Montresor 1757-1778." *Collections of the New York Historical Society for the Year 1881.* New York: New York Historical Society, 1882.

Senter, Isaac. "The Journal of Isaac Senter, Physician and Surgeon to the Troops Detached From the American Army Encamped at Cambridge, Mass., on a Secret Expedition Against Quebec . . . ." *Bulletin of the Historical Society of Pennsylvania*, Vol I, No.5 (1846).

Shipton, Nathaniel N., and David Swain, eds. *Rhode Islanders Record the Revolution: The Journals of William Humphrey and Zuriel Waterman.* Providence: Rhode Island Publications Society, 1984.

Showman, Richard K. *The Papers of General Nathanael Greene.* 12 vols. to date. Chapel Hill: The University of North Carolina Press, 1976–.

Smith, Paul H., ed. *Letters of Delegates to Congress, 1774-1789.* 26 vols. Washington, D.C.: United States Government Printing Office, 1976-2000.

Stedman, Charles. *The History of the Origin, Progress and Termination of the American War.* 2 vols. London: 1794.

Stone, Edwin Martin, ed. *The Invasion of Canada in 1775: Including the Journal of Captain Simeon Thayer, Describing the Perils and Sufferings of the Army Under Colonel Benedict Arnold.* Providence, Rhode Island: Knowles, Anthony & Co., Printers, 1867.

Tatum, Edward H. *The American Journal of Ambrose Serle.* San Marino, California: The Huntington Library, 1940.

Wilkinson, James. *Memoirs of My Own Time.* 3 vols. Philadelphia: Printed by Abraham Small, 1816.

Willcox, William B., ed. *The American Rebellion, Sir Henry Clinton's Narrative of His Campaigns, 1775-1782.* New Haven: Yale University Press, 1954.

Winsor, Justin, ed. *Arnold's Expedition Against Quebec 1775-1776, The Diary of Ebenezer Wild With a List of Such Diaries.* Cambridge, Massachusetts: John Wilson and Son, 1886.

Würtele, Fred C., ed. *Blockade of Quebec in 1775-1776 by the American Revolutionists.* Quebec: Literary and Historical Society of Quebec, 1906.

Secondary Sources

Adams, Hannah. *A Summary History of New-England From the First Settlement at Plymouth, to the Acceptance of the Federal Constitution. Comprehending a General Sketch of the American War.* Dedham, Massachusetts: H. Mann and J. H. Adams, 1799.

Alden, John Richard. *General Gage in America.* Baton Rouge: Louisiana State University Press, 1948.

———. *The American Revolution, 1775-1783.* New York: Harper & Brothers, 1954.

Allyn, Charles. *The Battle of Groton Heights.* New London, Connecticut, 1882.

Arnold, Isaac N. *The Life of Benedict Arnold.* Chicago: Jansen, McClurg & Company, 1880.

Babits, Lawrence E. *A Devil of a Whipping: The Battle of Cowpens.* Chapel Hill, The University of North Carolina Press, 1998.

Bellesiles, Michael A. *Revolutionary Outlaw: Ethan Allen and the Struggle for Independence on the Early American Frontier.* Charlottesville: University Press of Virginia, 1993.

Berg, Fred Anderson. *Encyclopedia of Continental Army Units.* Harrisburg, Pennsylvania: Stackpole Books, 1972.

Billias, George Athan, ed. *George Washington's Opponents: British Generals and Admirals in the American Revolution.* New York: William Morrow and Company, Inc., 1969.

Blanco, Richard L., ed. *The American Revolution, 1775-1783.* 2 vols. New York: Garland Publishing, Inc., 1993.

Bland, Humphrey. *A Treatise of Military Discipline: In Which is Laid Down and Explained The Duty of the Officer and Solider, Through the Several Branches of the Service.* London: R. Baldwin, J. Richardson, T. Longman, S. Crowder & Co., 1762.

Brandt, Clare. *The Man in the Mirror: A Life of Benedict Arnold.* New York: Random House, 1994.

Buell, Miss Rowena. *The Memoirs of Rufus Putnam.* Boston and New York: Houghton, Mifflin and Company, 1903.

Burke, Edmund (attributed to). An *Impartial History of the War in America Between Great Britain and Her Colonies, From the Commencement to the end of the Year 1779.* London: R. Faulder, 1780.

Codman, John, 2nd. *Arnold's Expedition to Quebec.* New York: The Macmillan Company, 1901.

Coffin, Robert P. Tristram. *Kennebec, Cradle of Americans.* New York: Farrar & Rinehart Incorporated, 1937.

Dandridge, Danske. *Historic Shepherdstown.* Charlottesville, Virginia: The Michie Company, 1910.

Davis, Matthew. *Memoirs of Aaron Burr With Miscellaneous Selections From His Correspondence.* 2 vols. New York: Harper & Brothers, 1836 & 1837.

Duncan, Louis C. *Medical Men in the American Revolution.* New York: Augustus M. Kelley, 1970.

Egly, T.W., Jr. *History of the First New York Regiment.* Hampton, New Hampshire: Peter E. Randall, 1981.

Everest, Allan S. *Moses Hazen and the Canadian Refugees in the American Revolution.* Syracuse: Syracuse University Press, 1976.

Fenn, Elizabeth A. *Pox Americana: The Great Smallpox Epidemic of 1775-82.* New York: Hill and Wang, 2001.

Ferguson, E. James. *The Power of the Purse.* Chapel Hill: The University of North Carolina Press for The Institute of Early American History and Culture, 1961.

Ferling, John. *The Ascent of George Washington: The Hidden Political Genius of an American Icon.* New York: Bloomsbury Press, 2009.

——. *A Leap in the Dark.* Oxford and New York: Oxford University Press, 2003.

——. *The First of Men: A Life of George Washington.* Knoxville: The University of Tennessee Press, 1988.

Fischer, David Hackett. *Washington's Crossing.* New York: Oxford University Press, 2004.

Flexner, James Thomas. *The Traitor and the Spy.* New York: Harcourt, Brace and Company, 1953.

Freeman, Douglas Southall. *George Washington—A Biography*. 7 vols. New York: Charles Scribner's Sons, 1954-7.

French, Allen. *The Taking of Ticonderoga in 1775: the British Story*. Cambridge, Massachusetts: Harvard University Press, 1928.

——. *The First Year of the American Revolution*. Boston and New York: Houghton Mifflin Company, 1934.

Gerlach, Don R. *Proud Patriot: Philip Schuyler and the War of Independence, 1775-1783*. Syracuse, New York: Syracuse University Press, 1987.

Gordon, William. *The History of the Rise, Progress, and Establishment, of the Independence of the United States of America: Including an Account of the Late War*... 4 vols. London, 1788.

Graham, James. *The Life of General Daniel Morgan, of the Virginia Line of the Army of the United States*. New York: Derby & Jackson, 1859.

Hatch, Robert McConnell. *Thrust For Canada: The American Attempt on Quebec in 1775-1776*. Boston: Houghton Mifflin Company, 1979.

Hearn, Chester G. *George Washington's Schooners: The First American Navy*. Annapolis, Maryland: Naval Institute Press, 1995.

Heitman, Francis B. *Historical Register of Officers of the Continental Army*. Washington, D.C.: The Rare Book Shop Publishing Company, Inc., 1914.

Higginbotham, Don. *Daniel Morgan, Revolutionary Rifleman*. Chapel Hill: The University of North Carolina Press, 1961.

The History of the Civil War in America. London, 1780. (author unknown)

Humphreys, David. *An Essay on the Life of the Honorable Major-General Israel Putnam*. Hartford, Connecticut: Hudson and Goodwin, 1788.

Huston, James A. *Logistics of Liberty: American Services of Supply in the Revolutionary War and After*. Newark, Delaware: University of Delaware Press, 1991.

Jackson, John W. *The Pennsylvania Navy 1775-1781: The Defense of the Delaware*. New Brunswick, New Jersey: Rutgers University Press, 1974.

James, Captain W. M. *The British Navy in Adversity*. New York: Longmans, Green and Co. Ltd., 1926.

Katcher, Philip R. N. *Encyclopedia of British, Provincial, and German Army Units, 1775-1783*. Harrisburg, Pennsylvania: 1973.

Leake, Isaac Q. *Memoirs of the Life and Times of General John Lamb*. Albany, New York: Joel Munsell, 1850.

Lederer, Richard M., Jr. *Colonial American English, Words and Phrases Found in Colonial Writing, now Archaic, Obscure, Obsolete, or Whose Meanings Have Changed*. Essex, Connecticut: A Verbatum Book, 1985.

Lomask, Milton. Aaron Burr, *The Years from Princeton to Vice President 1756-1805*. New York: Farrar-Straus-Giroux, 1979.

Lossing, Benson J. *The Pictorial Field-Book of the Revolution*. 2 vols. New York: Harper & Brothers, 1860.

Main, Jackson Turner. *The Social Structure of Revolutionary America*. Princeton: Princeton University Press, 1965.

Marshall, John. *The Life of George Washington, Commander in Chief of the American Forces.* 5 vols. Philadelphia: C.P. Wayne, 1804-1807.

Martin, James Kirby. *Benedict Arnold, Revolutionary Hero: An American Warrior Reconsidered.* New York: New York University Press, 1997.

Martyn, Charles. *The Life of Artemas Ward, The First Commander-in-Chief of the American Revolution.* Port Washington, New York: A. Ward, 1921.

Mayer, Holly A. *Belonging to the Army: Camp Followers and Community During the American Revolution.* Charleston: University of South Carolina Press, 1996.

Merwin, Henry Childs. *Aaron Burr.* Boston: Small, Maynard & Company, 1899.

Miller, Nathan. *Sea of Glory: The Continental Navy Fights for Independence.* New York: David McKay Company, Inc., 1974.

Morton, Doris Begor. *Philip Skene of Skenesborough.* Granville, New York: The Grastorf Press, 1959.

Murray, James A. H., et al., eds. *Oxford English Dictionary.* 20 vols. Oxford: Clarendon Press, 1989.

Neimeyer, Charles Patrick. *America Goes to War: A Social History of the Continental Army.* New York: New York University Press, 1996.

Neumann, George C. *Battle Weapons of the American Revolution.* Texarkana, Texas: Scurlock Publishing Co., Inc.

Oliver, Sandra L. *Saltwater Foodways: New Englanders and Their Food, at Sea and Ashore, in the Nineteenth Century.* Mystic, Ct.: Mystic Seaport Museum, Inc., 1995.

Palmer, Dave R. *George Washington and Benedict Arnold: A Tale of Two Patriots.* New York: Regnery Publishing, Inc., 2006.

Parkman, Francis. *A Half Century of Conflict.* 2 vols. Boston: Little, Brown and Company, 1892.

———. *Count Frontenac and New France Under Louis XIV.* Boston: Little, Brown, and Company, 1896.

———. *Montcalm and Wolfe.* Boston: Little, Brown and Company, 1955. (reprint)

Parmet, Herbert S., and Marie B. Hecht. *Aaron Burr: Portrait of an Ambitious Man.* New York: The Macmillan Company, 1967.

Peterson, Harold L. *Round Shot and Rammers.* New York: Bonanza Books, 1969.

———. *The Book of the Continental Soldier.* Harrisburg, Pennsylvania: The Stackpole Company, 1968.

Ramsay, David. *The History of the American Revolution.* 2 vols. Trenton, New Jersey: James J. Wilson, 1811. (reprint of the original 1789 edition)

Reynolds, Paul R. *Guy Carleton, A Biography.* New York: William Morrow and Company, Inc., 1980.

Richardson, Edward W. *Standards and Colors of the American Revolution.* Philadelphia: The University of Pennsylvania Press, 1982.

Rossie, Jonathan Gregory. *The Politics of Command in the American Revolution.* Syracuse: Syracuse University Press, 1975.

Rowe, William Hutchinson. *The Maritime History of Maine.* Gardiner, Maine: The Harpswell Press, 1989.

Royster, Charles. *A Revolutionary People at War: The Continental Army and American Character, 1775-1783.* Chapel Hill, North Carolina: The University of North Carolina Press, 1979.

Sellers, Charles Coleman. *Benedict Arnold: The Proud Warrior.* New York: Minton, Balch & Company, 1930.

Shelton, Hal. T. *General Richard Montgomery and the American Revolution.* New York: New York University Press, 1994.

Smith, Captain George. *An Universal Military Dictionary.* London: Printed for J. Millan, 1779.

Smith, Justin H. *Arnold's March From Cambridge to Quebec.* New York: G.P. Putnam's Sons, 1903.

———. *Our Struggle For the Fourteenth Colony: Canada and the American Revolution.* 2 vols. New York: G.P. Putnam's Sons, 1907.

Smith, Samuel Steele. *Fights for the Delaware, 1777.* Monmouth Beach, New Jersey: Philip Freneau Press, 1979.

Sparks, Jared. *The Life and Treason of Benedict Arnold.* Boston: Billiard, Gray, and Co., 1835.

Stanley, George F. G. *Canada Invaded, 1775-1776.* Toronto: A.M. Hakkert Ltd., 1973.

Stevenson, Roger. *Military Instructions for Officers Detached in the Field.* Philadelphia: R. Aitken, 1775.

Tillotson, Harry Stanton. *The Exquisite Exile: The Life and Fortunes of Mrs. Benedict Arnold.* Boston: Lothrop, Lee & Shepard Co., 1932.

Wallace, Willard. *Traitorous Hero: The Life & Fortunes of Benedict Arnold.* New York: Harper & Brothers, 1954.

Wandell, Samuel H., and Meade Minnigerode. *Aaron Burr.* 2 vols. New York: G.P. Putnam's Sons, 1925.

Ward, Christopher. *The War of the Revolution.* 2 vols. New York: The Macmillan Company, 1952.

Warren, Mrs. Mercy Otis. *History of the Rise, Progress and Termination of the American Revolution.* 3 vols. Boston: Printed by Manning and Loring, For E. Larkin, 1805.

Weber, Ralph E., ed. *Masked Dispatches: Cryptograms and Cryptology in American History, 1775-1900.* National Security Agency, 1993.

Wood, Gordon S. *The American Revolution, A History.* New York: The Modern Library, 2002.

Wright, Robert K., Jr. *The Continental Army.* Washington, D.C.: Center of Military History, United States Army, 1989.

Monographs, Articles, Dissertations and Exhibition Catalogs

Allen, William. "Account of Arnold's Expedition." *Maine Historical Society Collections*, 1 (1831), 499-532.

Bell, Richard G. "The Court Martial of Roger Enos." *Connecticut Bar Journal*, Vol. 73, No.6.

Boylston, Arthur W., M.D. "Clinical Investigation of Smallpox in 1767." *The New England Journal of Medicine*, Vol. 346, No. 17 (April 25, 2002).

"Colonel Christopher Greene." *The Magazine of History*, vol. XXIII, July 1916, No. 1.

Crist, Robert Grant. *Captain William Hendricks and the March to Quebec* (1775). Carlisle, Pennsylvania: The Hamilton Library and Historical Association of Cumberland County, 1960.

Dworetzky, Murray, M.D. "Smallpox, October 1945." *The New England Journal of Medicine*, vol. 346, No. 17 (April 25, 2002).

Gerlach, Don R. "Philip Schuyler And The Road to Glory: A Question of Loyalty and Competence." *The New York Historical Society Quarterly*, vol. XLIX, number 4, October 1965.

Heth, William. "The Diary of William Heth." Winchester, *Virginia Historical Society Annual Papers*, vol. 1 (1931), 27-118.

Huston, James A. "The Logistics of Arnold's March to Quebec." *Military Affairs*, vol. 32, issue 3 (Dec., 1968), 110-124.

McAuliffe, Mary C. Timothy Bigelow, *The Patriot of Worcester*. Master of Education thesis, The State Teachers College at Hyannis, Massachusetts, 1941. (A copy of this thesis is at Bridgewater State College, Bridgewater, Massachusetts)

"Maine Indians in the Revolution." *Sprague's Journal of Maine History*, vol. six, no. 3 (Jan. 1919).

Nelson, William. Edward Antill, *A New York Merchant of the Seventeenth Century, and His Descendants*. Paterson, New Jersey: The Press Printing and Publishing Company, 1899.

Ogden, Matthias. "Journal of Major Matthias Ogden, 1775 in Arnold's Campaign Against Quebec." *Proceedings of the New Jersey Historical Society*, New Series, vol. XIII (1928).

Roch, John F., ed. "Quebec Under Seige, 1775-1776: The 'Memorandums' of Jacob Danford." *The Canadian Historical Review*, vol. L, No.1 (March 1969).

Saunders, Robert. "When Newfoundland Helped to Save Canada." *Newfoundland Quarterly*, vol. 49, no. 3, 1949.

Squier, Frank, ed. "Diary of Ephraim Squier." *Magazine of American History*, No. 2, part 2 (1878).

Whiteley, W. H. "The British Navy and the Siege of Quebec, 1775-6." *Canadian Historical Review*, vol. LXI, no. 1, March 1980.

Index